W9-ABL-128

DISCARDED

822.009
R32

128570

| DATE DUE | | | |
|---|---|---|---|
| | | | |
| | | | |
| | | | |
| | | | |
| | | | |
| | | | |
| | | | |
| | | | |
| | | | |
| | | | |
| | | | |
| | | | |
| | | | |

The *Revels*
History of Drama
in English

GENERAL EDITOR
*T. W. Craik*

# The *Revels*
# History of Drama
# in English

GENERAL EDITOR
*T. W. Craik*

# The Revels
# History of Drama
# in English

VOLUME V 1660-1750

*John Loftis, Richard Southern*
*Marion Jones & A. H. Scouten*

CARL A. RUDISILL LIBRARY
LENOIR RHYNE COLLEGE

Methuen & Co Ltd
London

822.009
R32
12 8570
cyn. 1984

First published 1976 by Methuen & Co Ltd
11 New Fetter Lane, London EC4P 4EE
© 1976 John Loftis, Richard Southern,
Marion Jones, A. H. Scouten
Printed in Great Britain by
Richard Clay (The Chaucer Press), Ltd
Bungay, Suffolk
ISBN (hardbound) o 416 13060 7
ISBN (paperback) o 416 81370 4

This title is available in both hardbound and paperback editions. The
paperback edition is sold subject to the condition that it shall
not, by way of trade or otherwise, be lent, resold, hired out, or
otherwise circulated without the publisher's prior consent in any form
of binding or cover other than that in which it is published and
without a similar condition including this condition being imposed
on the subsequent purchaser.

Distributed in the USA by
HARPER & ROW PUBLISHERS, INC.
BARNES & NOBLE IMPORT DIVISION

# Contents

Contents vii

# List of illustrations

Figures

# Chronological Table

This table draws freely on the relevant volumes of *The London Stage* (see Bibliography) edited by W. van Lennep, E. L. Avery and A. H. Scouten. The editor is grateful to Miss Marion Jones and to Professor Scouten for their help in its compilation.

Non-dramatic writings are listed under the date of publication, and plays under the date of first performance. A conjectural date is preceded by a question mark.

| 1 | 2 | 3 | 4 |
|---|---|---|---|
| Date | Historical events | Theatrical events | Non-dramatic literary events |
| 1656 | | Davenant permitted to offer *The First Day's Entertainment* at Rutland House | |
| 1657 | | | |
| 1658 | Cromwell d. | | |
| 1659 | | Actors arrested for performing at the Red Bull | |
| 1660 | Restoration of Charles II | Introduction of actresses on the English stage; creation of King's Company and Duke's Company by royal patent | Pepys begins his diary; Royal Society founded |
| 1661 | | Duke's Company begins acting at Lincoln's Inn Fields Theatre | |
| 1662 | Act of Uniformity | | Butler, *Hudibras*, I; Fuller, *Worthies of England* |
| 1663 | | King's Company opens new Theatre Royal in Bridges St | Butler, *Hudibras*, II |
| 1664 | | Nell Gwyn joins King's Company; Walter Clun murdered | |
| 1665 | Second Dutch War; plague year | All theatres closed by plague | |
| 1666 | Great Fire of London | Theatres reopened 29 Nov. | Bunyan, *Grace Abounding* |
| 1667 | Clarendon dismissed | Theatres closed in July for Dutch War | Milton, *Paradise Lost*; Sprat, *History of Royal Society* |

| 5 Birth and death dates of non-dramatic writers | 6 Dates of notable plays | 7 Birth and death dates of playwrights | 8 Continental theatrical events |
|---|---|---|---|
| | Davenant, *The Siege of Rhodes* | | |
| | | Dennis b. | |
| | Davenant, *The Cruelty of the Spaniards in Peru* | | Arrival of Molière in Paris |
| | | | Molière, *Les Précieuses ridicules* |
| | Tatham, *The Rump* | Southerne b.; Motteux b. | Corneille, *Discours* |
| Defoe b. | Davenant, *The Siege of Rhodes*, I & II | | Domenico Biancolelli becomes Harlequin for the Fiorelli troupe in Paris |
| entley b. | Howard, *The Committee*; Porter, *The Villain* | | Molière, *L'École des femmes*; opening of Smock Alley Theatre, Dublin |
| | Tuke, *The Adventures of Five Hours*; Rhodes, *Flora's Vagaries* | | |
| or b. | Howard and Dryden, *The Indian Queen*; Etherege, *The Comical Revenge* | Vanbrugh b.; Mountfort b. | |
| | Orrery, *Mustapha*; Dryden, *The Indian Emperor* | | |
| | | Shirley d. | Molière, *Le Misanthrope* |
| wift b. | Dryden, *Secret Love*; Newcastle and Dryden, *Sir Martin Mar-All*; Dryden and Davenant, from Shakespeare, *The Tempest* | Cowley d. | Molière, *Tartuffe*; Racine, *Andromaque* |

| 1 | 2 | 3 | 4 |
|---|---|---|---|
| *Date* | *Historical events* | *Theatrical events* | *Non-dramatic literary events* |
| 1668 | | Betterton and Harris become managers of Duke's Company | Cowley, *Works* |
| 1669 | | Theatres closed six weeks on death of Queen Henrietta-Maria; Elizabeth Boutell joins King's Company | W. Penn, *No Cross, No Crown* |
| 1670 | | | Walton, *Lives of Donne, Wotton, Hooker, Herbert* |
| 1671 | | Dorset Garden Theatre opened | Milton, *Paradise Regained; Samson Agonistes* |
| 1672 | Third Dutch War | Bridges St Theatre burned | |
| 1673 | The Test Act | Elizabeth Barry begins acting career; Fiorelli troupe in London | |
| 1674 | | Drury Lane Theatre opened by King's Company; T. Jevon joins Duke's Company | |
| 1675 | | | |
| 1676 | | | |
| 1677 | | Charles Killigrew replaces Thomas Killigrew as manager of King's Company | |
| 1678 | The Popish Plot | French troupe in London | Bunyan, *Pilgrim's Progress*, I |
| 1679 | Duke of York sent from England | Anne Bracegirdle joins Duke's Company | Burnet, *History of the Reformation*, I |

| 5 Birth and death dates of non-dramatic writers | 6 Dates of notable plays | 7 Birth and death dates of playwrights | 8 Continental theatrical events |
|---|---|---|---|
| | Etherege, *She Would If She Could*; Shadwell, *The Sullen Lovers* | Davenant d. | |
| Denham d. | | Stapylton d. | |
| | John Caryll, *Sir Salomon*; Dryden, *The Conquest of Granada*, I & II | Congreve b. | Racine, *Bérénice* |
| | Buckingham, *The Rehearsal* | Colley Cibber b. | |
| | Ravenscroft, *The Citizen Turned Gentleman*; Dryden, *Marriage à la Mode* | Addison b.; Steele b. | |
| | Settle, *The Empress of Morocco* | | Molière, *Le Malade imaginaire*; Molière d. |
| Milton d. Clarendon d. | | Tuke d.; Rowe b. | |
| | Crowne, *Calisto*; Wycherley, *The Country Wife*; Dryden, *Aureng-Zebe* | | Giovanni Gherardi begins career in Paris |
| | Etherege, *The Man of Mode*; Shadwell, *The Virtuoso*; Wycherley, *The Plain Dealer* | | |
| Barrow d. | Lee, *The Rival Queens*; Dryden, *All for Love* | | Racine, *Phèdre* |
| Marvell d. | Dryden and Lee, *Oedipus* | ? Flecknoe d.; ? Farquhar b. | |
| Hobbes d.; Parnell b. | | Boyle (Earl of Orrery) d. | |

| 1 | 2 | 3 | 4 |
|---|---|---|---|
| *Date* | *Historical events* | *Theatrical events* | *Non-dramatic literary events* |
| 1680 | Duke of York returns from Scotland | | Roscommon, trans. of Horace's *Art of Poetry*; Bunyan, *Mr Badman*; Burnet, *Life and Death of the Earl of Rochester* |
| 1681 | Charles II dissolves Oxford Parliament | Susanna Percival Mountfort Verbruggen joins King's Company | Dryden, *Absalom and Achitophel* I |
| 1682 | Monmouth Rebellion | Creation of United Company under Betterton and Smith | Dryden, *MacFlecknoe*; *Religio Laici*; Dryden and Tate, *Absalom and Achitophel*, II; D'Urfey, *Wit and Mirth* (*Pills to Purge Melancholy*) |
| 1683 | Rye House Plot | Charles Hart d. | Oldham, *Poems* |
| 1684 | | Michael Mohun d.; Cardell Goodman retires from stage | |
| 1685 | Death of Charles II; accession of James II | Theatres closed three months on death of Charles II | |
| 1687 | | Nell Gwyn d. | Dryden, *The Hind and the Panther* |
| 1688 | Flight of James II | T. Jevon d. | Halifax, *The Character of a Trimmer* |
| 1689 | Accession of William and Mary | | |
| 1690 | Battle of the Boyne | C. Cibber and T. Doggett begin acting careers | Locke, *An Essay concerning Human Understanding* |
| 1691 | | | Rochester, *Poems on Several Occasions* |
| 1692 | | W. Mountfort murdered; A. Leigh d. | |

| | 6 | 7 | 8 |
|---|---|---|---|
| *irth and death dates of non-dramatic writers* | *Dates of notable plays* | *Birth and death dates of playwrights* | *Continental theatrical events* |
| amuel Butler d.; ochester d. | Otway, *The Orphan*; Dryden, *The Spanish Friar*; Tate, from Shakespeare, *History of King Lear*; Lee, *Lucius Junius Brutus* | Porter d. | Founding of the Comédie Française; Fiorelli troupe moves to the Hôtel de Bourgogne |
| | Banks, *The Unhappy Favourite* | Lacy d. | |
| | Otway, *Venice Preserved* Banks, *Virtue Betrayed* | | |
| oung b. | Crowne, *City Politiques* | Killigrew d. | |
| | Tate, *A Duke and No Duke* | | |
| erkeley b.; Handel | Crowne, *Sir Courtly Nice*; Dryden, *Albion and Albanius* | Gay b.; Hill b.; Otway d. | |
| 'aller d. | Behn, *The Emperor of the Moon* | Buckingham d. | |
| unyan d.; Pope b. | Shadwell, *The Squire of Alsatia* | | New Italian troupe established in Paris |
| ichardson b. | Dryden, *Don Sebastian* | Aphra Behn d. | |
| | Betterton and Purcell, *The Prophetess*; Southerne, *Sir Anthony Love* | | |
| orge Fox d. | D'Urfey, *Love for Money*; Dryden and Purcell, *King Arthur*; Southerne, *The Wives Excuse* | Etherege d. | Racine, *Athalie* |
| | Settle and Purcell, *The Fairy Queen* | Lee d.; Shadwell d.; Mountfort d. | |

| 1 | 2 | 3 | 4 |
|---|---|---|---|

| Date | Historical events | Theatrical events | Non-dramatic literary events |
|---|---|---|---|
| 1693 | | Skipwith and Rich acquire control of United Company | Rymer, *A Short View of Tragedy* |
| 1694 | Queen Mary d. | Theatres closed for death of Queen Mary | Fox, *Journal* |
| 1695 | | Betterton and other players secede to act in Lincoln's Inn Fields; William Smith d. | Blackmore, *Prince Arthur* |
| 1696 | | Lord Chamberlain requires all plays to be fully licensed | |
| 1697 | Treaty of Ryswick | Mary Porter joins L.I.F. Company; Elizabeth Boutell retires | Dryden, *Alexander's Feast* |
| 1698 | | Robert Wilks joins Drury Lane Company | Collier, *A Short View of the Immorality and Profaneness of the English Stage* |
| 1699 | | Samuel Sandford retires | |
| 1700 | | First appearance of Anne Oldfield; Barton Booth joins L.I.F. Company | Dryden, *Fables* |
| 1701 | Pretender recognized by Louis XIV; war with France | | |
| 1702 | Death of William III; accession of Anne | | Defoe, *The Shortest Way with the Dissenters* |
| 1703 | Great Storm | | |
| 1704 | Battle of Blenheim | | Swift, *A Tale of a Tub* |

| *...rth and death dates non-dramatic ...iters* | 6<br>*Dates of notable plays* | 7<br>*Birth and death dates of playwrights* | 8<br>*Continental theatrical events* |
|---|---|---|---|
| | Congreve, *The Old Bachelor*; D'Urfey, *The Richmond Heiress*; Congreve, *The Double Dealer* | Lillo b. | |
| ...llotson d.; ...esterfield b. | Southerne, *The Fatal Marriage* | | Bossuet, *Les Maximes et Réflexions sur la comédie* |
| ...alifax d. | Congreve, *Love for Love*; Southerne, *Oroonoko* | Purcell d.; Killigrew d. | |
| | Cibber, *Love's Last Shift*; Vanbrugh, *The Relapse* | Wilson d. | |
| ...brey d. | Congreve, *The Mourning Bride*; Vanbrugh, *The Provoked Wife* | Ravenscroft d. | Italian players expelled from Paris |
| | | Howard d. | |
| ...emple d. | Farquhar, *The Constant Couple*; Cibber, from Shakespeare, *Richard III* | | |
| | Congreve, *The Way of the World*; Cibber, *Love Makes a Man* | Dryden d.; Thomson b. | |
| | Rowe, *Tamerlane* | Sedley d. | |
| | | | Creation of an office of censorship in Paris |
| ...pys d.; John ...esley b. | Rowe, *The Fair Penitent* | T. Cibber b.; Dodsley b.; ? Crowne d. | |
| ...cke d. | Cibber, *The Careless Husband* | | |

| 1 | 2 | 3 | 4 |
|---|---|---|---|
| Date | Historical events | Theatrical events | Non-dramatic literary events |
| 1705 | | Queen's Theatre in Haymarket opened; *Daily Courant* begins printing playbills | Mandeville, *The Grumbling Hive* |
| 1706 | | | |
| 1707 | Union of Scotland and England | Anne Bracegirdle retires | Isaac Watts, *Hymns* |
| 1708 | | Union of companies at Drury Lane | |
| 1709 | | Betterton's players return to Queen's; Rich expelled from Drury Lane | Rowe (ed.), *Works of Shakespeare*; Steele begins *The Tatler* |
| 1710 | Trial of Sacheverell | Companies united under Cibber, Doggett and Wilks; Betterton d.; Elizabeth Barry retires | Berkeley, *Principles of Human Knowledge* |
| 1711 | | Queen's Theatre in Haymarket restricted to operas | Addison and Steele, *The Spectator*; Shaftesbury, *Characteristics*; Pope, *An Essay on Criticism* |
| 1712 | | Richard Estcourt d. | Pope, *The Rape of the Lock* |
| 1713 | Treaty of Utrecht | Heidegger becomes manager of Queen's Theatre; Doggett retires | |
| 1714 | Death of Anne; accession of George I | Rich's company opens at new L.I.F.; Steele becomes governor of Drury Lane; Quin joins Drury Lane company | |
| 1715 | Jacobite Rebellion | Steele given royal patent for Drury Lane | Pope, trans. of *The Iliad*, I |
| 1716 | | | Gay, *Trivia* |

|  | 6 | 7 | 8 |
|---|---|---|---|
|  | Centlivre, *The Gamester*; Vanbrugh, *The Confederacy* |  |  |
| *elyn* d. | Farquhar, *The Recruiting Officer* | Banks d. |  |
|  | Farquhar, *The Beaux' Stratagem* | Farquhar d.; Fielding b. | Le Sage, *Crispin rival de son maître* |
|  |  |  | Regnard, *Le Légataire universel* |
| *hnson* b. | Centlivre, *The Busy Body* |  |  |
|  | C. Shadwell, *The Fair Quaker of Deal* |  |  |
| *ume* b. |  |  |  |
|  | Phillips, *The Distressed Mother* | Moore b. |  |
| *mer* d.; Sterne b. | Addison, *Cato* |  |  |
|  | Rowe, *Jane Shore* |  |  |
|  |  | Tate d. |  |
| *ay* b. | Bullock, *A Woman is a Riddle* | Wycherley d. | Riccoboni's company opens at the Théâtre du Palais Royal |

| 1 | 2 | 3 | 4 |
|---|---|---|---|
| *Date* | *Historical events* | *Theatrical events* | *Non-dramatic literary events* |
| 1717 | | | |
| 1718 | | French comedians at L.I.F. | Prior, *Poems on Several Occasions* |
| 1719 | | | Defoe, *Robinson Crusoe*, I |
| 1720 | South Sea Bubble | Steele removed from Drury Lane; new theatre opened in Haymarket | Defoe, *Captain Singleton* |
| 1721 | Walpole becomes Lord Treasurer | French comedians at Little Theatre in the Haymarket | |
| 1722 | | | Defoe, *Moll Flanders* |
| 1723 | | | |
| 1724 | | W. Pinkethman retires | Swift, *The Drapier's First Lette.* |
| 1726 | | | Swift, *Gulliver's Travels*; Thomson, *Winter* |
| 1727 | Death of George I; accession of George II | | Gay, *Fables*, I |
| 1728 | | A third acting troupe forms at the Little Haymarket; Booth retires | Pope, first *Dunciad* |
| 1729 | | New theatre in Goodman's Fields, under Odell; début of Kitty Raftor Clive | Swift, *A Modest Proposal* |
| 1730 | | Anne Oldfield d. | |
| 1731 | | H. Giffard becomes proprietor of Goodman's Fields | |

| | 6 | | 7 | 8 |
|---|---|---|---|---|
| ·th and death dates *non-dramatic iters* | | *Dates of notable plays* | *Birth and death dates of playwrights* | *Continental theatrical events* |
| race Walpole b. | | Gay, Pope and Arbuthnot, *Three Hours after Marriage* | Garrick b. | |
| in d.; Parnell d. | | | Rowe d.; Motteux d. | |
| | | | Addison d. | |
| | | | Foote b. | |
| or d.; Smollett b. | | Young, *The Revenge* | | |
| art b. | | Steele, *The Conscious Lovers* | | |
| | | Fenton, *Mariamne* | D'Urfey d. | |
| | | | Settle d. | |
| | | | Vanbrugh d. | |
| vton d. | | | Murphy b. | Destouches, *Le Philosophe marié* |
| | | Cibber and Vanbrugh, *The Provoked Husband*; Gay, *The Beggar's Opera* | | |
| ke b. | | Johnson of Cheshire, *Hurlothrumbo* | Congreve d.; Steele d. | |
| | | Thomson, *Sophonisba*; Fielding, *The Author's Farce*; Fielding, *Tom Thumb* | | Marivaux, *Le Jeu de l'amour et du hasard* |
| oe d.; Cowper b. | | Lillo, *The London Merchant*; Coffey, Mottley and T. Cibber, *The Devil to Pay* | | |

| Date | Historical events | Theatrical events | Non-dramatic literary events |
|------|-------------------|-------------------|------------------------------|
| 1732 | | H. Giffard opens new theatre in Ayliffe St., Goodman's Fields; John Rich opens new Covent Garden Theatre; R. Wilks d. | |
| 1733 | Walpole's Excise Bill | T. Cibber leads actors to secede from Drury Lane | Pope, *An Essay on Man* |
| 1734 | | C. Fleetwood becomes proprietor of Drury Lane | |
| 1735 | | | Pope, *Epistle to Dr Arbuthnot* |
| 1736 | | Fielding's company acts at Little Haymarket | |
| 1737 | Death of Queen Caroline; debates in Commons over war with Spain | Stage Licensing Act | Wesley, *Psalms and Hymns* |
| 1738 | | Riot against French troupe at Little Haymarket | Pope, *Epilogue to the Satires* |
| 1739 | War with Spain | W. Hallam's company acts at New Wells, Goodman's Fields | Swift, *Verses on the Death of Dr Swift* |
| 1740 | | H. Giffard's company resumes acting at Goodman's Fields; début of Margaret Woffington | Richardson, *Pamela* |
| 1741 | | Début of David Garrick | |
| 1742 | | Giffard's company moves to L.I.F. | Fielding, *Joseph Andrews*; Young, *Night Thoughts* |
| 1743 | | Secession of Garrick and Macklin; last performance of Mary Porter | Pope, revised *Dunciad* |
| 1744 | | Riots at Drury Lane over prices; début of George Anne Bellamy | |

| th and death dates on-dramatic ters | 6 Dates of notable plays | 7 Birth and death dates of playwrights | 8 Continental theatrical events |
|---|---|---|---|
| | Kelly, *The Married Philosopher* | Gay d.; Cumberland b.; Colman b. | Voltaire, *Zaïre* |
| | | | Nivelle de La Chaussée, *La Fausse Antipathie* |
| | | Dennis d. | Goldoni, *Belisaire* |
| | J. Miller, *The Man of Taste*; Aaron Hill, *Zara* | | |
| | Fielding, *Pasquin*; Lillo, *Fatal Curiosity* | | |
| bbon b. | Dodsley, *The Miller of Mansfield*; Fielding, *The Historical Register*; Carey, *The Dragon of Wantley* | | |
| | | George Lillo d. | |
| swell b. | | Southerne d. | |
| | Garrick, *The Lying Valet* | | |
| tley d. | | | |
| | | Carey d. | |
| e d. | | | |

| 1 | 2 | 3 | 4 |
|---|---|---|---|
| *Date* | *Historical events* | *Theatrical events* | *Non-dramatic literary events* |
| 1745 | Jacobite Rebellion | Fleetwood leaves; James Lacy made manager of Drury Lane; W. Hallam takes his company to Shepherd's Market, Mayfair | |
| 1747 | War with France | Garrick and Lacy purchase Drury Lane; Foote offers 'concerts' at Little Haymarket | |
| 1748 | | John Hippisley d. | Richardson, *Clarissa*; Smollett, *Roderick Random* |
| 1749 | | Riot at Little Haymarket | Fielding, *Tom Jones*; Johnson, *The Vanity of Human Wishes* |

| 6 | | 7 | 8 |
|---|---|---|---|
| *Birth and death dates of non-dramatic writers* | *Dates of notable plays* | *Birth and death dates of playwrights* | *Continental theatrical events* |
| Swift d. | Thomson, *Tancred and Sigismunda* | | La Place, *Théâtre anglais* |
| | Hoadly, *The Suspicious Husband* | | Goldoni, *Arlequin serviteur de deux maîtres* |
| | Moore, *The Foundling* | Thomson d. | |

# I The social and literary context

*John Loftis*

# 1 The court and the stage

In the prologue to *Marriage à la Mode* (1672), John Dryden alludes to the three major components of the Restoration audience: 'the Town, the City, and the Court',[1] three groups of unequal importance to the dramatists and the theatre managers, whose relative importance changed with the passing of years. An assessment of the impact of the three groups on the theatres and on the plays produced in them is at the same time one of the most important and one of the most subtle tasks confronting anyone who attempts to understand the dramatic history of the century following the Restoration.

In the first dozen years of the reign of Charles II, the decisive group seems to have been the court. For much of that time, two personal friends of the king presided over the theatres; a number of the best and most influential plays were written by persons who had direct access to the king; the king, then as throughout his twenty-five-year reign, took an interest in the new plays produced, frequently making suggestions to dramatists that shaped their plays. As we look for distinguishing qualities of Restoration comedy, we note at once its social orientation, an orientation that seems to have been influenced if not determined by the alliance between the court and the stage. James R. Sutherland has noted the youth of the Restoration court, the youth

[1] *The Poems of John Dryden*, ed. James Kinsley (Oxford, 1958), I, p. 145.

of the king himself as well as that of many of the most influential men around him, and he has called attention to the 'surprisingly large number of upper-class men and women who wrote with distinction: men like Buckingham, Orrery, Sir Robert Howard, Rochester, Dorset, Mulgrave, Roscommon, Sedley'.[1] Several of these men wrote plays, and all of them were patrons of the drama.

The combination of youth, rank and ability no doubt contributed to the self-confidence – even over-confidence – that characterizes much of Restoration criticism, the attitude of complacency to which Dryden gave tactless expression when in the epilogue to the second part of *The Conquest of Granada* (1671) he compared the drama of his own time with that of the Renaissance:

> Wit's now arriv'd to a more high degree;
> Our native Language more refin'd and free.
> Our Ladies and our men now speak more wit
> In conversation, than those Poets writ.[2]

This was extravagant, and it apparently provoked the censure it deserved; Dryden was moved to write a *Defence of the Epilogue: or an Essay on the Dramatic Poetry of the Last Age*, an analytical comparison of drama in his own time with that in the time of Shakespeare and Jonson. Compelled to defend an untenable position, Dryden is not at his best in this essay: he passes critical judgements that are neither sound nor consistent with opinions he elsewhere expressed. Yet he provides a contemporary examination of Restoration drama in its relation to the society that produced it.

Dryden insists, as at the time he had reason to do, that Restoration drama is a courtiers' drama, taking its distinctive qualities, and its distinctive excellencies, from the king and from men who looked to the king as a literary arbiter. As at few other times in English history, Dryden suggests, the court was dominated by men of rank who enjoyed literary conversation: 'And this leads me to the last and greatest advantage of our writing, which proceeds from *conversation*. In the age wherein those poets [of Shakespeare's time] lived, there was less of gallantry than in ours; neither did they keep the best company of theirs.'[3] This is more than the rhetoric of the royalist laureate: he undervalues the great Renaissance dramatists, of course, and yet he would

[1] Cf. James R. Sutherland, 'Restoration Prose', in *Restoration and Augustan Prose*, William Andrews Clark Memorial Library (Los Angeles, 1956), pp. 3–5.
[2] *Poems*, I, p. 135.
[3] *Defence of the Epilogue*, in *Essays of John Dryden*, ed. W. P. Ker (Oxford, 1926), I, p. 175.

seem to be accurate in describing what he saw about him. If he exaggerates the importance of the king's example, there is reason enough to believe that, more than any other sovereign since Queen Elizabeth I, Charles II did indeed help to shape dramatic history. As will be explained below, a number of dramatists, including Dryden himself, conversed with him on literary subjects, and collectively these men convey an impression of the king as knowledgeable about continental as well as English drama. He was a man of large intellectual capacity, and the drama was one among many subjects, apart from politics, which attracted him.[1]

Others than Dryden wrote about the king's attainments. Samuel Tuke, who had shared the royal exile, published a character of Charles II soon after the Restoration. 'Amongst his acquir'd endowments', he wrote,

> these are the most eminent, He understands *Spanish*, and *Italian*; speaks and writes *French* correctly; He is well vers'd in ancient and modern *History*, has read divers of the choicest Peeces of the *Politicks*, has studied some useful parts of the *Mathematicks*, as *Fortification*, and the knowledg of the *Globe*; but his chief delight is in *Navigation*, to which his *Genius* does so incline him, that by his frequent conversation with Mariners, and his own observation whilst he rid six weeks in the *Downes*, and in his passage into *Scotland*, he has arriv'd to so much knowledg in this Science, that I have heard many expert Seamen (whose discourses are not steer'd by the compass of the Court) speak of it with delight and wonder; in *General*, here is a true friend to *Literature*, and to *Learned Men*.[2]

If Tuke's devotion to his sovereign led to a generous estimate of his accomplishments, Charles's activities in the quarter-century that followed provide corroboration of his essential accuracy. The king proved indeed to be 'a true friend to *Literature* [meaning learning in general, including but not restricted to imaginative literature], and to *Learned Men*'.

In assessing his knowledge of literature, it is important to remember that he had spent many years on the continent in the middle of the seventeenth century, a period of remarkable accomplishment in France, the Netherlands and Spain. He had left England in 1646 and, except for the interval of his alliance with the Scots in 1650 and 1651, he did not return until May 1660.

[1] Godfrey Davies, *Essays on the Later Stuarts* (San Marino, California, 1958), pp. 20–4; James Sutherland, 'The Impact of Charles II on Restoration Literature', in Carroll Camden (ed.), *Restoration and Eighteenth-Century Literature* (Chicago, 1963), pp. 251–63.
[2] *A Character of Charles II* (London, 1660), p. 6.

# 6 The social and literary context

The earlier years of his exile, until 1654, he spent mainly in France and Holland; the later years in Germany and the Spanish Netherlands (modern Belgium).[1] He had, as Dryden remarks, 'an opportunity which is rarely allowed to sovereign princes . . . of travelling, and being conversant in the most polished courts of Europe';[2] and he set an example of cosmopolitanism to the courtiers of the Restoration. 'By his being abroad,' Lord Halifax wrote, 'he contracted a Habit of conversing familiarly, which added to his natural Genius, made him very *apt to talk*; perhaps more than a very nice judgment would approve'.[3] Among those to whom he talked were men who wrote plays: Samuel Tuke, the Earl of Bristol, the Earl of Orrery, Tom D'Urfey, John Crowne, as well as John Dryden.

In the first year of the Restoration, presumably with French tragedy in mind, he commanded the Earl of Orrery to write an English play in rhyme.[4] In this, as in his subsequent patronage of Orrery, Sir Robert Howard and Dryden, he provided an impetus to the development of the rhymed heroic play, a dramatic sub-genre that celebrates a conception of kingship altogether consistent with that of the Stuarts.[5] A year or so later the king gave Samuel Tuke a suggestion that resulted in *The Adventures of Five Hours* (1663), the first highly successful play of the Restoration. His plot, Tuke writes in the preface to the third edition (1671), 'was taken out of *Dom Pedro Calderon*, a celebrated *Spanish* Author, the Nation of the World who are the happiest in the force and delicacy of their *Inventions*, and recommended to me by *His Sacred Majesty*, as an *Excellant Design*'. It cannot be determined where Charles saw the Spanish play (which Tuke and others at the time erroneously attributed to Calderón). Still, in some four years' residence in the Spanish Netherlands, he had opportunity enough to gain a knowledge of the *comedia*.

That the king had a certain sophistication in neoclassical literary theory is implied by a remark of Dryden's in the preface to *Secret Love* (published in 1668). Charles particularly liked this play, giving it, Dryden writes with understandable pride, 'the Title of His Play'; and if his pleasure in it was heightened by Nell Gwyn's performance of a principal role, he did not relax

---

[1] For a detailed account of Charles II's experiences on the Continent, see Eva Scott, *The King in Exile* (London, 1905) and *The Travels of the King* (London, 1907). See also Maurice Ashley, *Charles II : The Man and the Statesman* (London, 1971), pp. 17–103.

[2] *An Essay on the Dramatic Poetry of the Last Age*, in *Essays*, I, p. 176.

[3] George Savile, Marquis of Halifax, *A Character of King Charles the Second : And Political, Moral and Miscellaneous Thoughts and Reflections* (London, 1750), p. 30.

[4] Thomas Morrice, *Memoirs of Roger Boyle, Earl of Orrery*, in Orrery's *Collection of State Letters* (1742), p. 39.

[5] John Loftis, *The Politics of Drama in Augustan England* (Oxford, 1963), p. 14.

his critical faculties. He concurred, Dryden writes, in a censure 'of the last Scene of the Play, where *Celadon* and *Florimell* are treating too lightly of their marriage in the presence of the Queen, who likewise seems to stand idle while the great action of the *Drama* is still depending'. This would seem to be an echo of conversation at court, notable in that the objection, in which the king concurred, turns on a subtle aspect of literary theory: the doctrine of decorum. Yet he had a taste for farcical comedy, as is suggested among other ways by the even more active interest he took, to judge from a remark in a letter Dryden wrote in July 1677, in another of Dryden's comedies: 'the Kings Comedy lyes in the Sudds [i.e. in difficulties]: . . . it will be almost such another piece of businesse as the fond Husband, for such the King will have it, who is parcell poet with me in the plott; one of the designes being a story he was pleas'd formerly to tell me . . .'. Charles E. Ward has identified the comedy as *The Kind Keeper*, which resembles Tom D'Urfey's farcical *A Fond Husband*, to which Dryden here alludes.[1] One of the least attractive of Dryden's comedies, *The Kind Keeper* scarcely does credit to the royal taste – though a desire to satirize political opponents may have provided an extraliterary motive for some of the more distasteful qualities of the play.

Even at the end of his life, Charles was making suggestions to dramatists: to John Crowne, whose most successful comedy, *Sir Courtly Nice; or, It Cannot Be* (1685), was based on a Spanish play recommended to him, and to Tom D'Urfey, whose *The Banditti* (1686) was based on a translation from the Spanish also recommended by the king. Crowne wrote in his dedicatory epistle, published soon after the king's death: 'The greatest pleasure he [Charles] had from the Stage was in Comedy, and he often Commanded me to Write it, and lately gave me a *Spanish* Play called *No Puedeser: Or, It Cannot Be*. out of which I took part o' the Name, and design o' This.' And D'Urfey wrote in his preface: 'The distress of the *Story* was hinted to me by the *Late Blessed King* of ever-glorious Memory, from a Spanish Translation' (probably Lord Bristol's lost *Worse and Worse*, based on a play by Calderón to which D'Urfey's *The Banditti* has important resemblances).[2]

These examples of Charles's intervention in dramatic affairs emphasize the importance to him, and to Restoration drama, of his exposure to Spanish and French drama during the exile. Some of the dramatists, too, had been impressed by plays they had read or seen on the continent, and, soon after the

[1] *The Letters of John Dryden*, ed. Charles E. Ward (Durham, N.C., 1942), pp. 13–14.
[2] In his preface D'Urfey specifies the kingdom of Naples (under Spanish rule) as the place of action in his source. This is the locale of Calderón's *Peor está que estaba*, of which Bristol's play was presumably an adaptation. *The Banditti* has similarities of plot to the Spanish play.

Restoration, they wrote plays based on French or Spanish models. Sir William Davenant adapted his last play, *The Man's the Master* (1668), from Paul Scarron's *Jodelet, ou le maître-valet* (itself an adaptation from the Spanish), which was first performed about 1643 and published in 1645. Since Davenant was in France from 1645 until early in 1650, when Scarron was at the height of his career, he probably became acquainted then with Scarron's work. He may have met Scarron personally: both of them were socially prominent and moved in court circles. The Duke of Newcastle's collaboration with Dryden in *Sir Martin Mar-All* (1667) is perhaps, in its origin, to be traced to the duke's experiences in exile. *Sir Martin Mar-All* is a close adaptation of two French plays, Molière's *L'Étourdi* and Philippe Quinault's *L'Amant indiscret*, both of them having a common source in the Italian *commedia dell'arte*, in Niccolò Barbieri's *L'Inavvertito*. The two French plays were written and acted in the 1650s. It is likely that Newcastle saw or read them while he was on the continent and, a decade later, enlisted Dryden's aid in completing *Sir Martin Mar-All*, a brilliantly successful farcical comedy, one of the closest approximations in Restoration England to the *commedia dell'arte*.[1] The Earl of Bristol's three adaptations from Calderón (of which only one, *Elvira; or, The Worst Not Always True*, survives) may result from his residence in Spain during the Interregnum, though he had been born there early in the century, the son of the English ambassador.

These probable instances of courtiers' plays deriving from the experiences of royalists in exile provide a reminder that the strong native English dramatic tradition was altered, in some small and immeasurable degree, by continental importations. The literary conversations so gracefully represented by Dryden in his *Essay of Dramatic Poesy* (1668) would seem to reflect current topics of conversation at court and in the theatres; and, if so, men of letters were preoccupied with a reassessment of English drama, Renaissance as well as Restoration, in the light of their expanded knowledge of continental drama. The *Essay of Dramatic Poesy* is in the strictest sense an essay in comparative literature; and if the fundamental theme is a comparative evaluation of ancient and modern drama, the theme is expanded to embrace evaluations of French and Spanish drama. The references to Spanish drama are consistently depreciatory; those to French drama vary in tone from one interlocutor to another. The essay reflects an ambiguity in Dryden's own attitude towards the French dramatists: admiration, above all for Corneille, but recognition as well that the English had finally to go their own way, with only limited at-

[1] *The Works of John Dryden*, IX, ed. John Loftis and Vinton A. Dearing (Berkeley, California, 1966), pp. 354–67.

tention to French precept and example.[1] In reading the *Essay of Dramatic Poesy* we come as close as is possible to the frame of mind of the first generation of Restoration dramatists, in which a new cosmopolitanism, engendered by the experiences of royalists in exile, blends with a hard-headed awareness of the intractable nature of English taste.

Both of the men Charles II chose to preside over the Restoration playhouses, Thomas Killigrew of the King's Company and Sir William Davenant of the Duke's, had shared the exile. In their experiences, their abilities and their personalities, they epitomize much that is distinctive about at least the earlier years of the Restoration, and their careers – especially their experiences during the Interregnum – will repay brief attention in our effort to understand the conditions under which Restoration drama was written and performed.

Killigrew wrote while on the continent a fictional account of the royalists' experiences, *Thomaso, or The Wanderer* (published 1664), a long and loosely constructed semi-autobiographical drama which certainly includes reference to political events and apparently to his own and his friends' social intrigues as well. However prolix and clumsily constructed *Thomaso* may be, it provides insight into the conditions of life the Cavaliers had encountered: the demoralizing poverty, the enforced freedom from responsibility and the frequent travel from one country to another – in short, the conditions of life which reinforced if they did not occasion the sophisticated cosmopolitanism as well as the moral laxity that found expression in Restoration comedy. Killigrew was known for his easy good humour as well as for the comedies he had written before the civil wars. He had long known the king and his principal courtiers; he had shared their adventures and their sufferings; he knew their taste and was prepared to offer the kind of drama they wanted.[2]

Davenant, a much more important dramatist and man of letters than Killigrew, was like him in having written plays before the wars and in having shared the exile.[3] I have already referred to his last play, *The Man's the*

[1] Pierre Legouis, 'Corneille and Dryden as Dramatic Critics', in *Seventeenth Century Studies Presented to Sir Herbert Grierson* (Oxford, 1938), pp. 269–91; Frank Livingstone Huntley, *On Dryden's 'Essay of Dramatic Poesy'* (Chicago, 1951), pp. 6–8; John M. Aden, 'Dryden, Corneille, and the "Essay of Dramatic Poesy"', *Review of English Studies*, N.S., VI (April 1955), pp. 147–56.

[2] The standard biography is Alfred Harbage, *Thomas Killigrew, Cavalier Dramatist, 1612–83* (Philadelphia, Pa., 1930).

[3] As early as 26 March 1639 Charles I had granted Davenant a patent to build a new theatre, though nothing seems to have come of the grant, which in any event was soon revoked: see Alfred Harbage, *Sir William Davenant, Poet, Venturer 1606–1668* (Philadelphia, Pa., 1935), p. 67.

*Master*, as a probable consequence of his residence in France. A more important literary consequence of his residence there was the unfinished poem *Gondibert*, intended as a new form of epic which would embody some of the structural qualities of drama. In *Gondibert* there is an accommodation between epic and tragic theory anticipating that in the later heroic play, of which, we have it on Dryden's authority, Davenant's *The Siege of Rhodes* (1656; 1658) is the first example.[1] And in the conversations Davenant carried on with Abraham Cowley, Edmund Waller and Thomas Hobbes, as Davenant wrote *Gondibert*[2] – conversations of which his preface to the poem (1650) and Hobbes's published reply to it (1650) are a systematic formulation – he gave preliminary expression to major themes in Restoration dramatic criticism even as he provided systematic reformulation of much of Renaissance criticism. The vagaries of fortune took Davenant back to London in the 1650s, where beginning in 1656 he produced a series of semi-dramatic performances, including the operatic version of *The Siege of Rhodes*. If a man of more energy and ability than Killigrew, as he certainly was the more accomplished writer, Davenant seems nevertheless to have been like him temperamentally. In choosing the governors of the London theatres, Charles, even while rewarding men who had been faithful in the adversity of exile, had an eye to their capacity to meet his own and his courtiers' taste in drama.

Killigrew and Davenant gave the king what he wanted. Restoration drama is directed to the tastes and interests of a court which was, in the opinion of John Dennis, 'the most polite that ever *England* saw'.[3] As already suggested, many of the plays were written by men who were prominent socially and had access to the king. In the first decade of the Restoration (to choose a manageable period for analysis), a time when the new drama moved to its distinctive forms, the important playwrights were, with the single exception of Thomas Shadwell, men who had some claim to social distinction. In addition to Killigrew and Davenant, I have already alluded to the Earl of Orrery, who shared credit with Davenant, Dryden and Sir Robert Howard for the early vogue of the rhymed heroic play; the Duke of Newcastle, who collaborated with Dryden in *Sir Martin Mar-All*; and the Earl of Bristol, who adapted plays from

---

[1] Dryden, 'Of Heroic Plays', published as a preface to *The Conquest of Granada* (1672). On the background in literary theory for the heroic play, see *The Works of John Dryden*, VIII, ed. John Harrington Smith, Dougald MacMillan and Vinton A. Dearing (Berkeley, California, 1962), pp. 284–9.

[2] Arthur H. Nethercot, *Sir William D'avenant, Poet Laureate and Playwright-Manager* (Chicago, 1938), pp. 241 ff.

[3] *A Defence of 'Sir Fopling Flutter'*, in *The Critical Works of John Dennis*, ed. E. N. Hooker (Baltimore, Md., 1943), II, p. 243.

the Spanish. Sir Robert Howard and his brothers Edward and James, sons of the Earl of Berkshire (and after 1663 brothers-in-law of Dryden), all produced plays. At least one of the comedies of the Honourable James Howard, *The English Monsieur* (*c.* 1663), merits the attention of literary historians as an early approximation of the Restoration pattern of the comedy of manners.

The two most important dramatists of the first decade, Dryden and Sir George Etherege, repaid royal friendship and patronage with comedies achieving the conversational brilliance to which the court aspired. It is in Etherege's second play, *She Would If She Could* (1668), that the Restoration comedy of manners is conventionally said to come to maturity, and in his third, *The Man of Mode; or, Sir Fopling Flutter* (1676), that it reaches one of its peaks.

The latter comedy assumed in the writings of Richard Steele early in the following century the status of typicality, providing a target for what was in fact an assault on Restoration comedy as a whole. All this will require our attention later. Of present relevance is contemporary or near-contemporary testimony to the accuracy of Etherege's portrayal of Restoration courtiers. Dryden wrote the epilogue to the play and thought fit to include in it a disclaimer that Etherege, in his title character, had any one person in view. 'Yet none Sir Fopling him, or him can call,' Dryden wrote; 'He's Knight o'th' Shire, and represents ye all.'[1] Yet a disclaimer is evidence of the impression of authenticity conveyed by the play,[2] and certainly some members of the audience identified characters with prominent persons. Peter Killigrew, brother of the leader of the King's Company, reported in a letter written just three days after the first performance 'the generall opinion' that Sir Fopling represented 'Mr Villiers, L^d Grandisons eldest son' and that Dorimant represented the famous Duke of Monmouth.[3] The latter, to say the least, would seem improbable, and in any event is contradicted by the speculations of others, including Saint-Évremond, who alluded to the resemblance of Dorimant to the Earl of Rochester.[4] John Dennis later wrote more fully on this

[1] *Poems*, I, p. 159.
[2] Captain Alexander Radcliffe criticized Etherege for merely transcribing, with literary heightening, the conversation he heard at a fashionable tavern: *The Ramble* (1682), p. 5, quoted in *The Dramatic Works of Sir George Etherege*, ed. H. F. B. Brett-Smith (Oxford, 1927), I, p. lxx.
[3] In *Joseph Spence, Observations, Anecdotes, and Characters of Books and Men*, ed. James M. Osborn (Oxford, 1966), II, p. 638.
[4] *A Memoir of the Life of John Wilmot, Earl of Rochester*, in *The Works of the Right Honourable Earls of Rochester and Roscommon* (1707), Sig. b5, as cited in Jocelyn Powell, 'George Etherege and the Form of a Comedy', in John Russell Brown and Bernard Harris (eds), *Restoration Theatre* (London, 1965), pp. 68–9.

subject. His remarks repay quotation, not because they establish an intention on Etherege's part to portray Rochester (for it would seem on balance that Dryden's disclaimer is accurate), but because they convey Dennis's conviction that there was a resemblance between the characters of the comedy and the court wits. In *A Defence of 'Sir Fopling Flutter'* (1722), written in rebuttal to Steele's *Spectator*, No. 65 (1711), Dennis includes a historical line of argument, an attempted justification of controversial qualities in Etherege's characters as faithful depictions of life. '*Dorimont*', Dennis writes, 'is an admirable Picture of a Courtier in the Court of King *Charles* the Second.' And then he becomes more specific:

> Now I remember very well, that upon the first acting this Comedy, it was generally believed to be an agreeable Representation of the Persons of Condition of both Sexes, both in Court and Town; and that all the World was charm'd with *Dorimont*; and that it was unanimously agreed, that he had in him several of the Qualities of *Wilmot* Earl of *Rochester*, as, his Wit, his Spirit, his amorous Temper, the Charms that he had for the fair Sex, his Falshood, and his Inconstancy; the agreeable Manner of his chiding his Servants, which the late Bishop of *Salisbury* takes Notice of in his Life; and lastly, his repeating, on every Occasion, the Verses of *Waller*, for whom that noble Lord had a very particular Esteem. . . .[1]

This is the testimony of a contemporary (Dennis was born in 1657), the more plausible because of its specifics; and it is useful historical evidence, whatever the unknowable facts may have been about Etherege's intentions in writing the play. Dennis obviously thought of *The Man of Mode* as a play about the 'Court and Town' – that is to say, about the noblemen and gentlemen of Charles's court and the fashionable parts of London.

[1] In *Critical Works*, II, pp. 244, 248.

# 2 The audience

Following the remarkable accomplishments in drama of the 1670s, attendance at the theatre dropped off to the point that in 1682 the two companies, the King's and the Duke's, were merged into a single United Company, and for thirteen years, until 1695, London supported only one theatre. It is scarcely coincidental that this period is that of the Revolution – as well as of a diminished production of distinguished plays.[1] James II shared his brother's liking for the theatre, if not his acuity of mind and his taste, but his short and troubled reign is a parenthesis in dramatic history, a time when the most able men were otherwise engaged than in writing and seeing plays.

Under William and Mary the theatre lost its special relationship with the court: King William, a Dutchman who was his own prime minister and commander-in-chief in a time of war, had other things on his mind. It would indeed seem surprising that he took even a minimum of interest in the theatre (as he did, for example, when in 1695 he personally received Thomas Betterton and other discontented actors from the United Company and gave them a licence to form their own company).[2] Queen Mary occasionally attended the

---

[1] Cf. George W. Whiting, 'The Condition of the London Theaters, 1679–83: A Reflection of the Political Situation', *Modern Philology*, XXV (November 1927), pp. 195–206.

[2] John Downes, *Roscius Anglicanus* (London, 1708), p. 43; Cibber, *An Apology for the Life of Mr Colley Cibber*, ed. Robert W. Lowe, 2 vols (London, 1889), I, pp. 192n–193n.

public theatre,[1] but, pious lady as she was, she was temperamentally incapable of the enthusiasm for the drama shown by her royal uncle. And her sister Queen Anne, who in 1702 succeeded King William, had even less capability and taste for the role of theatre patron.

Although the theatre remained the preserve of the affluent, the audience had changed, and John Dennis, among others, commented on the fact. Dennis was a man of strong prejudices, and his remarks must be read with an awareness that they are coloured by his own frustrations, but he is nevertheless a useful witness because more than any other person of the time he attempted detailed analysis of social reasons for what he regarded as a decline in the quality of drama. In an essay of 1702 he praises the Restoration audience:

> ... in the Reign of King *Charles* the Second, when People had an admirable taste of Comedy, all those men of extraordinary parts, who were the Ornaments of that Court: as the late Duke of *Buckingham*, my Lord *Normanby*, my Lord *Dorset*, my late Lord *Rochester*, Sir *Charles Sidley*, Dr *Frazer*, Mr *Savil*, Mr *Buckley*, were in Love with the Beauties of this Comedy [*The Merry Wives of Windsor*].[2]

Moved by pique at the recent failure of his adaptation of Shakespeare's comedy, he turns later in the essay to a comparative analysis of 'the taste of *England* for Comedy' in King Charles's reign, when in his opinion it was good, to that at the time he was writing, when it was 'excessively bad'. His disappointment leads him to overstatement, of course; and yet his nostalgic remarks about the taste of the Restoration court repay attention:

> ... in the Reign of King *Charles* the Second, a considerable part of an Audience had such an Education as qualified them to judge of Comedy. That Reign was a Reign of Pleasure, even the entertainments of their Closet were all delightful. Poetry and Eloquence were then their Studies, and that human, gay, and sprightly Philosophy, which qualify'd them to relish the only reasonable pleasures which man can have in the World, and those are Conversation and Dramatick Poetry. In their Closets they cultivated at once their Imaginations and Judgements, to make themselves the fitter for conversation, which requires them both.

---

[1] The warrants for payment for her box provide a detailed record of her attendance: P.R.O., L.C. 5/149, p. 368; L.C. 5/151, p. 369; quoted in Allardyce Nicoll, *A History of English Drama, 1660–1900*, 6 vols (Cambridge, 1952–9) (Nicoll, *HED*), I, p. 352.
[2] *A Large Account of the Taste in Poetry, and the Causes of the Degeneracy of It*, in *Critical Works*, I (1939), p. 279.

And the Conversation of those times was so different from what it is now, that it let them as much into that particular knowledge of Mankind, which is requisite for the judging of Comedy, as the present Conversation removes us from it. The discourse, which now every where turns upon Interest, rolled then upon the Manners and Humours of Men.[1]

Whether literary taste had indeed degenerated may be doubtful, though there were to be many in the next generation, including Alexander Pope and Henry Fielding, to say so, but Dennis would seem to be accurate in emphasizing the increased preoccupation with business and politics in the years after King Charles's death. Probably he is accurate also in stressing, as he does, the increased heterogeneity of the theatre audience, which, he writes, included 'Several People who made their Fortunes in the late War; and from a state of obscurity, and perhaps of misery, have risen to a condition of distinction and plenty.'[2] He does not precisely say that persons of inferior rank were attending the theatre; rather, that some persons with new fortunes, as well as some who were working to acquire them, were doing so:

. . . in the present Reign, a great part of the Gentlemen have not leisure, because want throws them upon employments, and there are ten times more Gentlemen now in business, than there were in King *Charles* his Reign. Nor have they serenity, by Reason of a War, in which all are concerned, by reason of the Taxes which make them uneasie. By reason that they are attentive to the events of affairs, and too full of great and real events, to receive due impressions from the imaginary ones of the Theatre.[3]

We may supplement Dennis's contemporary but prejudiced comments on the nature and causes of the changes in the theatrical audience with the findings of modern historical research. J. H. Plumb, in an analysis of 'The Role of the Executive', provides an account of the changing relationship between the court and the major administrative departments which helps to explain the increased professionalism that prompted Dennis's complaint:

Between 1680 and 1720, the executive underwent a number of profound changes. . . . The most striking, perhaps, is the changed relation-

[1] Ibid. I, p. 292.
[2] Ibid. I, p. 293.
[3] Ibid. I, p. 294.

ship between the Court and the Departments of State. In contrast with the seventeenth century, by the early eighteenth the Court was dwarfed in size of personnel employed by the Admiralty, the War Office, and the Treasury (including the Exchequer, Customs, and Excise). The Court had, in fact, diminished absolutely as well as relatively. . . . William III and Anne had abolished a number of offices – Esquires of the Body as well as various sporting offices. Some offices, although in theory they still existed, were not filled; others had ceased to have much importance.[1]

And just as the court diminished in size and influence, the governmental bureaucracies grew enormously:

The number of men employed by the government grew faster between 1689 and 1715 than in any previous period of English history, and perhaps at a rate not to be equalled again until the nineteenth century. The volume of government business grew equally fast, and in so doing touched directly the lives of more people than ever before.[2]

Not all the men employed in transacting the business resided in London, but obviously very many of them did live there, and, to judge from Dennis's comments, some of them attended the theatre. By the time of Queen Anne's reign, the institutions of government were conducted by a large core of professional civil servants.[3]

What Dennis says about the occupations of theatregoers in the year Queen Anne succeeded is convincing enough and is supported by Professor Plumb's researches. What about Dennis's reflections on the audience in Charles II's time?

Our information about the Restoration audience is most complete for the period covered by Pepys's diary, 1660–9, the early years of the reign. Pepys's record of the people he saw in the audience provides detailed, even statistical, confirmation for our generalizations about royal patronage of the theatres: during these years, Emmett L. Avery writes, 'there were at least 130 occasions when royalty witnessed plays in the public theaters or at Court.'[4] Yet if Pepys's diary (which can be supplemented by scattered public and private records) includes many references to the king and queen, the Duke and

---

[1] J. H. Plumb, *The Origins of Political Stability* (Boston, 1967), p. 108.
[2] Ibid. p. 112.
[3] Ibid. pp. 112–25.
[4] Emmett L. Avery, 'The Restoration Audience', *Philological Quarterly*, XLV (January 1966), p. 55. For an account of performances at court, see Eleanore Boswell, *The Restoration Court Stage (1660–1702)* (Cambridge, Mass., 1932).

Duchess of York, and the royal mistresses, as well as lords and gentlemen of high rank, it also establishes the fact that professional men and bureaucrats, in whose number Pepys himself is to be counted, went to the theatres. Pepys's colleagues in the Navy Office were often in the audience, and presumably they would have had no more liking for the drama than men employed in other branches of government service. A close examination of his diary, and of such other records as remain, provides a caution against assuming that the prominence of the courtiers precluded the presence of persons of modest wealth and intermediate social position.[1]

To be sure, the tone of references to 'citizens' by Pepys as well as by the dramatists would suggest that at least the humbler members of the business community were regarded as aliens in the playhouse. Thus Pepys on 26 December 1668 referred disparagingly to the fact that the house was filled with 'ordinary citizens',[2] and Dryden in the prologue of *Marriage à la Mode* (1672) alluded mockingly to their preference for entertainments other than those provided by the theatres:

> Our City Friends so far will hardly come,
> They can take up with Pleasures nearer home;
> And see gay Shows, and gawdy Scenes elsewhere:
> For we presume they seldom come to hear.[3]

The mere distance of the playhouse, in this instance Lincoln's Inn Fields, from the mercantile City, as Dryden here implies, kept members of the business community away. However, Dryden acknowledges in this prologue that the theatre had recently lost much of its fashionable clientele in consequence of the war (the Third Dutch War, in which many young gentlemen served in the army and navy), and in a bantering vein Dryden appeals to the citizens to make up the vacancies. On the evidence of the Restoration prologues and epilogues, Pierre Danchin has indeed suggested that the theatrical season 1671–2 is a transitional one, a time when the dramatists and managers, having lost a portion of their audiences from the upper classes, were forced to seek more broadly based support, and notably support from the

---

[1] Avery, op. cit. pp. 58–61. See also Helen McAfee, *Pepys on the Restoration Stage* (New Haven, Conn., 1916); Nicoll, *HED*, I, pp. 5–19; Harold Love, 'The Myth of the Restoration Audience', *Komos*, I (1967), pp. 49–56; Leo Hughes, *The Drama's Patrons: A Study of the Eighteenth-Century London Audience* (Austin, Texas, 1971).

[2] Quoted from *The London Stage*, Part 1, ed. William van Lennep (Carbondale, Ill., 1965), p. 150. Cf. A. S. Bear, 'Criticism and Social Change: The Case of Restoration Drama', *Komos*, II (1969), p. 27.

[3] *Poems*, I, pp. 144–5.

*public bourgeois*.¹ Certainly Wycherley's prologue to *The Gentleman Dancing-Master*, also recited in 1672, was addressed 'To the CITY, Newly after the Removal of the Dukes Company from *Lincoln-Inn-fields* to their new Theatre, near *Salisbury*-Court':² that is, to Dorset Garden Theatre, east of their former site and thus closer to the residences of the citizens. Some broadening in the social range of the audience there may have been, but I can see no evidence of a major and lasting change until after the Revolution.³ In an epilogue spoken in 1674 at the opening of the new Drury Lane Theatre, Dryden alluded to its favourable location, near the residences of the gentry, in comparison with that of Dorset Garden.⁴ In any event, when members of the business community had the time, inclination and money to attend the theatre, they found themselves the butts of contemptuous allusions in the dialogue of the plays as well as in prologues and epilogues. The type character of the merchant cuckold – Alderman Gripe, Alderman Fondlewife, Sir Jealous Traffic – persisted into King William's and even Queen Anne's reigns, and so did satirical references to citizens in the audience.⁵

Many of the satirical glances at citizens turn on the seating arrangements in the late seventeenth-century theatres, arrangements that seem to have remained largely constant from the Restoration well into the eighteenth century:⁶ the customary fourfold divisions of box, pit, middle gallery and upper gallery. Only the price of admission determined where a man could sit, but there seem nevertheless to have been well-established habits of division along social lines. The several contemporary accounts of the social groups who sat in the different areas were written in the final years of the seventeenth and in the early years of the eighteenth centuries, but they would nevertheless seem to be applicable to the theatres of Charles II's reign as well. Among other descriptions of the audiences is a playful one by Jonathan Swift in *A Tale of a Tub*, written in King William's reign though not published until 1704, an analysis of the theatre's clientele that is not the less informative for its wit:

¹ Pierre Danchin, 'Le Public des théâtres Londoniens à l'époque de la Restauration d'après les prologues et les épilogues', in Jean Jacquot (ed.), *Dramaturgie et société* (Paris, 1968), II, pp. 878–9.
² Ibid. II, p. 879.
³ Cf. Eric Rothstein, *Restoration Tragedy : Form and the Process of Change* (Madison, Wisconsin, 1967), pp. 43–4.
⁴ *Poems*, I, pp. 379–80.
⁵ John Loftis, *Comedy and Society from Congreve to Fielding* (Stanford, California, 1959), *passim*.
⁶ Cf. Danchin, op. cit. II, p. 857.

... the Pit is sunk below the Stage ... ; that whatever *weighty* Matter shall be delivered thence (whether it be *Lead* or *Gold*) may fall plum into the Jaws of certain *Criticks* (as I think they are called) which stand ready open to devour them. Then, the Boxes are built round, and raised to a Level with the Scene, in deference to the Ladies, because, That large Portion of Wit laid out in raising Pruriences and Protuberances, is observ'd to run much upon a Line, and ever in a Circle. The whining Passions and little starved Conceits, are gently wafted up by their own extreme Levity, to the middle Region, and there fix and are frozen by the frigid Understandings of the Inhabitants. Bombast and Buffoonry, by Nature lofty and light, soar highest of all, and would be lost in the Roof, if the prudent Architect had not with much Foresight contrived for them a fourth Place, called *the Twelve-Peny Gallery*, and there planted a suitable Colony, who greedily intercept them in their Passage.[1]

Despite Swift's proposition that 'Air being a heavy Body ... must needs be more so, when loaden and press'd down by Words', his fourfold division of the audience is more than a jest; it is corroborated by less witty descriptions.

One of the most detailed accounts of the late seventeenth-century theatres appeared in a travel narrative written in French and published in 1698:

Il y a deux Théatres à Londres, l'un grand & beau, où se fait tantôt l'Opera, tantôt la Comédie: l'autre Théatre, qui est plus petit, n'est que pour la Comédie. Le Parterre est en Amphithéatre, & rempli de bancs sans dossiers; garnis & couverts d'une étofe verte. Les hommes de qualité, particulierement les jeunes gens; quelques Dames sages & honnêtes; & beaucoup de Filles qui cherchent fortune, s'asseyent tous là pesle mêle; causent, joüent, badinent, écoutent, n'écoutent pas. Plus loin, contre le mur, sous la premiere Galerie, & vis à vis de la Scene, s'éléve un autre Amphithéatre qui est occupé par les personnes de la plus haute Qualité, entre lesquelles on voit peu d'hommes. Les Galeries, dont il y a seulement un double rang, ne sont remplies que de gens du commun, particulierement celles d'en haut.[2]

Approximately the same pattern of division is suggested in 1714 by John Macky, who in a travel narrative described the audience of the three theatres then in operation:

[1] *A Tale of a Tub*, ed. Herbert Davis, in *The Prose Works of Jonathan Swift*, I (Oxford, 1939), pp. 36–7.
[2] Henri de Valbourg Misson, *Mémoires et observations faites par un voyageur en Angleterre* (La Haye, 1698), pp. 63–4.

... the *Parterre* (commonly call'd the *Pit*) contains the Gentlemen on Benches; and on the first Row of Boxes sit all the Ladies of Quality; in the second, the Citizens Wives and Daughters; and in the third, the common People and Footmen. ...[1]

As already noted, this would seem to have been the usual pattern of division throughout the period with which we are concerned; and it would not suggest a democratization of the audience, though affluent business and professional men were becoming less conspicuously different from the gentry.[2]

Part of our difficulty in understanding the relations among the different components of the audience arises from imprecisions in terminology. The word 'citizen' was notoriously vague in its application. If Alderman Gripe of Wycherley's *Love in a Wood* (1671) was a wealthy man of importance in commerce, he was a 'citizen' just as were the shopkeepers and apprentices who filled humble roles in both drama and life. Throughout the seventeenth century dramatists persisted in depicting business figures as variants of the dramatic type of the citizen, notwithstanding the immensity of the range in accomplishment and power that in actual life lay between the positions of an overseas trader, on the one hand, and a shopkeeper, on the other. Even in the final decade of the century, Congreve in *The Old Bachelor* (1693) and Farquhar in *The Constant Couple* (1699) pass social judgements on 'citizens', undifferentiated as to wealth and status, not unlike those of Dryden and Wycherley a generation before.

The sustained raillery directed against the business community and the subsequent modification of it in the eighteenth century require brief explanation. Behind the hostility to the business community of the Restoration dramatists who played variations on the theme of merchant cuckoldry lay a political premiss: that the business community of London had supported the usurpers during the Interregnum, and that after the Restoration it perpetuated the political and religious attitudes of the mid-century Puritans. Whatever the complicated facts of social allegiances in the mid-seventeenth-century wars (and few subjects have been so ably and vigorously contested in the last generation),[3] the dramatists assumed that the merchants were loyal to

---

[1] John Macky, *A Journey Through England*, 2nd ed. (London, 1722), I, pp. 170–1.
[2] Cf. Lawrence Stone, 'Social Mobility in England, 1500–1700', *Past and Present*, XXXIII (April 1966), pp. 52–3. See below, pp. 36–7.
[3] The publications on this important subject are too numerous to list; it will suffice to name three principal contributors to the debate: R. H. Tawney, H. R. Trevor-Roper and Lawrence Stone.

the 'good old cause'. Wycherley's Alderman Gripe is typically described as 'a prying Common-Wealthsman, an implacable Majestrate, a sturdy pillar of his cause' (I.i). In a comedy directed to a king whose father had been beheaded by Cromwell, such a character was fair game.

The inequities of property transfers – forced sales, confiscations – during the Interregnum, the consequences of which persisted into the Restoration, exacerbated the social tensions. Although crown lands and those of certain favoured persons were restored, it proved to be impossible to make general restitution for the property losses of the royalists.[1] Comedies contain frequent references to gentlemen who have suffered in the king's cause. The clever servant Warner in Dryden and Newcastle's *Sir Martin Mar-All* (1667), for example, turns out to be a gentleman and the kinsman of a lord – and thus an appropriate husband for an heiress. 'I cannot refuse to own him for my Kinsman,' says Lord Dartmouth (V. ii), 'though his Father's sufferings in the late times have ruin'd his Fortunes.' There would have been many in the Restoration audience who had, or thought that they had, similar cause for complaint, and they would have found to their taste satirical caricatures of rich businessmen, some of whom retained the lands they had bought from impoverished royalists.[2]

The tradition of contempt for the citizens, unbroken in the theatre until Queen Anne's reign, implies that the dramatists and prologue writers were not concerned lest they offend and alienate a profitable part of their audience. Yet some business figures attended the theatre: even in the 1660s Pepys mentions seeing them there.[3] Presumably, however, the businessmen of prominence, in life if not on the stage, became less easily identifiable as such – or at any rate less conspicuously different from the doctors and lawyers and government functionaries who attended the theatres. They were therefore less vulnerable to the satirical assaults that assumed the status of a formal convention in Restoration comedy. Some humble folk, whether shopkeepers, apprentices, clerks or servants, sat in the middle and upper galleries, but they were not very important financially to the dramatists and theatre managers because they did not pay much for admission. The audience that mattered to the dramatists, determining their rewards in money and prestige, was that seated in the pit and the boxes, and well into the eighteenth century it seems

---

[1] David Ogg, *England in the Reign of Charles II* (Oxford, 1963), I, pp. 161–4; Paul H. Hardacre, *The Royalists during the Puritan Revolution* (The Hague, 1956), pp. 145–69.
[2] Ogg, op. cit. I, p. 163.
[3] Avery, op. cit. p. 60.

to have been a fashionable audience, even if progressively it included affluent businessmen, who paid high prices for admission.[1]

Perhaps the strongest argument against believing that the theatre audience in the Restoration and even in the first half of the eighteenth century came to include large numbers of persons of middle and inferior social rank is a simple statistical one: the capacity of the theatres was so limited that only a small fraction of London's rapidly growing population could be accommodated in them. As already noted, the two companies were fused into one in 1682, an arrangement that lasted thirteen years. Only two theatres operated consistently between 1695 and the mid-eighteenth century, Drury Lane and Lincoln's Inn Fields, the latter replaced in 1732 by Covent Garden, though in the years before the Licensing Act of 1737 additional theatres operated intermittently: the Haymarket from 1705, the Little Theatre in the Haymarket from 1720, Goodman's Fields from 1729 and, even after it was replaced by Covent Garden, Lincoln's Inn Fields.

Information about the numbers of people attending the Restoration theatres is severely limited, but the editors of *The London Stage*, working with a few scattered documents, have provided estimates pertaining at least to Drury Lane:

> The capacity of this playhouse during the two and one-half decades of its use in the seventeenth century is not known, but a few clues exist in two documents recording the receipts there on 12 and 26 December 1677. On the first evening the pit held 117 spectators; on the second, 191. On the first evening the gallery held 63 auditors; on the second, 144. In the upper gallery, on the first day, were 33 spectators; on the second, 119. The probable attendance in the boxes on 12 December 1677 was 38 spectators; on 26 December, 60 persons.[2]

[1] John Harrington Smith has offered rebuttal to the frequently expressed opinion that there was an important and influential change in the composition of the audience in the late seventeenth and early eighteenth centuries: 'Writers on the change in comedy have regularly attributed some influence to the "middle class", but it is difficult to know just what this term means. If Shadwell, Collier, Steele, Colley Cibber are considered to belong to this class, then its influence was great indeed. I am disposed, however, to doubt that the London tradesman and mercantile classes had much to do with the change. One may think of the make-up of the audience changing after the Glorious Revolution – more and more cits attending the theater, and by their preferences helping to bring about a change in the theatrical fare afforded there. But it is my impression that although they attended, at least in some number, they exerted little influence. I should be more inclined to believe in effectual pressure by a bloc of middle-class patrons if the plays have more evidence that the writers wished to conciliate "the city". But in fact there is very little of this.' (*The Gay Couple in Restoration Comedy* (Cambridge, Mass., 1948), p. 229.)

[2] *The London Stage*, Part 1, pp. xlii–xliii.

These figures are small indeed for a city that already numbered about half a million;[1] and if they are larger for the early eighteenth-century theatres, so was London, and hence the percentages of the total population in the audience, though perhaps larger, were not of a different order of magnitude. The utmost capacity of Lincoln's Inn Fields at the time of *The Beggar's Opera*, no doubt with much crowding, seems to have been about 1400.[2]

H. W. Pedicord's calculations of theatre attendance in the mid-eighteenth century, when records are more plentiful, will suggest at least the approximate proportion of Londoners who attended the theatre in the late seventeenth and the early eighteenth centuries. Referring to London, Westminster, Southwark and their adjoining parts as the area from which Drury Lane and Covent Garden, the two patent houses, drew their audiences, he writes that the population 'is estimated to have been 676,250 by 1750, rising to 900,000 by the end of the century. If we relate our audience estimates to the total population from 1750 on, we discover that 1.7 per cent of the people . . . attended these theatres during the period of Garrick's management.'[3] There were undoubtedly fluctuations in the percentage of attendance during the Restoration and first half of the eighteenth century, downwards between 1682 and 1695, for example, and upwards in the mid-1730s, but this figure would seem to be approximately accurate. Admission prices were high in relation to incomes, too high for most Londoners to pay even if they had been interested in the drama.

As on so many other theatrical subjects, Dennis is our most useful contemporary witness to the prices charged for admission. In an essay directed against Steele's *The Conscious Lovers*, Dennis early in 1723 provided a review of prices since the Restoration. His argument characteristically includes supporting detail:

> Sir *William Davenant* was the first who brought Scenes upon the Stage, towards the Middle of the last Century; and to defray the Expence of them, from time to time, rais'd the Theatrical Receipt about a third Part higher than it was before. The Pit, which was before but eighteen Pence, was rais'd to Half a Crown; The Boxes, which were Half a Crown before,

[1] Gregory King estimated the population of London in 1688 as 540,000. Cf. David Ogg, *England in the Reigns of James II and William III* (Oxford, 1969), pp. 30–1.
[2] Paul Sawyer, 'The Seating Capacity and Maximum Receipts of Lincoln's Inn Fields Theatre', *Notes and Queries*, CXCIX (July 1954), p. 290, cited and discussed in *The London Stage*, Part 2, ed. Emmett L. Avery (Carbondale, Ill., 1960), pp. xxxiii–xxxiv.
[3] Harry William Pedicord, *The Theatrical Public in the Time of Garrick* (New York, 1954), pp. 16–17.

were advanc'd to four Shillings; the first Gallery from a Shilling to eighteen Pence; and the upper Gallery, from Sixpence to a Shilling. So that . . . there is above a third Part of each Night's Receipt, even at the common Prices, allow'd for the Scenes.[1]

The actor-managers had raised the prices for Steele's play even above these figures, Dennis complains, and they had used as the excuse for doing so the cost of the new 'Scenes' – that is, new stage properties and painted scenery. Whether Dennis's anger was justified is beside the point here; what is relevant is the analysis of prices in the different portions of the theatre, an analysis that reveals they were high indeed if we take into account the value of money in the late seventeenth and eighteenth centuries. Without attempting any conversion to the equivalent in modern money, we may gain a sense of how high they were by recalling that some forty years later Samuel Johnson's pension, which permitted him ease and even a certain modest luxury, was only three hundred pounds. Charges for admission, in brief, reinforce our impression that the audience was dominated by the affluent.

Even if the fraction of the population as expressed in percentages of those who attended the theatre remained more or less constant, the number of people involved increased markedly in consequence of the growth of London. E. A. Wrigley has recently estimated the rapidity of growth, emphasizing in doing so that the figures can be only approximations: about 200,000 at the beginning of the seventeenth century, about twice that number by mid-century, about 575,000 by 1700, 675,000 by 1750 and 900,000 by 1800.[2]

By the end of the seventeenth century, he points out, London was the largest city in Europe and furthermore included a larger percentage of the inhabitants of the nation of which it was the capital than any other city of Europe with the possible exception of Amsterdam. Here is the statistical basis for the many satirical comments in Restoration and eighteenth-century comedy on the expansion of the suburbs.

The suburbs grew in well-defined patterns: so far as the theatres were concerned, notably to the west, since it was there that the fashionable and the increasing numbers of persons, formerly resident in the country or in the City, built their houses.[3] Continuous building had reached to St James's Palace by the end of the seventeenth century and, by 1738, to the eastern

---

[1] *Remarks on . . . 'The Conscious Lovers'*, in *Critical Works*, II, p. 254.
[2] 'A Simple Model of London's Importance in Changing English Society and Economy 1650–1750', *Past and Present*, XXXVII (July 1967), pp. 44–70.
[3] Cf. John Summerson, *Georgian London* (London, 1945), *passim*.

boundary of Hyde Park. Dennis in 1719 attributed the prosperity of Drury Lane Theatre to the growth in 'the Numbers of the Nobility and Gentry of the Town, and consequently of their Dependants';[1] and Colley Cibber about twenty years later attributed the rise in value of the location of the Haymarket Theatre in the years since the theatre was constructed in 1705 to 'the vast Increase of the Buildings' near it.[2] If the theatres remained the preserve of the quality, the number of the quality, or of those who had sufficient wealth to aspire to that condition,[3] increased throughout the period with which we are concerned.

The wealth of the nation, graphically represented in the patterns of building in the suburbs, increased markedly. Lawrence Stone explains, however, that the consequences for changes in individual social status are not fully understood. It is by no means clear that social mobility increased; rather, he points out, there is some evidence to the contrary:

> As for the post-Restoration period, the remarkable commercial expansion of the late seventeenth century clearly created a great deal of new wealth. What is not so certain, however, is how it was distributed. Was it concentrated in the hands of a few men like Sir Josiah Child and Sir John Banks, or was it spread over the mercantile community as a whole? The closing down of the land market suggests that, however it was distributed, less of this wealth than before was being converted into social status by the purchase of an estate, and more of it was being reinvested in long-term mortgages, commerce and banking. Thus neither the expansion of the bureaucracy nor the expansion of trade are incompatible with the hypothesis of an increasingly immobile society.[4]

Yet if the social consequences of the commercial expansion are ambiguous, the consequences for theatre attendance are not: many more bureaucrats and merchants, whatever the gradations in their social ranks and prestige, had money enough to see plays, and they helped to provide the large audience to which Dennis, Cibber and other observers alluded.

---

[1] 'To Judas Iscariot, Esq., on the Present State of the Stage', in *Critical Works*, II, p. 166.
[2] Cibber, *Apology*, I, p. 322.
[3] Mr Alan Everitt has employed the useful term 'pseudo-gentry' to designate 'that class of leisured and predominantly urban families who, by their manner of life, were commonly regarded as gentry, though they were not supported by a landed estate.' ('Social Mobility in Early Modern England', *Past and Present*, XXXIII (April 1966), p. 71.)
[4] Stone, op. cit. p. 34.

# 3 Governmental control of the theatres

The small size and the distinctive social orientation of the audience were consequences of the theatrical monopoly established by Charles II. When in the summer of 1660, soon after his return to England, he granted patents to Killigrew and Davenant, authorizing them to lead theatrical companies, he forbade the organization of other companies;[1] and thus he forestalled the development of theatres, and of drama, which might have had a broader and more representative social base. The royalist and aristocratic bias of the Restoration theatres was enforced by legal sanctions.

Theatrical law in the Restoration and early eighteenth century reveals all the ambiguity, pragmatism, compromise and traditionalism that we associate with the English constitution. Its structure results from Charles II's engrafting of a system of patent monopoly on the system of state supervision by the Lord Chamberlain and his subordinate the Master of the Revels inherited from the period before 1642. In the same summer that he granted patents to Killigrew and Davenant, the king confirmed the authority of Sir Henry Herbert, who survived as Master of the Revels from the earlier part of the century.[2] The king made no clear distinction between Herbert's authority and that of Killigrew and Davenant, and indeed he seems not to have con-

[1] For an account of Killigrew and Davenant's successful effort to enforce their monopoly, see John Freehafer, 'The Formation of the London Patent Companies in 1660', *Theatre Notebook*, XX (Autumn 1965), pp. 6–30.

[2] Joseph Quincy Adams (ed.), *The Dramatic Records of Sir Henry Herbert* (New Haven, Conn., and London, 1917), pp. 85–7.

sidered the legal complexities of his action, with the result that almost from the beginning there was tension between individuals representing the two aspects of stage supervision: the patentees, on the one hand, and, on the other, the Lord Chamberlain and the Master of the Revels.[1] The tension persisted until the Licensing Act of 1737, which clarified ambiguities in theatrical law that had plagued the theatres since the Restoration.

The legal details of the long sequence of manoeuvrings for power in the theatres are irrelevant here; they may be read in litigation extending to the eve of the Licensing Act of 1737, which, despite its damaging effects, at least defined separate authorities and responsibilities. Here we must examine the pattern of stage supervision that emerged in the 1660s and the modifications in it prior to the legislative action of 1737.

The patentees, Killigrew and Davenant and their successors (for the theatrical grants were theoretically perpetual and could be and were, in whole or in part, assigned to or inherited by other persons), proved to be the dominant figures in the life of the theatres. They were the managers and entrepreneurs who personally or by deputy decided theatrical policy: the choice of plays for production, the hiring of actors and the assignment of roles. The Lord Chamberlain retained authority over the theatres, and intermittently in the later seventeenth and early eighteenth centuries some individuals who held that office did indeed intervene in the internal affairs of theatrical companies, but usually only in response to some real or alleged political offence. Soon after the Restoration, for example, the Lord Chamberlain stopped a revival of *The Maid's Tragedy*, presumably because its catastrophe bore too close a resemblance to the closing events of Charles I's reign;[2] and in December 1680 he silenced Nathaniel Lee's *Lucius Junius Brutus* after a run of a few nights, citing its 'Scandalous Expressions & Reflections vpon ye Government'.[3] The duty of censoring and of licensing plays before production fell to the Master of the Revels – and after 1737 to a stage censor established by law. Such responsibility as the Master of the Revels retained after 1660 was largely that of censor.[4]

---

[1] Leslie Hotson, *The Commonwealth and Restoration Stage* (Cambridge, Mass., 1928), pp. 204–6, 210–13; Arthur F. White, 'The Office of the Revels and Dramatic Censorship during the Restoration Period', *Western Reserve University Bulletin*, XXXIV (1931), pp. 7–11; Nicoll, *HED*, I, pp. 316–18.

[2] Cibber, *Apology*, II, p. 12.

[3] P.R.O., L.C. 5/144, p. 28. Quoted in Nicoll, *HED*, I, p. 10n.

[4] For a summary of such information as we have about the Lord Chamberlain and the Master of the Revels's performance of their duties, see *The London Stage*, Part 1, pp. lxii–lxv; Part 2, pp. xxxix–xliii.

Both the severity of the censorship and the direction it took changed with the passing of the years. In Charles's reign it was permissive – notoriously so – on sexual subjects, but it was at least intermittently severe on political and religious subjects. In a surviving manuscript copy of John Wilson's *The Cheats*, produced by Killigrew's company in March 1663, we may follow in detail Sir Henry Herbert's decisions as to what could not be permitted on the stage, and we find him understandably sensitive to passages that presented, even ironically and satirically, arguments sympathetic to 'the good old cause'. In spite of his diligence in expunging political sentiments as well as oaths, the performance of the play occasioned such protest that the king subsequently issued an order to suppress it.[1] A similar sequence of events accompanied the performance of Edward Howard's *The Change of Crowns* by Killigrew's company in April 1667. A manuscript copy of the play, bearing Herbert's autograph licence, reveals the deletion of passages that were politically dubious. Yet when the play was performed, Pepys writes, the comedian 'Lacy did act the country-gentleman come up to Court, who do abuse the Court with all the imaginable wit and plainness about selling of places, and doing every thing for money'. Some of Lacy's offensive remarks may have been his own interpolations into the text. In any event, the king took offence and temporarily silenced the company and imprisoned Lacy.[2] Other instances of the suppression of plays in Charles II's reign arose from political meanings that could be discovered by an audience bent on finding them, whether intended by the author or not. Among the old plays not permitted owing to their susceptibility to dangerous applications were Nahum Tate's adaptation of *Richard II* and John Crowne's of *1 Henry VI*.[3]

Instances of the suppression of plays, or passages from plays, on political grounds could be multiplied, but these are sufficient to suggest the pattern that censorship assumed before the Revolution. However callous the patentees, the Lord Chamberlain and the Master of the Revels may have been to the exploitation of sexual subjects, they were sensitive indeed to dramatic situations or allusions which might be offensive to a king whose father had been beheaded by a faction which had closed the theatres.

Not until the theatres lost the protection of Charles, and of James, was the censorship directed in a sustained way at moralistic offences. Earlier there had been lip-service to good manners and morals and occasional complaints

[1] See the edition by Milton C. Nahm (Oxford, 1935).
[2] Pepys, *Diary*, 15 and 16 April 1667. See *The Change of Crownes*, ed. F. S. Boas (London, 1949). For the suppression of *The Country Gentleman* (1669), see p. 165 below.
[3] Frank Fowell and Frank Palmer, *Censorship in England* (London, 1913), pp. 102–6; White op. cit. pp. 15–16.

about the licentiousness of drama, such as that of Shadwell in the preface to *The Sullen Lovers* (1668). The patents to Killigrew and Davenant had contained admonitions that they expunge from plays 'all Prophanenesse and Scurrility'.[1] But Restoration comedy survives as testimony to the easiness of their response to the royal command.

'O wretched We!' wrote Dryden in self-condemnation a year after Charles's death,

> why were we hurry'd down
> This lubrique and adult'rate age,
> (Nay added fat Pollutions of our own)
> T' increase the steaming Ordures of the Stage ?[2]

Not until William and Mary came to the throne was there a sustained governmental effort to repress the 'immorality and profaneness' of the stage, and even this only after pamphleteers, of whom Jeremy Collier was the most persuasive, had aroused broadly based support for a reform movement.[3]

In the wake of the Collier controversy, the sensitivity of public officials to licentiousness and irreligion in the drama was intensified, if we may judge by surviving records of orders and prosecutions.[4] The Master of the Revels, for example, was commanded by the Lord Chamberlain in 1704 to read diligently the plays submitted to him.[5] The meagreness of theatrical records does not permit us to know how systematically he responded to the order. Certainly the old comedies in the repertory continued to be performed, and the complaints of the reformers were repeated. Yet in a surviving prompt copy of two plays of 1710, Charles Johnson's *The Force of Friendship* and *Love in a Chest*, in which we may follow the Master of the Revels's cancellations in detail, he deleted all passages that could be considered irreligious or disrespectful towards the clergy.[6]

There was a weakening, or even a breakdown, in the Master of the Revels's exercise of censorship in the period following 1715, when Steele was granted a theatrical patent. 'The Patent granted by his Majesty King *George* the First

---

[1] Adams (ed.), op. cit. p. 88.
[2] *To the Pious Memory of . . . Mrs Anne Killigrew*, in *Poems*, I, p. 461.
[3] Joseph Wood Krutch, *Comedy and Conscience after the Restoration* (New York, 1949), *passim*.
[4] *The London Stage*, Part I, pp. lxiv–lxv.
[5] P.R.O., L.C. 5/153, p. 434. Cited in Nicoll, *HED*, II, p. 282.
[6] E. N. Hooker, 'Charles Johnson's *The Force of Friendship* and *Love in a Chest*: A Note on Tragi-Comedy and Licensing in 1710', *Studies in Philology*, XXXIV (July 1937), pp. 407–11.

to Sir *Richard Steele* and his Assigns, of which I was one,' wrote Cibber in the *Apology*, 'made us sole Judges of what Plays might be proper for the Stage, without submitting them to the Approbation or License of any other particular Person.'[1] When, soon after the patent came into force, the Master of the Revels demanded his usual fee for licensing a new play, Cibber went to see him and in effect denied that he retained authority over the company.[2] For several years the company persisted in what amounted to defiance of the Master of the Revels and thus indirectly of the Lord Chamberlain. They persisted, in fact, until the season of 1719–20, when the Lord Chamberlain, then the Duke of Newcastle, decisively reasserted his authority by suspending first Cibber and later Steele.[3]

Yet even this episode ended inconclusively, with the reinstatement of Cibber and, after an interval of more than a year, of Steele. The jurisdictional issues remained unresolved. Little systematic censorship seems to have been practised in the 1720s. In the celebrated instance of censorship in 1729 when the Lord Chamberlain forbade the production of Gay's *Polly*, he acted by way of a direct order to the theatre manager (as Gay explains in the preface to the published play), not through the Master of the Revels as an intermediary. The severely critical temper of political satire in the 1730s prior to the Act of Parliament suggests a total abandonment of licensing before production. When officers of the government acted against the theatres, as in several episodes involving Henry Fielding's plays, usually they did so after performances rather than before.[4] Certainly there is reason enough to assume that Fielding's *The Welsh Opera*, *Pasquin* and *The Historical Register of 1736* did not undergo censorship prior to production.

The sequence of events leading to the Licensing Act has often been described:[5] the growing audacity of dramatic satirists in the years after Gay's *Beggar's Opera*, the theatrical experimentation of Fielding in the 1730s and his eventual union with the literary opposition to Walpole, the scurrilous play called *The Golden Rump* read from manuscript by Walpole in the House of Commons as demonstration of the need for new legislation – and parliamentary and royal approval of the legislation. Fielding and the anonymous

---

[1] Cibber, *Apology*, I, pp. 276–7.
[2] Ibid. I, p. 278.
[3] John Loftis, *Steele at Drury Lane* (Berkeley, California, 1952), pp. 121–80.
[4] Cf. Wilbur L. Cross, *The History of Henry Fielding* (New Haven, Conn., 1918), I, pp. 110–12.
[5] See in particular P. J. Crean, 'The Stage Licensing Act of 1737', *Modern Philology*, XXXV (February 1938), pp. 239–55; *The London Stage*, Part 3, ed. Arthur H. Scouten (Carbondale, Ill., 1961), pp. xlviii–lx.

author of *The Golden Rump* were indeed the proximate causes of the Licensing Act, but much more was involved than several over-bold plays of the 1730s, much more even than the growing strength of the opposition to Walpole. Since the Restoration, as I have already said, there had been confusion in the stage regulatory machinery, an ill-defined and changing relationship between the patentees and the Lord Chamberlain. Since the accession of George I the authority of the Lord Chamberlain, and under him the Master of the Revels, had ceased to be exercised systematically, and this notwithstanding the temporary show of strength by the Duke of Newcastle against Drury Lane between 1719 and 1721. There was furthermore an abandonment, in practice if not in law, of the older pattern of theatrical monopoly, as the number of theatres operating grew larger, until in the years just before the Licensing Act, when Fielding led his 'Great Moguls Company of Comedians' at the Little Theatre in the Haymarket, as many as five companies often performed plays simultaneously. This resulted in a highly competitive situation, which in turn resulted in dramatic innovation, of which Fielding's burlesques are but one of several important expressions.[1] It would seem in retrospect that an important era of drama was opening, a more promising departure from the older dramatic and theatrical conventions than had come about since the turn of the century. Yet it would amount to an anachronistic projection of modern attitudes about the beneficial effects of unregulated competition to assume that most contemporary observers thought that the weakening of the governmental machinery of regulation was desirable. Cibber deplored the effects of theatrical competition.[2] Dennis urged closer supervision of the stage by the Lord Chamberlain, in order to prevent the exploitation of drama by theatre managers bent on making large profits.[3] Lewis Theobald expressed a widely held opinion when in a periodical of 1717 he wrote 'that the noblest and most instructive Diversion may be lost, for Want of the State's taking it under its Direction, and commissioning Officers to see it kept up to the Dignity, and Decorum of its first Design. . .'[4] The controversial and repressive aspects of the Licensing Act notwithstanding, it eliminated the jurisdictional conflicts, and it provided the reduction in theatrical competition and the closer governmental supervision that many articulate men had long advocated.

The Act had two major provisions: a restriction of theatres to those which

---

[1] *The London Stage*, Part 3, pp. xlviii, lxxiv, lxxx–lxxxix.
[2] *Apology*, I, p. 297.
[3] Dedication to *The Invader of His Country* (1720), in *Critical Works*, II, p. 179.
[4] *The Censor*, No. 87 (11 May 1717).

held royal patents (Drury Lane and Covent Garden) or were granted licences by the Lord Chamberlain; and a requirement that all new plays, epilogues, prologues and additions to old plays be submitted at least two weeks in advance for review by a stage licenser.[1] As everyone knows, Fielding was forced out of business, and the period of theatrical expansion and dramatic experiment of which he is the most important representative came to an end. Copies of new plays were faithfully submitted to the Licenser (the copies which are how housed in the Huntington Library in California),[2] who effectively tamed the dramatic satirists and allegorists. Not until 1739 did the Licenser prohibit a play: Henry Brooke's *Gustavus Vasa*, a political allegory in a familiar vein of the literary opposition to Walpole. Despite Samuel Johnson's ironical protest in *A Complete Vindication of the Licensers of the Stage* against the infringement of freedom of expression, the play could plausibly be interpreted as seditious. In the earlier years, at least, the censorship seems not to have been excessively restrictive, though in at least one instance – that of the denial of a licence for William Paterson's *Arminius* – the denial seems to have been capricious.[3] Occasional violations of the monopolistic provisions of the Licensing Act were tolerated. Henry Giffard, for example, led a company during the season of 1740–1 at the theatre in Goodman's Fields, using the transparent subterfuge of presenting a play free of charge in the interval between two parts of a concert, for which admission was charged.[4] But no company could have any sense of permanence or security under the necessity of such evasive tactics, with the result that the patent houses dominated the mid-century theatrical situation.[5] Freed from the necessity of meeting competition except from each other, and perhaps even discouraged from accepting new plays by the knowledge that audiences resented the licensing to which new plays were subjected,[6] the managers of Drury Lane and Covent Garden revived old plays at the expense of the ambition of aspiring new dramatists.

[1] Crean, op. cit. p. 254.
[2] They are described in a catalogue prepared by Dougald Macmillan, *Catalogue of the Larpent Plays in the Huntington Library* (San Marino, California, 1939).
[3] *The London Stage*, Part 3, p. liii.
[4] Ibid. pp. lii–liii.
[5] James J. Lynch, *Box, Pit, and Gallery: Stage and Society in Johnson's London* (Berkeley, California, 1953), *passim*.
[6] Cf. Arthur H. Scouten, 'The Increase in Popularity of Shakespeare's Plays in the Eighteenth Century: A *Caveat* for Interpreters of Stage History', *Shakespeare Quarterly*, VII (Spring 1956), p. 197.

# 4 Drama and society

In the preface to *Historia Histrionica* (1699), James Wright described one of the uses of drama:

> Old plays will be always Read by the *Curious*, if it were only to discover the Manners and Behaviour of several Ages; and how they alter'd. For Plays are exactly like *Portraits* Drawn in the Garb and Fashion of the time when Painted. You see one Habit in the time of *King Charles I.* another quite different from that, both for Men and Women, in Queen *Elizabeths* time; another under *Henry* the Eighth different from both; and so backward all various. And in the several Fashions of Behaviour and Conversation, there is as much Mutability as in that of Cloaths.

The perennial claim that drama is history, more precisely social history, is one that falls within the limits of almost self-evident validity. Yet there are limits to the usefulness of drama as a record of society, narrower limits than are sometimes acknowledged, and the failure to recognize them can render suspect the validity of a potentially important body of historical information.

We must differentiate between the permanent in experience, which is not the subject of history because it does not change, and the aspects of experience which do indeed change. The coexistence in a play of strict honesty in the depiction of human nature with limited honesty in the depiction of the contemporary scene provides a difficulty in the interpretation of Restoration drama. The best Restoration comedies, those, say, by Etherege, Wycherley, Congreve and Vanbrugh, carry in the colloquial idiom of their dialogue and in their determined avoidance of emotional cant an impression of authenticity. If the dramatists were so honest in analysing the emotional ambiguities of courtship, we reason, ambiguities that we know are faithfully represented because we have experienced them, then the dramatists must have been similarly honest in representing the society they saw about them. The conclusion may be justified – but how do we know that it is? How do we know that Restoration comedy does not portray, in Charles Lamb's phrase, 'a utopia of gallantry', a fantasy land having no close relationship to any society that ever existed?

The problem of verifying, or more precisely of correcting, the dramatist's view of society is troublesome, but it is not hopeless. Despite the difficulties and dangers in using literary evidence as an aid to understanding Restoration and eighteenth-century life, the potential value of that evidence cannot be ignored. The drama of the period provides a voluminous record of society written by intelligent and well-informed men. The comic dramatist does nothing at all, John Dennis wrote in reference to Molière, 'if he does not draw the Pictures of his Contemporaries'.[1] Restoration and eighteenth-century comedy includes a large body of conversation, much of it directed to what the dramatists saw about them and only tangentially conditioned by the dramatic medium. Both comedy and tragedy turn on themes that represent judgements about contemporary life. Yet if we are to read drama for valid historical insights, we need to keep in mind methodological difficulties.

The difficulties may be illustrated by reference to the sexual licence of many of the dramatic characters. That the sexual attitudes controlling Restoration comedy are unrepresentative of those of the nation at large in the later seventeenth century has often been noted: Earl Miner has said as much in one of the best critical discussions of the subject.[2] How unrepresentative they are of the nation, if not necessarily of the fashionable part of London who attended the theatres, has recently been described in statistical detail. The comedies of Etherege and of most of the other important Restoration dramatists depict a society of sexual freedom, for men under a very liberal code, and for women as well except for young true wits like Harriet in *The Man of Mode*, who are the matrimonial prizes to be carried off by the young

[1] *Remarks on . . . 'The Conscious Lovers'*, in *Critical Works*, II, p. 259.
[2] Miner (ed.), *Restoration Dramatists* (Englewood Cliffs, N.J., 1966), pp. 2–8.

rakes such as Dorimant. The dramatists frequently assume extramarital sexual experience, for men if not for all women, as a condition of life; and certainly, as Jeremy Collier charged at the end of the century, they are ready enough to forgive the licentiousness of their male characters, to depict libertines appreciatively and provide rich heiresses for them at the play's end. Yet a recent study by Peter Laslett suggests that there was in fact less sexual licence in Restoration England than in almost any other period of English history.

Laslett's evidence is largely derived from records of illegitimacy, based on ratios of births out of wedlock to the total number of births. Using figures derived from parish records, where illegitimacy was customarily noted, Laslett concludes that bastardy rates in Restoration England were at a lower level than in most of the periods for which data are available.[1] To be sure, illegitimacy ratios for the peerage are somewhat higher than those for the country at large, though not strikingly so.[2] Given the social orientation of Restoration drama, the peerage figures are the more relevant here. Yet they may be higher merely because illegitimacy, of considerable importance in property settlements, was more carefully recorded for noble families. Neither set of figures, however, is consistent with the impression conveyed by an uncritical reading of Restoration drama that the age was one of libertinage. Apparently John Evelyn and Daniel Defoe were more representative of the sexual mores of the later seventeenth century than were Samuel Pepys and the Earl of Rochester or the comedies of Etherege, Dryden and Wycherley.

The disparity between historical fact (as suggested by the statistical tables of illegitimacy) and social conduct (as portrayed by the drama) cautions against the uncritical use in historical study of literary evidence, but it does not, I think, invalidate that evidence. Restoration comedy began as a courtiers' drama, a coterie drama directed to the tastes of the king and the noblemen and gentlemen surrounding him, a group so small as to be statistically insignificant. Charles II's sexual behaviour is scarcely debatable, nor for that matter is the Duke of Buckingham's, the Earl of Rochester's, Sir Charles Sedley's and Samuel Pepys's, to name but a few conspicuous members of the theatre audience. The records of bastardy, in short, provide merely an added dimension to what we have known all along – that Restoration comedy gives only a partial and selective view of English life.

[1] Peter Laslett's statistical tables are published in the French translation of his book *The World We Have Lost* (London, 1965; New York, 1966), under the title, *Un Monde que nous avons perdu* (Paris, 1969), p. 146.
[2] See Thomas Hollingsworth, 'The Demography of the British Peerage', *Supplement to Population Studies*, XVIII (1964). Reference from Peter Laslett.

One of the liveliest topics in recent debates among social historians has been social mobility, a subject that is central to Restoration and early eighteenth-century comedy. Preoccupation with rank and status, as in the writings of, say, Wycherley, Vanbrugh and Steele, is a distinguishing quality of the comedy of manners, a dramatic form that is concerned above all with social relationships, between classes as well as between individuals. Dramatic characters are frequently intended to represent the classes, of status or of occupation, to which they belong. The dynamics of the social and financial change that produced the tensions animating the rivalries portrayed by the dramatists are now better understood, owing to the researches of social historians, though many uncertainties remain. Lawrence Stone, for example, has described in statistical detail for the period before the civil wars 'the inflation of honours', which stemmed in part from the selling of titles to raise money for the crown.[1] The consequences of all this are reflected in the prominence of foolish knights, such characters as Dryden's Sir Martin Mar-All, in early Restoration comedy. The loss of prestige in the rank is pointed out by Dapperwit in Wycherley's *Love in a Wood* (II. i): 'your true wit despises the title of Poet, as much as your true gentleman the title of Knight; for as a man may be a Knight and no Gentleman, so a man may be a Poet and no Wit.' We are easily convinced of the truth of his remark as we observe Sir Simon Addleplot in the play.

In an analysis of social mobility in sixteenth- and seventeenth-century England, which is comprehensively documented in non-literary sources, Lawrence Stone makes no reference to the drama.[2] Much of what he says, however, supplements and often corroborates observations made by dramatic characters. Compare, for example, Stone's comment on the rise in status of professional men and businessmen with a famous statement on a related subject by Mr Sealand of Steele's *The Conscious Lovers*. The twentieth-century historian describes a structural change in society as

> ... the rise of the commercial and professional classes in numbers and wealth, and their consequent acquisition both of a share in political decision-making and of social recognition. ...
> Along with their admission to the political nation went a rise in their social status. There was a slow but steady shift of attitudes on the part of the landed classes, a growing recognition that the previously anomalous

---

[1] Stone, 'The Inflation of Honours, 1558–1641', *Past and Present*, XIV (November 1958), pp. 45–70.
[2] Stone, 'Social Mobility', pp. 16–55.

occupational categories [merchants, lawyers, clergy and administrators] formed a series of semi-independent and parallel status hierarchies.[1]

The eighteenth-century dramatic character asserts (IV. ii) that

... we Merchants are a Species of Gentry, that have grown into the World this last Century, and are as honourable, and almost as useful, as you landed Folks, that have always thought your selves so much above us.

The historian helps us to believe what the dramatic character says; the character helps us to understand the personal and emotional consequences of the changes that are the subject of the modern analysis. Mr Sealand's boastful remark was not, after all, unprovoked.

The search for corrective or validating evidence with which to read the drama for insights into social history is not limited to twentieth-century investigation. The drama of the period was written against a background of critical commentary. The responses evoked by the plays from contemporary critics, some of whom forthrightly described 'distortions' of the social realities the dramatists purported to represent, provide at once a source for social history and a check on present-day assumptions about historical veracity in the drama. The body of contemporary criticism is very much larger than that for English drama in any earlier period; we can compare our own response to the plays with those of the first audiences as it is impossible to do with Renaissance drama.

In reading dramatic criticism, as in reading the plays themselves, we must take into account the prejudices of the writer and the literary strategies – raillery, hyperbole, irony – he employs. Jeremy Collier, for example, in his famous polemic of 1698 repeatedly censures dramatists for distorted representations of occupational groups and social classes such as clergymen, merchants, lords and squires. Because he is both voluminous and specific, Collier provides information about the distance between drama and social reality. Yet the interpretation of his comments requires an allowance for his own bias, imperceptiveness and special purpose. In his denunciation of Vanbrugh's *The Relapse*, for example, he insists that the country squire of the play, Sir Tunbelly Clumsey, is not at all representative of his class in real life: 'This Gentleman the *Poet* makes a *Justice of Peace*, and a *Deputy Lieutenant*, and seats him fifty Miles from *London*: But by his Character you would take him for one of *Hercules*'s Monsters, or some Gyant in *Guy* of

[1] Ibid. pp. 52–3.

*Warwick.'*[1] How, we may ask in wonderment, could even so fanatical a critic as Collier have failed to recognize that Vanbrugh had employed broad stage caricature in the service of satire? And yet Collier, his critical obtuseness notwithstanding, suggests in the long paragraph devoted to Sir Tunbelly and his dealings with Lord Foppington the relationships between the squire-archy and the nobility, a subject that has recently been of intense interest to social historians.

The social biases of the critics and the dramatists are for the most part clear and apparent, and we may easily take them into account in reading their works. The playwrights of Charles II's reign were nearly all royalists writing for a small audience including the king and his courtiers. They can be expected to provide, not a comprehensive and objective view of English life, but rather a view from the vantage of bureaucrats and gentlemen and noblemen who shared the king's interpretation of recent English history. Political animosities aroused during the Interregnum and exacerbated by transfers of property, some of them irreversible, had not yet cooled; they found expression in comedy: in the satirical edge of dramatic dialogue, in the harsh depiction of character types – citizens and Puritans who were inimical to courtiers – and even in the shape of plots, many of which were contrived for the discomfiture of citizens and Puritans. We would search Restoration comedy in vain for a fair-minded portrayal of Englishmen who had supported Oliver Cromwell, some of them still alive and presumably not totally penitent. Among the major dramatists only Thomas Shadwell broadens the social range, providing engaging portraits of men outside fashionable society and venturing to criticize gentlemen not only for social affectation. Shadwell is a solitary instance of a playwright whose vision transcended the prejudices of the court circle, and even his plays impose severe limits on social toleration. For example, the sagacious London merchant in *The Squire of Alsatia* proves to be the son and brother of rich country squires. Restoration drama is a record of the prejudices, preoccupations, manners and social values of a group that was numerically small. Yet because the dramatists' angle of vision is well defined, we need not be misled by it.

The value of drama as historical record is the more obvious in comedy, but it can be seen in tragedy as well. Tragic dramatists supplied less specific comment on the times, since characters and locales were associated with remote times and places; and yet they too wrote with an awareness, albeit a prejudiced awareness, of the passing scene. The themes of tragedy from the

---

[1] Jeremy Collier, *A Short View of the Immorality and Profaneness of the English Stage* (London, 1698), p. 215.

Restoration to 1688 are, with a few significant exceptions, royalist; the term 'Tory' applies for the period after the Popish Plot. Consider, for example, the dramatic treatment of the implausible episode which convulsed the nation after Titus Oates committed audacious perjury in 1678. At least two of the best tragedies of the later seventeenth century, Nathaniel Lee's *Lucius Junius Brutus* and Thomas Otway's *Venice Preserved*, have political themes that derive from the Popish Plot, the former providing a Whig commentary on the constitutional issues posed by it, and the latter a Tory commentary.[1] Again, the biases of the dramatists are so obvious that we have no trouble in recognizing them, and in doing so gaining an insight into the patterns of current political thought and into the emotional dimension of the theoretical debates. *Lucius Junius Brutus* (1680) provided a cautionary example of royal tyranny in Tarquin and, in the title character, a devoted admirer of the rule of law – all this a full decade before Locke published *Two Treatises of Government*. As Locke's editor has demonstrated, the *Two Treatises* were written about 1681, roughly the same time as the play, though they were revised after the Revolution, before publication in 1690.[2] Lee's political theme was too bold to be tolerated, and his play was promptly and permanently prohibited by order of the Lord Chamberlain. On the other hand, Otway's theme in *Venice Preserved* was acceptable. The political meaning of the play is much more subtly revealed than that of *Lucius Junius Brutus*, and yet, as the subtitle, 'A Plot Discovered', implies, *Venice Preserved* turns on an episode that in 1682 would have had inescapable relevance to the Popish Plot. The play's theme of political conservatism, of the need for stability in government even at the cost of corruption and injustice, yields an insight into the frame of mind that could accept the inequities of Restoration England rather than risk the horrors of revolution.

When revolution did come in 1688, the themes of tragedy changed abruptly.[3] Whereas earlier royal tyranny had been a rare subject of tragedy (in part because of the operation of censorship, in part because of the biases of both dramatists and audiences), it became commonplace after King William's accession. The rule of law in a constitutional monarchy is an ideal that animates scores of eighteenth-century tragedies, some of them employing a cautionary strategy of depicting the results of royal tyranny, others a strategy that is direct and exemplary. In the Walpole era, at least before the Stage Licensing Act of 1737, there was added to the Whig burden of tragedy the

---

[1] Loftis, *Politics of Drama*, pp. 15–17, 18–19.
[2] John Locke, *Two Treatises of Government*, ed. Peter Laslett (Cambridge, 1960), pp. 45–61.
[3] Loftis, *Politics of Drama*, pp. 22–5.

additional theme of the perversion of royal justice by an ambitious and corrupt minister, a 'prime minister' in the phrase that still carried opprobrium.

In reading the plays as evidence of political attitudes, we must adjust the angle of our corrective lens to take into account the altered assumptions of the dramatist, reinforced as they were by the operation of censorship. Again the correction for the dramatist's prejudices is easy to make, and having made it we can gain from the tragedies knowledge of English thought. We must remember, however, that we find, not comprehensive or objective representations of opinion, but rather passionate dramatizations of the working out of political propositions that were acceptable to the censors.

The dramatists are prejudiced witnesses, and their prejudices must be recognized in any attempt to evaluate the evidence they supply. We do not, in courts of law, bar witnesses who are well informed on certain aspects of a subject from giving testimony because they are prejudiced or because they do not know all aspects of the subject. Rather, we listen to what they have to say, make allowances for their point of view and their limited knowledge, and check their assertions with such other evidence as is available. We should, I think, proceed in the same manner in evaluating historical evidence from Restoration and eighteenth-century drama.

# 5 Dramatic theory

Restoration dramatists and critics wrote about dramatic theory as few of their predecessors, of whom Ben Jonson is the most conspicuous, had done. The prestige enjoyed by Jonson in the later seventeenth century derived, in part at least, from the fullness with which he anticipated the Restoration preoccupation with the neoclassical theory of drama.[1] He had expressed many of the opinions later held by the French theorists. I have already referred to the travels of the exiled royalists which brought them a knowledge of mid-century French drama and critical theory, and to the *Essay of Dramatic Poesy*, which would seem to embody the kind of conversation Dryden heard around him in the mid-1660s as gentlemen, with an enlarged knowledge of foreign precedent, attempted a reassessment of English drama. The admiration for

Cf. Louis I. Bredvold, 'The Rise of English Classicism: Study in Methodology', *Comparative Literature*, II (1950), pp. 253–68.

The adjective 'neoclassical' has recently become controversial – at least as a general term describing the literature produced in England from 1660 to 1800. Cf. especially Donald Greene, 'What Indeed Was Neo-Classicism?', *Journal of British Studies*, X (November 1970), pp. 69–79. Yet in discussing the history of drama, a much more restricted subject than general literary or intellectual history, I am reluctant to give it up, so accurately does it describe a set of assumptions that writers from Dryden to Sheridan took as the point of departure for the innovations that give their plays individuality.

French critical theory, already apparent in the *Essay of Dramatic Poesy*, became more pronounced in the 1670s after Thomas Rymer began to write.

In his preface to his translation of Rapin's *Réflexions sur la Poétique d'Aristote*, Rymer provides a succinct account of the history of neoclassical criticism in Renaissance Europe:

> For this sort of Learning, our Neighbour Nations have got the start of us; in the last *Century*, *Italy* swarm'd with Criticks, where, amongst many of less note, *Castelvetro* opposed all comers; and the famous Academy *La Crusca* was alwayes impeaching some or other of the best Authors. *Spain*, in those dayes, bred great Wits, but, I think, was never so crowded, that they needed to fall out and quarrel amongst themselves. But from *Italy*, *France* took the Cudgels; and though some light strokes passed in the dayes of *Marot*, *Baif*, &c. yet they fell not to it in earnest, nor was any noble Contest amongst them, till the *Royal Academy* was founded, and Cardinal *Richlieu* encouraged and rallied all the scattered Wits under his Banner. Then *Malherb* reform'd their ancient licentious Poetry; and *Corneille's Cid* rais'd many Factions amongst them. At this time with us many great Wits flourished, but *Ben Johnson*, I think, had all the Critical learning to himself; and till of late years *England* was as free from Criticks, as it is from *Wolves*, that a harmless well-meaning Book might pass without any danger. But now this priviledge, whatever extraordinary Talent it requires, is usurped by the most ignorant: and they who are least acquainted with the game, are aptest to bark at every thing that comes in their way. Our fortune is, *Aristotle*, on whom our Author makes these *Reflections*, came to this great work better accomplished.[1]

There is more to be said on the subject than these acid remarks, and there are important qualifications to be added; modern scholarship has provided both the amplitude and the correctives needed.[2] Yet Rymer's emphasis is just: the movement of critical learning from Italy, in the sixteenth century, to France,

[1] *The Critical Works of Thomas Rymer*, ed. Curt A. Zimansky (New Haven, Conn., 1956), pp. 1–2.

[2] Modern writings on this subject are too numerous to be listed. The most authoritative account of neoclassicism in its relationship to English drama is to be found in the editorial apparatus of *The Critical Works of John Dennis*, ed. E. N. Hooker, 2 vols (Baltimore, 1939 and 1943). For the background in Italy, see Bernard Weinberg, *A History of Literary Criticism in the Italian Renaissance*, 2 vols (Chicago, 1961). The French background is well represented in an anthology: Scott Elledge and Donald Schier (eds), *The Continental Model: Selected French Critical Essays of the Seventeenth Century in English Translation*, rev. ed. (Ithaca, N.Y., 1970).

in the earlier seventeenth century, and to England, at the time of the Restoration – though certain English writers, including Sidney and Jonson, had already expressed critical ideas that were widely accepted after the Restoration.[1] Rymer errs, we would say, in omitting reference to Dryden, who had already written an important group of essays informed by a knowledge of Corneille and other French theorists, and perhaps in omitting reference to Davenant and Hobbes, who in their exchanges of 1650 on *Gondibert* had adumbrated the major concerns of the later seventeenth century. Yet he is right in his implication that, before he began to write, Restoration criticism had not been rigorously and systematically influenced by neoclassical doctrines.

The fact that the first of Rymer's three important works was his translation, with the preface already cited, of René Rapin's *Réflexions sur la Poétique d'Aristote* emphasizes the origin of the two principal strains in Rymer's critical thought: Aristotle's *Poetics* and the writings of the French formalist critics, above all Rapin.[2] Rymer turned with a devotion that to the modern mind may seem fanatical to the exposition of French opinion, which was grounded – sometimes closely, sometimes remotely if at all – in Aristotle; and he succeeded to a remarkable degree in convincing his countrymen that the opinion was worth taking seriously. This is not to say that they were not more strongly influenced by the native English tradition or that they were not already familiar with many of the French critical ideas. The king and a number of his courtiers, as already explained, passed years of their exile in mid-seventeenth-century France. Davenant dated his preface to *Gondibert* 'From the Louvre in Paris, January 2, 1650'; and it was in France in the same year that Hobbes wrote his 'Answer' to Davenant's preface.[3] This exchange reveals an insistence on Aristotle's conception of the ideal truth of poetry as superior to the particularized truth of history, the conception from which the doctrine of decorum in characterization was derived; an insistence on the commonsensical and probable and a criticism of Renaissance poets for flights of fancy damaging to verisimilitude; an insistence on the didactic function of poetry; and careful attention to the relationships between the literary genres.[4]

---

[1] For the English Renaissance, see J. E. Spingarn, *A History of Literary Criticism in the Renaissance*, 2nd ed. (New York, 1908), and Madeleine Doran, *Endeavors of Art: A Study of Form in Elizabethan Drama* (Madison, Wisconsin, 1954).
[2] Cf. G. B. Dutton, 'The French Aristotelian Formalists and Thomas Rymer', *PMLA*, XXIX (June 1914), pp. 152–88; *Critical Works of Rymer*, Introduction, pp. xxix–xxx.
[3] These essays are reprinted in J. E. Spingarn (ed.), *Critical Essays of the Seventeenth Century*, II (Oxford, 1908), pp. 1–67.
[4] Cf. C. M. Dowlin, *Sir William Davenant's 'Gondibert', its Preface, and Hobbes's Answer* (Philadelphia, Pa., 1934).

The last part of Davenant's preface is an 'apology for poetry' in the Renaissance manner of Sidney, but the earlier paragraphs, if read in conjunction with Hobbes's answer, foreshadow the critical themes of Dryden and Rymer. Again as already noted, Dryden's criticism as well as his plays of the 1660s show him to have been an assiduous student of the French: 'He who writ this,' goes his boast in the prologue to *Secret Love* (1667),

> not without pains and thought,
> From *French* and *English* Theaters has brought
> Th' exactest Rules by which a Play is wrought.

It was not to the uninitiated that Rymer addressed himself.

What then is the explanation of the impact made by Rymer in his first independent work, *The Tragedies of the Last Age Consider'd and Examin'd by the Practice of the Ancients, and by the Common Sense of All Ages* (1677)? The answer is perhaps to be found in the systematic rigour with which he brought all aspects of dramatic composition into coherent relationship with a set of premises the validity of which he claimed to demonstrate. He reveals in utmost clarity the 'uniformitarianism' that was to be a mark of English critical thought for the next century: the assumption that all men in all places, in so far as they think justly about literature as well as about everything else, think alike.[1] 'Certain it is, that *Nature* is the same,' he wrote,

> and *Man* is the same, he *loves*, *grieves*, *hates*, *envies*, has the same *affections* and *passions* in both places [Athens and London], and the same *springs* that give them *motion*. What mov'd *pity* there, will *here* also produce the same effect.[2]

Dryden's Crites in the *Essay of Dramatic Poesy* had said much the same thing a decade before (and the idea was not new then). But Crites' opinions were after all opposed by those of Eugenius and Neander. Rymer pursued the principle of uniformity with rigour, and he was the more effective by reason of his bantering style. Here was a persuasive argument for the relevance of French formalist principles to the criticism of English tragedy and an application of them to the criticism of Renaissance tragedy.

Like Davenant and Hobbes before him, Rymer objected to implausibilities in plot and characterization. He criticized John Fletcher for violations of probability. He shows in its fullest extension the emphasis on judgement over

---

[1] Arthur O. Lovejoy, 'The Parallel of Deism and Classicism', *Essays in the History of Ideas* (Baltimore, Md., 1948), pp. 79–82.
[2] *Critical Works*, p. 19.

fancy for which Hobbes in 1650 had provided a reasoned explanation.[1] This emphasis, frequent in neoclassical criticism, is not specifically Aristotelian. On the other hand, Rymer's consistent – one might almost say obsessive – preoccupation with the principle that the poet should be concerned with ideal truth can indeed be traced to the *Poetics*,[2] though his detailed applications of the principle derive from the French critics, from François Hédelin and René Rapin, among others.[3] It was this principle that provided a rationale for his insistence on poetic justice. Discrepancies between the moral quality of characters' behaviour and the fortunes they experienced in the fifth act would imply departures from the ideal world order, which was assumed to embody justice.[4] So too Rymer's insistence on decorum in all aspects of characterization derived from the assumption that dramatic characters should be, not idiosyncratic human beings, but just representatives of their social ranks, occupations and ages. Horace and many after him had provided precedent for the opinion.[5] As Rapin had put it, in Rymer's own translation:

> The painter draws faces by their features, but the poet represents the minds of men by their manners, and the most general rule for painting the manners is to exhibit every person in his proper character: a slave, with base thoughts and servile inclinations; a prince, with a liberal heart and air of majesty; a soldier, fierce, insolent, surly, inconstant; an old man, covetous, wary, jealous.[6]

Rymer says much the same thing at length, and so do many English critics after him, including Dryden and Dennis. (As late as 1723 Dennis objected

---

[1] Cf. Hobbes, 'Answer to Davenant's Preface to *Gondibert*', in Spingarn (ed.), *Critical Essays*, II, pp. 59–60.

[2] Cf. *Poetics*, Ch. IX.

[3] G. B. Dutton, op. cit.

[4] Sarup Singh observes that 'Poetic Justice is one of the most fundamental tenets of the theory of drama in the Restoration period', and in differentiating the conception of justice evident in Renaissance drama from that in the later period, he asserts that the Restoration 'preferred to think that the universe was divinely planned and controlled. Whatever the reasons for such a comfortable view of life, whether sociological, political or religious, the fact remains that a sharp gulf came to exist between the Restoration age and Shakespeare and his contemporaries. . . . It must be realized that the incapacity of the age to understand and appreciate the temper of Shakespearean tragedy is to be attributed to this gulf rather than to any changes in the theory of drama. . . . Poetic justice is a Renaissance creed and the Restoration age simply accepts it. The old creed, however, has suddenly acquired a new meaning and has come to satisfy a psychological necessity.' (*The Theory of Drama in the Restoration Period* (Bombay, 1963), pp. 64–5.)

[5] Cf. Horace, *Ars poetica*, ll. 153–78.

[6] *Reflections on Aristotle's Treatise of Poesy in General*, in Elledge and Schier (eds), op. cit. p. 285.

that Steele in *The Conscious Lovers* had endowed Bevil Junior, a young man, with qualities inconsistent with his age and physical vigour.)[1] There are hidden and unquestioned assumptions in all this, including assumptions about social and political subordination; the conclusions do not follow as inevitably from the premisses as Rymer assumed. Yet, drawing on the French writers, he transmitted to England a coherent, systematic and persuasive set of critical ideas which could be and promptly were transformed into a method of practical criticism.

The impact made by Rymer may be gauged by Dryden's response to him. In a letter written to a nobleman (apparently the Earl of Dorset) about September 1677, Dryden refers to Rymer's recently published *The Tragedies of the Last Age*: 'which has been my best entertainment hetherto: tis certainly very learned, & the best piece of Criticism in the English tongue; perhaps in any other of the modern.'[2] This is curiously high praise of a critic who has seemed to later readers opinionated, imperceptive and even obtuse. That Dryden's admiration was sincere, though qualified, is demonstrated by his subsequent critical and dramatic writings.[3] (I think it is possible that Dryden might have been prejudiced in Rymer's favour by a high compliment paid to him in the preface to Rapin: Rymer compared, to Dryden's advantage, a description of the night in *The Indian Emperor* with passages on similar subjects in ancient and modern languages.)[4] If he was never as censorious as Rymer of English infringement of the dramatic unities and decorum in characterization, language and plots, he nevertheless, in *All for Love* (performed late in 1677 and published early the following year), produced one of the closest – and finest – approximations in English to the kind of tragedy that Racine had made his own. Yet he included a petulant reference in his preface to *All for Love* to the excessive 'nicety of manners' in French tragedy, with an illustrative reference to *Phèdre*, first published in 1677. (Dryden had obviously followed developments in French drama closely since at least the mid-1660s.) In his most systematic exposition of dramatic theory, 'The Grounds of Criticism in Tragedy', published in 1679 together with his preface to his adaptation of *Troilus and Cressida*, he cites Rymer's criticism of Fletcher with approbation. In the preface to the play he explains, in a manner

---

[1] *Remarks on . . . 'The Conscious Lovers'*, in *Critical Works*, II, pp. 265–6.
[2] *Letters of Dryden*, pp. 13–14.
[3] Cf. Robert D. Hume, 'Dryden's "Heads of an Answer to Rymer", Notes Toward a Hypothetical Revolution', *Review of English Studies*, N.S., XIX (November 1968), p. 374n.
[4] *Critical Works*, pp. 10–16.

reminiscent of Rymer, the principles by which he had proceeded in his adaptation of Shakespeare:

> ... because the play was Shakespeare's, and ... there appeared in some places of it the admirable genius of the author, I undertook to remove that heap of rubbish under which many excellent thoughts lay wholly buried. Accordingly, I new-modelled the plot, threw out many unnecessary persons, improved those characters which were begun and left unfinished, ... and added that of Andromache. After this, I made, with no small trouble, an order and connexion of all the scenes; removing them from the places where they were inartificially set; and, though it was impossible to keep them all unbroken, because the scene must be sometimes in the city and sometimes in the camp, yet I have so ordered them, that there is a coherence of them with one another, and a dependence on the main design. . . .[1]

However arrogant this may seem to modern sensibilities, the rationale underlying it is intelligible as an expression of the intensified concern with verisimilitude, propriety and neatness of structure that Dryden shared with Rymer. *Troilus and Cressida* becomes in Dryden's version a tragedy of young lovers separated by the fortunes of war. Perhaps remembering Rymer's observation that a distinguishing characteristic of a woman is modesty,[2] and certainly desiring to simplify and clarify the patterns of characterization and dramatic conflict, he depicts a chaste Cressida, steadfast in her love for Troilus. (It is relevant to recall that his Cleopatra is tamer and more faithful to her lover than her Shakespearian predecessor.) Audacities of language are eliminated. Thersites is subdued to the extent that his satirical function disappears. The ignobility of Achilles' killing of Hector receives little notice. In short, clarity and decorum of characterization and language replace the ambiguities of Shakespeare.

In face of the deference Dryden showed in his published writings to Rymer's opinions, it has come as a surprise to many students to read his *Heads of an Answer* to Rymer, written in the endpapers of his copy of *The Tragedies of the Last Age*: an author's notes to himself, not published in Dryden's lifetime, though some of the ideas expressed reappear in altered form in 'The Grounds of Criticism in Tragedy'.[3] In the notes the respectful

---

[1] In *Essays*, I, pp. 203–4.
[2] *Tragedies of the Last Age*, in *Critical Works*, p. 64.
[3] For a comprehensive analysis of the 'Heads of an Answer', stressing their continuity with Dryden's other critical work, see Robert D. Hume, *Dryden's Criticism* (Ithaca, N.Y., 1970), pp. 102–23.

tone of admiration for Rymer reappears, but this time it is qualified by more combativeness: specifically, by an emphasis on the emotional dimension of the audience's experience of drama:

> And here Mr Rymer's objections against these plays are to be impartially weighed, that we may see whether they are of weight enough to turn the balance against our countrymen.
>
>   'Tis evident those plays which he arraigns [*The Bloody Brother, A King and No King, The Maid's Tragedy*] have moved both those passions [pity and terror] in a high degree upon the stage.[1]

The temper of these jottings is less rationalistic, more prudential, than that of 'The Grounds of Criticism in Tragedy'; Dryden's criticism of the French, and in this instance of the Greeks as well, is less restrained than in the published essay. In his forthright attention to the limitations of Greek drama, he indeed echoes the strictures of his interlocutor Eugenius in the *Essay of Dramatic Poesy*.

Dryden's *All for Love* and *Troilus and Cressida* as well as the title of Rymer's *The Tragedies of the Last Age Considered* provide a reminder that neoclassicism as an operational force conditions the response to the plays of the English Renaissance. Beaumont and Fletcher enjoyed great popularity, notwithstanding such critical censure as Rymer's, in part perhaps because their plays had been widely read during the Interregnum.[2] Shakespeare retained a favoured place in the repertory, despite the critics' preference for Ben Jonson,[3] but often his plays were performed in radically revised form. To be sure, some of them were acted regularly without major changes: *1 Henry IV, Julius Caesar, Hamlet* and *Othello*.[4] Yet a number underwent the

---

[1] In *Of Dramatic Poesy and Other Critical Essays*, ed. George Watson (London, 1962), I, p. 213.

[2] Louis B. Wright, 'The Reading of Plays during the Puritan Revolution', *Huntington Library Bulletin*, VI (1934), pp. 73–108. About forty of the plays attributed to Beaumont and Fletcher were performed between 1660 and the end of the seventeenth century: *The London Stage*, Part 1, p. cxxviii.

[3] Gerald Eades Bentley provides a summary statement about the relative popularity enjoyed by Shakespeare and Jonson in the seventeenth century: 'Jonson's general popularity was greater than Shakespeare's from the beginning of the century to 1690; Shakespeare's reputation was growing more rapidly than Jonson's in the last two decades. Throughout the century Jonson was unchallenged in most critical writings as the greatest English dramatist, his popularity in critical writings being greater than his over-all popularity.' (*Shakespeare and Jonson: Their Reputations in the Seventeenth Century Compared*, 2 vols (Chicago, 1945), I, p. 138.)

[4] George C. Branam, *Eighteenth-Century Adaptations of Shakespearean Tragedy* (Berkeley, California, 1956), p. 1.

kind of alteration we have observed in Dryden's *Troilus and Cressida*: alteration calculated to remove ambiguities of language and characterization,
clarify plots and make them symmetrical, and introduce poetic justice.[1]
Shadwell's remarks in the dedication of his version of the *History of Timon of
Athens* (1678) catch the ambivalence of the response to Shakespeare: the
original play, he wrote, 'has the inimitable hand of *Shakespear* in it, which
never made more Masterly strokes than in this. Yet I can truly say, I have
made it into a Play.' The devotion to the principle of order – to the proposition that the dramatist should imitate ideal truth – is nowhere more evident
than in Nahum Tate's famous adaptation of *King Lear* (1681), in which
poetic justice is achieved, and in which orderliness of dramatic action is
enhanced by consolidation of the subplot with the main plot by the expedient
of Cordelia's marriage to Edgar rather than the King of France. The fondness
for symmetry animates the alterations in Davenant and Dryden's *The Tempest*,
Davenant's *Macbeth*, Otway's *Caius Marius* (*Romeo and Juliet*) and, at the end
of the century, Cibber's *Richard III*.[2]

[1] For discussion of the neoclassical adaptations, see Hazelton Spencer, *Shakespeare
Improved* (Cambridge, Mass., 1927), and Branam, op. cit.
[2] Branam, op. cit. pp. 1–2. For a discussion of changes in emphasis in tragic theory, see
Rothstein, op. cit. pp. 3–23.

# 6 The reform movement and the theory of dramatic genres

Much of the criticism of comedy in the final decade of the seventeenth century and the earlier decades of the eighteenth was pre-empted by debate about the alleged licentiousness of the stage. Systematic dramatic criticism, only as old as the Restoration, grew much more voluminous when it received the stimulus provided by the Jeremy Collier controversy, which was conducted on both sides, despite the passions engendered, as a critical controversy.[1] The general acceptance by reformers and dramatists alike of a common set of literary premisses provides a measure of the influence neoclassicism had achieved in England. The voluminous tracts written by Collier and the other reformers and the answering tracts written by the dramatist in self-defence[2] merit attention as theoretical formulations by contemporaries of the nature of comedy and of its relationship to the society that produced it.

In the epilogue to *The Pilgrim* (1700) Dryden alludes to the Jeremy Collier

[1] J. E. Spingarn's summary statement is relevant: 'In a word, Collier has adopted Rymer's critical method and his theory of poetry, and has transferred them both from the field of Elizabethan tragedy to that of Restoration comedy. "Poetical justice" is the basis of his theory, and he is more consistent than Rymer himself in refusing to accept the fashionable theory that pleasure is the end of poetry.' (*Critical Essays of the Seventeenth Century*, I (1908), Introduction, p. lxxxvi.)

[2] For a bibliography of the controversy, see Krutch, op. cit. pp. 264–70.

controversy, writing with candour about the sexual subjects of Restoration
comedy:

> Perhaps the Parson stretch'd a point too far,
> When with our *Theatres* he wag'd a War.
> He tells you, That this very Moral Age
> Receiv'd the first Infection from the Stage.
> But sure, a banisht Court, with Lewdness fraught,
> The Seeds of open Vice returning brought.
> Thus Lodg'd, (as Vice by great Example thrives)
> It first debauch'd the Daughters and the Wives.
> London, a fruitful Soil, yet never bore
> So plentiful a Crop of Horns before.
> The *Poets*, who must live by Courts or starve,
> Were proud, so good a Government to serve;
> And mixing with Buffoons and Pimps profain,
> Tainted the Stage, for some small Snip of Gain.[1]

Dryden refuses, even in the intensity of the Collier controversy, to deny that
Restoration comedy was licentious, and indeed at about the same time he
wrote in a similar vein in his final critical essay, the preface to his *Fables*.[2] Yet
in one of the 'fables' in his volume he reveals, in a satirical assault on Collier,
something of his old pugnacity. 'He makes me speak the Things I never
thought', Dryden complains in the opening passage of *Cymon and Iphigenia*,
and after referring to the incongruity between Collier's 'Cloth' and the tenor
of his book, Dryden offers a qualified rebuttal to *A Short View*:

> The World will think that what we loosly write,
> Tho' now arraign'd, he read with some delight;
> Because he seems to chew the Cud again,
> When his broad Comment makes the Text too plain:
> And teaches more in one explaining Page,
> Than all the double Meanings of the Stage.
>     What needs he Paraphrase on what we mean?
> We were at worst but Wanton; he's Obscene.
> I, nor my Fellows, nor my Self excuse;
> But Love's the Subject of the Comick Muse. . . .[3]

[1] *Poems*, IV, pp. 1759–60.
[2] *Essays*, II, pp. 272–3.
[3] *Poems*, IV, p. 1741.

'We were at worst but Wanton': not a denial of the charges but a justifiable assertion that Collier was intemperate in framing them. Long before Collier had published *A Short View of the Immorality and Profaneness of the English Stage* in 1698, Dryden had acknowledged his own guilt, as I have said, in his *To the Pious Memory of . . . Mrs Anne Killigrew* of 1686. He did not contest the fact that, to those who accepted the premisses of Christian morality, many Restoration plays were offensive in their tolerant depiction of sexual irregularities and in their blasphemous and profane language.

Dryden would seem to be justified in attributing the moral laxity of the Restoration stage to its close connections with Charles's court. As I have already explained, there is some evidence that in the country at large sexual permissiveness was less common than in other periods. Yet the sexual permissiveness of the court is too well known, from the diary of Pepys, the diary of Evelyn, the memoirs of the Count of Gramont, the poems and deathbed confession of the Earl of Rochester, to mention only sources external to the plays, to require demonstration. As I have said, the king took a special interest in two of Dryden's comedies, *Secret Love* and *Mr Limberham* (perhaps indeed writing part of the latter),[1] and both of them reveal, though in different ways, the characteristic lack of inhibition in sexual relationships. The king of course took an interest in actresses also; and it has been well suggested that the best-known of the royal mistresses, Nell Gwyn, may have contributed to Dryden's idea for the effervescent wit of his heroines.[2] She had the role of Florimel in *Secret Love*, and there may be a description of the actress herself embedded in the dialogue of the play (I. ii). At any rate, Celadon's catalogue of her features fits the portraits of Nell Gwyn. Several of Dryden's later heroines are variations on the splendid model he had created in Florimel, an irreverent, impious, if witty model. And thus we may plausibly trace one of the most attractive strains in his comedies to the king's own bedchamber.

Although there had been occasional complaints before the Revolution about the licentiousness of the drama, such as that of Thomas Shadwell in the preface to *The Sullen Lovers* (1668) and that of Dryden in the Killigrew ode, it was not until a few years before Jeremy Collier published *A Short View of the Immorality and Profaneness of the English Stage* in 1698 that the complaints became prominent and frequent. Only after the Revolution, when the theatres had lost their royal patrons Charles II and James II, was it prudent for pamphleteers to risk the identification with the mid-century

---

[1] *Letters of John Dryden*, pp. 11–12. See above, p. 7.
[2] John Harold Wilson, *All the King's Ladies* (Chicago, 1958), pp. 99–100.

Puritan regicides that was inherent in an attack on the theatres. A critic made the identification of Collier and Puritan explicit in his rebuttal to *A Short View*, *A Defence of Dramatic Poetry* (1698): 'A profane *Comedy* or *Tragedy*, were all Heathen and Antichristian [to the Puritans], but Pious *Regicide* and *Rebellion*, were Religion and Sanctity with them'.[1] Elkanah Settle, John Dennis, Thomas Baker and Colley Cibber, among others, said much the same thing.[2] Still, in the political climate of William's reign, and later of Anne's, there was no danger in the association, and the complaints of the reformers assumed the nature of a concerted effort to enforce change.

Despite his hostility to the existence of the theatre and his heavy moralistic bias, Collier was almost as devoted an adherent of neoclassical formalism as Rymer – in his advocacy of poetic justice and his attacks on the dramatists for violations of it and in his use of the principle of decorum to rationalize his objections to the depiction of certain character types. He was as fond of citing classical precedent as Dryden and Dennis. Consider his distinction between dramatic genres in his *Defence of the Short View* (1699):

> Now as the Business of *Tragedy* is to represent Princes and Persons of Quality; so by the Laws of Distinction, *Comedy* ought to be confin'd to the ordinary Rank of Mankind. And that *Aristotle* ought to be thus interpreted appears from the Form of *New Comedy*, set up in the Time of this Philosopher. And tho' we have none of these *Comedies* extant, 'tis agreed by the Criticks that they did not meddle with Government and Great People; The *Old Comedy* being put down upon this Score. And tho' *Menander* and the rest of that Set are lost, we may guess at their Conduct from the Plays of *Plautus* and *Terence*, in all which there is not so much as one Person of Quality represented.
>
> Farther, Mr *Congreve*'s reason [in *A Defence of Dramatic Poetry*] why *Aristotle* should be interpreted by *Manners*, and not *Quality* is inconclusive.[3]

Later in the same pamphlet he explains the relevance of this allusion to

---

[1] p. 13.

[2] Thomas Baker's remarks in the dedicatory epistle of his *An Act at Oxford* (1704) will illustrate the political temper of the dramatists' response to the reformers: 'Whatever Reformation the Stage wanted, 'tis plain, that FACTION is now it's bitterest Adversary. To prove this, your Lordship [Lord Dudley] may observe, the Quarrel is chiefly manag'd by Enemies to the Establish'd Church, headed by the Author of the SHORT VIEW, who we all know to be a profess'd One to our Constitution, and rather than want Materials, borrows the old Phanatical Arguments to sharpen his Invectives.'

[3] pp. 6–7.

classical authority: 'I had charg'd our Modern Dramatists, and particularly Mr *Congreve* with being too free in exposing the Nobility under Characters of Lewdness and Contempt.'[1] This is literary theory in the service of Christian morality – and of social conservatism. Collier's most influential criticism of the comic dramatists turns on his acceptance of the principle that ideal and not historical truth is the poet's subject. 'The Lines of Virtue and Vice are Struck out by Nature in very Legible Distinctions', he writes at the beginning of Chapter IV in *A Short View*, a chapter to which he prefixed a thematic statement: 'The Stage-Poets make their Principal Persons Vitious, and reward them at the End of the Play.'[2] If all this may now seem pedantic and literal-minded, it was criticism in the current idiom, grounded on widely accepted premisses, and carrying a heavy load of documentation.

Most of the replies elicited by *A Short View*, such as those of Congreve and Vanbrugh, are shrill, petulant and superficial. Tempers were too hot to permit the careful discourse needed to counter such a strong indictment. Farquhar includes a harsh reference to Collier in *The Constant Couple* (1699), satirically suggesting that he had been subsidized by hypocritical City merchants (V. ii); and Congreve attributes to Lady Wishfort in *The Way of the World* a fondness for the writings of Collier: 'There are Books over the Chimney,' she tells Mrs Marwood (III. iv), '*Quarles* and *Pryn*, and the *Short View of the Stage*, with *Bunyan*'s Works to entertain you.' But more than satire was needed to counter Collier; the closest approach to an adequate rebuttal came from Dennis.

His *The Usefulness of the Stage, To the Happiness of Mankind, To Government, and To Religion* (1698) is the most learned, the most systematic and the most compelling of the contemporary replies, though the essay makes heavy reading today. Much of it is devoted, not to the 'immorality and profaneness' of the drama, but rather to a closely reasoned exposition of the function of theatres in civilized society, for Dennis recognized Collier's hostility to the stage as an institution. In his deliberate exposition of much that we now take for granted about the function of the stage, we may detect an effort to counter a resurgence of the widespread hostility to the stage that called to his mind the eighteen-year ban on theatrical performances in the middle of the century. The political implications of Collier's book are not far from his thoughts:

---

[1] p. 25.
[2] In *Critical Essays*, III (1909), p. 253. A paragraph in *A Project for the Advancement of Religion, and the Reformation of Manners* (1709) reveals that Jonathan Swift had read this chapter with attention and approbation: Swift, *Prose Works*, ed. Herbert Davies, II (1939), pp. 55–6.

And this seems very remarkable, that since the Drama began first to flourish among us, we have been longer at quiet, than ever we were before, since the Conquest; and the only Civil War which has been amongst us since that Time, is notoriously known to have been begun, and carried on by those, who had an utter Aversion to the Stage; as on the other side, he who now discovers so great an Aversion to the Stage, has notoriously done all that lay in his little Power, to plunge us in another Civil War.[1]

This last is an allusion to the fact that Jeremy Collier, a High Church Anglican clergyman, had after the Revolution refused to swear the oaths of allegiance to the new sovereigns. Dennis answers Collier's 'Objections from Authority' at length. No doubt the citations had their weight at the time, but they are likely to seem mere pedantry today. Dennis is less illuminating on the theory of drama than he was to be later in replying to Collier's defender and popularizer, Richard Steele.

Steele began his career soon after the publication of *A Short View*, and from the first he revealed sympathy for the reformers. The theme of his *The Christian Hero* (1701) is summarized in its subtitle, 'No Principles but those of Religion are sufficient to make a Great Man'; and the pious strain in his thought, animated by his redeeming wit, appears at least intermittently in the three comedies he wrote in the early years of the century. We have his word for it that he was attentive to the reformers. Recalling in his *Apology* his second play, *The Lying Lover* (1703), he refers to *A Short View*:

Mr *Collier* had, about the Time wherein this was published, written against the Immorality of the Stage. I was (as far as I durst for fear of witty Men, upon whom he had been too severe) a great Admirer of his Work, and took it into my Head to write a Comedy in the Severity he required.[2]

He quotes from his preface to the play, in which he had anticipated ideas and even phrases about stage reform that reappear in his periodicals; and with his characteristic and saving capacity to avoid the solemn, he concludes with a reference to the failure of his play: 'And considering me as a Comick Poet, I have been a Martyr and Confessor for the Church; for this Play was damn'd

---

[1] In *Critical Works*, I, pp. 167–8.
[2] In *Tracts and Pamphlets by Richard Steele*, ed. Rae Blanchard (Baltimore, Md., 1944), p. 311.

for its Piety.'[1] Here, in his gift for a neatly turned and deliberately incongruous phrase of self-criticism, coupled with an acceptance of most of Collier's programme, may be seen the combination of wit and piety that made Steele, 'the Censor of Great Britain '(as he became known after the great success of *The Tatler*), the most effective popularizer of Collier's ideas in Queen Anne's England.

The theatre is a frequent topic in the papers that he contributed to *The Tatler, The Spectator* and *The Guardian*, and often, though not always, the papers advance reformist principles.[2] A successful dramatist, a friend of the actors, a playgoer and a witty man, he did not submerge an awareness of aesthetic quality in moralistic zeal. Frequently his purpose is analogous to that of Dennis in *The Usefulness of the Stage*: the demonstration of the salutary function of theatrical performances when properly supervised. Like Dennis in *The Usefulness of the Stage*, though far less ponderously, he looks closely at the psychology of audience response – in *The Guardian*, No. 43, on Addison's *Cato*, for example – attempting to explain the power of drama to influence men's minds.

Two of his essays would seem to have a particular relevance to the theory of comedy he self-consciously evolved (with attention to Collier's arguments), *The Tatler*, No. 182 (1710), and *The Spectator*, No. 65 (1711). The essays are complementary, and both of them are related to his plan for *The Conscious Lovers*, though the play did not reach the stage until 1722. The essay in *The Tatler* includes what is apparently a preliminary account of the play, which then had 'only the Out-Lines drawn'; that in *The Spectator* is a sharply censorious attack on Etherege's *The Man of Mode*, representative to Steele of the type of Restoration comedy that had provoked Collier's attack. Isaac Bickerstaff of *The Tatler* explains that his young pupil, presumably Steele himself, is writing a play, in which there are to be displayed 'all the reverend Offices of Life; such as Regard to Parents, Husbands, and honourable Lovers, preserved with the utmost Care' and in which 'Agreeableness of behaviour, with the Intermixture of pleasing Passions as arise from Innocence and Vertue', is to be 'interspersed in such a Manner, as that to be charming and agreeable shall appear the natural Consequence of being virtuous.' The comedy is to be organized as a recommendation of virtue by example rather than as a satirical review of vice and folly.

The essay in *The Spectator* on *The Man of Mode* condemns Etherege's play, deploring, in a vein reminiscent of Collier and even of Thomas Shad-

[1] Ibid. p. 312.
[2] Loftis, *Steele at Drury Lane*, pp. 13–25.

well much earlier in the preface to *The Sullen Lovers* (1668), the portrayal of debauchery in the guise of witty and attractive characters. The line of continuity even from the first decade of the Restoration merits emphasis for its implications in critical theory.[1] Shadwell had written, referring perhaps to Dryden's early plays:

> but in the *Playes* which have been wrote of late, there is no such thing as perfect Character, but the two chief persons are most commonly a Swearing, Drinking, Whoring, Ruffian for a Lover, and an impudent ill-bred *tomrig* for a Mistress, and these are the fine people of the *Play*...

And Collier had written about Valentine in Congreve's *Love for Love*:

> He is a prodigal Debauchee, unnatural, and Profane, Obscene, Sawcy, and undutiful, And yet this Libertine is crown'd for the Man of Merit, has his Wishes thrown into his Lap, and makes the Happy *Exit*.[2]

Steele says much the same thing, at greater length and with equal vehemence, about Dorimant: 'a direct Knave in his Designs, and a Clown in his Language'. Steele does not acknowledge in *The Spectator*, No. 65, the cautionary theory of comedy – that comedy provides in depraved characters admonitions against misconduct – the theory that had provided the basic argument of the dramatists who at the turn of the century had replied to Collier. Steele was therefore vulnerable to rebuttal.

When *The Conscious Lovers* was finally ready for the stage in 1722, Dennis, who by then had personal grievances against Steele, struck hard, writing just before the play was first performed his *Defence of Sir Fopling Flutter* and, soon after it had begun its successful run, his (and the full title is significant) *Remarks on a Play, Call'd, The Conscious Lovers, a Comedy*. In this pair of essays there is perhaps the clearest of all the English expositions of the neo-Aristotelian theory of comedy, a much clearer account than Dennis had provided a quarter of a century earlier when he replied to Collier. Dennis recognized that Steele's theory of comedy was inconsistent with the neo-classical conception of genre. It is indeed his recognition of this fact, and his learned exposition in rebuttal of Steele's theory of comedy, which gives his pair of essays their special significance as a reaffirmation of the doctrine of dramatic genres.

In *A Defence of Sir Fopling Flutter*, published five days before *The*

---

[1] Cf. John Harrington Smith, 'Shadwell, the Ladies, and the Change in Comedy', *Modern Philology*, XLVI (August 1948), pp. 22–33.

[2] *A Short View*, pp. 142–3.

*Conscious Lovers* was first acted, Dennis writes more about comic theory than about Steele's play, which as yet he knew only by reputation. But he knew a lot about it by reputation. Over a period of years Steele had included puffs preliminary for it in his essays. Dennis knew that the comedy (which before it reached the stage went by the title 'The Gentleman' or 'The Fine Gentleman')[1] would display an exemplary young hero, intended to provide an edifying contrast to the dissolute rakes of Restoration comedy. Dennis proceeds by way of praise of Etherege's play, writing with indignation about *The Spectator*, No. 65: 'The Knight certainly wrote the foremention'd Spectator, tho' it has been writ these ten Years, on Purpose to make Way for his fine Gentleman, and therefore he endeavours to prove, that Sir *Fopling* is not that genteel Comedy, which the World allows it to be.'[2] Turning to the theory of 'genteel comedy', the term then used to designate comedy depicting the affairs of the gentry,[3] Dennis argues that whether or not characters are faithful representatives of characters from fashionable life is finally beside the point. He is illuminating on the reputation of *The Man of Mode* as an accurate representation of Restoration court society, but his most compelling argument, reinforced with references to Jonson and Molière as well as Aristotle and Horace, turns on the cautionary strategy of comedy:

> How little do they know of the Nature of true Comedy, who believe that its proper Business is to set us Patterns for Imitation: For all such Patterns are serious Things, and Laughter is the Life, and the very Soul of Comedy. 'Tis its proper Business to expose Persons to our View, whose Views we may shun, and whose Follies we may despise; and by shewing us what is done upon the Comick Stage, to shew us what ought never to be done upon the Stage of the World.[4]

This is a theory of comedy applicable to Jonson and Molière, but not as comprehensively applicable to Etherege's *The Man of Mode* as Dennis implies. Sir Fopling Flutter is indeed a cautionary character, as Dennis explains, but what about Dorimant, who was the target of Steele's attack? Dennis evades this crucial point, deflecting the argument into a historical review of Dorimant's reputation as an accurate depiction of a Restoration courtier. By implication Dennis is tolerant of Dorimant's licentiousness,

[1] It is called 'The Gentleman' in *Applebee's Original Weekly Journal*, 21 November 1719. Dennis calls it 'The Fine Gentleman' in *A Defence of Sir Fopling Flutter*.

[2] In *Critical Works*, II, p. 244.

[3] Cf. F. W. Bateson, 'Contributions to a Dictionary of Critical Terms: I. "Comedy of Manners" ', *Essays in Criticism*, I (1951), pp. 89–93.

[4] In *Critical Works*, II, p. 245.

explaining it historically by reference to the manners of Charles's court. Yet he fails to come to terms with the central charge in Steele's indictment of the play. But he is unequivocal in rejecting Steele's arguments for exemplary comedy.

In *Remarks on The Conscious Lovers* Dennis confronted the disruptive consequences for the theory of dramatic genre of the inclusion in comedy of pathetic episodes – the kind of episode of which the recognition scene in the last act of *The Conscious Lovers* is a classic example. Since the essay appeared after *The Conscious Lovers* had reached the stage and had been published, he could examine the play and its preface in detail. This second essay has a discursiveness absent in the more tightly organized defence of *The Man of Mode*; but if some passages seem mere pedantic fault-finding, others explain the significance of Steele's critical and dramaturgical innovations. Dennis confronts Steele's defence, in the preface to *The Conscious Lovers*, of emotionally charged situations. Steele had written:

> But this Incident [the quarrel in the fourth act], and the Case of the Father and Daughter, are esteem'd by some People no Subjects of Comedy; but I cannot be of their Mind; for any thing that has its Foundation in Happiness and Success, must be allow'd to be the Object of Comedy, and sure it must be an Improvement of it, to introduce a Joy too exquisite for Laughter, that can have no Spring but in Delight, which is the Case of this young Lady.

If one of the earliest authorial defences of a 'sentimental' episode in comedy, this statement is not remarkable for clarity of analysis. Dennis's rejoinder turns on Steele's imprecision of terminology. As in his earlier essay Dennis grounds his objection in the theory of genre:

> When Sir *Richard* talks of a Joy too exquisite for Laughter, he seems not to know that Joy, generally taken, is common like Anger, Indignation, Love, to all Sorts of Poetry, to the Epick, the Dramatick, the Lyrick; but that kind of Joy which is attended with Laughter, is the Characteristick of Comedy; as Terror or Compassion, according as one or the other is predominant, makes the Characteristick of Tragedy, as Admiration does of Epick Poetry.[1]

And thus in the first quarter of the eighteenth century, before the term 'sentimental comedy' had gained currency,[2] Steele and Dennis differed on

[1] In *Critical Works*, II, p. 260.
[2] For a review of the eighteenth-century use of the term, see Arthur Sherbo, *English Sentimental Drama* (East Lansing, Mich., 1957), pp. 1–14.

the emotional range of comedy, anticipating conflicts that would find expression in critical essays and in plays for the rest of the century. If Dennis would seem to have won the round in clarity of analysis, Steele expressed, however imprecisely, the opinion that was to be the more influential in later eighteenth-century comedy. The measure of the enlargement in the emotional range of comedy may be read in Oliver Goldsmith's complaint, in his *Essay on the Theatre; or, A Comparison between Laughing and Sentimental Comedy* (1773), about 'a new species of Dramatic Composition' by then known as '*Sentimental* Comedy', 'in which the virtues of Private Life are exhibited, rather than the Vices exposed; and the Distresses, rather than the Faults of Mankind, make our interest in the piece.'[1]

Steele's literary partner in his major periodicals, Joseph Addison, was a more systematic critic than Steele, better informed in neoclassical theory and more deeply influenced by it, though he too had differences of opinion with Dennis. It is curious that the two men, Addison and Dennis, who in retrospect seem the most considerable literary critics of early eighteenth-century England, should so often have been antagonists, as they were in writing about Milton's *Paradise Lost* and on the folk ballad as well as on such a dramatic topic as poetic justice. The cause of their disagreements is at least in part to be sought in their personalities and social positions rather than in their ideas, for in many of their theoretical assumptions they were alike. At the time of *The Spectator*, 1711 and 1712, the contrast between them in their manners of life and their personal appearances must have been striking: Addison, a handsome man just forty years old, socially and politically prominent, already famous; Dennis, fifty-five and not handsome, poor and, as a conventional representative of 'the critic', becoming a favourite target of abuse. Small wonder that he was irascible and resentful, and that he was quick to strike when Addison turned a vulnerable side to him, as he did in his theatrical criticism and in his tragedy *Cato* (1713).

Addison's theatrical criticism reveals his philosophical turn of mind, his preference for general principles over detailed analysis. His preoccupation with first principles is in this instance the more notable because it stands in contrast with the practice of Steele, who customarily wrote about plays which were about to be or recently had been performed. Steele was a journalistic critic of the theatre, the first important one in England; whereas Addison was a dramatic theorist. Even at the time of *The Spectator*, Steele had written three plays, and he was long and well acquainted with the leading actors,

[1] In the *Collected Works of Oliver Goldsmith*, ed. Arthur Friedman (Oxford, 1966), III, p. 212.

whose performances provided the subjects of some of his essays. Addison had not yet completed his first play, and he did not habitually go to the theatre. Even when he writes about a current theatrical issue, in the essay on the dramatic reform movement (No. 446), for example, he promptly introduces comparisons with the drama of antiquity and relates current practice to neo-classical theory: in this instance, to the obligation of the dramatist to instruct as well as to entertain his audience. Such comments as he makes on English dramatists and their plays, though well informed and illuminating, are typically brief *obiter dicta* such as the comments on Nathaniel Lee and Thomas Otway in No. 39.

Addison's four essays on tragedy (Nos. 39, 40, 42 and 44) appeared in April 1711 and thus just two years before the first performance of *Cato*, in April 1713. At the time he wrote the essays he had already written most of the tragedy.[1] We are justified in looking to the criticism for insight into the theory that shaped the play, which was, in the restricted sense of its fortune on the stage, a pre-eminently successful adaptation of French conceptions of dramatic form. We may read Addison's recommendation (in No. 39) of 'a noble Sentiment', and his criticism of English dramatists for their indulgence in a 'Sense either very trifling or very common', as a commentary on the frame of mind that led to the earnestness of *Cato*, in which sentiments are noble to the point that they lose credibility. We may read the recommendation (in No. 44) that violent action performed before the audience be sharply reduced or eliminated as an expression of the theory that led to the passages of expository narration in *Cato*. Addison presumably thought that he was providing in *Cato* the kind of tragedy of strong good sense, undamaged by melodramatic spectacle, that he had recommended in his essays.

His discussion of 'poetical Justice' (in No. 40) would also seem to be relevant to *Cato*. The title character of the play, though a figure of legendary nobility and virtue, meets his death by suicide, as the army of the victorious Caesar approaches. It would appear that Addison, not convinced by current arguments in support of the doctrine of poetic justice, undertook in *The Spectator* a justification for the planned catastrophe of his still unfinished tragedy. In any event, both the essay on poetic justice and the exemplification of it in the tragedy two years later brought him under severe attack from Dennis.[2]

Addison may have failed to see the full implication of his argument on

[1] Peter Smithers, *The Life of Joseph Addison* (Oxford, 1954), pp. 45, 77, 241, 250-3.
[2] Cf. Richard H. Tyre, 'Versions of Poetic Justice in the Early Eighteenth Century', *Studies in Philology*, LIV (January 1957), pp. 29-44.

poetic justice, at least as stated in *The Spectator*, No. 40, without the qualifications that he later supplied: he may have failed to see, that is, the difficulty
with which his conception of tragedy, based as it was on the observation both
of the human experience that provided its subject and the audience to which
it was directed, could be reconciled with the doctrine that literature should
imitate the ideal order of nature. His remarks on poetic justice show an unresolved tension between empirically observed life, on the one hand, and the
hypothetical conception of an orderly and just nature, on the other, which,
according to Thomas Rymer, who had originated the term 'poetical Justice',[1]
it was the business of the poet to imitate.

Dennis was prompt in reminding him of his inconsistencies. In a published
letter *To the Spectator*, *Upon His Paper on the 16th of April*, Dennis used in
rebuttal both citation of authority, notably that of Aristotle, and systematic
argument. 'For what Tragedy can there be without a Fable?' Dennis asks
rhetorically, 'or what Fable without a Moral? or what Moral without poetical
Justice? What Moral, where the Good and the Bad are confounded by Des-
tiny, and perish alike promiscuously.'[2] A later *Spectator* (No. 548), not signed
in Addison's customary way and not certainly written by him, provides a
vindication of his original position by redefining it. Whereas Dennis, citing
Aristotle, had insisted that only an imperfect man was a fit protagonist for
tragedy since only such a man could be subjected to catastrophe without
damage to the didactic effectiveness of the play, Addison or some unidentified
collaborator now argued that any man – an exceptionally good as well as an
imperfect man – has enough of evil about him to qualify for the role of tragic
hero: 'Our goodness being of a comparative, and not an absolute Nature.'
This later essay reveals clearly enough that Dennis had scored and that Addison or his defender was attempting to reinterpret his position in a manner
approximating that held by Dennis.[3]

Addison, like Dennis, accepted neoclassical conceptions of dramatic
genres; Steele, perhaps without fully understanding the theoretical implications of what he was doing (and certainly without acknowledging them),
weakened the conception of genre, at least in comedy. A decade after *The
Conscious Lovers*, George Lillo enlarged and altered the conception of genre
in tragedy.

Perhaps more than Steele, even though he lacked Steele's university

---

[1] *Critical Works*, pp. xxviii–xxix.
[2] In *Critical Works*, II, p. 19.
[3] For an interpretation of the debate more critical of Dennis and more sympathetic to
Addison, see Singh, op. cit. pp. 89–92.

education, Lillo was critically self-conscious. 'Considering the Novelty of this Attempt,' he wrote in the dedicatory epistle to *The London Merchant* (1731), 'I thought it would be expected from me to say something in its Excuse'; and in fact the epistle is a succinct critical essay in defence of his choice of a figure from common life, an apprentice, as his protagonist. Lillo's argument, which has resemblances to Samuel Johnson's later defence of biography in *The Rambler*, No. 60, turns on the assumption that the didactic efficacy of tragedy could be improved by broadening the social range of its subjects: 'Tragedy is so far from losing its Dignity, by being accommodated to the Circumstances of the Generality of Mankind,' he wrote, 'that it is more truly august in Proportion to the Extent of its Influence, and the Numbers that are properly affected by it'; and perhaps it will aid us in considering the argument without prejudice to recall how similar was Johnson's claim for biography:

> Our passions are . . . more strongly moved, in proportion as we can more readily adopt the pains or pleasure proposed to our minds, by recognizing them as once our own, or considering them as naturally incident to our state of life. It is not easy for the most artful writer to give us an interest in happiness or misery, which we think ourselves never likely to feel, and with which we have never yet been made acquainted.

If, as many have assumed, Lillo overemphasizes the importance of external correspondences between the subject and the audience of literature, then perhaps Johnson cannot be wholly acquitted of doing so, though Johnson qualifies his argument, as Lillo does not, by going on to insist on the essential similarity of men in all ranks.

The resemblance to Johnson is not in itself important. Yet it may serve to suggest that Lillo had thought systematically about critical theory. Certain ineptitudes in *The London Merchant* may lead us to underestimate his literary sophistication and his knowledge of dramatic history. This tragedy, like his later *Fatal Curiosity*, often echoes earlier drama, notably that of Shakespeare.[1] His adaptation of *Arden of Feversham*, acted and printed posthumously, demonstrates that he was familiar with at least one of the Renaissance domestic tragedies. His prologue to *The London Merchant* includes knowledgeable reference to more recent experiments in the adaptation of

[1] See the editions prepared by William H. McBurney: *The London Merchant* (Lincoln, Nebraska, 1965) and *Fatal Curiosity* (Lincoln, Nebraska, 1966). For an account of Lillo's personal library, see McBurney, 'What George Lillo Read: A Speculation', *Huntington Library Quarterly*, XXIX (May 1966), pp. 275–86.

tragedy to familiar life: 'Upon our Stage indeed', he writes, personifying the tragic muse,

> with wish'd Success,
> You've sometimes seen her in an humbler Dress;
> Great only in Distress. When she complains
> In *Southern*'s, *Rowe*'s or *Otway*'s moving strains. . . .

Southerne, Rowe and Otway: he isolates (metre rather than chronology determines the order) his most significant predecessors, men who had reduced the social rank of their characters, not to the merchant class but to the gentry, and who had furthermore anticipated Lillo in the luxuriant exploitation of pathetic emotion in tragedies in which the protagonists, by earlier standards at least, are passive: victims rather than challengers of their fatal destinies.

Although tragedies controlled by neoclassical conceptions of decorum continued to be written long after *The London Merchant*,[1] Lillo's theory and practice of tragedy represent a kind of schematic culmination of trends observable since the later years of Charles II's reign – in emotional structure as well as in enclosure within a familial situation. Lillo went beyond his predecessors in writing in prose (which in its rhythms, however, is sometimes disguised blank verse)[2] and in taking his characters, as well as the code of conduct by which their actions are measured, from the business community. These are bold, innovatory steps, and they are not consistent with the conceptions of tragedy held by Rymer and Dryden. They may be regarded as signalling a preliminary effort in the transformation of a dramatic genre to adapt it to new conditions of social organization: specifically, to the conditions of a society in which commerce had become very important.

As its title implies, *The London Merchant* is a tragedy of business life: the word *merchant* meant 'businessman',[3] a term used loosely and broadly for persons ranging in status and accomplishment from such overseas traders as George Barnwell's master, Thoroughgood, to shopkeepers. The play is dedicated to a rich merchant, Sir John Eyles, 'Member of Parliament for, and Alderman of the City of *London*, and Sub-Governor of the *South-Sea* Company'. In dialogue that is only tangentially relevant to the dramatic action, the play carries an account of the usefulness of merchants to the nation. The

---

[1] Cf. Clarence C. Green, *The Neo-Classic Theory of Tragedy in England during the Eighteenth Century* (Cambridge, Mass., 1934), *passim*.
[2] Cleanth Brooks and Robert Heilman, *Understanding Drama* (New York, 1957), pp. 32, 185.
[3] Lewis B. Namier, *The Structure of Politics at the Accession of George III*, 2nd ed. (London 1960), p. 49n.

standards of success and failure as well as the criteria by which personal honour is evaluated are those of a commercial society.

And it is more than coincidence that Steele, too, in *The Conscious Lovers* and in his critical writing aimed at modifying the structure of comedy, included as an aspect of his programme a propagandistic, and controversial, defence of the merchants. His Mr Sealand is not so sententious and long-winded as Mr Thoroughgood, but he is as firmly convinced of the dignity and usefulness of his profession as is Lillo's merchant. These characters echo opinion that had been expressed in Whig propaganda since the final years of Queen Anne's reign, when differences between the moneyed as opposed to the landed interests were exacerbated by the effort to end the War of the Spanish Succession. Whig opinion had been expressed by the fictional merchant Sir Andrew Freeport of Addison and Steele's *The Spectator*, and it had occasionally been expressed in comedies of the earlier years of George I's reign. But it is more emphatic in *The Conscious Lovers* than it had been in earlier drama, and in *The London Merchant* it enters tragedy.

# 7 'Sentimentalism'

Steele, Lillo, the exploitation of pathetic situations, the weakening of the barriers between comedy and tragedy, the calculated praise in drama of the business community – all this leads inevitably to one of the most difficult concepts of eighteenth-century scholarship, that which is signified by the ambiguous word 'sentimentalism'. Argument about the nature of it, and about the evaluation of literary expressions of it, continues.[1] Final agreement may not be possible: perhaps we can merely devise a conceptual framework within which to organize our thought on this subject as it is related to literary history.

We need a conception of eighteenth-century sentimentalism, I think, that will allow us to see some gains as well as the manifest losses that came with the heightened emphasis on episodes of emotional intensity. For there are some fortunate literary results, though they are easier to see in the novel than in the drama. Sterne's *A Sentimental Journey*, for example, provides a famous instance of what could be accomplished within the literary patterns established by the earlier sentimentalists. The fact that Sterne provides an ironical evaluation of the sentimental feelings and conduct of Yorick (his classic

[1] Notable recent contributions to the debate appear in Arthur Sherbo, op. cit., and Paul E. Parnell, 'The Sentimental Mask', *PMLA*, LXXVIII (December 1963), pp. 529-35.

exemplar of the 'unreliable narrator') should not obscure the fact that the novel derives force from the intensity of the exploration of thought and emotion.[1]

In its earlier expressions in comedy, in, say, the plays of Cibber and Steele, sentimentalism led to a more inward view of dramatic characters. Restoration comedy had treated its characters externally, emphasizing social relationships – rather than individual emotional experience. The emotional range of Restoration comedy is limited indeed, almost as limited as the narrow social range of its characters – most of them members of the wealthier gentry and lesser nobility. Even in one of the first instances of sentimentalism in Restoration drama, in Lee's *The Princess of Cleve* (1681),[2] there is a broadening of the moral and emotional range. Sometimes, as in Cibber's plays, there would seem to be a deliberate exploration of the consequences for the personality of certain intense experiences. Sentimental comedy has an experimental aspect, psychological as well as literary, that has not been fully acknowledged. The implausibilities of Cibber's plots, and his tasteless violations of consistency in tone, should not obscure the originality of some of his psychological experimentation.

We have approached sentimentalism in drama with too narrow a conception of our task. We have confined ourselves too closely to English literature and to those plays in which there is a crude and excessive exploitation of poignant situations. Perhaps we should broaden our investigation to take in French as well as English drama, and tragedy as well as comedy.[3] For it is apparent that in France as in England tragedy moved to an increasing inwardness of emotion,[4] and intensified luxuriance of passion, in its progression from Pierre Corneille's great plays of the 1640s to Racine's of the 1660s and 1670s. The change is not unlike that which we see in Dryden's career, in the movement from his early heroic plays to his final one, *Aureng-Zebe* (1675), and to the tragedies in blank verse he wrote later.[5] The intensified luxuriance of feeling in Dryden's later tragedies resembles qualities in the tragedies of

---

[1] Cf. *A Sentimental Journey*, ed. Gardner D. Stout, Jr (Berkeley, California, 1967).

[2] Cf. Thomas B. Stroup, '*The Princess of Cleve* and Sentimental Comedy', *Review of English Studies*, XI (April 1935), pp. 200–3.

[3] Eric Rothstein aptly writes that 'The critic of English or of French literature might do well to frame his hypotheses about his own field of interest in the light of its analogue' (op. cit. p. 45n).

[4] George H. Nettleton noted the relevance of Otway and Southerne to the developments culminating in 'sentimental comedy': *English Drama of the Restoration and Eighteenth Century* (New York, 1914), p. 119.

[5] Arthur C. Kirsch, *Dryden's Heroic Drama* (Princeton, N.J., 1965), pp. 118–28; Rothstein, op. cit. pp. 24–47.

Lee and Otway. From Lee and Otway the next step would seem to be sentimentalism: that is, an excess of emphasis, in comedy as well as in tragedy, on
qualities already apparent in their work. The consistency with which the
curve of acceleration in emotional intensity rises would suggest that sentimentalism is merely the final working out of literary patterns long established.

The interpretative problem is in part one of definition. In any effort to
describe or define 'sentimental drama', we must remember that the term did
not come into popular use until the mid-eighteenth century, after the neoclassical doctrine of kinds or genres had lost some of its hold on the minds of
literary theorists. The earlier eighteenth-century dramatists were ignorant of
the term; and the eighteenth-century plays that exploit emotional situations
conspicuously are heterogeneous in structure as well as in social and moral
assumptions. It would seem to be futile to attempt a structural or formalistic
account of the plays that traditionally have been called 'sentimental'.[1]

A more profitable mode of approach to literary sentimentalism, in the drama
as in other forms of literature, has resulted from the study of seventeenth-
and eighteenth-century theories of ethics.[2] Samuel Johnson alluded to speculations on the subject in his preface to Shakespeare. In Shakespeare's time,
he wrote,

> The contest about the original benevolence or malignity of man had not
> yet commenced. Speculation had not yet attempted to analyse the mind,
> to trace the passions to their sources, to unfold the seminal principles of
> vice and virtue, or sound the depths of the heart for the motives of all.
> All those enquiries, which from that time that human nature became the
> fashionable study, have been made sometimes with nice discernment,
> but often with idle subtilty, were yet unattempted.[3]

Some of those inquiries were carried on in dramatic form. Drama then, as
always, was sensitive to changes in the interpretation of behaviour, and the
late seventeenth and early eighteenth centuries happened to be a period when
the changes came rapidly – notably, from ethical theories assuming human
depravity to theories assuming human benevolence. Non-dramatic literature,
as well as comedy and tragedy, reflects, not steadily but fitfully, new, secular-

---

[1] For expression of a divergent opinion, see Sherbo, op. cit.
[2] Cf. Ernest Bernbaum, *The Drama of Sensibility* (Boston, 1915); Ronald S. Crane, 'Suggestions toward a Genealogy of "The Man of Feeling"', *ELH, A Journal of English
Literary History*, I (December 1934), pp. 205–30; Ernest L. Tuveson, 'The Importance
of Shaftesbury', *ELH*, XX (December 1953), pp. 267–99.
[3] Arthur Sherbo (ed.), *Johnson on Shakespeare*, in *The Yale Edition of the Works of Samuel
Johnson*, VII (New Haven, Conn., 1968), p. 88.

ized attitudes and psychological explorations. The second and third epistles of Pope's *Essay on Man*, among many other documents, provide an exposition of the ideological background for the passages in drama which we commonly call 'sentimental':

> And Reason raise o'er Instinct as you can,
> In this 'tis God directs, in that 'tis Man. (III. 97–8)

We can scarcely neglect these lines – and the vast literature in ethical theory of which they are an epitome[1] – if we would understand the intent of eighteenth-century dramatists and of novelists and non-dramatic poets in focusing attention on the emotional reactions of their characters. There are important affinities between expressions of sentimentalism in drama and cognate expressions in non-dramatic literature: to take a famous example, between *The School for Scandal* and *Tom Jones*, in both of which brothers are evaluated according to their possession, or lack, of an intuitive benevolence.

It is necessary, I think, that we distinguish between two referents of the adjective 'sentimental': the one a quality of emotional excess in literature of any period; and the other a quality characteristic of a movement in literary history which in England began late in the seventeenth and ran through most of the eighteenth century. The two meanings are related, and both of them are applicable to many eighteenth-century plays. But they are distinct, and the confounding of them can only prevent us from understanding the full significance of some important innovations in eighteenth-century drama.

A more comprehensive conception of sentimentalism would reduce the force of evidence linking it with the increased prominence of the business community as patrons of the theatre. In any event, that evidence is slight indeed, consisting largely of a coincidence in time.[2] In considering sentimentalism in relation to changes in the social orientation of drama, we must guard against the logical error of 'after this, therefore because of this'. In any event, it was the novel rather than the drama which captured the enlarged audience provided by the expansion of commerce.

---

[1] For discussion of this ethical theory, see Maynard Mack (ed.), *Essay on Man*, in *Poems of Alexander Pope*, III, Pt 1 (London, 1951).
[2] Cf. Smith, *The Gay Couple*, p. 229; Sherbo, *English Sentimental Drama*, pp. 13–14.

# 8 The drama and the novel

The period under consideration is the last in which the drama, printed as well as acted on the stage, was the most popular form of non-devotional literature, the period in which the supremacy of the novel was won. The declining vigour of drama and its replacement in popularity by the novel constitutes a chief fact of eighteenth-century literary history, a fact sufficiently obvious in outline and yet difficult to describe closely and to explain. The most important reasons for the change are perhaps legal and sociological: the narrowing of opportunities for new plays to be performed that followed the Licensing Act of 1737, and the emergence of a large and profitable audience for the novel.[1] The economy of the literary market-place may have been decisive.

A merely literary explanation will scarcely suffice. If possible variations on the formalized pattern of Restoration comedy had largely been played out by the end of the seventeenth century, other promising veins in comedy had been opened. Even *The Way of the World* has about it an innovatory quality – in the intricacy of its plot, the depth of the moral evil explored, the complex-

---

[1] On the growth of the reading public, see Ian Watt, *The Rise of the Novel* (London, 1957), pp. 35–59.

ity of the characters.[1] The depravity of Fainall and Mrs Marwood and the resulting difficulty of Mrs Fainall's position, though not without precedent, are unconventional aspects of comedy of that time and ones to which we are more accustomed in the later novel than in the earlier drama. *The Relapse*, acted four years before *The Way of the World*, has about it a quality we may describe, perhaps anachronistically, as 'novelistic': a departure from comic conventions of plot and character in a manner anticipating the mid-eighteenth-century novel. It is idle to speculate about Vanbrugh's intention: how much of the unconventional quality of the play is due to its rapid composition and its origin as a parody of *Love's Last Shift*; how much to premeditated design. (It presents theoretical problems analogous to those we encounter in Fielding's *Joseph Andrews*, like it originating in parody and to some undetermined extent a work of brilliant improvisation.) In any event, Vanbrugh's characters Amanda and Worthy seem curiously different from the other characters of the play: Miss Hoyden, Sir Tunbelly Clumsey, Lord Foppington and the rest, who are cut to familiar Restoration patterns. Amanda's obstinate and high-minded virtue, enduring to the end of the play and in face of Worthy's plausible claim on her affections, has something about it of the idealism of Richardson's heroines; and Worthy's own final soliloquy about his motives is difficult to reconcile with the comic and satiric tone of the play.

The history of comedy reveals indeed a movement to particularity of character, plot, language and setting analogous to that which Ian Watt finds in prose fiction.[2] If the characters of comedy, unlike those of the novel, retain their conventional and adjectival names, they acquire, at least by the time of Fielding, an individuality of motive and a variety of occupation that separate them from the true wits and the would-be wits of Restoration comedy; and the dramatic fables in which they act out their roles become more varied than those of the love-game comedy of Etherege, Wycherley and Congreve. If dialogue becomes less witty, it also becomes a closer approximation to the language men speak, and the settings of the plays cease to be so exclusively the fashionable areas of London. The extent of innovation in early eighteenth-century comedy has been obscured by the fact that the subsequent history of comedy was not more impressive. As I have already said, the reasons for the later failures were in part legal ones – consequences of the Licensing Act. It is significant that the best dramatist of the 1730s, Henry Fielding, anticipated

---

[1] Clifford Leech, 'Congreve and the Century's End', *Philological Quarterly*, XLI (January 1962), pp. 275–93.
[2] Watt, op. cit. pp. 9–34.

in his five-act comedies literary themes and methods that he later developed more fully in his novels.

His *The Modern Husband* (1731) holds special interest as an anticipation of the later and more important phase of Fielding's career, for it would seem, *in retrospect*, to represent a movement in the drama towards the form of the novel. However qualified any critical assessment of the play must be (a stronger case for it can be made than has yet been attempted),[1] it is strikingly original in its conception,[2] original in the manner of Fielding's novels, more specifically the last of them, *Amelia*. If from the time of Vanbrugh and Congreve there had been an assimilation in comedy of complex characters involved in difficult domestic situations, in *The Modern Husband* there is a fullness of characterization as well as direct confrontation with problems of matrimony and of economic survival that represent a break with the conventions inherited from Restoration comedy. If Fielding retains the conception of comedy as instructive through the depiction of corrupt, cautionary characters, he can scarcely be said to have retained a generic conception of comedy as witty or humorous. In this grim play, in which the title character lives by pimping for his wife, the notion of laughter as the appropriate response is no more relevant than it is in *Amelia*. So too the older conception of decorum in characterization is abandoned in the treatment of the debauched Lord Richly, formerly a purchaser of Mrs Modern's favours, now grown weary of her and attempting, with her bribed assistance, to seduce the virtuous Mrs Bellamant. Mr and Mrs Bellamant anticipate the marital problems of Captain Booth and his wife Amelia of the novel: he in need of money and succumbing to lust for another woman despite his love for his wife, and she magnanimously forgiving him even as she repulses the advances of a rich man who would use his prominence in an effort to seduce her. (The specific detail of Captain Booth's quest for assignment to an active regiment is here represented, not by Mr Bellamant, but by Captain Merit, who is forced to the humiliation of attending the despicable Lord Richly's levee.)

It will already be apparent that the tone of the play, and notably the implied judgement on illicit sexual behaviour, by men as well as by women, has little in common with that typical of late seventeenth-century comedy. In its serious and cautionary treatment of sexual licence, it is indirectly a celebration of marital fidelity: Fielding's firm though not fanatical nor unrelenting moral control, apparent in the novels, is already present, and so is

[1] F. W. Bateson is notably severe in his judgement of the play: *English Comic Drama, 1700–1750* (Oxford, 1929), pp. 115–16.
[2] Cross, *The History of Henry Fielding*, I, pp. 118–19.

his admiration for the manly independence of people in subordinate positions towards their superiors who would abuse their rank. His tone is altogether too sombre for the 'wit' of the earlier comedy to appear. Rather, he attempts, in the reduced metaphorical content of the dialogue, a closer approximation to the rhythms and the diction of unrehearsed conversation. The characters are occasionally banal, as those of the best Restoration dramatists are not, but their commonplaces are similar to those we are accustomed to in mid-eighteenth-century novels, and they derive from a similar preference for an appearance of authenticity over rhetorical virtuosity.

Even in its amplitude *The Modern Husband* seems – and again I emphasize in retrospect, in the light of subsequent literary history – novelistic. Years before the Licensing Act of 1737 terminated his career as a dramatist and led him to write novels, Fielding had broken with earlier conventions in plotting as well as in characterization and in dramatic dialogue. However full of promise in the sense of dramatic innovation the play may be, it is a qualified success, its character relationships too numerous and complex to be fully assimilated, the sordidness of its subject not fully compensated for by analysis of character and society. Fielding had not yet worked out solutions to the problems confronting him in consequence of his break with precedent. And yet if we would understand the evolution of literary theory as it found expression in the drama of the decade before the novel came into its own, we find it a curiously revealing work, one which reminds us how different the subsequent history of drama might have been but for the interruption of Fielding's career in 1737.[1]

---

[1] For an account of the background in the drama for Samuel Richardson's novels, see Ira Konigsberg, *Samuel Richardson and the Dramatic Novel* (Lexington, Kentucky, 1968).

# 9 Theatrical records and the rise of theatrical scholarship

English theatrical history can scarcely be written in detail for periods earlier than the eighteenth century. If we know much about isolated actors, dramatists, plays and theatres, our information exists haphazardly and with large omissions. The difference in scale between the single volume of *The London Stage* devoted to the last forty years of the seventeenth century and the several volumes devoted to a similar span starting at the beginning of the eighteenth testifies to the sudden increase in the quantity of historical sources. In order to assemble even a partial and incomplete calendar of performances in the Restoration, the editors of *The London Stage* had to draw on widely scattered sources of very different kinds and on the one brief history of the theatres written by a man who had personal knowledge of them, John Downes's *Roscius Anglicanus* (published in 1708).

The scarcity of information about the Restoration theatres reflects the indifference to literary history before the eighteenth century.[1] Such scattered information as exists (conveniently assembled for us in *The London Stage*) is to be found in diaries, letters, advertisements in newspapers,[2] theatrical

---

[1] Cf. René Wellek, *The Rise of English Literary History* (Chapel Hill, N.C., 1941), *passim*.
[2] Sybil Rosenfeld, 'Dramatic Advertisements in the Burney Newspapers 1660–1700' *PMLA*, LI (March 1936), pp. 123–52.

documents, court records, preliminaries to published plays and Downes's history. From 1660 until 1669 there is Pepys, the most readable, trustworthy, and – in theatrical matters – informative of diarists, who loved the drama and wrote about the plays he saw with a spontaneity unimpaired by critical dogma.[1] For the whole of the Restoration there is Evelyn's diary, not at all comparable to Pepys's in theatrical interest, but still useful at unpredictable intervals. There are other diaries, such as Robert Hooke's, and there are occasional letters containing relevant material, but not many, for leisurely and literary personal letters did not come into their own until later. A number of legal documents pertaining to the theatres survive, notably those originating in the offices of the Lord Chamberlain and the Master of the Revels, and they provide information about performances of plays as well as insight into the structure of theatrical organizations.

Systematic catalogues, histories of the theatre and memoirs of actors have their beginnings in the late seventeenth and early eighteenth centuries.[2] If occasional play lists had been published since the time of Queen Elizabeth I,[3] English dramatic bibliography properly begins, as W. W. Greg has explained, with Gerard Langbaine's *A New Catalogue of English Plays* (better known by the title of *Momus Triumphans*) of 1687 and his greatly enlarged *An Account of the English Dramatic Poets* of 1691.[4] Langbaine made use of the earlier catalogues compiled by Francis Kirkman, Edward Phillips and William Winstanley,[5] but he is much more accurate than any previous scholar who attempted a comprehensive account of English drama; and his later work embodies research on aspects of drama, above all on literary sources, that is wider-ranging and, frequently though by no means always, more accurate than has been carried out since the seventeenth century. Perhaps alone among seventeenth-century students of English drama, Langbaine continues to be cited not merely as a contemporary or near-contemporary witness but as an authority whose opinion is valued by reason of his research. The search for the sources of plays was not for him so much an antiquarian exercise as a matter of reading the popular literature, English and foreign, of his time and that of the two or three preceding generations. He is sometimes inaccurate, in his source studies as in his biographical and bibliographical passages;

---

[1] McAfee, op. cit.
[2] W. W. Greg, 'Notes on Dramatic Bibliographers', in Malone Society *Collections*, I, Pts 4 and 5 (1911), pp. 324–40.
[3] Carl J. Stratman, *Dramatic Play Lists, 1591–1963* (New York, 1966).
[4] Greg, op. cit.
[5] *Momus Triumphans*, introduction by D. S. Rodes (Los Angeles, 1971), pp. i–ii.

always we must use his work with attention to later investigation. Yet we can rarely ignore him.

Although Langbaine makes frequent reference to having seen performances of plays in London and writes appreciatively of the art of acting, his approach to the drama is that of the literary scholar, working from printed texts, rather than that of the man of the theatre. The distinction will become clear if we consider his *Account* alongside John Downes's slightly later *Roscius Anglicanus* of 1708, a work that like Langbaine's is in its own way a pioneering effort, this time not in dramatic biography and bibliography, but in theatrical history. In his preface, Downes describes himself as having been '*Book-keeper and Prompter*' in Davenant's company, a position, as he explains, that entailed copying out the parts for the actors and attending rehearsals and performances. He differentiates between his reliability on matters pertaining to Davenant's company (the Duke's), which he knew at first hand, and those pertaining to Thomas Killigrew's (the King's), which he had '*from Mr Charles Booth sometimes Book-keeper there*'. He is understandably more complete and anecdotal in his account of the Duke's company, though even here he is not free from ambiguity and occasional error. His point of view reflects his position; it is not at all that of a scholar or critic but that of a professional man of the theatre. Such few aesthetic comments as he makes lead habitually to financial judgements. 'It took well', he says about Etherege's *She Would If She Could*, 'but Inferior to Love in a Tub',[1] and it is clear that he is thinking not about the quality of the plays but about the money they brought in. His is a matter-of-fact view from behind the scenes, a commercial view of the drama. And yet it is his unimaginativeness, his businesslike preoccupation with the continuing routine of the theatres, that makes him so useful a witness. It is after all factual material of the kind he provides that is in short supply, and often his prosaic fact can be translated into literary history. His play lists and his reports of the money made or lost provide evidence about the taste of Restoration audiences and can lead us to conclusions about the rise and decline of dramatic sub-genres. Without him we should know little indeed about theatrical finance influential in shaping late seventeenth-century drama.

Langbaine made use of his own large collection of printed plays in compiling his catalogues;[2] Downes, on the other hand, seems to have worked from theatrical records (perhaps a collection of playbills, perhaps a promp-

[1] *Roscius Anglicanus*, introduction by John Loftis (Los Angeles, 1969), p. 29.
[2] *An Account of the English Dramatic Poets*, introduction by John Loftis (Los Angeles, 1971), p. i.

ter's book): the detailed lists of the casts of plays give the appearance of having been copied verbatim. Downes's history, like the Lord Chamberlain's records and the accounts of performances by diarists and letter writers, is largely independent of the published drama of the Restoration. Yet most of the plays referred to in Downes and the other records have survived in printed form. They were customarily published soon after first performance.[1] A few plays were either not printed at all or have since been lost: for example, the Earl of Bristol's *'Tis Better than It Was* and *Worse and Worse*. Yet for plays produced at the patent houses, these are unusual instances. Manuscripts of plays rarely survive of a date prior to the Licensing Act of 1737, which led to the establishment of a comprehensive file of manuscripts submitted to the Licenser.[2] In the absence of manuscripts for the Restoration plays, we cannot always feel confident that the printed texts record what was said on stage at the première. Yet little has been lost of the performed drama of the Restoration – and perhaps even less of the first half of the eighteenth century – apart from afterpieces and incidental entertainments.

Downes is of unique importance in recording the plays produced in the Restoration theatres. But there are other near-contemporary accounts of theatrical affairs. James Wright in *Historia Histrionica* of 1699 provides, in the words of his subtitle, 'An Historical Account of the English-Stage, Shewing the ancient Use, Improvement, and Perfection, of Dramatick Representations, in this Nation', all this 'In a Dialogue, of Plays and Players' of thirty-two pages. Not at all comparable to Downes's *Roscius Anglicanus* in information conveyed about the Restoration theatres, the work covers a longer time-span in shorter space, moving with the discursiveness of conversation over a range of topics connected with the theatres; in any event it is most informative on the theatrical history of the period before the Restoration. Giles Jacob's *The Poetical Register : or, The Lives and Characters of the English Dramatic Poets* (1719) is of especial usefulness because, just as in a modern *Who's Who*, many of the subjects contributed information about themselves. One of the early histories of the theatre, *The History of the English Stage, from the Restauration to the Present Time* (1741), is attributed on its title page, wrongly it would appear, to Thomas Betterton; the true authors seem to have been William Oldys and Edmund Curll, who worked from Betterton's notes.[3] W. R. Chetwood's *A General History of the Stage . . . with*

---

[1] Cf. Rosenfeld, op. cit. pp. 126–7.

[2] For a guide to this valuable collection of manuscripts, see MacMillan, *Catalogue of the Larpent Plays* (above, p. 32, n. 2).

[3] F. W. Bateson (ed.), *Cambridge Bibliography of English Literature*, II (Cambridge, 1940), p. 403.

*the Memoirs of most of the principal Performers that have appeared on the English and Irish Stage for these last Fifty Years* (1749) falls far below, in its discursiveness, the promise of its title, and yet it records a body of theatrical fact and anecdote that would otherwise be lost.

After the beginning in 1702 of London's first long-lived daily newspaper, *The Daily Courant*, we have complete and dependable knowledge at least of the theatres' routine operations and often of much more. In the years after censorship of the press ended in 1695, and especially after the success of *The Daily Courant*, journalism in all its forms gained enormously in strength; and in the early years of the eighteenth century it came to include the theatres within its range of subjects habitually treated, with happy results for stage historians. A glance at the relevant volumes of *The London Stage* will reveal that most of the daily entries come from the newspapers.

It was Richard Steele who first introduced periodical criticism of drama (as distinguished from advertising and news reporting),[1] in genial reviews of current plays written avowedly to attract profitable audiences to the theatre. In *The Tatler*, and to a lesser extent in *The Spectator*, *The Guardian* and *The Theatre*, Steele reviewed plays and also considered theatrical problems: those, for example, of stage morality and of governmental responsibility for the theatres. We have it on Cibber's word that Steele's notices of plays were effective in drawing crowds.[2] Yet after its promising beginnings with Steele, periodical criticism of drama met no favourable conditions for growth, largely because the journals were pre-empted by political debate. Since most of them were supported by partisan groups, theatrical criticism was excluded or was made to serve the ends of political argument. Not until Aaron Hill's *Prompter* of 1734–6 was theatrical criticism comparable in frequency and quality to Steele's again included in a periodical.[3]

Some of the historical works about the theatres include, as their titles suggest, biographical information about actors: at times brief notices, at other times extended memoirs, such as one of Anne Oldfield appended to the history attributed to Betterton.[4] There are other biographies, collections of biographies and autobiographies of actors, the most notable of which is *An Apology for the Life of Mr Colley Cibber, Comedian* (1740). Cibber's name is

---

[1] Charles Harold Gray, *Theatrical Criticism in London to 1795* (New York, 1931), pp. 1, 37–9.
[2] *Apology*, II, p. 162.
[3] See the recent edition of selections from *The Prompter* prepared by William W. Appleton and Kalman A. Burnim (New York, 1966).
[4] For an account of theatrical biography in the eighteenth century, see Donald Alfred Stauffer, *The Art of Biography in Eighteenth Century England* (Princeton, N.J., 1941).

tarnished by his role as Pope's king of the dunces, a role for which his position as Poet Laureate after 1730 made him seem ironically appropriate as the symbol of an alleged degeneracy in national culture. And no doubt we may believe Pope and Henry Fielding and many other contemporary witnesses who testified to his vanity and personal insensitivity. Yet he wrote a good autobiography, which is in fact a comprehensive though not unbiased account of theatrical affairs from about 1690, when he became an actor, until 1738. The existence of the histories to which I have alluded notwithstanding, the *Apology* is the closest approximation to a satisfactory contemporary account of the theatres in the period just before Garrick.

It is informative to contrast the widespread resentment aroused by Cibber's social prominence with the more general approval of David Garrick's greater social prominence a generation later. The status of the successful actor rose in the eighteenth century: from the time in Queen Anne's reign when Richard Steele wrote about Thomas Betterton's funeral in *The Tatler*, using a eulogy of the most distinguished actor of the Restoration as the occasion for a reply to those such as John Dennis who considered actors as little better than hired menials; to the time of Barton Booth and Colley Cibber, both of whom had friendships among the nobility; to the time of Garrick, whose personal correspondence recalls that of Pope, in the frequency with which the recipients of his letters were famous or titled persons.

It is not entirely coincidence that the first English actor whose correspondence is of sufficient quality and bulk to have achieved multivolume publication[1] was the pupil of the man who is the subject of the first great English biography. The circumstances that Garrick was born eight years after Samuel Johnson and that Garrick's family resided in Lichfield at the time Johnson kept his school there may owe something to a kindly providence. Yet Garrick shared the conviction Johnson passed on to Boswell that literary history and biography were subjects worthy of cultivation, and, if he was primarily an actor and theatre manager, he also assumed a role as custodian and popularizer of English theatrical history. The first Shakespeare jubilee, conceived and organized by Garrick in 1769, testifies to a reverence for Shakespeare's plays and the circumstances that shaped the man who wrote them that has something in common with the more severely scholarly interest in historical criticism exhibited in Johnson's great edition of Shakespeare, published four years earlier.

This is not to say that Garrick, for all his reverence for Shakespeare and

[1] *The Letters of David Garrick*, ed. David M. Little and George M. Kahrl, 3 vols (Cambridge, Mass., 1963).

dramatic history, was responsible for the Shakespeare 'revival' of the eighteenth century. The great popularity of the plays antedates Garrick's career. Arthur H. Scouten has argued, with convincing statistical analysis of performances, 'that Garrick could not have been the chief cause of the Shakespearian revival and instead of one "revival" there was a series of revivals.' The influence of Garrick was great, of course, but much more was involved in the general rise in the number of performances of Shakespeare's plays, both absolutely and in percentages of total performances – the relative weakness of the new plays offered to the managers, the opposition of audiences after 1737 to new plays which had been approved by the Licenser, the interest in Shakespeare engendered by the frequent printings of his plays. The patentees of the mid-eighteenth-century theatres were largely freed from competition, except from one another, and they could produce the old plays without payment to an author, and Garrick at Drury Lane and John Rich at Covent Garden found it profitable to take advantage of the popularity of Shakespeare. The economy of theatrical management, that is to say, provided reinforcement for the broadly based mid-eighteenth-century revaluation of the literature of the English Renaissance which came with the interest in and improved knowledge of literary history. The Shakespeare 'revival' was in part a corollary of the rise of theatrical scholarship in the eighteenth century.[1]

[1] Scouten, 'The Increase of Popularity of Shakespeare's Plays', pp. 189–202.

# II Theatres and actors

# 1 Theatres and scenery

## (i) Founding of the scenic theatre in England

A spectator might have supposed in the year 1640 that theatrical presentation generally in England was in a satisfactory and even flourishing state and that no revolutionary change was imminent. In that year the court masque had reached unprecedented development in Sir William Davenant's *Salmacida Spolia* for which Inigo Jones had devised his most advanced designs; the great acting tradition of the Elizabethan public playhouse was still close enough to its fertile days to be vivid – indeed it had not long before branched into a new tradition of performances in roofed playhouses; and the work of the boy companies and the strolling players was expanding so as to carry touring productions to some of the continental centres.[1]

But by 1649 the Puritan rebellion crushed the whole activity or at least forced all presentations to be either clandestine or politic in message. And so, when in 1660 the English court returned from exile in France and the restoration of the monarchy took place, the tradition of theatrical presentation had a gap of eleven years to make good, through which it may have persisted but only very precariously. But one advantage in the new situation was that King Charles II favoured the theatre. Within months of his return

[1] See for example the articles on 'The English Comedians' and 'George Jolly' in *The Oxford Companion to the Theatre*, ed. Phyllis Hartnoll (London, 1951), pp. 234–5, 429.

two of his courtiers took advantage of the moment and openly began the theatre afresh. It is this 'beginning afresh' – with all the features of a new era and all the controversies about novelties supplanting traditions – that particularly marks this period in British theatre history. The two men received royal patents to conduct public theatrical performances; one of them, Thomas Killigrew (1612–83), named his company 'The King's Men' and their theatre 'The Theatre Royal', while the other, Sir William Davenant (1606–68), instituted 'The Duke's Men' and their theatre was known as 'The Duke's Theatre' after the Duke of York.

Of the two, Killigrew led Davenant by a matter of a month or two in exercising his patent right from the king to open a new theatre. There would appear to have been some feeling of hurry about this, for the two men were rivals, each anxious to make his theatre more successful than the other's. Perhaps it was for this reason that they both began with temporary premises pending the opportunity and the means to create special theatre buildings, and both took the same type of premises, namely an indoor tennis court. It is perhaps significant to note that neither turned to one of the surviving Elizabethan playhouses; that era was ended.

One of the regrettable gaps in our present knowledge of theatre history comes at this point. We know the tennis court that Killigrew chose, and its situation, and similarly we know the tennis court Davenant chose, but we have no record of exactly what either man did to equip his tennis court for the revival of the theatrical art. This much, however, is believed: that Killigrew, in his Gibbons's Tennis Court in Vere Street, off Clare Market (opened November 1660), revived something based on the tradition of the open platform stage of the Elizabethan public playhouse or, at least, of the Jacobean indoor playhouse; that is to say it is supposed that – whether intentionally or perforce – he did not, any more than any other regular English professional theatre manager before him, use scenery.

On the other hand we know, and now upon more dependable evidence, that Davenant in adapting Lisle's Tennis Court in Portugal Street, Lincoln's Inn Fields (opened June 1661), did in fact prepare it for an opening production which had in the first place been categorically written for 'Representation by the Art of Prospective in Scenes' (see the title page of the 1656 edition of *The Siege of Rhodes*). This opening production at Davenant's tennis court was his own specially expanded version of *The Siege of Rhodes*, based on a private performance he had staged at his home at Rutland House, Aldersgate Street, London, in 1656, and at the Cockpit Theatre in Drury Lane in 1658–9. There survives information of this show which will be outlined in section

(iii) below since it offers some significant suggestions to help in forming a picture of a Restoration performance.

But to continue the outline of principal events: in 1663 Killigrew (apparently forced by the public success of Davenant's rival theatre with its scenery) abandoned his Gibbons's Tennis Court and opened an old riding school in Bridges Street off Drury Lane; here he probably used scenery. But Davenant countered by engaging an architect to plan a specific new kind of building to house his new type of theatre show. The architect was Sir Christopher Wren. And so in 1671 Davenant's Duke's Men transferred from Lisle's Tennis Court, Lincoln's Inn Fields, to this new Duke's Theatre, Dorset Garden (which stood near the River Thames just south of Fleet Street). The occasion must have been the achievement of his ambition, but he did not live to see his achievement for he died in 1668 while his new theatre was still being built.

In 1672, the year after Dorset Garden opened, Killigrew's Bridges Street Theatre was burnt; the next step in competition was therefore his, and he responded with the sincerest form of flattery – he commissioned the same architect to build for him also a special theatre designed to take scenery, and close to the site of his last one in Bridges Street; this theatre became the ancestor of all the succeeding Drury Lanes. The site available to him was 112 feet long and 59 feet wide, and among Wren's drawings now at All Souls College, Oxford, is a longitudinal scale section of a building labelled 'Playhouse' and agreeing in length with the length of that site (see Plate 8).[1] This coincidence in size is the only evidence to connect Wren's drawing with Killigrew's Drury Lane, but however that may be the drawing is a representation by a Restoration mind of the Restoration idea of a theatre, and its form agrees well with the forms of the theatres that followed as the period developed; thus it may be considered as offering dependable evidence for visualizing the primal form of the Restoration playhouse. The drawing itself has been torn across once and then (apparently) the two pieces put together and torn across again. By whom we do not know, but if by Wren, then the suggestion is that this scheme was abandoned. For ideas concerning possible other sources among Wren's drawings which might refer to Drury Lane, see Graham Barlow's essay 'Sir James Thornhill and the Theatre Royal, Drury Lane, 1705'.[2]

[1] Cf. Hamilton Bell, 'Contributions to the History of the English Playhouse', in *The Architectural Record*, XXXIII (1913), pp. 359 ff.
[2] In Kenneth Richards and Peter Thomson (eds), *The Eighteenth-Century English Stage* (London, 1972).

Fig. 1

With these two buildings, Dorset Garden and Drury Lane, a new era in English theatrical presentation had opened.


## (ii) The theatres up to 1732

To summarize the main events of the next seventy-five years: the situation in which Dorset Garden and Drury Lane ran simultaneously as rivals lasted only until 1682 when, for reasons that do not concern the development of staging, the two companies, Duke's Men and King's Men, combined; what is of some significance is that of the two buildings the combined companies made Drury Lane their headquarters and not Dorset Garden. The general impression is that Wren's second theatre was more convenient than his first, and acoustically superior.

In 1695 the leader of the combined companies, Thomas Betterton, quarrelled with the manager of Drury Lane, Christopher Rich, and broke away to return to Lincoln's Inn Fields. His 'New Theatre' (as he called it) was presumably a modernization of Davenant's old tennis court but little is known of its details.

In 1705 Betterton left Lincoln's Inn Fields for the Haymarket where a comparatively large new Opera House, designed by the architect and playwright John Vanbrugh, was opened. The building made a considerable step historically as providing a house specifically intended for opera, but was less successful theatrically since it was soon found to be too big and too resonant for straightforward spoken drama – as well as having a stage too wide for the stocks of scenery that had been made for Drury Lane – demonstrating thus early in our history how nearly impossible it is to make an opera theatre that is also a good dramatic playhouse.

In 1714 a fresh theatre was built in Lincoln's Inn Fields, sometimes called the New Theatre and sometimes the Little Theatre (a source of possible confusion for students). It was planned by an architect who was to make some mark in theatre history as well as on the London scene in general, Edward Shepherd, after whom Shepherd's Market in Mayfair is named. Its manager was John Rich, son of the late Christopher Rich of Drury Lane.

In 1720 a builder named John Potter put up another theatre in the Haymarket nearly opposite the Opera House. It was named (even more confusingly for students) the New Theatre, or the Little Theatre, or the French Theatre in the Haymarket. It survived until 1820 when the present Haymarket Theatre was built on the neighbouring site, and a pleasant print of its interior was published showing it as it was in 1807 (see Plate 1).

In 1729 a theatre opened at Ayliffe Street, Goodman's Fields, and this was replaced in 1732 by a new theatre designed by Shepherd. Also in 1732, Shepherd made his greatest contribution to the story by planning the first Covent Garden to which John Rich transferred (see below p. 115).

Some brief notes on the dates of the above theatres are published in *Theatre Notebook*, I (1945–6), pp. 2, 17, 35 and 48–50. As for the interior appearance and scenic arrangements of these theatres, our information is very patchy but some attempt can be made at a provisional picture in the remainder of this chapter.

### (iii) The first scenery at Lincoln's Inn Fields

The following is an attempt to deduce (as far as available evidence will allow) what kind of scenic system Davenant may have instituted on the stage of his tennis court theatre – the theatre that is regarded today as the first playhouse in English history equipped to present regularly shows with scenery to the general public.

The opening production was his own play *The Siege of Rhodes* but now expanded by the introduction of a new character, Roxalana, the consort of Solyman, and by the addition of a complete new 'Second Part' which was presented on the second day and thereafter alternated with the First Part.[1]

Both parts were printed together in 1663 and on the title page of this edition we read:

> The Siege of Rhodes The First and Second Part; As they were lately Represented at His Highness the Duke of York's Theatre in *Lincoln's-Inn-Fields*. The First Part being lately Enlarg'd. . . .

The important point that concerns the history of staging is that this title implies that the stage directions and scenic descriptions in the subsequent text are all properly relevant to the stage of Lisle's Tennis Court in Lincoln's Inn Fields. But the scenic descriptions in the First Part are word-for-word *unchanged* from those in the earlier 1656 edition of the First Part alone when it was presented at Rutland House. The implication then is that the same scenic arrangements were used for the two productions (though possibly expanded to fit a larger stage, since an indoor tennis court is some 30 feet

---

[1] Detailed discussion can be found in the opening pages of Montague Summers, *The Playhouse of Pepys* (London, 1935), and in Richard Southern, *Changeable Scenery* (London, 1952), ch. 7.

wide whereas the Rutland House stage was only 22 feet 4 inches wide). And the scale plans for these arrangements as well as the designs for the scenes survive today in drawings by John Webb, the former in the British Museum and the latter in the Devonshire Collection at Chatsworth. It is therefore worth considering Webb's scheme as most probably exemplifying the scenic system used in Davenant's first Restoration theatre.

John Webb (1611–72) was nephew and assistant to Inigo Jones, and closely acquainted with court masque techniques before the Commonwealth. His designs for *The Siege of Rhodes* have been discussed at length by William Grant Keith, who identified the plans in *The Burlington Magazine*,[1] and in the present writer's *Changeable Scenery*. Briefly, the scenes consist of four main elements: (1) a group of backscenes or 'shutters' about half-way up the depth of the stage, each scene being divided vertically down the centre so as to present a right half and a left half which could be slid open and drawn out of sight or shut to and displayed; (2) framing these at either side of the stage a number of pairs of wings or side scenes parallel with the front; (3) continuing the framing along the top, a number of hanging borders joining the opposite wing-tops; and (4) a quite different group of elements set up behind the back shutters on the deeper half of the stage and consisting of a fixed backcloth and in front of it a series of two or more cutout groundrows which could be changed as required.

Thus two varieties of scene were possible. The first was one in which a pair of closed shutters formed the back. It was called a *shutter scene* by Inigo Jones and later a *flat scene* (for example in Orrery's *Guzman*, Lincoln's Inn Fields, 1669, III. ii, discussed in *Changeable Scenery*, p. 144). The two sliding elements made up a *pair of flats*, whence derives our present noun a *flat* to designate the basic canvassed frames of which a full scene is made up. The significance of the original term is that the scene is painted on the flat. The second variety of scene could only be revealed, or discovered, when all the shutters were drawn back to show the farther part of the stage; it was called a *scene of relief*, that is 'in relief' (for example in Inigo Jones's note on his plan for *Florimène* (1635), where this part of the scenery is labelled 'works of Relevo to Remouv'[2]). It was so named because in contrast to the flat scene it was made up of separate cutout planes set in succession before a backcloth, thus giving a sense of third dimension or 'relief'. This variety of scene, since its elements had to be *set* in place before discovery, came later to be called a

---

[1] Vol. XXV (1914), pp. 29 ff.
[2] B. M. Lansdowne MS. 1171, ff. 5b and 6. See also Southern, *Changeable Scenery*, p. 58 and Plates 4 and 6.

*set scene*. The distinction between the two varieties is discussed in more detail in *Changeable Scenery*, ch. 13.

This distinction between flat scene and set scene is essential to an understanding of Restoration scenery. Since all the scene changes were effected in full open view of the audience and not concealed by a curtain, it followed that any number of flat scenes could be shown in direct succession merely by opening or closing a pair of flats, but that all set scenes had to be preceded and followed by a flat scene so that the pieces might be set up or removed, and that therefore no two set scenes could come in succession.

The device by which the flat scenes were enabled to slide on and off was a framework consisting of a grooved timber lying face up on the stage floor, with uprights at either end supporting a similar timber with grooves facing downwards at the level of the top of the shutters. The opposite halves of a pair of shutters were entered into the extremity of their groove through intervals in the uprights. The grooves were soaped to assist easy sliding.

At first the side wings seem to have been fixed and therefore to have remained unchanged whatever the scene. They were so in Webb's scheme for the first *Siege of Rhodes*. But before long they too became changeable and ran in grooves as the shutters did, but the idea that wings and backscene must necessarily match and form one pictorial composition was not as important as it became later, the wings being merely a framing element to the backscene. Because of this consideration it followed that if the wings were 'standing wings' (that is unchanged throughout all the scenes of a play), then there was no need for them to be simple pieces in one plane; they could be three-dimensional or 'Serlian' wings – each wing could be made up of two pieces, one parallel with the stage front, and the other at an angle to it, facing towards the centre-line of the stage, so presenting a corner like the corner of a house. The tree-and-cottage wings designed by Inigo Jones for *Florimène* at Whitehall in 1635 had been of this sort – what today would be termed 'booked wings'. The special advantage of this kind of wing was that it 'masked' the sides of the stage more effectively than the simple wing parallel with the stage front, since it prevented cross-glances from the audience into the offstage areas more effectually.

The reason for making the above point in detail is that it is possible that such bipartite wings persisted in London theatres as late as 1731 as they are apparently represented in the illustration to *Harlequin Horace* referred to near the end of this chapter.

This system of scenery was used for the first private production of *The Siege of Rhodes*, and since the second edition prepared for the production at

Lisle's Tennis Court in Lincoln's Inn Fields repeats the original scene descriptions unchanged, it is to be inferred they applied equally to the system of scenery used in this first regular public theatre in England to present shows graced by 'the Art of Prospective in Scenes'.

Apart from this hypothesis of its scenic system, can anything else be deduced about its stage? There is one point of considerable significance; in the First Part of *The Siege of Rhodes* there is no mention of any *door* for the entrance of characters, nor is there any sign whatever of a door in the plans of the stage or in the designs for the scenes that Webb made; at Rutland House the characters entered between the wings (as they had done in Inigo Jones's court masques). But in the Second Part of *The Siege*, written for the new stage in Lincoln's Inn Fields, there is specific mention of doors. A direction in the opening scene reads '*A shout within, and a Noise of forcing of Doors*'. One of the characters goes out and then a further direction reads 'Enter *Ianthe* and her two Women at the other Door'. Thus we have not only direct reference to an entrance door for use by the characters but a clear implication that there were at least two such doors.

The signification is that one of the most striking technical features of the English theatre was now in use at Lisle's Tennis Court – that is, the combination of the new system of scenery with a survival of the two-door entry system for actors that characterized the Elizabethan stage, a system where the doors were quite independent of any scenic picture and were positive features of the architecture of the public playhouse stage. Such a combination of two so disparate things argues the existence of a third element, a portion of the stage independent of the scenic part upon which the doors can give. In other words, a forestage.

What size was this forestage and how was it used in the presentation of a Restoration play? There is not much direct evidence relating to Davenant's first theatre in Lincoln's Inn Fields but in the texts of plays presented there we can find particular and perhaps surprising inferential evidence.

One such play is Sir Samuel Tuke's *The Adventures of Five Hours* shown at this theatre in January 1662–3, in which it is clear that at least four such doors would be needed (see my examination of the play in *Changeable Scenery*, ch. 8). It is also clear that, whatever the scenery at the back of the stage was painted to represent, the considerable area in front served by these four doors was regarded as a relatively unparticularized and independent acting area (as was the stage of an Elizabethan playhouse). To such an extent was this true that a character might leave the stage by one of these doors and immediately enter by another door and be understood to have left one room and gone into another *even though the scenery at the back remained unchanged.* For an example see *The Adventures of Five Hours*, V. iii. During a chase through rooms in Don Carlos's house, Antonio and Octavio are directed to '. . . *retire fighting off the Stage*; Henrique *and his Men pursuing them*, . . . *Exeunt.*' Then '*Enter presently* Antonio *and* Octavio *at another Door, which* Antonio *bolts.*' Antonio then says –

> Now we shall have a breathing while at least,
> *Octavio*, and time to look about us;
> Pray see yon other Door be fast.
>     Octavio *steps to the Door where they went out*, . . .
>     Antonio *goes to both the Doors, to see if they be fast.*

– and immediately he has done so Antonio gives a sigh of relief, 'So, 'tis now as I could wish it . . .' But no change of scene whatever takes place during this passage; the flats at the back of the stage still represented – or shall we say 'stood for' – a room in Don Carlos's house.

This loose regard for any relationship of a visual sort between the scenery and the action that went on in front of it is one of the salient features of the Restoration stage. In effect it meant that the forestage was regarded practically as a sort of transpicuous hall where the major action of the play took place under the lights of the candle-hoops. One side of this hall was replaced by the auditorium, lit in much the same key; the other side was occupied by the deeper part of the stage with its scenes, lit only by candles behind the wings and with no light at all from above, in consequence probably relatively dim. At either end of this hall were the walls flanking the forestage, with their doors below and their balconies above, directly related in architectural style to the sides of the auditorium and continuous with them, so that the forestage and its acting area were thus part of the auditorium and not part of the scenery. The lit actor was related to the spectator and the auditorium, not to the shadowy painting on the flats behind him.

Since the Restoration forestage had to serve so important a theatrical purpose, it needed to be of considerable size. The one shown in Wren's sectional drawing of a playhouse is some twenty feet deep; moreover, there are indications that six doors might on occasion be implied in a play. In Edward Howard's *The Man of Newmarket* (Drury Lane, 1678) there twice occurs the direction '*Enter* Jockeys *at several Doors*'. There are five jockeys in the play: hence, even if each jockey does not have a door to himself (in which case symmetry would dictate six doors?), at least four doors would seem to be required.

It is not uninteresting to notice that a stage direction implying six doors may not be inconsistent with a stage possessing only four doors, because the extra pair might well be added by placing stock door wings upstage of the regular proscenium sides. That such door wings existed at any rate in 1731 is proved by the very clear representation of one in Hogarth's meticulously exact painting of the juvenile performance of Dryden's *The Indian Emperor* at Mr Conduitt's house (now in the possession of Teresa, Viscountess Galway).

The use of this Restoration forestage as the main acting area corresponded with the use of the stage platform in the Elizabethan playhouse. It is significant that in Johannes De Witt's well-known drawing of the Swan Theatre (*c.* 1596) this area of platform is distinctly labelled with a name – the *proscaenium*. By this word is presumably meant the area *pro* (in front of) the *skene* building (or tiring house). Thus actors coming out from the tiring-house doors to act would come out and act upon the *proscaenium*. Following this approach it is not difficult to see how the doors giving on to this area came to be called the 'proscenium doors' and the walls themselves the 'proscenium sides', with a 'proscenium ceiling' above.[1] And finally how in the course of time, when the whole feature had been developed and had lost some of its original integrity and purpose, the 'non-existent' far side through which one saw the scenery came to be called the 'proscenium opening' – and ultimately (whatever its shape) the 'proscenium arch' or even quite simply (though incorrectly) the 'proscenium'. This seems a safer derivation of the modern term than to trace it back to the 'frontispiece' of the Stuart court masques.

It should be remembered that it was at the *back* of this forestage, that is, on the far side of the acting area, that what we call today the 'front curtain' rose and fell in the Restoration theatre. This curtain was generally of the festoon type and traditionally of green material. It was very rarely used during the course of a play. It was down when the audience entered the theatre and remained down while the prologue was being spoken in front; it then rose on the first scene of the play and did not fall again until after the epilogue at the end of the performance. The transition between one scene and another was marked by visibly changing the scenery – that is, by opening or closing the flats – and the interval between one act and another was simply marked by leaving the stage empty of action but with the curtain still up. Any scene change that might be required for the opening scene of an ensuing act occurred after the interval and immediately before the action of the scene

---

[1] As described in *The Revels History of Drama in English*, VI (London, 1975), pp. 61 ff., 'The Lost Remains at King's Lynn'.

began. Scene changes were signalled by the stage manager's whistle or by ringing a bell.[1]

With scenery thought of and used in this particular way, it was of course by no means necessary for actors to leave the stage at a scene change; frequently a character might stay in sight at the end of a scene while the character to whom he had been speaking would 'go within the scene' (that is, retire into the scenic area) and the flats would close over him, while the first actor was left on the forestage to continue the action straight into the next scene. The stage direction to mark this remaining on the stage, in contrast to an 'exit' or an 'enter', was *manet* (let him remain).[2]

This seems to be as far as it is possible to go in hazarding a reconstruction of the scenic system of the early Restoration stage, but a certain amount of further light may be reflected from a study of the first two major buildings put up specially to present shows with full scenery, Dorset Garden and Drury Lane.

### (iv) Dorset Garden and *The Empress of Morocco*

Though Wren's surviving drawings for theatres do not include any that can be certainly ascribed to Dorset Garden, there are three other pieces of evidence on which to base an idea of its interior. The first is a series of five engravings of scenes on its stage illustrating a play by Elkanah Settle entitled *The Empress of Morocco* and presented on that stage in 1673 (also, according to the dedication in the 1673 edition, previously '*presented* . . . *in a* Court-Theater, *& by persons of* . . . *Birth and Honour* . . .'). The second is a statement by a French visitor, François Brunet, in his *Voyage en Angleterre, 1676*,[3] that the *parterre* (or pit) was *en Amphitheatre*, by which is presumably meant that the rows of seats were curved and on a sloping floor; and that there were only seven boxes each holding twenty persons, with a like arrangement in the circle above, and a gallery to top them all. The third is the evidence (mentioned above) that there were at least four doors to the forestage.

[1] As early as Inigo Jones the whistle was used, see in Ben Jonson's *Expostulation* (1631), l. 66, the reference to 'Inigo, the whistle, and his men'. For scene-change whistles marked in a prompt book, see 'The Scene Plot of *The Change of Crownes*' (Edward Howard, Drury Lane, 1667) by the present writer in *Theatre Notebook*. IV (1950), pp. 65–8. For the bell, see W. J. Lawrence, *Old Theatre Days and Ways* (London, 1935), p. 37; and also the 'curtain bell' and 'thunder bell' mentioned in the Covent Garden inventory of scenery and properties of 1743, discussed in *Changeable Scenery*, p. 201.

[2] For further discussion and examples, see *Changeable Scenery*, pp. 137–42.

[3] Unpublished, B.M. Add. MS. 35, 177.

The illustrations to *The Empress of Morocco* show the frame to the scene with its very elaborate carving, a projecting music room above, and at the sides a glimpse of part of a door either side with part of a balcony above (Plates 2 to 7).

It is not unprofitable to give some consideration to what survives of the show itself in the script. In five of the six illustrations (the sixth is a view of the theatre exterior) we have the first known pictures of scenes in action on an English public stage. Two of the plates have been widely reproduced, those of the prison scene and of the torture scene. The whole set of five are not so frequently seen together.

The plates in the original are a little clumsy. Each shows a scene as viewed behind the proscenium, and though the scenes vary the proscenium frame is the same in each illustration. It is, however, so cropped that very little of the sides of the frame is shown. In some plates this little is enough to carry clear indications of the door and balcony. Now, as stated above, it is clear from the stage directions of several plays produced at this theatre that Dorset Garden had four doors, two on each side of the forestage. It is almost certain that the two pairs of doorways would be similar in decorative character and that this similarity would apply also to the balconies above the doors. If this is correct we may take one of the plates – the one which shows most of these side features – mount it and draw on the mount an extension of the design so as to complete the door, shown in part, and also the balcony above it (Fig. 2). The purpose of such a tentative reconstruction is to gain a truer idea of the theatre interior in one particular respect than the untouched plate alone provides, severely cropped as it was in publication; this particular respect is in the matter of the forestage. The plates as they are give a radically wrong impression of the theatre because they suggest (1) that it was a picture-frame theatre like the orthodox theatre of today; (2) that all the action took place behind the picture-frame; and (3) that practically no depth of stage floor projected forward through the frame. The present intention in extending the drawing is to remove this impression and to see what the theatre might look like when that impression was removed.

It seems now that, once the complete door is represented, it might not be too hazardous to go on to repeat the pilaster that is shown above it, but now on the near side thus framing the door between two pilasters. After this one may be emboldened to a further development – to represent the second door with its balcony on the near side of the new pilaster, and beyond this again to add a third pilaster in front of all – without infringing either the laws of architecture or of probability.

Fig. 2

Such a procedure may seem only a more or less harmless amusement un-less it can be shown that among Christopher Wren's drawings for theatres such an arrangement as has been described was actually, and in every detail, present. It is because precisely such an arrangement can be found (see the drawing of Wren's discussed below in section (v) and Plate 8) that there seems justification for undertaking such a reconstruction. The result was first pub-lished as Illus. 42 in the second edition of *The Oxford Companion to the Theatre* (1957) but, by some curious error, wrongly and misleadingly cap-tioned, and in later editions withdrawn. This reconstruction is therefore reproduced again here with the above elucidation.

Taking in its suggestion of the size of the Dorset Garden forestage with the four doors giving on to it, one may turn now to the illustrations of the scenery and ask what light they throw on the nature of a Restoration performance. It should perhaps be said first that in Fig. 2 the centre portion down to the bottom of the scene itself is entirely untouched; only the sides and the empty forestage have been added.

Settle's play begins: 'The First Act, Scene the First. | *Scene opens*, Muly Labas *appears bound in Chains, attended by Guards.*'

The words '*Scene opens*' present a problem. After consideration of many Restoration stage directions one is led to suppose that the word 'opens' should be read literally as signifying that a pair of flats slid apart and actually 'opened'. But the usage in the instance above seems to be exceptional, for the words come at the very beginning of a play when, presumably, there had been no previous scenery to open. The common practice, as has been said, was that the prologue was delivered before the green curtain, and it was this curtain which, as it rose after the prologue, would reveal the first scene. But here it appears, if the rubric is correct, that the prologue may have been spoken on the forestage but before a painted 'scene' instead of the curtain. If so, what was painted on this scene at Dorset Garden, which took the place of a curtain, we do not know.

With regard, however, to this particular problem of the ambiguity of the word 'opens', the following passage from Congreve's *The Old Bachelor* (1693, but written originally in 1689) is worth quoting before going on. In V. x Belmont says to Belinda:

> Alas! Courtship to Marriage, is but as the Musick in the Play-House, 'till the Curtain's drawn; but that once up, then opens the Scene of Pleasure.

This would indicate that at the beginning of a play the expression 'the scene opens' might be used without any implication of shutters parting but simply to mean 'the scene begins'.

It should perhaps be said here that there is nothing in our present knowledge to forbid the idea that the Duke's Theatre had a painted front curtain possibly derived from the painted curtains used behind the frontispieces in so many of the masques that Inigo Jones, with Webb as his assistant, had designed. In Webb's original scheme for *The Siege of Rhodes* the show opened with a 'Curtain being drawn up', but we have only the indecisive fact that no design has been found for it to support an opinion that it was not a pictorial curtain.

However this may be, what appeared on the stage when the 'scene' opened is clearly stated: it was a prison scene and it is depicted in the plate which faces the opening page of the script (Plate 2). It was most probably made up on the same lines as Davenant's previous scenery at Lincoln's Inn Fields – that is to say, the sides of the prison would be represented on a series of wing pieces (comparable to the prison wings in Hogarth's *Indian Emperor* paint-

ing), the roof on a series of arch borders (comparable to those very faintly to
be distinguished in the under-painting of that picture), and the far wall on a
pair of flats. This last is confirmed by the words at the beginning of the next
act which read '*The Scene opened . . .*'.

The action in the prison scene is that Muly Labas, son of the Emperor of
Morocco and heir to the throne, is held captive by his father. To him comes
his lover Morena – also a prisoner, and daughter to a neighbouring king who
is at war with Morocco. To them there enters Laula the reigning Empress of
Morocco, played by Mrs Betterton, who announces the Emperor's death and
the pardon of both the captives. Next, there enters the villainous Crimalhaz –
which must have been a sensational moment, for he was played by no less a
person than the great Betterton himself. The released lovers go out and the
Empress and the villain are left to reveal to the audience that they are hatch-
ing a plot to betray the young lovers and take the throne themselves. Now
follows:

Act the Second, Scene the First.

*The Scene opened, is represented the Prospect of a large River, with a
glorious Fleet of Ships, supposed to be the Navy of* Muly Hamet, *after the
Sound of Trumpets and the Discharging of Guns.*
*Enter* King, Young Queen, Hametalhaz *and Attendants.*[1]

(Muly Hamet is Muly Labas's general.)

Of this scene also there is an illustration on the facing page (Plate 3), but its
technical make-up is less easy to guess than that of the last. It is to be supposed that the prison scene would have been left in place through the interval
between Acts I and II, and that when Act II was ready to begin the prison
flats opened and discovered what may have been a 'scene of relief'. It is made
up of architectural wings framing what were possibly water-rows (or 'groundrows' representing water), with four ships and a small boat riding over or
between them. No indication at all is given of any backscene or of any
borders – these may have been a plain skycloth with matching sky borders.
Three remarks are due here. First, we find some confirmation of the idea that
the action of a scene took place on the forestage and not among the scenery,
by the fact that there is no ground to stand on represented in this scene at
all – only water. Second, it is pretty clear that more wings than the two shown
would be needed to mask-in the scene; such further wings might have been

[1] The entry direction is to be understood as completing the statement which begins *after
the Sound of Trumpets and the Discharging of Guns*; that is, the visual effect is followed by
the sound effect which in turn is followed by the entry.

repetitions of these column wings, or they might have been sky wings or cloud wings with or without water painted on the lower part to match the water-rows. Third, it is also pretty certainly implied here that a system existed on this stage for changing the wings and borders as well as the flat backscenes, for the prison wings and borders certainly do not seem to be left framing the prospect of the '*large River*'. This system would very probably be a revival or development of Inigo Jones's method of wing-grooves in *Salmacida Spolia*.

In the action of the scene the new young king, Muly Labas, welcomes and honours his victorious general, Muly Hamet, and bestows on him the hand of his sister Mariamne – a scene of great rejoicing. At the end of this passage there occurs something that may be of technical significance. It is the leaving of Crimalhaz on the stage to soliloquize for fourteen lines, followed by the words 'The Scene opened' and a description of the scene to come. Now it is impossible technically that it could have been the river scene that 'opened' if (as seems unavoidable) that scene was a relief scene. The situation implied here is to be found elsewhere in the play; what is suggested is that a pair of flats of some unspecified kind was closed over the river scene and that the actor soliloquized before them while a new scene was being prepared behind. If this were so then the next scene should turn out to be another relief scene or to have some element of the 'set scene' about it. This we shall find it has.

It is interesting to note that this next scene, though quite different in locale from the preceding one, is *not* called Scene Two. There seems to be some impression that the two highly different events which are the subjects of the two scenes are to be thought of as contributing equally to the development of the plot and thus the script does not indicate any second scene in the act but retains the heading 'Act the Second, Scene the First' right to the opening of the third act. However this may be, the description which follows is:

> The Scene opened.
> *A State is presented, the King, Queen and* Mariamne *seated,* Muly-Hamet, Abdelcador *and Attendants, a Moorish Dance is presented by* Moors *in several Habits, who bring in an artificial Palm-tree, about which they dance to several antick Instruments of Musick; in the intervals of the Dance, this Song is sung by a Moorish Priest and two Moorish Women; the Chorus of it being performed by all the* Moors.

Opposite a plate shows this scene with the tree and the full chorus (Plate 4). What is remarkable is that it shows us no wings and no borders and no backscene at all! Indeed the illustration is one of the most curious in scenic history. Among the things it does not show is any trace at all of the '*State*' or royal seat. Presumably this state is a property of some size for three people are described as seated when the scene begins – they are therefore presumably discovered. Since two of them are king and queen, they are presumably seated on that state. And as a final presumption, they must have been arranged in position behind the scene which opened and thus on the scenic part of the stage, not on the forestage, and so should properly have been included in the illustration.

But in this illustration the figures are shown somewhat larger than those in the first scene of the prison and therefore it is possible that a sort of partial 'close-up' was intended by the illustrator, in which he concentrated on the dance spectacle while the scenery surrounding it was ignored together with that part of the stage on the extreme sides where the state and the attendant court would have been distributed.

In any case it seems that the spectacle of this court would have been all that the audience would have been able to see in the opening moments of the scene, for we read that the palm tree was not discovered with the court but was an artificial tree brought in by the dancers and singers. What could have been visible on the stage behind the court before the tree was brought in to them? In other words, what scenery was in the background which the illustration leaves blank?

The very fact of this leaving-blank may just possibly imply that the chief scenic elements were simply left over from the previous scene (that is to say the sky backing, the borders and possibly even the architectural wings) when the ships and water-rows had been removed.

For the opening of the third act there is no illustration and only the stage directions remain to help until the middle of Act IV; but the directions alone are of some value. They show one of the typical Restoration scenic conventions, that of presenting alternately the inside and outside of the same room so that persons may be seen approaching it and leaving it as well as what is happening inside.

The opening direction of the act is quite simple:

Act the Third, Scene the First.
*Enter* Muly Hamet, *Scene the Palace.*

Muly Hamet has only three lines to speak, in which he expresses the hope that the Queen Mother (the old Empress) will bless his betrothal to Mariamne, and '*Exit*'. There follows immediately:

CARL A. RUDISILL LIBRARY
LENOIR RHYNE COLLEGE

Scene a Bed-Chamber.

*The Scene opens, and discovers* Crimalhaz *and Queen Mother sleeping on a Couch, a Table standing by, with* Crimalhaz's *Plume of Feathers, and his Drawn Sword upon it.*

Thus there is first a non-particularized pair of flats representing some part of the palace interior – 'Scene the Palace' – perhaps a corridor or an anteroom; then Muly Hamet walks in by a proscenium door, speaks and goes out. Then the palace flats open and uncover the perfidious occupation of the Empress of Morocco with her courtier and gallant. Immediately follows 'Re-enter Muly Hamet'; he makes suitable comment without waking the couple but appropriates Crimalhaz's sword to use in evidence against him and 'Exit'.

The Scene changes to an Anti-Chamber.

Muly Hamet *re-enters with the same Sword, and in passing over the Stage is overtaken by the* King.

Thus the flats close over again, presumably the same flats as at the beginning of the act; Muly Hamet enters once more and begins to cross, '*passing over the Stage*' back to his first entrance, when he is suddenly overtaken by the young King, who calls to him and asks him what he is doing. Muly Hamet regretfully conveys the perfidy of the King's mother; the King swears vengeance and exits; Muly Hamet has a brief soliloquy and then follows him off. Then:

*The Scene changes again to the Queen Mothers Bed-Chamber, where She and* Crimalhaz *appear hand in hand; She in a Morning Dress.*

– the lovers are now awake and she has donned the equivalent of a dressing gown. He discovers that his sword has been taken and calls for a eunuch servant from whom he learns the name of the intruder. Thereupon the Queen Mother '*Stabs the Eunuch, who falls and dies*'. They then plot how to avoid Muly Hamet's imminent unmasking of them and, following on the Queen Mother's ingenious suggestion, '*Here* Crimalhaz *stabbs himself in his right Arm, which immediately appears bloody.*' (Presumably here is the old trick of a bladder of red liquid.) He then '*Throws away the Dagger*' – and not a moment too soon, for immediately '*Enter to them the King and* Muly Hamet'. The couple turn the evidence in such a way as to accuse Muly Hamet himself, at which the King is completely bewildered, but finally has Muly Hamet '*led out by the Guards*' while he himself goes away by a separate door ('*Exeunt* King *and* Muly Hamet *severally*'). The couple are left to exult for fourteen lines and then '*Exeunt*'.

Scene the Second, the Scene a Prison.
*The Scene opens*, Muly Hamet *appears bound.*

So then the bedchamber flats open and a prison (possibly the same scenery
as that in I. i) is discovered. The wings of the bedchamber may have remained unchanged. Mariamne enters to her lover and has a sad scene with
him in which she at first believes that it was he who was with the Empress but
is finally convinced of his innocence. During this passage there '*Enter King,
and young Queen*' but only, it is noted in a subsidiary marginal direction, '*To
the Door*' – that is, they come just inside the proscenium door and stand
listening. The King hears Mariamne forgive Muly Hamet and is scandalized
at such treatment to a man he supposes to be his mother's would-be ravisher.
He starts forward from the door where he has been eavesdropping, and is
followed by his court; and although he had already entered '*To the Door*'
some fourteen lines ago, he is included again in the direction: '*Enter to them
King, Young Queen, Q. Mother*, Crimalhaz, Hametalhaz *and Attendants*'.
Thereafter the case against Muly Hamet strengthens until the end of the act.
He is banished. The Old Queen inspires Crimalhaz to ransack the treasury
and make off into the mountains taking the bulk of the King's troops with
him; she will then spur the young King to follow him, ostensibly to be
revenged but actually to be ambushed.

Next follows an act with some scenic surprises; the opening rubric is
simply:

Act the Fourth, Scene the First.
*Enter* King *Attended.*

– but there is no description of the scene at all. In the action the old Queen
Mother bids farewell to the King her son as he sets out for the trap she has
laid for him. The scene behind could quite suitably be the same as that used
for an anteroom in the palace. Whatever it was, it now opened to something
of a sensation as the next direction suggests:

Scene the Second.
*The Scene open'd, is presented a Prospect of a Clouded Sky, with a Rain
bow. After a shower of Hail, enter from within the Scenes* Muly Hamet *and*
Abdelcador.

Unfortunately there is no illustration for this scene, and so the 'Prospect of a
Clouded Sky' affords a task for the imagination; it might be right to see a dim
sky-painting with a painted rainbow across it – or even a rainbow effected by
means of a 'transparency', such as Inigo Jones had known – and, since this

was probably a relief scene, there might have been a low line of ground in profile across the bottom, with the whole framed in rock wings from stock. Through these wings ('*enter from within the Scenes*') there come the exile and his friend; the doors of entrance on the forestage are here not used but it is most likely that the two players left the 'scenes' and advanced on to the forestage as they began their dialogue, coming down through the hailstorm as from a distance. By a quirk of plot Mariamne enters to them '*with a small Attendance*'. Next comes a posse of villains disguised as priests and led by Crimalhaz's minion, Hametalhaz. Danger threatens. And at this point comes the longest direction in the play.

> *Here a Company of Villains in Ambush from behind the Scenes discharge their Guns at* Muly Hamet, *at which* Muly Hamet *starting and turning,* Hamettalhaz *from under his Priests habit draws a Sword, and passes at* Muly H. *which pass is intercepted by* Abdelcader. *They engage in a very fierce Fight, which*[1] *the Villains, who also draw and assist* Hametalhaz, *and go off several ways Fighting; after the discharge of other Guns heard from within, and the Clashing of Swords, Enter again* Muly Hamet, *driving in some of the former Villains, which he Kills.*

Here clearly might be, with adequate rehearsal, opportunity for sensational effect. But in the dialogue that follows it turns out that Mariamne has been abducted, and Muly Hamet and his friend *exeunt* in despair. There follows:

> Scene the Third, the Scene a Tent.
> *Enter Queen Mother and young Queen.*

The old Empress with malice aforethought broaches the subject of a masque entertainment in the camp with the Young Queen taking part; she agrees and they go out to discuss details. The King and Hametalhaz now enter, and a marginal direction reads 'Scene *continues*'. During it the Queen Mother returns to persuade the King to act the part of Orpheus in the masque, in which he will have to rescue Eurydice from the underworld. He falls in with the suggestion and exits. Then the Young Queen returns and is similarly persuaded to play Eurydice, but here the plot thickens, for she is told that the Orpheus who will be playing in his disguise opposite her will really be Crimalhaz and that he will take her and ravish her at the end of the performance. And so she is subtly counselled to carry a knife and stab him at the climax of the show. All go out. But we are not long held in suspense for there immediately follows:

[1] For *with*. Corrected in Errata at the end of the play.

The Mask.

*The Scene open'd; is presented a Hell, in which* Pluto, Proserpine, *and other Women-Spirits appeared seated, attended by Furies; the Stage being fill'd on each side with* Crimalhaz, Hamet, *Q. Mother, and all the Court in Masquerade: after soft Musick Enter* Orpheus.

At this point there is fortunately no need to imagine the picture presented, or on the opposite page is the fourth illustration showing the Hell scene in detail (Plate 5). Of some interest is the fact that this picture alone of all the series shows a glimpse of the ends of two tableau curtains drawn up on either side towards the top of the frame. One would very much like to know whether this was part of the scenic effect of the masque or was the regular front curtain of the theatre which had been unintentionally omitted from the other illustrations.

The scene itself consists of a rocky hill surmounted by a sort of rustic temple belching smoke. To one side is a figure in a long Persian coat with a wand – presumably a master of ceremonies – and to the other a woman with a florid turban headdress – perhaps the Queen Mother dressed '*in Masquerade*'. A three-headed dragon writhes before the hill; demons fly around and emerge from traps near the front. No wings or borders are indicated but presumably these would show rocks and clouds respectively. The masque proceeds to its climax and:

*Here a Dance is perform'd, by several infernal Spirits, who ascend from under the Stage; the Dance ended, the King Offers to snatch the Young Queen from the Company, who instantly draws her Dagger, and stabs him.*

– crying as she does so 'Take that Ravisher.' Too late she recognizes him upon his '*undisguising himself*' and she 'Faints away, and falls into the hands of some Women; who run in to her Assistance. *Here all the Masquers undisguise, and run in to the Kings assistance.*' The King dies. The Young Queen '*Offers to stab her self, but is detain'd by* Crimalhaz; *and the Dagger snatcht from her.*' The Queen Mother denounces her as having murdered the King intentionally. The King's body is removed. Much plotting and cross-accusation follow. Then:

*Exeunt Q.M. &* Ham.
Manent Crimalhaz *and Y. Queen.*

Crimalhaz offers to get the Young Queen out of the accusation if she will let him 'have more than Thanks for a reward'; she at first contemptuously refuses, then on second thoughts feigns to agree. They go out.

The Fifth Act.
*Enter* Crimalhaz *attended as King.*

There is no further description of this scene; indeed, the technique of the play now seems to revert to that of the Elizabethan public playhouse stage, for there follows a series of warlike alarums and excursions in which news is brought that Morena's father King Taffalet is attacking the town. In a panic Crimalhaz and the Queen Mother indulge in mutual recrimination and he orders the Guards to seize her. She turns king's evidence and kneels to beg forgiveness of the Young Queen but only, in fact, to get near enough to stab her, and then she turns the dagger upon Crimalhaz. But she is '*stopt by the Guards*' and instead '*stabs her self*'. News comes that the exiled Muly Hamet is approaching at the head of Morena's father's army and that the people of Morocco have gone over to the side of the advancing conquerors. No indication is given of the removal of the two women's bodies, apart from an order to that effect from Crimalhaz, who leaves with Hametalhaz to engage the enemy at the gates.

Immediately they have gone (but without any note of a scenery change), '*Enter* Muly Hamet, *and* Attendants *with* drawn Swords, *after a sound of Trumpets*' – presumably from one of the opposite doors. He declaims and all go out again. Then:

> *The Trumpets continue Sounding, and dashing of Swords is heard from within.*
> *Enter* Crimalhaz, Hametalhaz, *and Attendants, with drawn Swords, as pursued.*

– they cry warnings and rush off. Then no more detail, but simply:

The Scene Changes.
*Enter* Muly Hamet *and* Abdelcador *Attended.*

And now the atmosphere has altered; the noise has died down and victory is assured. Whatever flat scene may have backed the last few sensational episodes, it has now changed. The new backscene is not specified any more than was the last one, but this is clearly not considered a great matter. The whole of the fifth act is concerned with action, not with scenery; if all went well with the presentation, the audience would have little time to bother with what might be seen behind the figures. The thought at that time may well have been much the same as Boaden was to express in his *Memoirs of Mrs Siddons* (1827, ch. 19), 'When we have such a being as Mrs Siddons before us in Lady Macbeth, what signifies the order or disorder of the picture of a castle behind her . . . ?' Admittedly here it was no Mrs Siddons playing Lady Macbeth, but it *was* Thomas Betterton playing Crimalhaz – and '*attended as King*'.

However this was, there comes now in *The Empress of Morocco* a clear example of a dramatic change of tension – silence after storm. The villains are routed. They rush off. In this silence 'The Scene Changes'. What could be a more suitable employment of the new possibilities of the scenic stage? It did not greatly matter to what the scene changed; it changed. Any relatively inoffensive pair of flats from stock would do.

Before these new flats Muly Hamet is awarded the throne of Morocco for his victory; and then, suitably, '*Here* Mariamne *appears from the Balcone above*'. So, at the climax of the show, dramatic use is made of one of the balconies that surmounted the proscenium doors and whose character and relation to the forestage area we have reconstructed from the hints at the edge of the illustrations. It must have been a not unengaging spectacle to watch the two men in their triumph under the candlelight of the forestage, and see them turn their faces up as, from one of the balconies unused until that moment, there came the movement of a feminine gown and Mariamne leaned over the rail to receive the passionate tribute of her victorious lover and to hear him offer to share his throne with her.

But more is to follow. There is a rustle behind her and a second figure slips through on to the same balcony. It is Crimalhaz and he '*Draws and points his Sword at* Mariamnes *Breast*'. No wonder poor agonized Muly Hamet from below exclaims,

Here I my baffled hopes of Vengeance lose:
To right my King my Mistress I expose.

Crimalhaz says he will spare her if Muly Hamet will give up the throne to him, adding,

If not, prepare to see her amorous Breast,
Give entertainment to this *Iron* Guest.
To this your Answer.

– and he goes blood-wild with visions of his conquest. Then like a *deus ex machina*, no less a person than a reformed Hametalhaz, disgusted at his master's Neronian excesses, enters '*in the Belcone with Guards, who seizes* Crimalhaz *and disarmes Him*'. He is brought down on to the stage, curses his captors and is led away. Mariamne follows down on to the forestage where Muly Hamet embraces the reformed Hametalhaz, who then goes off.

Now follows, very suitably, the last scenic effect and the greatest piece of butchery. How it was worked is still a puzzle, but the description is striking:

> *Here the Scene opens, and* Crimalhaz *appears cast down on the Gaunches, being hung on a Wall set with spikes of Iron. Enter again* Abdelcador.

The nondescript scene that had closed in after the battles is clearly no longer suitable here, and so it opens upon a great spectacular *finale*. There is no direction for either Muly Hamet or Mariamne to leave the stage; they presumably remain through the change. But once the old flats open there returns Hamet's faithful friend Abdelcador to assist in the final two speeches. Every member of the audience must have watched intently as the scene gradually opened and discovered what is recorded for us in the last of the illustrations to the play which faces this page of text (Plate 6).

It would seem that this is a set scene. The '*Gaunches*', or ganches, are the means of death by impalement. What the spectators were offered was a sort of dungeon-well with iron spikes set in wooden frameworks lining the walls. Into this the victim is flung down, his body catching on the spikes where it may, to join the rotting remains of previous victims. Down at the bottom lie the bleached bones of such as had been cast down still longer ago. There is no reason that I know of to doubt that the figures were not painted on the scene but were actual three-dimensional bodies like those in the horror chamber of a waxworks. And, just as Crimalhaz's arm in III. i '*immediately appears bloody*', so it might be supposed that the red paint would not have been spared here.

In front of this spectacle, which could have looked still grimmer under the candlelight from the sides, the faithful Abdelcador exchanges one speech with his triumphant friend Muly Hamet, the new king, and so the play ends – incidentally with a gay and witty Epilogue recommending the audience's charity towards a play which 'To please You, lost its Maidenhead at Court' but has since become 'a Miss o'th'Town' and 'Yours for half a Crown'.

### (v) Wren's Drury Lane

In 1674, a year after *The Empress of Morocco*, Wren's Drury Lane opened. Supposing Bell's ascription of Wren's section at All Souls College, Oxford, to be correct (see Plates 8 and 9; but compare the opposite view expressed by Graham Barlow[1]), then his scheme comprised a sloping pit containing ten

---

[1] 'Sir James Thornhill and the Theatre Royal, Drury Lane, 1705', in Richards and Thomson, op. cit. pp. 179–93.

rows of benches curved, as Colley Cibber gives us to understand in his *Apology* (1740),[1] to match the curve indicated at the front of the forestage. Access to this pit from the theatre entrance at the front of the house was by stairs down to a sunk corridor running under the side boxes, thence by a doorway near the stage and up four steps into the front of the pit and so to the benches. This pit is flanked by raking side walls converging slightly towards the stage and running up the stage for some seventeen feet. The walls are broken by six great pilasters in Corinthian style, between which are either doors on to the forestage or boxes for spectators. The wall as a whole is designed in perspective with its intervals and heights all decreasing as it runs on to the stage. Above both pit and forestage is a continuous raked ceiling. Facing the stage, behind the pit, is an open 'circle' with four rows of benches; above it, a second; and above again a third. Access to these circles is by a system of stairs in the corridors across the front of the house. Above the auditorium ceiling is a large void in the roof which was possibly used as a scenic workshop.

At the back of the stage are dressing rooms on three floors, so arranged as to leave a central recess or extension of the stage area, reaching right to the back of the building or, to use a contemporary term, 'to the end of the house'. This is to accommodate the occasional spectacular 'long scenes' that developed out of the system of 'scenes of relief' and were chiefly useful in the presentation of processions.

In the matter of scenic arrangements for this stage Wren is not very informative. It would seem that he considered the planning of scenery not his business – indeed it is the scenic designer's business – and Wren does no more than indicate the positions of four wings and three back shutters, but gives no hint of the machinery for working them. He does, however, make one additional suggestion regarding the back shutters that is important: above each of the three he carries up a line extending it to the ceiling level. These three extension lines are somewhat different in character from the lines above the wings representing borders, and it is probable that they are intended to signify *upper back shutters* like those used in Inigo Jones's masques, where it was possible to open the sky independently of the landscape below and reveal a glimpse into heaven. (See for example Jones's sectional drawing for the scenery of *Salmacida Spolia* where 'the vpper back shutters' are designated by the letter 'V'. Discussed in *Changeable Scenery*, p. 48.)

One can calculate a seating capacity that is according to present-day

[1] Ch. xii, pp. 339–40. Everyman ed. (London, 1914), p. 212.

standards relatively low for a capital theatre – somewhat in the region of 600–800 persons. It would seem then that a typical English Restoration playhouse was deliberately and specifically smaller in size than the theatres on the continent, and this difference has tended in general to remain to this day. There is a reason for it; namely, that English playhouses were distinctly planned for the dramatic side of entertainment, not the operatic. The English were to build their own Opera House as mentioned above (p. 88), but some people – certainly in those early days – regarded any opera presented on continental lines with a considerable measure of hostility, as a pretentious entertainment involving foreigners and threatening to put native actors and dramatists out of work. And for drama in the English tradition, a small house was far more suitable to the relatively more delicate effects of voice nuance and facial expression that belong to spoken dialogue, as against the tones and gestures of an opera singer. Moreover, a dramatic play could at a pinch proceed undiminished with no scenery at all – or the simplest – while opera without its spectacular effects on the largest possible scale was opera shrunken and at a disadvantage.

### (vi) Thornhill's scenes for *Arsinoe* at Drury Lane

In January 1705 there was presented at Drury Lane an opera called *Arsinoe, Queen of Cyprus*, composed by Thomas Clayton, and adapted from the Italian by the ingenious Peter Motteux (who finished Urquhart's translation of Rabelais and produced one of the most spirited versions of *Don Quixote*). The opera has no particular pretensions as an opera but it is worth consideration here for three reasons. First, it was produced at Wren's Drury Lane and thus in a theatre whose interior we can to some extent picture – always remembering that the alterations of 1692 referred to by Colley Cibber had by then taken place (see p. 109 n. above). Second, it is one of the first operas by an English composer framed in the classical Italian fashion. Third, most important of all, it is the only English show in the first half of the century for which we can study some at least of the original designs for scenery. The designs are by Sir James Thornhill, one of whose other scenic drawings is discussed at length in *Changeable Scenery* ('The 1st Great flat Scene' reproduced as Plate 29). There are four surviving *Arsinoe* designs; they are in the Victoria and Albert Museum, and have been published in James Laver's *Drama* (1951) and, with some detailed discussion, in Graham Barlow's essay referred to above.

Motteux's script can be studied in Volume III of a bound collection of *Old*

*Plays* in the Forster Collection of plays in the Library of the Victoria and Albert Museum (Press mark, 6976.3). It opens with the following description:

> Act 1. Scene 1. Arsinoe *sleeping in a garden. The time Night, the Moon shining.*
> *Enter* Ormondo *and* Delbo.

Ormondo is a general in the Queen of Cyprus's army (though his true name and status are different, as the plot reveals). Delbo is his man.

We can identify Thornhill's design for this scene with certainty since it is inscribed 'Arsinoe sleeping / Act 1st Scene 1st / by moonlight' (Plate 10). It shows a lawn with a central fountain playing and, in the middle distance, the classic portico and wings of a country house framed in trees. In the far distance are mountains. Of particular interest in this scene design is the central jet of the fountain; mingled with the lines of the spray is a vertical dotted line reaching from the stage into the sky but stopping short at the point where it reaches a line of clouds. This dotted line is clearly an indication of the join between a pair of flats, and this again means that the backscene is all to be painted on the flat, no item is cut out in the form of groundrows, and the design is in fact for a shutter scene. Framing the backscene, there appear to be three pairs of wings, but the stage-left wings of the front two pairs are different from those on the stage-right. (A similar difference in the wings on the two sides of the stage is to be seen again in the second drawing.) I think that it is not to be supposed that Thornhill intended them to be thus differently painted in the finished scene on the stage, but that he was simply concerned to see which of two alternative schemes he – or the manager for whom he was working – found the more suitable. Finally one of the two would be abandoned.

Thornhill has clearly drawn these wings with an experimental hand. On the reader's right the wing bases have, sketched across them, straight lines which appear to be slightly at an angle with the horizontal, suggesting that Thornhill might have been considering the advantages of setting the wings not parallel with the stage front but at an angle. This would indeed be a sensible idea if the wings could be set at will – as they can be today – but on the eighteenth-century stage one of the disadvantages that hampered work for decades was that the wings had to be slid in grooves, and that these grooves were parallel with the stage front. Some attempt might admittedly be made to arrange grooves at an angle, but if the stage floor on which they lie is raked – that is, sloping up towards the back in the interests of perspective effect – then the vertical appearance of the wings will be upset, and they will appear to tip outward at the top. This rigidity of wing position was one of the objections to be levelled against the scenic machinery of the period, but so long as visible scene change was the fashion little could be done about the objection.

In Thornhill's drawing the upstage pair of wings – those in front of the back shutters – are of a different design. No attempt is made here at representing any retreating face; instead the profiling (or shaped edge) is wide and deeply cut, and at the foot of each a profiled balustrade piece extends inwards.

How far an actual moonlight effect would be simulated in 1705 is not certain. Inigo Jones had managed it in his court masques. Possibly coloured glasses were put over the candles behind the side wings; but any lowering of the footlights or extinguishing of the hoops over the forestage would have surely cast the actors into virtual obscurity.

During this scene Ormondo sees the Queen sleeping in the garden and falls in love with her. She wakes, gives him her scarf as a token and goes out. He closes the action by renouncing his previous love (by name Dorisbe, whom the dramatis personae describes as 'Pretender to the throne, in love with Ormondo'). All the above action has been divided by the author into five 'scenes' and so what next follows is –

SCENE VI.    Dorisbe's *Apartment, enter* Feraspe.

– but no drawing has been found for this scene and it might have been most likely a simple pair of flats, perhaps taken out of stock.

For the next scene a design does survive and it has some interesting features. It is inscribed 'Act 1st. Sc 3d / A Room of State, with statues & Bustoes' and 'Arsinoe on a Couch' (Plate 11). There are three pairs of architectural wings; once again those on the left differ from those on the right, and hanging above them is one elaborate drapery border. This one border alone would presumably be insufficient to mask the upper workings over the stage. There would be needed in addition a couple of high-arched architectural borders behind, joining the pairs of wing tops. These are partly suggested in the drawing.

It is at the back of the scene, however, that the chief problem comes. This backscene is more imposing in proportion than the pair of flats in Scene i; more of its upper part is to be seen under the border than was the case with the flats in Scene ii. In addition, the perspective line of the cornice at the tops of the wings (particularly on the reader's right) would, if produced to cut the backscene, strike it well below the top of the scene. Whereas the perspective line of the top corners of the garden wings in Scene i would if produced strike the back shutters right at the top. Since the upper flat grooves in an early eighteenth-century theatre were normally suspended at the same height as (or even a little below) the last pair of wing-grooves, this feature of the drawing described is worth attention. What appears to be shown is a *high* scene, employing not only a pair of lower back shutters (as did the garden scene) but also a pair of upper back shutters hanging above them, and now disclosed by the highly arched borders. The division between the two 'storeys' was probably along the line of the moulding below the central bust in the upper arch.

This design may then have made a varied and effective scene on the stage for a room of state. The action in it proceeds with the direction '*Enter Ormondo kneeling with a wreath of Lawrel in his Hand, as from Battle. The Scarfe upon his Arm.*' Arsinoe sees the scarf and gives him her picture. Act II opens with '*A Great Hall looking into a Garden. Ormondo with the Picture in his Hand and* Delbo.' Here again we have a design; it is inscribed simply 'Act 2nd. Sc. 1st.' (Plate 12.) Again there are three pairs of wings and again arched borders; at the back is a perspective formal garden of lesser extent than that in Act I, but similarly marked upon it at the centre of the lower edge of the backscene is a vertical line extending upwards and ending in a couple of dots suggesting continuance. The indication seems clear that here again is a shutter scene. There follows a change to a 'Palace Hall', but for this no design has been found.

But for the third scene of this act a design survives. The direction in the script simply reads 'Arsinoe *alone. A* Garden.' The drawing is inscribed more fully 'Act 2nd. Sc. 3d. Arsinoe in a fine Garden, with Ships, Haven &c. as [*sic*] a distance.' (Plate 13.) The design shows no division of the backscene and this, together with a certain specific tone in the words 'as a distance', strongly suggests that this is a scene of relief with either three or four cutout planes in the distance. This impression is strengthened by certain preliminary chalk lines still visible through the ink lines of the drawing of the trees seeming to intend continuing the trees of the wings directly into the backscene. But such high trees would clearly be undesirable on a groundrow, and destructive of any effect of distance. And presumably Thornhill has changed them in the development of his drawing into small, more distant trees of a different kind. In this scene Ormondo prevents Dorisbe from murdering Arsinoe but is mistaken himself for the assassin, and ordered to the Tower.

Act III opens with the Queen's apartment again – possibly the same stock flat scene as that for I. vi. Feraspe tries unsuccessfully to get Ormondo in trouble with Arsinoe.

For the next scene there survives no drawing. It is '*A Prison*. Ormondo *in Chains, with a Letter in his Hand.*' He is sleeping. Arsinoe enters to forgive him but before she does so she finds from the letter that he is really Pelops, a prince. They go out. From the next direction we learn that the prison must have been a flat scene (possibly a pair of flats from stock) because

> *The Scene opens and discovers* Arsinoe *and* Pelops *on a Throne. A Dance. After which an Epithalamium Song.*

It might be that the scene of the room of state was used again here. All seems to be going well for the couple when 'Dorisbe *looks out of a Balcony of the Castle with a Dagger in her hand*'. It is to be noted from the words '*a Balcony of the Castle*' how closely the eighteenth century associated the scenes of its dramas with the auditorium it sat in. She stabs herself and throws the dagger over on to the stage. Arsinoe cries 'Make hast, break up the Door'. Dorisbe calls down

> O Feeble Arm.
> What must I live?
> Give me the Dagger back
> I'll strike again.

Feraspe faints. The Guards bring in Dorisbe slightly wounded, and all is forgiven.


### (vii) Some scenic systems to 1750

In the above there is no particularly outstanding feature either in the play directions or in the scene designs, but instead a number of small items that all go together with the impression of Drury Lane stage and auditorium to make some beginning of a picture of the period. To this picture we may add now a curious piece of chance information from about the 1730s. It comes in two editions of a work in verse by the Rev. James Miller, playwright and rector of Upcerne in Dorset. The work carries a comment on the theatrical devices of John Rich – the son of the notorious Christopher Rich who had left the management of Drury Lane to take over that of the New Theatre, Lincoln's Inn Fields. Christopher died and John Rich succeeded as manager. John was not very literate by some accounts, and presumably was despised by the fastidious: a failure as a tragic actor and yet despite all this an inspired showman, a brilliant Harlequin, an innovator of the English pantomime and the presenter of the London première of *The Beggar's Opera* in 1728. He assumed the stage name of Lunn, or Lun.

Miller's comment on John Rich is entitled *Harlequin Horace* and it was first published in 1731 with a somewhat scurrilous frontispiece illustrating a scene in Rich's Lincoln's Inn Fields Theatre (Plate 14). In 1735 a third edition was published with a more respectable frontispiece, again illustrating a scene in Rich's theatre (Plate 15); but the point of interest in the present context is that between the two editions – specifically in 1732 – Rich moved from the New Theatre, Lincoln's Inn Fields, to Shepherd's new theatre in Covent Garden. Thus the two frontispieces can be assumed to show respectively the old and the new theatres.

The first plate of 1731 is a fairly crude piece of work with some poor drawing and possibly some inaccuracies. The second of 1735 is by the elegant Van der Gucht and is far more skilful though probably idealized, particularly with regard to the scenery. But it is possible to check its architectural details as recording the first Covent Garden; for in 1763 G. P. M. Dumont published in Paris a volume entitled *Parallèle de Plans des plus belles salles de spectacles...*, in which is included an engraving inscribed 'Coupe prise sur la longueur du Théatre de Coven Garden, à Londres'. (See Plate 16.) This shows the proscenium side in detail, and on comparing it with Van der Gucht's frontispiece the features are seen to be the same even to the caryatid figures flanking the proscenium balconies.

Beside its frontispiece, *Harlequin Horace* is informative in its text as well. In the 1731 edition there is a quotation from Horace – 'Pictoribus atque Poetis / Quidlibet audendi semper fuit aequa potestas...' – which is translated by Miller as 'Painters and Poets ... have ever had an equal right to bold device ...', and glossed or expanded by him under the title 'Horace Imitated' as follows –

Well, Bards (you say) like Painters, Licence claim
To dare do anything for Bread, or – Fame.
'Tis granted – therefore use your utmost Might,
To gratify the Town in all you write;
A Thousand jarring Things together yoke,
The *Dog*, the *Dome*, the *Temple*, and the *Joke*,
Consult no Order, but for ever steer
From grave to gay, from florid to severe.

In a 'Note of Explanation' to this passage in the 3rd edition we read:

> *The Dog, the Dome.* In the farce of Perseus and Andromeda, a most obscene Dance was performed in a temple, before a handsome audience of Priests and Bishops, at the same Time the ingenious Mr Rich deported himself very naturally in the Shape of a Dog, till a Dome rising voluntarily from under the Stage, gave him Room for another transformation by standing on the Top of it in the Guise of a Mercury, to the high Admiration and Delight of a British Audience.

And so this 1731 print is in some sense a faithful record of a contemporary English show, as well as being an example of how the medieval freedom to depict successive happenings in one picture was maintained even at this late date. Thus Rich is shown deporting himself 'very naturally in the Shape of a Dog' upon a despondent Muse at the bottom of the picture while, at the top, he is shown simultaneously in the character of an allegedly unclothed Mercury new lighted on a Heaven-kissing Temple. And we are told that the temple did in fact rise 'voluntarily' from beneath the stage.

The 1735 print also shows that in addition to the two proscenium doors with their balconies and caryatids, Covent Garden had two profile statues just inside the opening (seen also in Hogarth's sixth and last version of his *Beggar's Opera* painting as expanded for the larger stage of Rich's new theatre – the painting now in the Tate Gallery), and behind these an inner frame with the motto *Vivitur ingenio* over it. This frame was presumably painted on the two proscenium wings shown in plan (but not in the section) in the Dumont engraving. And so, reinforcing Van der Gucht's illustration with Dumont's evidence, this picture of Rich in his theatre can be accepted as a guide for visualizing the interior and stage of the first Covent Garden. Some licence is presumably taken in both frontispieces in the matter of width; they certainly show a narrower opening than was in the theatre, in order to accommodate picture to book page.

But what is a final note of very curious interest indeed is that in the 1731 print, naïve as it may be, there are three lines at the top of the wings on the stage-right that can hardly be explained save by accepting their suggestion that on the stage of the New Theatre, Lincoln's Inn Fields, it was still the custom to use Serlian, or booked, wings on the lines of those Jones planned in *Florimène.*

One other technicality of the period deserves mention; this is the *transparent scene.* Anyone who has visualized the dim Restoration scenery with its candles behind each wing will appreciate that if a shape were cut out from the canvas of any piece of scenery and the shape backed with a translucent linen patch, then any light behind this shape would gleam through very effectively from the rest of the surface. And if the linen were dyed a bright colour, the shape would gleam much like stained glass in a window. And if a variety of dyes were applied in a pattern, the effect would be still more like a luminous coloured window. A 'transparent scene' was one designed to make use of such a possibility.

Thomas Lediard, an Englishman on the embassy staff at Hamburg, made many such scenes for the Opera House there (among others for operas by Handel), and in 1732 he designed a scene of this sort for the Little Theatre in the Haymarket, London, to mark the coronation of George II (Plate 17). A book of the show survives, entitled *Britannia, An English Opera . . . With the . . . Description of a Transparent Theatre . . . embellish'd with Machines, in a manner entirely new. By Mr Lediard . . . MDCCXXXII.* It states that the scene represented a Temple of Honour masked by 'Transparent Pillars' for wings, with transparent 'arches' as borders, with a triple vista in the backscene, and a profile equestrian cutout of the king in front. All these elements were fretted and filled in with transparent 'Emblems, Devices and Inscriptions, which . . . not only divert, but instruct the Mind' and (of course) 'delight the Eye'.[1]

In conclusion there is a curious reflection to be made on all these events if one compares them with what was happening in the Japanese theatre at just this time. In a period corresponding roughly with our early medieval performances, say about 1400, Zeami Motokiyo (1363–1443) had been consolidating in Kyoto the technique of the Noh performance. This was a theatrical system that, like the Elizabethan, has always used an open stage without representational scenery. In the precise year of the death of Queen Elizabeth I (1603) a Japanese dancer named Okuni inaugurated in the same city what was to become (in contradistinction to the Noh) the scenic performance *par excellence* of Japan, namely the Kabuki theatre – incidentally the only regular national scenic system of theatre outside Europe. There were and still are quite striking parallels between the non-scenic Noh and the Elizabethan stage. And on the other hand there are parallels between their respective rivals, the scenic Kabuki stage and the scenic European Renaissance stage; moreover, both the Kabuki and the Restoration stages coincided with revolutionary changes in the systems of government of the two countries.

But since those days the Noh and Kabuki have developed side by side in Japan and both exist today. The curious reflection is that – but for the

[1] For a description of Lediard's work, see *Theatre Notebook*, II (1948), pp. 49–57.

interruption of the Commonwealth and if Killigrew had persisted with his non-scenic methods instead of following Davenant's lead and introducing scenery – there might have survived in England also two separate methods side by side; the new, and the old as used in Shakespeare's theatre – the latter as religiously preserved for the English as the Noh is today for the Japanese, and no more superseded by the progress of the scenic tradition than the Noh is superseded by the Kabuki.

As it was, the rivalry in England between the scenic ideas and the non-scenic ideas of presentation (in spite of Killigrew's capitulation to the scenic) remained surprisingly acrid. Although the non-scenic system showed no sign of practical revival for some two centuries, through the whole of that time a certain body of opinion in the English theatre has heavily criticized stage scenery. And even among the writers who have justified it are those who insisted that it must be 'subservient to the actor' and must help, not hinder, that mysterious thing 'theatrical illusion'.[1]

---

[1] A study of the origin and development of this conflict appears in *Changeable Scenery*, ch. 6, under the heading of 'The Great Scenic Controversy'.

# 2 Actors and repertory

## (i) Companies and management

> As soon as the King was restord by the People, and Two of The Theaters by the King, tis incredible with what Ardour the people returnd and flew to their old pleasures. All sorts of persons were charmd to that Degree with the True entertainments of the stage, that Two Companies of exellent Actours started upon a sudden as it were out of the ground, such as had never appeard in England before nor in all likely Hood will ever appear again.[1]

In these terms, looking back in 1725 to an already legendary heyday, the stiff old critic John Dennis (1657–1734) saw fit to praise the rival patent companies created by Charles II in the autumn of 1660 – the King's Men under Sir Thomas Killigrew (1612–83), and the Duke's Men under Sir William Davenant (1606–68).[2] In his anxiety to show a subsequent decline, Dennis rather overstated his case: the acting profession in England had already boasted Richard Burbage and Edward Alleyn, and in spite of the eighteen-year gap in stage practice imposed by Cromwell's closing of the theatres there

[1] John Dennis, *The Critical Works of John Dennis*, ed. E. N. Hooker, 2 vols (Baltimore, 1943), II, p. 276.
[2] Documents cited by Leslie Hotson, *The Commonwealth and Restoration Stage* (Cambridge, Mass., and London, 1928) (Hotson, *CRS*), pp. 199–202, 400.

was more continuity of manpower from the pre-war companies than Dennis suggests. What he does very well convey is the glamour and prestige of the theatre revival.

The new managers, Killigrew and Davenant, were men of means and education, both courtiers, both playwrights, both with experience of the theatre before the Civil War. Killigrew, who belonged to a distinguished Cornish family, enjoyed rather more of the king's personal favour;[1] but Davenant, who was Shakespeare's godson and Jonson's successor as Poet Laureate, had more recent and immediate acquaintance with members of the renascent theatrical profession – he had been mounting musical spectacles with texts of his own composition from time to time since 1656, disarming suspicion by terming them operas.[2] Acting had begun again, sometimes with temporary official consent, about a year before the Restoration proper.[3] Veteran actors who had fought for the king formed the nucleus of a company at the old Red Bull:[4] headed by the king's favourite, ex-Major Michael Mohun (c. 1620–84), whom Pepys heard described as the best actor in the world,[5] this company was the obvious choice for Killigrew's King's Men. Two other mushroom companies, both headed by theatre veterans, were playing at the king's return. The first, under John Rhodes, wardrobe-keeper turned bookseller, used the Cockpit, Drury Lane; the second, under William Beeston, son of the pre-war actor-manager Christopher Beeston who had built the Cockpit, used Salisbury Court.[6] For a month's stand at the Cockpit in October 1660 Killigrew was able to supplement the Mohun group by employing some good men from the other companies: Rhodes supplied two of his own former apprentices – Thomas Betterton (c. 1635–1710) and Edward Kynaston (c. 1650–1706), a boy-player who took women's parts to perfection.[7] When Davenant began to enrol the Duke's Men, he drew mainly on the Rhodes company, to which Betterton returned to become its leading actor and the most famous theatrical personality of the period.

Dennis saw the policy of both patentees in a favourable light: 'Their chief aim was to see that the Town was well entertaind and The Drama improvd.

[1] See Montague Summers, *The Playhouse of Pepys* (London, 1935), pp. 65–145.

[2] Hotson, *CRS*, pp. 133–66.

[3] John Freehafer, 'The Formation of the London Patent Companies in 1660', *Theatre Notebook*, XX (Autumn 1965), pp. 6–30.

[4] Evidence reviewed by Allardyce Nicoll, *A History of English Drama 1660–1900*, 6 vols (Cambridge, 1952–9) (Nicoll, *HED*), I (4th ed. rev. 1952), pp. 287–9.

[5] Pepys, *Diary*, 20 November 1660.

[6] Hotson, *CRS*, pp. 89–100; Nicoll, *HED*, I, pp. 289–92.

[7] John Downes, *Roscius Anglicanus* (1709), facs. ed. M. Summers (London, n.d. [1928]), pp. 17–19; Pepys, *Diary*, 18 August 1660.

They alterd all at once the whole Face of the stage by introducing scenes and Women, which added probability to the Dramatick Actions and made evry thing look more naturally.'[1] The idea that a theatre manager should try to direct and educate public taste was not congenial to many of the men who followed Killigrew and Davenant in the capacity of patentees, though it was dear to Dennis half a century later. There was a businesslike ambition about Killigrew and Davenant which controlled them more surely than any aesthetic principles: certainly the increased natural effect of using changeable scenery and female talent on stage was not the chief motive behind these innovations. The personal taste of the king for foreign fashions, and the holiday humour, eager for any novelty, which Londoners were displaying to welcome his return, together suggested and endorsed these successful experiments, which had a great and permanent effect on the choice of repertory and the nature of the acting profession. Thereafter many a silly play was carried by its settings, and many a feeble performance by the actress's personal charms. In England, however, the taste for scenic spectacle as such, and the taste for female beauty as such, were indulged as separate wanton whims, scarcely affecting the literary and artistic standards by which the plays and performances were judged. On the big apron stages the actors went on acting in their established style as the scenes changed behind them, and those few actresses who were ambitious to act, rather than anxious to put their goods into the shop-window, modelled their acting style on that of the men. Literary value in a play, and technical skill in a performance, were keenly debated, and honoured where found.

Though the gentlemanly patentees had secured a joint monopoly of theatre management, Rhodes, Beeston and another dogged professional, George Jolly (*fl.* 1640–73),[2] went on working with whatever actors they could muster, and survived several attempts to suppress them or banish them to provincial touring.[3] The struggle to enforce monopoly was complicated by the anomalous but active authority of Sir Henry Herbert, Master of the Revels, who exercised his right to collect fees for licensing play-texts, and his duty to bespeak royal entertainments, in such a way as to secure as many as possible of his office's traditional pickings at the expense of the patentees.[4]

Once the initial difficulties were adjusted, however, the two patent

[1] Dennis, *Critical Works*, II, p. 278.
[2] Hotson, *CRS*, pp. 167–94; B. M. Wagner, 'George Jolly at Norwich', *Review of English Studies*, VI (October 1930), pp. 449–52.
[3] Nicoll, *HED*, I, pp. 308–16.
[4] Ibid. I, pp. 316–18; see J. Q. Adams (ed.), *The Dramatic Records of Sir Henry Herbert* (New Haven, Conn., and London, 1917).

companies enjoyed nearly twenty years of security, rivalled only by each other. Killigrew remained in charge of the King's Men until his increasing mismanagement led to such disaffection that his son Charles took over the company in February 1677: their chief actors were Mohun, Kynaston and Charles Hart (*c.* 1627–83).[1] Davenant personally attended to the management of the Duke's Men until his death in 1668, and was succeeded by his widow and sons, advised by his chief actors Betterton and Henry Harris (*c.* 1634–1704).[2] Young recruits for both companies were trained in a Nursery Company, managed by Jolly and others.[3] Over in Dublin, the management of John Ogilby (1601–76) and his successor Joseph Ashbury (*c.* 1638–1720) provided a parallel repertory and valuable professional engagements for actors from London or on their way there.[4]

The King's Men had bad luck with their theatre premises: they used the Vere Street Theatre, once Gibbons's Tennis Court, until their Theatre Royal, Bridges Street, was built; but the new house was in use only from 1663, when they opened with Fletcher's *Humorous Lieutenant*, to 1672, when it burnt down. They were then obliged to make shift with Lisle's Tennis Court in Lincoln's Inn Fields, recently vacated by Davenant's company, until yet another new house could be erected for them. This was the Theatre Royal, Drury Lane, which opened with Fletcher's *Beggars' Bush* in March 1674, and survived with only minor alterations and vicissitudes until 1791.

The Duke's Men began less ambitiously with a spell at Salisbury Court while Lisle's Tennis Court was being renovated as a scenic house: they opened this with *The Siege of Rhodes*, one of Davenant's musical spectacles revived, in June 1661, and worked there for ten years. Davenant was in his grave before they began to build their grand new spectacle-house, Dorset Garden, which opened with Dryden's *Sir Martin Mar-All* in 1671. Dorset Garden rivalled Drury Lane until 1682, when the collapse of the King's Company gave Betterton and his fellows the chance to take over Drury Lane. Some of the King's Men joined him, and a new United Company was formed under the joint management of Betterton and William Smith;[5] it opened at Drury Lane, probably with Fletcher's *Rule a Wife and Have a Wife*, in November 1682.[6]

[1] Hotson, *CRS*, pp. 242–67; Nicoll, *HED*, I, pp. 294–9, 320–5.

[2] Hotson, *CRS*, pp. 217–28.

[3] Ibid. pp. 186–94; P. H. Gray, 'Lenten Casts and the Nursery', *PMLA*, LIII (September 1938), pp. 781–94.

[4] See W. S. Clark, *The Early Irish Stage* (Oxford, 1955).

[5] Hotson, *CRS*, pp. 267–73; Nicoll, *HED*, I, pp. 326–30; E. Langhans, 'New Restoration Theatre Accounts', *Theatre Notebook*, XVII (Summer 1963), pp. 118–34.

[6] Acted at court on 15 Nov. (Nicoll, *HED*, I, p. 356: Item 6); Drury Lane opened 16 Nov.

London had only one company for the next dozen years, though two new entrepreneurs bought their way into its management. Christopher Rich (*c.* 1658–1714), a lawyer, whose character recalls that of Philip Henslowe a century earlier, and his associate, Sir Thomas Skipwith, were both keen businessmen rather than lovers of drama. They covertly bought up the Davenant interest between 1687 and 1690,[1] and began to alienate the players by cutting salaries and juggling with profits. A period of squabbling and mutinous resentment ended in a formal petition to the Lord Chamberlain by Betterton and most of the best actors in December 1694.[2] Concessions were offered too late, and Betterton secured a licence for his Seceded Company in March 1695:[3] he had remodelled Lisle's Tennis Court, dark since 1674, in readiness, and was able to open with the immensely successful première of Congreve's *Love for Love* at the end of April.[4] The breakaway company played here for the next ten years.

Left behind at Drury Lane, Rich gathered such actors and entertainers as were available into his company, which still held both the original patents. Young Colley Cibber (1671–1757), who had aspirations as playwright and actor too, remained with Rich and became well known rather than popular.[5] Noting his master's difficulties after the dispute with Betterton, Cibber learned a lesson that stood him in good stead years later when he himself came to manage Drury Lane: 'I laid it down as a settled Maxim that no Company could flourish while the chief Actors and the Undertakers were at variance. I therefore made it a Point, while it was possible upon tolerable Terms, to keep the valuable Actors in humour with their Station.'[6]

Rich and Skipwith were bullies and exploiters; but Betterton's company also had its disputes and jealousies. The popular but touchy comedian, Thomas Doggett (*c.* 1670–1721), who had played Ben in *Love for Love*, deserted to Rich within a year, though the dashing Jack Verbruggen (*c.* 1671–1708) was allowed to transfer from Drury Lane in exchange.[7] Unhappily, as Cibber put it, 'Experience in a Year or two shew'd them that they had never been worse govern'd than when they govern'd themselves'.[8] The actors'

---

[1] Hotson, *CRS*, pp. 296–7.
[2] Nicoll, *HED*, I, pp. 333 ff., 368–79.
[3] Ibid. I, pp. 361 ff.
[4] Ibid. I, pp. 335–6.
[5] For Cibber's career see R. H. Barker, *Mr Cibber of Drury Lane* (New York, 1939).
[6] Colley Cibber, *An Apology for the Life of Mr Colley Cibber* (1740), ed. R. W. Lowe, 2 vols (London, 1889), I, p. 190.
[7] Nicoll, *HED*, I, pp. 338–40; for Verbruggen see Thomas Davies, *Dramatic Miscellanies*, 3 vols (London, 1784), III, pp. 418–24.
[8] Cibber, *Apology*, I, p. 228.

republic ended when Betterton took over sole management in November 1700.

The fortunes of theatre were at a very low ebb as the century turned. In 1698 Jeremy Collier (1650–1726) had launched his virulent attack on the immorality and profaneness of the English stage, and the question of stage reform was brought before a general public of which many classes and interests were on Collier's side. The total suppression of theatre was freely canvassed, and regulations for excising indecent, profane and politically obnoxious material from plays and performances received ever stricter enforcement.[1]

Queen Anne, with sensible moderation, supported reform of abuses, but decided to endorse theatre itself on a no-gamekeeper-like-a-retired-poacher system: she issued a new patent to William Congreve (1670–1729) and Sir John Vanbrugh (1664–1726), both playwrights who had come under Collier's fire, to establish a new company and manage it creditably.[2] Congreve soon retired from public life, but Vanbrugh obeyed the Queen's command by taking over Betterton's Seceded Company and transferring it to his newly built Queen's Theatre in the Haymarket. The house opened with a new opera in April 1705,[3] and offered an ambitious programme of time-honoured revivals, favourites of more recent date and brand-new pieces. The acoustics of the Queen's, however, proved unsatisfactory for spoken drama, and despite dogged efforts the company was increasingly unsuccessful. In 1706 Vanbrugh sold out to Owen Swiney (c. 1675–1754), an Irishman secretly acting for Rich. Swiney and Rich were soon at loggerheads; Colley Cibber and several other straight actors joined Swiney at the Queen's, where things began to improve. Rich kept up his competition with a range of undignified but popular entertainments at Drury Lane.[4]

Sir Thomas Skipwith had made over his interest at Drury Lane to an old friend of Cibber's, Colonel Henry Brett (c. 1677–1724),[5] who proposed to the Lord Chamberlain a scheme to unite the companies and divide repertories, giving plays to one house and operas to the other.[6] Rich, who had been under

---

[1] Documents and a full account are given by J. W. Krutch, *Comedy and Conscience after the Restoration* (New York, 1924), especially at pp. 150–91; see also pp. 264–70 for a bibliography of the Collier controversy.

[2] Nicoll, *HED*, II (3rd ed. rev. 1952), p. 275.

[3] For the prologue by Sir Samuel Garth (1661–1719) which Mrs Bracegirdle spoke on this occasion, see 'Thomas Betterton', *The History of the English Stage* (1741), pp. 117–18.

[4] The evidence for this transition period is well reviewed by Barker, op. cit. pp. 64 ff.

[5] See documents in *Skipwith v. Brett*, given by Hotson, *CRS*, pp. 386–97.

[6] Cibber, *Apology*, II, pp. 31–46.

a cloud since the Lord Chamberlain had silenced him in March 1707,[1] was obliged to acquiesce, and Betterton's company accepted the union in January 1708. By arrangement with the Lord Chamberlain the united company of actors was based at Drury Lane, leaving Swiney at the Queen's with the Italian opera, to which the acoustics of that house were best suited.

In June 1709 Rich again offended the Lord Chamberlain, Drury Lane was silenced, and the whole company went back to the Queen's for one season.[2] Now well over seventy, but game to the end, Betterton was seen as Hamlet, Othello and Macbeth: he took what proved to be his last bow in Beaumont and Fletcher's *Maid's Tragedy*, presented for his own benefit in April 1710. Wearing a slipper on his gouty foot, he exerted more than ordinary spirits, and received great applause.[3] A fortnight later he died and – a signal honour – was buried in Westminster Abbey.[4]

In the meantime, Rich, who had bought up the old Lisle's Tennis Court with a view to renovating its fabric, remained sulking in a dark and barricaded Drury Lane. Thence he was expelled by William Collier, a lawyer and M.P. who, having acquired legal rights in the lease of the building and a licence to set up a company there, burst into Drury Lane on 22 November 1709.[5] With Aaron Hill (1685–1750) as director, in partnership with seven actors including Barton Booth (1681–1733), Collier's company opened with Dryden's *Aureng-Zebe* on the following night. Stirred up by George Powell (*c.* 1658–1714), always a storm centre, the actors grew out of hand, and brought the Lord Chamberlain's wrath upon the house by beating up Hill in June 1710.[6] The season had been indifferent, both houses suffering from their rivalry: Collier persuaded the Haymarket company, headed since Betterton's death by Cibber, to leave him the Queen's for opera, and return to Drury Lane to form one company under the management of Cibber, Doggett and Robert Wilks (*c.* 1670–1732).[7]

The new arrangement lasted only a season, after which Collier gave the Queen's back to Swiney (whom it soon ruined), and returned to claim his share of the Drury Lane profits.[8] Contriving to satisfy both Collier and their

[1] Nicoll, *HED*, II, p. 282: Item xi.
[2] Ibid. II, pp. 282 f.: Item xii; Cibber, *Apology*, II, pp. 72–3.
[3] Cibber, *Apology*, I, pp. 117–18.
[4] See Steele, *The Tatler*, No. 167 (2–4 May 1710).
[5] Cibber, *Apology*, II, pp. 91–3; Steele, *The Tatler*, No. 99 (24–6 November 1709).
[6] Nicoll, *HED*, II, p. 292: Item xvii; for Hill's career and influence, see D. Brewster, *Aaron Hill* (New York, 1939).
[7] Cibber, *Apology*, II, pp. 101–5.
[8] Agreement of 6 December 1712 cited in Collier's 'Memorial against Cibber and Others', Nicoll, *HED*, II, p. 283: Item xv; see Cibber, *Apology*, II, pp. 107–9.

company, the triumvirate of actor-managers went on ruling with success for the rest of Queen Anne's reign.

In 1714 Queen Anne died, and with her Collier's licence. It was Sir Richard Steele (1672–1729), the distinguished essayist, who became the new governor of Drury Lane.[1] He gave his support to the triumvirate, in which after some unpleasantness Doggett had been replaced by Booth. Their regime continued to prosper, though they had trouble with the Lord Chamberlain in 1720, and Steele had less to do with the theatre for some years before his death in 1729. Not until 1732 was the triumvirate dissolved.

Christopher Rich died in 1714, just before his splendidly remodelled Lincoln's Inn Fields Theatre was completed. His son, John Rich (1692–1761), an accomplished Harlequin, opened the new house with a straight play, Farquhar's *Recruiting Officer*, in December 1714, but soon made it the home of popular pantomime.[2] The most striking success of his management there, which lasted until 1732, was the production of Gay's *Beggar's Opera* in 1728, which, as the town said, made Gay rich and Rich gay. It achieved over sixty performances in its first season, including the unprecedented initial run of thirty-two nights, and set a fashion both for ballad opera and for theatregoing.[3] The rival house also gained by this – Cibber's recension of Vanbrugh's *Provoked Husband* ran for twenty-eight nights in the same season.

The competition between Rich and the Drury Lane triumvirate was complicated after 1720 by the erection of a new theatre in the Haymarket – not to be confused with the sometime Queen's, now the King's but still given over to the Italian opera. The first ten years of this new house offered only sporadic entertainment by foreign troupes – rope-dancers, acrobats and the like – with an occasional production of the revue type by actors out of regular employ; but after 1730 when Henry Fielding (1707–54) began to put on his popular burlesques there, the 'Little Theatre in the Hay' became a serious rival to the patent houses.[4]

---

[1] For a full account, see John Loftis, *Steele at Drury Lane* (Berkeley and Los Angeles, 1952).

[2] See E. L. Avery, 'The Defense and Criticism of Pantomimic Entertainments in the Early Eighteenth Century', *ELH, Journal of English Literary History*, V (June 1938), pp. 127–45.

[3] For a comprehensive survey, see W. E. Schultz, *Gay's Beggar's Opera* (New Haven, Conn., 1923).

[4] See F. H. Dudden, *Henry Fielding, His Life, Works and Times*, 2 vols (Oxford, 1952), I, pp. 163–211.

In 1729 the playwright and lampoonist Thomas Odell (1691–1749) obtained letters patent to build a new theatre in Ayliffe Street, Goodman's Fields: despite local opposition it opened with Farquhar's *Recruiting Officer* on 31 October of the same year. Though silenced for a fortnight in 1730 after the Lord Mayor of London had appealed to the king, Odell was able to keep the house open until May 1732. His chief actor, Henry Giffard (1694–1772), who had been trained in Dublin, took over the management in the autumn of 1731, and chose Lillo's *London Merchant*, a sober piece calculated to mollify local citizens, for his first production. Giffard soon began to build a new and very elegant theatre in the same neighbourhood: it was finished within a year, and his company opened there with *1 Henry IV* in October 1732. It would appear that, whatever Odell's legal position at this time, Giffard for one had no licence to play; but for the moment no action was taken.[1]

This season was notable for a choice of miscellaneous entertainments from visiting performers at the Little Theatre in the Hay. Signora Violante, a rope-dancer, brought her troupe of Irish teenagers there with a version of *The Beggar's Opera* in September 1732: Macheath, Mrs Peachum and Mrs Diana Trapes were all played by one talented colleen – Peg Woffington (*c.* 1714–60).[2] A month later the expert in trick illuminations and pyrotechnics, Thomas Lediard (1684–1743), staged his *Britannia* there, an English opera featuring a 'Transparent Theatre'.[3]

John Rich had meanwhile been busy putting some of his *Beggar's Opera* profits into the erection of a sumptuous new theatre in Covent Garden:[4] after tiresome delays, his company from Lincoln's Inn Fields opened there with Congreve's *Way of the World* in December 1732.[5] Things were going badly at Drury Lane after the dissolution of the Cibber–Wilks–Booth triumvirate. Steele's patent for the theatre expired in September 1732, three years after his death, but was replaced by a patent in favour of the three actor-managers. A wealthy dilettante called John Highmore bought himself half Booth's share; Wilks died, and his widow sold half her inherited share to the painter John Ellys; and the venal Theophilus Cibber (1703–58) began to administer

[1] See F. T. Wood, 'Goodman's Fields Theatres', *Modern Language Review*, XXV (October 1930), pp. 443–56, and P. J. Crean, 'The Stage Licensing Act of 1737', *Modern Philology*, XXXV (February 1938), pp. 239–55.

[2] *Daily Post*, 4 September 1732; see Schultz, op. cit. pp. 49–50.

[3] See R. Southern, 'Lediard and Early Eighteenth Century Scene Design', *Theatre Notebook*, II (Summer 1948), pp. 49–54; see also Section II, ch. 1, pp. 116–17, above.

[4] See H. P. Vincent, 'John Rich and the First Covent Garden Theatre', *ELH*, XVII (December 1950), pp. 296–306.

[5] 7 December 1732: the same piece was performed in rivalry at Drury Lane on both 6 and 7 December. See Plate 22.

his father's interest.[1] After storms all round, old Colley Cibber cannily sold out to Highmore for 3000 guineas; Booth soon died, and the patentees – now the two widows, Ellys the painter and Highmore – staged a lockout of the actors, who were headed by Theophilus Cibber, on 28 May 1733 (see Plate 23). This dispute received nationwide publicity, and in the canvassing of ideal managerial policy that ensued, public sympathies were seen to be very mixed. The breach became permanent when Cibber took his followers to the Little Theatre in the Hay that autumn, opening with Congreve's *Love for Love* on 26 September.[2] Cibber had no licence to play, but did good business: Drury Lane struggled on with its few faithful actors, which luckily included Charles Macklin (*c*. 1700–97)[3] and Kitty Clive (1711–85). Giffard, who had bought up Mrs Booth's half-share in the management of Drury Lane, occasionally took a part there, though his own theatre required most of his attention.

London now had the choice of four companies – at Drury Lane and at Covent Garden licensed players, and at Goodman's Fields and the Little Theatre in the Hay encroaching entertainers. Though Theophilus Cibber and his followers returned to Drury Lane in March 1734, after Highmore had sold out to another rich amateur, Charles Fleetwood, the vacated Haymarket was soon in use again for occasional performances. Colley Cibber's remarkable daughter, Charlotte Charke (1713–60),[4] played there that season in a variety of parts including Macheath in Roman dress, George Barnwell and the gay Lothario.[5]

For the next couple of years the patent houses suffered from illegitimate competition, London was well amused, and those who distrusted theatre worked against it with ever-increasing ferocity. Fielding precipitated matters by a series of Haymarket satires with political implications.[6] After one attempt to get a bill for controlling the theatre through Parliament had failed in April 1735, the passing of the Licensing Act in June 1737 reduced the companies to two, playing at Drury Lane and Covent Garden, and clapped a

[1] This period of rapid transition is fully documented by Barker, op. cit. pp. 167–74.
[2] The choice of *Love for Love* deliberately recalled Betterton's opening at Lincoln's Inn Fields with the Seceded Company in 1695.
[3] See W. W. Appleton, *Charles Macklin: An Actor's Life* (Cambridge, Mass., 1961), for a carefully documented account of Macklin's career.
[4] Her autobiography, *A Narrative of the Life of Mrs Charlotte Charke* (1755), is of great interest to students of theatre and of human nature.
[5] 3, 17 and 19 June 1734.
[6] See E. L. Avery, 'Fielding's Last Season with the Haymarket Theatre', *Modern Philology*, XXXVI (February 1939), pp. 283–92.

rigorous censorship on new plays.[1] Giffard had been instrumental in bringing the ultimate in seditious drama, *The Golden Rump*, to Walpole's personal attention: his reward was £1000, but the Licensing Act closed Goodman's Fields. Fielding was also obliged to divert his energies, and the Little Theatre in the Hay remained closed until 1747, apart from an ill-fated visit in 1738 by a French troupe who were resentfully hooted from the stage. Drury Lane and Covent Garden shared the pickings.

At Drury Lane Fleetwood, with Macklin to help him, managed well enough till 1743; Rich, with his pantomimes and sponsorship of Peg Woffington in 1740, held his ground at Covent Garden. The disruptive factor was Giffard, who under the guise of holding concerts reopened his Goodman's Fields Theatre in 1740.

It was under Giffard's management at Goodman's Fields that David Garrick (1717–89), the central luminary of acting talent in the eighteenth century, made his first appearance on the London stage.[2] He had already played for Giffard at Ipswich, using Mrs Giffard's maiden name Lyddall to save the Garrick family face;[3] but soon his own name became the talk of the town. Such sensational success could not be ignored: both patent houses wanted his services, and after a visit to Smock Alley with Peg Woffington in the autumn of 1742[4] he threw in his lot with Drury Lane. The Goodman's Fields house closed at his loss: Giffard made a valiant effort to start again at the long-deserted Lincoln's Inn Fields, but was obliged to admit defeat.[5]

Fleetwood had by this time withdrawn his personal attention from the management of Drury Lane, and his manager, one Pierson, treated the players so badly that Macklin and Garrick were driven to secede in September 1743, hoping to be allowed to form a new licensed company. After a painful struggle, exacerbated because the Lord Chamberlain would not grant a licence and Fleetwood was able to replace the rebels by members of Giffard's disbanded company, Garrick gave way and Macklin was left high and

[1] See John Loftis, *The Politics of Drama in Augustan England* (Oxford, 1963), pp. 128–53.
[2] As Richard III, 19 October 1741; see Thomas Davies, *Memoirs of the Life of David Garrick Esq.*, 2 vols (London, 1780), I, pp. 39–43.
[3] *Ipswich Journal*, 25 July 1741; see Garrick's letters to relatives about his stage début, printed in David Garrick, *The Letters*, ed. D. M. Little and G. M. Kahrl, 3 vols (London, 1963), I, pp. 27–33.
[4] Garrick, *Letters*, I, pp. 40 f.
[5] For the move, see *Daily Advertiser*, 4 December 1742 (cited *The London Stage*, Monday, 6 December 1742); a benefit for the actor Milward's widow and children on 11 April 1743 was one of the last performances at Lincoln's Inn Fields.

dry.[1] The whole conflict was given much publicity, and Fleetwood's incompetence became so obvious that after audience riots in November 1744 he sold out to James Lacy (c. 1698–1774), formerly Rich's assistant at Covent Garden.[2] Lacy was a sensible and experienced manager: he weathered the ill consequences of the 1745 Jacobite rising, let Rich have Garrick at Covent Garden for a season, and then held out the prospect of a partnership if Garrick would return. Garrick returned, and the contract by which he became joint patentee and co-manager of Drury Lane was signed on 9 April 1747.[3] The theatre was enlarged by 250 seats before opening again with *The Merchant of Venice* on 15 September 1747: on this occasion the reconciled Macklin played Shylock and Garrick spoke Dr Johnson's specially commissioned prologue. With Lacy on the business side and Garrick in charge of production policy, Drury Lane entered a new era of prosperity, and Garrick's ascendancy there ended only with his retirement in 1776.[4]

Rich continued his career at Covent Garden, putting up rivals to Garrick in old James Quin (1693–1766) and young Spranger Barry (1719–77). In the hope of avoiding the Licensing Act, two new companies had begun to announce miscellaneous occasions for gatherings at which a play happened to be presented. Just as Macklin tried to smuggle *Othello* into the intervals of a musical concert,[5] William Hallam (*fl.* 1740–55) sold tickets for concerts at the New Wells, Goodman's Fields, from November 1744,[6] and Samuel Foote (1720–77), an immensely ingenious and unprincipled person who had made his début in Macklin's undercover *Othello*, gave concerts, tea and chocolate parties, and many other matinée gatherings at the Little Theatre in the Hay from 1747 onwards.[7] The vicissitudes of Foote's intransigent company, and the astonishing circumstances in which it obtained its royal patent in 1766, belong to another chapter.

---

[1] See Davies, *Memoirs of . . . Garrick*, I, pp. 66 ff.
[2] Garrick, *Letters*, I, pp. 45–7.
[3] Documents reproduced in Garrick, *Letters*, III, pp. 1344–50.
[4] See D. MacMillan, *Drury Lane Calendar 1747–1776* (Oxford, 1938).
[5] Haymarket, 6 February 1744; see C. B. Hogan, *Shakespeare in the Theatre 1701–1800*, 2 vols (Oxford, 1952–7), I, p. 367.
[6] See C. B. Hogan, 'The New Wells, Goodman's Fields, 1739–1752', *Theatre Notebook*, III (Autumn 1949), pp. 67–72.
[7] See A. H. Scouten, 'On the Origin of Foote's Matinées', *Theatre Notebook*, VII (Winter 1952), pp. 28–31.

## (ii) An actors' theatre

Even from this outline of the way in which the company system developed in London between the Restoration and 1750, it may be seen that theatre management was a demanding art, that acting as a career offered little security for man or woman and that aesthetic considerations were not those most useful to managers and players in selecting material for presentation to the public. Before examining in detail the motives that drew recruits to management and the stage, the conditions in which they worked and the repertories they maintained, we should bear in mind that for the whole of this period the theatre in England was an actors' theatre, as distinct from a playwrights' theatre, a directors' theatre or a designers' theatre. The basic reason for all developments and shifts of emphasis in the world of drama, and the factor by which all managerial, acting and repertory problems must be assessed, is the changing constitution and disposition of the audience, whose collective will the theatrical profession must gratify or be damned. Though the court coterie audience of the early Restoration period was replaced by a wider and less self-consciously sophisticated public, drawn increasingly from classes with far other social assumptions and standards, the collective demand upon the actors remained more or less constant. What began as a fashion embodying the narcissistic holiday humour of a small but powerful minority hardened into a tradition which perpetuated while extending the social attitude which had called it into being. At the Restoration, when theatre in London was a court toy managed by courtiers, the actors – and still more the actresses – were in a sense public playthings, bearing the stamp of royal approval at a time when it was fashionable to emulate the king. It was the personal glamour of the players that secured attention, not the intrinsic literary quality of their repertory. Because a liberal education and virtuous character were the time-honoured equipment of a courtier, plays of impeccable literary lineage and high moral tone were indeed felt to be *de rigueur* for court circles; but because the king himself and the tough, active men who stood about him were in reality impatient of pedantry and bored by too much talk of virtue, the plays that went down best were either frankly of a less edifying nature or carefully calculated in their staging and acting to provoke thoughts and emotions a good deal less edifying than the sentiments actually voiced by their dramatis personae. The work of Beaumont and Fletcher, which often provides just this possibility of ambiguity, was extensively revived, and Dryden in the new generation proved an expert in the same art. From the actors' point of view, this real preference of their public offered much the most promising acting opportunities – in comedy for the polished, or sometimes the knockabout, in tragedy for the high and passionate.[1] Their professional objective was the display of each actor's person and technique to the best advantage within the context of a given play's demands, not that submissive putting-over of an author's well-turned sentiments which had always characterized quite a separate branch of theatre in England, the academic stage. The good amateur actor in a school or university production tried to act as a mouthpiece for the text, and as a mobile lay-figure, piecing out the understanding of the audience by appropriate clothing and gestures – he gave a figuring-forth rather than a personal performance. Figuring-forth was a small part of the professional actor's ambition. One clue to what the professional companies thought they were doing on stage is the way in which they cut the texts of plays for performance: the early editions of plays performed in this period often follow the pre-war fashion of indicating which passages were omitted in representation, and sometimes also which passages were regarded as of exceptional poetic beauty – there is often a telling coincidence in the selection. For the modern reader, this process is perhaps most readily detected in the acting versions of Shakespeare, which sometimes entirely remodel the originals, but in any case freely dispense with lines sacred to our own ears, only to incorporate stage business we may judge ludicrous.[2] One instance of intrusive business can be documented very closely: in the closet scene of *Hamlet*, at the moment when the Ghost appears, all the early illustrations show Hamlet standing aghast, the chair from which he has sprung now lying overturned behind him (see Plate 24).[3] Betterton, Spranger Barry and Garrick in turn contrived this effective crash (Garrick by the use of a trick chair[4]), and the tradition remained unbroken till 1777, when John Henderson defied it and alienated the critics.

This was just the sort of 'point' which the audience watched for in comparing rival performances of the same role, and which received increasing attention when theatrical criticism began to develop as an art in the newspapers and periodicals of the early eighteenth century. The system whereby

[1] For acting style in this period, see J. H. Wilson, 'Rant, Cant and Tone on the Restoration Stage', *Studies in Philology*, LII (October 1955), pp. 592–8, and A. S. Downer, 'Nature to Advantage Dress'd: Eighteenth Century Acting', *PMLA*, LVIII (December 1943), pp. 1002–37.
[2] See A. C. Sprague, *Shakespeare and the Actors. The Stage Business in his Plays 1660–1905* (Cambridge, Mass., 1944).
[3] See R. Mander and J. Mitchenson, *Hamlet Through the Ages* (London, 1952), pp. 93, 95.
[4] John Ireland, *Letters and Poems by the late Mr John Henderson, with Anecdotes of his Life* (1786), pp. 207–9.

an actor 'possessed' a given part, having the first right to enact it whenever his company revived the play, however inappropriate an incarnation his advancing age or girth might have made him, of course consolidated this tendency to appraise the actor rather than submit to the play. Though members of the Restoration and early eighteenth-century audience were sometimes carried *out* – drunken, riotous, fainting or apoplectic – they were rarely carried *away*, in the sense of forgetting personal identity and accepting the illusion of the stage. The desire for stage illusion is something that springs up wherever the theatre is valued as a means of escape from the rigour or banality of everyday existence; but between 1660 and 1750 the audience for legitimate drama was extrovert and volatile, pleased with itself and life, relishing a heightened picture of both – even nobler in tragedy, even glossier in comedy, and swift to detect topical references both political and personal in the plays set before it, swift also to appropriate the players as human beings inhabiting the same busy, self-conscious world, and to seek security in the obvious continuity of the personalities behind the varying masks.

## (iii) Repertory policy

It is in this sense that the English theatre in this period was predominantly an actors' theatre, based on an intimate and complex relationship between the human beings on stage and in the house, rather than a literary theatre, where plays are judged on their own merits, or a theatre of illusion, where the personal identities of the actors are absorbed into the compelling verisimilitude of the characters they represent, while the separate intelligences of the audience are subsumed into a corporate act of faith in the world created on stage. Not until the late eighteenth century and the nineteenth century, when the forestage retreated behind the proscenium arch and an ever-increasing proportion of less educated and less sophisticated spectators frequented greatly enlarged playhouses, was the feeling of direct personal contact weakened, and the desire for stage illusion regularly gratified, at performances of legitimate drama. Between 1700 and 1750 the growth of audience interest in opera and pantomime did indeed constitute a threat to the legitimate drama and the actors' theatre, as was fully recognized and deplored at the time by those who took drama seriously: both opera and pantomime indulged and fostered that taste for escape into an exotic world of spectacle and music which had already revealed itself as a factor in the success of Restoration heroic drama, but which the Restoration tragic-acting tradition, at once formal in style and highly personal in direction, had strongly counterstated.

It was Garrick who by his own 'natural' acting style began to build up a new but equally engrossing actor–audience relationship, and who by his flair for finding Drury Lane a repertory of good stage-plays, including extensive revivals of Shakespeare, kept the power of first-class dramatic writing lively in the ears of his audience.

The story of Garrick's success in these directions, and of his attempts to integrate the audience's delight in scenic attractions into a full, delighted response to the play itself and its acting, belongs to the period after 1750: suffice it here to note that where acting style and revivals of Shakespeare were concerned Garrick marshalled theatre the way that it was going.[1] Macklin, whose own style of acting was 'natural', found himself at first unable to get a foothold in London theatres, but the tide began to turn in the 1730s, after Fielding's popular skit *Tom Thumb* had neatly deflated not only the implausibility and grandiloquence of the heroic tragedies but the turgid style of their delivery.[2] A taste for Shakespeare's romantic comedies, which had been out of fashion in the Restoration period, began to revive at the same time, just before Garrick made his début, and was supported by a steady growth of interest in Shakespeare's work as a whole, revealed in a series of new editions and critical writings.[3] Though Dryden had praised Shakespeare with only minor reservations,[4] Pepys was more true to his generation when he called *Twelfth Night* 'but a silly play'.[5] The calculated *double entendre* of Beaumont and Fletcher, and the trenchant scholar's wit of Jonson, had pleased the Restoration playgoer better than Shakespeare's more imaginative and less self-conscious art.[6] Of Shakespeare's great tragedies, only *Hamlet* and *Othello* held the stage in anything like their original form during the Restoration period. Davenant arranged *Macbeth* as a spectacular opera, Nahum Tate gave *King Lear* a happy ending, Dryden replaced *Antony and Cleopatra* by his regular and heroic *All for Love*.[7] Between 1700 and 1730,

---

[1] See A. H. Scouten, 'Shakespeare's Plays in the Theatrical Repertory when Garrick came to London', *Studies in English* (Texas University, 1944), pp. 257–68.

[2] See the edition by J. T. Hillhouse, *The Tragedy of Tragedies* (New Haven, Conn., and London, 1918).

[3] See A. H. Scouten, 'The Increase of Popularity of Shakespeare's Plays in the Eighteenth Century', *Shakespeare Quarterly*, VII (Spring 1956), pp. 189–202.

[4] As Neander in *Essay of Dramatic Poesy* (1668), in *Essays of John Dryden*, ed. W. P. Ker, 2 vols (Oxford, 1900), I, pp. 79–83.

[5] Pepys, *Diary*, 6 January 1662–3; see also 11 September 1661 and 20 January 1668–9.

[6] See A. C. Sprague, *Beaumont and Fletcher on the Restoration Stage* (Cambridge, Mass., 1926), and G. E. Bentley, *Shakespeare and Jonson: Their Reputations in the Seventeenth Century Compared*, 2 vols (Chicago, 1945).

[7] See Hazelton Spencer, *Shakespeare Improved* (Cambridge, Mass., 1927).

though Shakespeare in some version or other was still the staple of the tragic repertory, tragedy itself was substantially less popular, and subordinated in the playhouse programmes not only to comedy but increasingly to opera and pantomime.[1]

By 1731 a latter-day Horace had noted how John Rich trimmed his sails to this new wind:

> Long labour'd *Rich*, by Tragick Verse to gain
> The Town's Applause – but labour'd long in vain;
> At length he wisely to his Aid call'd in
> The *active Mime*, and *checker'd Harlequin*.[2]

Rich himself under his stage-name Lun was the first superlative English Harlequin. An epigram current at the time shows how his policy succeeded:

> *Shakespear, Rowe, Johnson*, now are quite undone,
> These are thy *Triumphs*, thy *Exploits*, O *Lun*![3]

Similar complaints against degenerating public taste were regularly made with reference to Italian opera and the ballad operas; but it should be observed that if Shakespeare had really ever been in danger of oblivion his name would not have figured so frequently as a type of neglected worth. Besides the increasing scholarly support that the roll-call of his editors in this period attests, Shakespeare had at least one theatrical fan club, 'Shakespeare's Ladies', who got up a subscription in 1737 towards the revival of his plays at Covent Garden.[4] By promoting revivals of Shakespeare at Drury Lane in the 1740s, Garrick deliberately set himself to further a trend which had already begun. The strident epilogue to *Tittle-Tattle*, 'A New Farce . . . By Timothy Fribble, Esq.', 1749, catches a tone which twenty years later Garrick and the public his work had helped to create were to take up triumphantly in the great Shakespeare Jubilee:

[1] For detailed analysis, see Nicoll, *HED*, II, pp. 55–60.
[2] James Miller, *Harlequin Horace, or, The Art of Modern Poetry*, dedicated to 'J—n R—h Esq.' (1731), p. 30.
[3] This couplet, perhaps by Theophilus Cibber, appears under an engraving by Van der Gucht tentatively dated 1729 (see *A Catalogue of Prints and Drawings in the British Museum*, Division I, Political and Personal Satires, II, Nos 1834 and 1838) which is bound with some copies of the 3rd edition of *Harlequin Horace* in 1735: the lines are inserted with others into the text of this 3rd edition on p. 34. See Allan S. Jackson, 'Little Known Theatrical Prints of the Eighteenth Century', *Theatre Notebook*, XXII (Spring 1968), pp. 113–16, for this and other caricatures of Rich as Lun.
[4] See E. L. Avery, 'The Shakespeare Ladies' Club', *Shakespeare Quarterly*, VII (Spring 1956), pp. 153–8.

*Rouze*, Britons, *rouze*, this modish Taste *despise*,
*And let* Good Sense *to its* Old Standard *rise*;
*Frequent your* luscious Pantomimes *no more*,
*But* SHAKESPEARE, *like your* Ancestors *adore*.[1]

The successful managers in this period were therefore those who sensed
or observed the general climate of varying public taste while it was still in
process of change, and who, having correctly predicted each tomorrow's
weather, had time to equip themselves to do it justice. The playwright-
managers – Davenant, Cibber, Hill – could try to set and promote fashions
for their own styles of piece, just as the actor-managers – Betterton, Cibber
again and, in his own way, John Rich – traded on their own special talents
and personalities within the context of the actors' theatre. The business-
managers – Killigrew (whose days of creative inspiration were over by 1660),
Christopher Rich, Lacy – succeeded by a combination of shrewdness and
*finesse*, directed towards the securing and profitable manipulation of attractions valued exactly (and only) to the extent that they pleased the public:
player, playwright, painter, singer, dancer or acrobatic dog, each had his
price, and each his box-office returns. As Dr Johnson put it in his prologue
for Garrick's opening of Drury Lane in 1747:

The Stage but echoes back the publick Voice.
The Drama's Laws the Drama's Patrons give,
For we that live to please, must please to live.[2]

## (iv) Players as people

It was this systematic wooing of fashion, however silly, and the glare of
publicity upon any individual connected with the stage, coupled with the
popular assumption (sometimes too well justified) that people with such a
public reputation lost all claim to reputation in their private lives, which led
to family opposition when young men and women of standing tried to enter
the acting profession. Garrick's successful struggle with his relatives has
already been noted: other well-educated and stage-struck young gentlemen
who managed to cut loose were Cardell Goodman (*c.* 1649–99), sent down
from Cambridge and aptly nicknamed 'Scum';[3] William Mountfort (*c.* 1660–

[1] 'Timothy Fribble', *Tittle-Tattle* (1749), p. 52.
[2] Samuel Johnson, *Poems*, ed. D. Nichol Smith and E. L. McAdam (Oxford, 1941), pp. 49–55.
[3] See J. H. Wilson, *Mr Goodman the Player* (Pittsburgh, Pa., 1964).

92), son of an army captain;[1] William Smith (*c.* 1620–95), a barrister 'whose character as a Gentleman could have been in no way impeach'd had he not degraded it by being a celebrated Actor';[2] Colley Cibber, son of a distinguished sculptor; Barton Booth, who left Westminster School to make his Dublin début as Oroonoko at the age of seventeen; and Tony Aston the stroller (*c.* 1682–*c.* 1749), the son of a respectable lawyer and himself bred for the law.[3] Betterton was the son of a royal cook, and destined for a career as bookseller: his education was wholly respectable.[4] Of unknown parentage and no particular education was James Nokes (d. 1696), who had been a boy-player and went on to excel in low comedy and harridan transvestite roles: he made a fortune and used it to buy a toyshop.[5] Henry Harris (*c.* 1634–1704) was a seal-cutter by profession, and his spectacular career on stage between 1660 and 1681 was a side-show to his official career as an engraver at the Royal Mint.[6] Thomas Doggett soared from the slums of Dublin to such affluence that he was able to found a prize-race for Thames watermen still rowed every August in honour of George II's accession.[7] Other Irish actors who rose to fame in this period were Wilks, Macklin and Spranger Barry: Wilks did not begin to prosper until he took over the murdered Mountfort's parts at Drury Lane in 1693; Macklin had a hard struggle in the English provinces before he reached London in 1725; but Barry had only two seasons at Smock Alley before he appeared at Drury Lane in 1746, and began to star with Garrick in *Venice Preserved* and other plays with twin contrasted heroes. Further recruits from Smock Alley were George Farquhar (1677–1707) and James Quin. Farquhar was born in Londonderry and educated at Trinity College Dublin: he made his Dublin début in 1696, but after accidentally injuring another actor turned his hand instead to writing plays, and went to London to get them staged.[8] His early death prevented him from seeing them become the backbone of the comic repertory by 1750. Quin was born in London, the natural son of an Irish barrister: he made his début at Smock

---

[1] See A. S. Borgman, *The Life and Death of William Mountfort* (Cambridge, Mass., 1935).

[2] See Cibber, *Apology*, I, pp. 78 f.

[3] See *A Sketch of the Life, etc., of Mr Anthony Aston ... Written by Himself* (*c.* 1720), reprinted with other material by Aston in Watson Nicholson, *Anthony Aston Stroller and Adventurer* (South Haven, Mich. 1920).

[4] See R. W. Lowe, *Thomas Betterton* (London, 1891).

[5] 'Thomas Betterton', *The History of the English Stage* (1741), p. 32.

[6] Harris became a close friend of Pepys, many of whose frequent references to him are collected by Helen McAfee, *Pepys on the Restoration Stage* (New Haven, Conn., 1916), pp. 218–23.

[7] See T. A. Cook and G. Nickalls, *Thomas Doggett Deceased* (London, 1908).

[8] See Clark, op. cit. pp. 103–4.

Alley in 1712, gravitated to London in 1714 and played there until his retirement in 1751.[1]

Of the earliest professional actresses, very few had an assured social background, though many achieved titles by marriage or selling their favours; certainly few actresses before 1750 even professed chastity.[2] Betterton's wife Mary, née Sanderson (d. 1711), was an honourable exception; their adopted daughter, Anne Bracegirdle (c. 1673–1748), was at least rigidly discreet; and the composer Arne's sister Susannah Maria Cibber (1714–66), though notoriously false to her venal husband Theophilus, was true to her lover, Sloper.[3] Of the other prime favourites in this period, Nell Gwyn (1650–87) was a semi-literate orange-girl, bastard daughter of a bawd and mistress to many besides the King of England; Elizabeth Barry (1658–1713), the daughter of a Cavalier barrister, was trained for the stage by her lover the Earl of Rochester; Anne Oldfield (1683–1730), daughter of a decayed guardsman, was apprenticed to a sempstress and 'discovered' by Farquhar at the Mitre Tavern; Kitty Clive (née Raftor) and Peg Woffington were Irish girls of impoverished stock. Of all these perhaps only Oldfield was genuinely stage-struck: 'I long'd to be at it, and only wanted a little decent Intreaties.'[4] She made a fortune, and was buried – 'in woollen! 'twould a saint provoke'[5] – in Westminster Abbey.

From the Restoration period onwards there was a tendency for players to marry and remarry within the profession, and for theatrical families to place and perpetuate themselves in key positions. Mountfort's widow, Susanna (née Percival, 1667–1703), married Jack Verbruggen; Barton Booth chose Hester Santlow (c. 1690–1773) for his second wife; once Colley Cibber was established at Drury Lane, the Cibber tribe multiplied its stage connections with brisk efficiency. Later in the period the Hallam family became powerful: Adam was a veteran of Smock Alley, Thomas was killed by Macklin in a backstage brawl in 1735, William ran an unlicensed theatre in the 1740s, and Lewis took English theatre to the New World in 1752.

The beating-up of Kynaston by hired bullies in 1669,[6] and the cold-

[1] See A. M. Taylor, 'The Patrimony of James Quin', *Tulane Studies in English*, VIII (New Orleans, 1958), pp. 55–106.

[2] Restoration actresses are fully discussed, with biographies, by J. H. Wilson, *All The King's Ladies* (Chicago, 1958).

[3] Evidence reviewed by Barker, op. cit. pp. 180–93.

[4] W. R. Chetwood, *A General History of the Stage* (London, 1749), p. 201.

[5] Oldfield was Pope's Narcissa in the deathbed scene of his *Moral Essays* (Epistle I, ll. 246–51).

[6] Pepys, *Diary*, 1, 2 and 9 February 1668–9.

blooded murder of Mountfort in 1692 by Lord Mohun and his agents, who got off scot-free, illustrate the unprotected status of the profession during this period, just as the Macklin–Hallam killing, provoked by nothing more serious than the allocation of a wig for stage wear, illustrates its internal clashes of violent temperaments.[1] Another, very public, example of jealous violence was the struggle on stage between Mrs Barry as Roxana and Mrs Boutell as Statira in a revival of Lee's *Rival Queens*: the dagger-blow demanded by the text was in one performance given with malice through the stays and into the flesh.[2]

Genuine accidents with stage weapons, like the one that so daunted Farquhar, were frequent between 1660 and 1750. Among the most serious were the thrust near the eye that left Philip Cademan, Davenant's stepson, disabled for life in 1673;[3] the property-man's error by which Samuel Sandford (*c.* 1640–*c.* 1705) stabbed George Powell with a real instead of a dummy dagger in 1692;[4] and the death of a minor actor in a Moorfields booth theatre in 1723, killed in earnest as he played a victim in the droll of *Darius*.[5] Though Philip Cademan could never act after the accident, his salary of thirty shillings a week was paid him as a pension until Christopher Rich first forced him to earn it by handing out tickets and then stopped it altogether. Cademan's petition against this treatment survives, and claims that normally all persons 'disabled from acting by Sickness or other Misfortunes' were granted a life-pension. Plainly, however, the responsibility for this kind of social security rested with the individual manager, and Rich was too hard a master. Another source of income to players and their families in misfortune was the occasional benefit performance on their behalf:[6] after William Milward (1702–42) died 'of a Spotted Feaver', his widow and four children received three separate benefits of this kind.[7] The division of players into sharers, taking a covenanted proportion of the net receipts, and hirelings, working for a fixed wage, was not so important after the Civil War: Betterton himself sometimes went on salary when times were bad. The Restoration laws against changing from one

---

[1] Court proceedings quoted by J. T. Kirkman, *Memoirs of the Life of Charles Macklin*, 2 vols (London, 1799), I, pp. 182 ff.
[2] 'Thomas Betterton', *History of the English Stage*, pp. 20–2; for Mrs Boutell, see *Covent Garden Drollery* (1672), ed. M. Summers (London, 1927), pp. 89–96.
[3] See Nicoll, *HED*, I, pp. 367–8: Item 4.
[4] Recorded by Narcissus Luttrell (1657–1732) on 15 October 1692 (cited *The London Stage*, Monday, 13 October 1692).
[5] *The London Journal*, 20 April 1723 (cited *The London Stage*, Monday, 15 April 1723).
[6] *The Benefit System* is fully explained by St Vincent Troubridge (London, 1967).
[7] Garrick, *Letters*, I, pp. 37–8; Milward died 6 February 1742. Benefits at Drury Lane, 9 March 1742, Covent Garden, 25 March 1742, and Lincoln's Inn Fields, 11 April 1743.

company to another, however, exposed the players to unscrupulous managements, and the frequent loss of playing-days by chance events that closed the
playhouses – bouts of plague, periods of court mourning, vagaries of censorship – made the actor's financial status very insecure. Bad debts, stealing, even
coin-clipping, sometimes brought players before the courts, as did political
offences. Drinking, gambling and whoring were allegedly only the least
malignant of the typical actor's vices throughout the period:

> A Pimping, Spunging, Idle, Impious Race . . .
> A nest of *Leachers* worse than *Sodom* bore . . .
> Diseas'd, in Debt, and ev'ry Moment dun'd;
> By all Good Christians loath'd, and their own Kindred shun'd.[1]

This unsavoury reputation was not altogether deserved: from such evidence as survives about members of the acting profession between 1660 and
1750 – and the habit of writing theatrical memoirs and anecdotes took strong
hold of the eighteenth century – it is obvious that most of them had much the
same disposition (warm-hearted, quick-tempered, vain, hard-working and
hopeful) as many actors before and since their day. Their careers were insecure and highly competitive, so that continual rivalries, jealousies and petty
feuds arose; but the companies lived from day to day like big squabbling
families, held together by group interests and group loyalty, capable under
stress of very great *esprit de corps*.

The much publicized quarrel in 1736 between Mrs Cibber and Mrs Clive
over the part of Polly in a revival of *The Beggar's Opera*, which gave rise to
the anonymous skit *The Beggar's Pantomime, or The Contending Columbines*,[2]
can be set against many examples of differences settled in the interests of the
company as a whole. Especially among the poorer players, and in the strolling
companies that served remote country districts, a practical good-fellowship
often triumphed over deprivation and misfortune.

### (v) Provincial conditions

The reminiscences of Charlotte Charke and Tony Aston eloquently testify
that the life of an itinerant player in the early eighteenth century could be one
of degrading poverty, hardship and makeshift. Many fell by the wayside: a
few survived the gruelling apprenticeship and made good in London, Dublin

---

[1] Robert Gould, 'The Play-house; a Satyr', *Works*, 2 vols (London, 1709), II, p. 251.
[2] See D. F. Smith, *Plays about the Theatre in England 1671–1737* (New York and London,
1936), pp. 177–85.

or one of the provincial cities that cared to build a playhouse before the Licensing Act restricted the performance of plays in the provinces. Bath, Bristol, York and Ipswich became centres of theatrical activity before 1737, though the grant of patents to provincial theatres and the rise of Theatres Royal all over the kingdom belong to the second half of the century.[1] Many London actors spent their summers on tour in the provinces, and some concerned themselves with the booth theatres billing short action-packed pieces or drolls which had become a popular feature of the London fairs, held regularly in their season throughout the period.[2]

All the evidence about the style of performance which went down best in provincial cities, country districts and fairgrounds goes to show that England at large was conservative in taste, enjoying a good costume and a *bravura* display of voice and gesture whenever available, but willing to tolerate many inadequacies and shortcomings in the presentation so long as the piece or evening's programme gave sufficient excitement, amusement or emotional release. A typical evening at Norwich in 1727 provided 'an Excellent PLAY call'd, DIDO and AENEAS', a Harlequinade 'The Pye-Dancer', an acrobatic turn and a 'moving Wax-Work' of Edward IV, Jane Shore and the Princes in the Tower. The main piece was often a standard favourite, old or new: in 1741 the *Norwich Gazette* advertised four plays by Shakespeare (*Hamlet, Henry IV, As You Like It* and *Twelfth Night*) and five later successes (Rowe's *Tamerlane*, Congreve's *Double Dealer*, Cibber's *Love's Last Shift*, Addison's *Cato* and, of course, *The Beggar's Opera*).[3]

## (vi) Professional training

In at least three important respects – training, rehearsal techniques and costume usage – the responsibilities of an actor before 1750 were different from those of his modern counterpart. Dramatic academies now offer recognized qualifications; serious professional productions are nowadays normally rehearsed, after careful casting, by a specially appointed director, who feels free to use methods like improvisation where appropriate; costume is now regularly settled in respect of each show by director and designer working together. This state of affairs, however, represents the end of a long process

[1] See Sybil Rosenfeld, *Strolling Players and Drama in the Provinces 1660–1765* (Cambridge, 1939).

[2] See Sybil Rosenfeld, *The Theatre of the London Fairs in the Eighteenth Century* (Cambridge, 1960).

[3] *Norwich Gazette* notices cited by G. A. Cranfield, *The Development of the Provincial Newspaper 1700–1760* (Oxford, 1962), pp. 217 f.

of evolution in the world of theatre. Even within the period 1660–1750 there was some change in all three fields; but, in them all, the ideas on which modern practices are based had no currency before the work of Macklin and Aaron Hill in the 1730s. At the high-water mark of the classical tradition which had developed since the Restoration stood the orotund Quin, with his great wig, tunic *à la romaine* and carefully maintained hierarchical dignity; against Smollett's malicious depreciation in *Peregrine Pickle*[1] has to be set a chorus of contemporary praise, including tributes even from Garrick. Quin retired in 1751, having registered his reaction to Garrick's triumph: he declared peremptorily that if the young fellow was right, he and the rest of the players had all been wrong.[2]

Garrick, who retained a full range of graceful set poses and never hesitated to exhibit demonstrative passion, was in many ways less revolutionary than Macklin, who not only jettisoned the 'hoity-toity tone' of the Quin brigade in favour of 'familiar' intonations and naturally broken utterances, but founded his own training-school for actors on this principle. His venture, conducted at the Haymarket after the 1744 quarrel with Drury Lane, put into practice ideas for a 'Tragic Academy' which had been mooted by Aaron Hill as early as 1735.[3] Among Macklin's pupils were the irrepressibly natural Foote and John Hill (*c.* 1716–75), whose treatise on *The Actor* (1750) gave Macklin's practice the formal support of recent French dramatic theory, and strongly attacked imitative and mechanical acting, in the cause of intuitive sensibility.[4] Up to this time the training of actors had been largely empirical, directed to the perfecting of techniques deemed appropriate to a whole class of roles rather than the imbuing of each individual with the spirit of his unique part. In practice, the best way to be sure of pleasing in any established role was to play it as exactly like its acknowledged master as possible, in the hope of falling heir to it at his retirement or death. At first the pre-1642 tradition was jealously recalled and entrenched, then the scope of new parts was fixed by their creators. Betterton, who was allowed an extra £50 a year for training young actors in the last years of his life,[5] set his own grave and stately stamp

[1] Tobias Smollett, *Peregrine Pickle* (1751), ed. J. L. Clifford (London, New York, Toronto, 1964), pp. 274 f., 652 ff. A full discussion of Smollett's grudge against Quin is given by H. S. Buck, *A Study in Smollett* (New Haven, Conn., 1925), pp. 65–81.

[2] Davies, *Memoirs of . . . Garrick*, I, p. 44.

[3] See L. B. Campbell, 'The Rise of a Theory of Stage Presentation in England during the Eighteenth Century', *PMLA*, XXXII (June 1917), pp. 163–200, especially pp. 178–82; for Aaron Hill's plan, see also Davies, *Memoirs of . . . Garrick*, I, pp. 143 ff.

[4] See E. R. Wasserman, 'The Sympathetic Imagination in Eighteenth Century Theories of Acting', *Journal of English and Germanic Philology*, XLVI (July 1947), pp. 264–72.

[5] Document of *c.* 1707, cited Nicoll, *HED*, II, p. 276.

on tragic acting; but only Barton Booth inherited his judicious restraint, and most of the younger generation relied to a far greater extent on sound and fury. Cibber, Powell and Wilks were among the ranters, whose exaggeration seems to have been the strongest influence on popular and provincial taste long after it was outmoded in London. It is perhaps only fair to note that everyday behaviour in this period was at once more formal and more noisily demonstrative than the code of modern manners allows for; but even so things were higher-pitched on stage.

The gentlemanly style of comic acting was always closer to living models, demanding grace and elegance of deportment rather than insight into character. Both Betterton and Cibber were capable of success in both kinds, though Betterton excelled in heroic parts and Cibber in fops. Nell Gwyn took saucy wenches to perfection, but as an Indian Emperor's daughter disgusted Pepys: '... a great and serious part, which she do most basely'.[1] Sandford was best received as an ugly villain,[2] Mrs Verbruggen as a hoyden or a minx.[3] When a playwright deliberately provided a vehicle for a given player, no extra training was necessary: Congreve wrote star parts for Bracegirdle, Cibber for Oldfield. Macklin, however, used independent insight and sensibility to derive his conception of Shylock from Shakespeare's text, and shocked his contemporaries even while they applauded. For his familiar acting style Macklin acknowledged a debt to William Rufus Chetwood (c. 1695–1766), who had been Ashbury's assistant at Smock Alley and became prompter at Drury Lane in 1722.[4] As Chetwood reveals in his General History of the Stage (1749), he was a devotee of the earlier tradition, and it may well be that from their own point of view he and Macklin were pointing actors back to the more restrained style of Betterton and his company.

### (vii) Rehearsals and preparation

'When I was a young Player under Sir *William Davenant*...', confided Betterton the year before his death, 'we were obliged to make our Study our Business, which our young Men do not think it their duty now to do; for they now scarce ever mind a Word of their Parts but only at *Rehearsals*, and come thither too often scarce recovered from their last Night's Debauch.'[5] His

---

[1] Pepys, *Diary*, 22 August 1667.
[2] See R. H. Ross, 'Samuel Sandford; Villain from Necessity', *PMLA*, LXXXVI (September 1961), pp. 367–72.
[3] See Tony Aston, *A Brief Supplement to Colley Cibber Esq.* (c. 1747), reprinted in Cibber, *Apology*, II, pp. 313 f.
[4] Davies, *Dramatic Miscellanies*, III, p. 441.
[5] Charles Gildon, *The Life of Mr Thomas Betterton* (1710), p. 15.

words remind us that there are three main cares of an actor in rehearsal, whatever the period – his lines, his stage business and his positioning while on stage. Obviously Betterton considered that lines should be understood as well as committed to memory, and that the process of reaching agreement on the business and blocking of any play ought to be undertaken with a clear head. Of course only new plays required to be worked through for the first time: normally with a revival all concerned knew the established routine; but if there had been any cast changes, or if some uncertainty revealed itself in rehearsal, the prompter could be consulted – he carried much information in his prompt-book, and more in his head. Aaron Hill was bitter about actors who scamped attention to business and blocking, and ran through their lines parrot-fashion instead of practising their delivery: 'these vain Men and Women ... have reduc'd a Rehearsal to a mere *muttering over* the Lines'.[1]

On the whole, however, at least in London, the standard of performance seems to have been respectable on most occasions, so that lapses were complained of. In emergencies, when an actor dropped out at the last minute, a substitute would crave the indulgence of the house and read in the part;[2] but normally actors were present and more or less correct, doing their best to avoid the prompter's whisper. Colley Cibber as a novice once lost his nerve and his lines: they put him on the salary-roll so that he could be fined five shillings.[3] A system of fines, and sometimes of rewards, kept discipline behind the scenes as far as humanly possible, and attendance at rehearsals was obligatory. A few glimpses of the individual player preparing a role survive for our amusement – Mrs Knepp eating fruit with Pepys as they went through her cues together backstage one afternoon,[4] Verbruggen raging on the river bank to the terror of highwaymen,[5] Doggett taking up residence in Wapping to get local colour for Ben in *Love for Love*.[6]

## (viii) Costume on stage

The idea that a king on stage need not be dressed in bona fide velvet robes, nor even in kingly guise at all, is a modern one, born of an expanding textile trade and a new aesthetic of stage design. The costumes used in medieval

[1] See Hill's bi-weekly paper, *The Prompter*, Nos 51 and 56 (6 and 23 May 1735).
[2] Davies, *Dramatic Miscellanies*, III, p. 114.
[3] Ibid. III, pp. 417 f., reprinted in Cibber, *Apology*, I, pp. 181 f.
[4] Pepys, *Diary*, 5 October 1667.
[5] Alexander Smith, *The History of the Lives of the Most Noted Highwaymen*, 2nd ed., 2 vols (1714), I, pp. 89–92.
[6] David Garrick, *An Essay on Acting* (1744), p. 10.

religious drama had been rich, where appropriate, to the glory of God, and from its Tudor beginnings the secular theatre in England took spectacle on the wardrobe side as seriously as it could afford. Shows financed by the monarch and court were naturally the most lavish, after the Restoration as before;[1] but there can be no doubt that on the public stage too throughout the period were seen costumes of considerable value and elaboration. Charles II lent his coronation robes to Betterton for Davenant's *Love and Honour*, and Aphra Behn provided genuine feather garments from Surinam for Dryden's *Indian Queen*; the royal loan was repeated for Orrery's *Henry V*, and the feather dresses used again for Dryden's *Indian Emperor* and Mrs Behn's own *Widow Ranter*; but other extravagant specialities and 'Forreigne-habits', like the Moorish costumes which can be seen in one of Dolle's engravings for the lavish 1673 edition of Settle's *Empress of Morocco* (see Plate 4), or the sumptuous robes for the coronation procession in *Henry VIII* at Drury Lane, October 1727, show what a theatre wardrobe could produce if required. The public enjoyed such spectacle – too much, according to one resentful author, Edward Howard:

> And though the ear be the principal sense to receive satisfaction from the Stage, yet we find, that of seeing has not seldom a greater predominancy, whilst Scenes, habits, dances, or perhaps an Actress take more with Spectators, than the best Dramatick wit, or contrivance of the Age, from which we may prognosticate, that the enterlude of *Punchinello* ... may be as long frequented as either Theatre. (Preface to *The Six Days' Adventure*, 1671)

Speaking in 1671, Edward Howard was a true prophet of early eighteenth-century tastes.[2]

Not every piece, however, was the occasion for fresh spectacle, and even at the houses that spent most on costumes, the majority of performances were dressed out of stock. This fact, together with the complaints about tawdry and inadequate costume that figure largely in accounts of strolling players,

---

[1] See Eleanore Boswell, *The Restoration Court Stage 1660–1702* (Cambridge, Mass., 1932).
[2] The coronation robe loans are mentioned by Downes, *Roscius Anglicanus*, ed. Summers, pp. 21 f., 27 f.; for the Surinam feather dresses, see Aphra Behn, *Works*, ed. M. Summers, 6 vols (London and Stratford-on-Avon, 1915), V, p. 130. A picture of Anne Bracegirdle attended by native boys in *The Widow Ranter*, Drury Lane, *c*. November 1689, shows how the feather motif was combined with the usual tragedy train of unwieldy length. (See Plate 27.) Nicoll, *HED*, I, pp. 49–51 and p. 51n, cites references in the Lord Chamberlain's order regarding the new Lincoln's Inn Fields Theatre to expense 'for a variety of Cloaths, Forreigne-habitts ... &c.'.

has sometimes been taken to indicate that shabbiness reigned on stage until Garrick and likeminded managers took to considering the total visual effect of their productions. Luckily there survive not only many pictorial records of actors bedecked with ample finery in appropriate roles, but a body of references by eye-witnesses who noted what was worn, and also a small but significant amount of evidence from wardrobe accounts kept by the playhouses. Christopher Rich, for example, put plenty of money into dressing his company, working down from the principals.[1] How much the individual actor was expected to provide varied from company to company: in 1660 Davenant supplied his men with basic suits of clothes but not hats, feathers, gloves, ribbons, sword-belts, collars, stockings or shoes;[2] while Killigrew, at His Majesty's behest, furnished the favoured Mohun, Hart and Kynaston with most of these accessories, including 'Three paire of Silke Stockins' and 'Two plumes of feathers' yearly apiece.[3]

As *The Spectator* remarked in 1711, 'The ordinary Method of making an Heroe, is to clap a huge Plume of Feathers upon his Head'[4] – or rather upon his helmet: Quin may be seen thus embellished in the well-known illustration to Thomson's *Coriolanus* (1749).[5] The stiff wide-skirted *tonnelet* and buskins which complete Quin's costume here represent the orthodox 'classical' tradition of dressing any tragic hero. Tragic actresses were also graced with plumes, but their gowns followed the trend of current fashion, lagging a little when cast-offs from a patroness or stock from an earlier production. Because comedy was acted in 'modern dress' and was in any case considered an inferior medium, tragedy had the first claim to special finery, a state of affairs resented by some comic actors: '*Dogget* . . . could not with Patience look upon the costly Trains and Plumes of Tragedy, in which knowing himself to be useless, he thought were all a vain Extravagance.'[6] But as Steele put it in his prologue to Vanbrugh's *The Mistake* in 1705:

> With Audiences compos'd of Belles and Beaux,
> The first Dramatick Rule is, Have good Cloathes . . .
> In Lace and Feather Tragedy's express'd,
> And Heroes die unpity'd, if ill-dress'd.

[1] See Sybil Rosenfeld, 'The Wardrobes of Lincoln's Inn Fields and Covent Garden', *Theatre Notebook*, V (Winter 1950), pp. 15–19.
[2] The agreement of 5 November 1660 is given by Adams, op. cit. pp. 96–100; see p. 99 for this wardrobe provision.
[3] Livery Warrant of 6 March 1671–2, given by Nicoll, *HED*, I, p. 365: Item 13.
[4] *The Spectator*, No. 42 (Wednesday, 18 April 1711).
[5] See Plate 28.
[6] Cibber, *Apology*, I, p. 229.

The swarthy Charles II objected to the custom of clapping a black periwig on every stage rogue;[1] Addison's mock inventory of the 'Moveables Of C—r R—h Esq.' in *The Tatler* over forty years later includes a Murderer's 'Cole-black Peruke' and goes on to list 'A Suit of Clothes for a Ghost, *viz.* a Bloody Shirt, a Doublet curiously pink'd, and a Coat with three great Eyelet-Holes upon the Breast';[2] the Jacob's Wells Theatre, Bristol, spent two guineas on a ghost dress among numerous items of wardrobe expenditure during the period 1741–8, and also twenty shillings for five yards of crape for Calista's veil;[3] it was over a wardrobe veil that Roxana and Statira had struggled in the 1680s. In short, stage fashions of a conservative and rather arbitrary kind gave most productions between 1660 and 1750 a hotchpotch look, wide open to champions of probability and good sense: the sporadic attempts at historical or local verisimilitude in costume which won publicity for certain special productions during the period merely contributed to a general effect of patchy but authentic splendour in the theatre. When opera and pantomime began to take over the 'fancy-dress' aspects of stage spectacle, the legitimate drama needed a new rationale of costume, and began to find it in the doctrines of Aaron Hill, who prescribed decorum based on historical research, and himself designed a set of '*old Saxon* habits' (never, alas, made up) for his tragedy *Athelwold* (1731).[4]

Both antiquarian zeal and the concept of decorum were to become more and more fashionable as the century rolled on, and with them grew the vogue for mounting historical plays in painstaking reconstructions of the costumes their characters would have worn in real life. The story of this immensely influential vogue, which still has its champions in professional theatre, belongs to a later period. Aaron Hill's suggestions, and Macklin's carefully documented experiment with his costume for Shylock, are straws in a wind which took another generation to reach gale force.[5] Both the novelty value of 'historical' costuming and a cheerful indifference to its aesthetic justification are revealed in a letter from Garrick to Lacy, outlining plans to challenge Rich and Shakespeare at Covent Garden in 1750:

[1] Ibid. I, pp. 133 f.
[2] *The Tatler*, No. 42 (14–16 July 1709).
[3] See Sybil Rosenfeld, 'Actors in Bristol 1741–48', *TLS*, 29 August 1936.
[4] Aaron Hill's letters to Wilks, 23 and 28 October 1731: see *The Works of the late Aaron Hill Esq.*, 4 vols (London, 1753), I, pp. 88–91.
[5] See L. B. Campbell, 'A History of Costuming on the English Stage between 1660 and 1823', *University of Wisconsin Studies*, II (Madison, 1918), pp. 187–223, especially pp. 198–203.

... if we can get out *King John* before 'em ... and dress the characters half old English, half modern, as in Edward the Black Prince, we shall cut their combs there too.[1]

## (ix) Transvestite playing

Transvestite playing in this period deserves special mention, because there was a good deal of it, and the popularity of plays that allowed for an ambiguous use of costume affected the repertory pattern. More than one excuse served to get actresses into breeches for the delectation of a predominantly male audience. First, of course, came revivals of old plays with parts written for boys playing women, where the plot demanded assumption of male disguises at times during the action: with the advent of actresses, titillating dénouements with bared bosoms and flowing tresses became popular, and new plays were written to exploit this 'disguise penetrated' motif. Next, increasingly popular after Nell Gwyn played the madcap Florimel in Dryden's *Secret Love* (1667),[2] came the 'roaring-girl' type of part, where the heroine adopted men's clothes as a free expression of her vivacious nature: prologues and epilogues were sometimes given by favourite actresses in men's clothes with no other apparent reason than to provide the same arbitrary thrill. Something akin to this was the practice by which an actress took the part of a male character just to amuse the audience: Peg Woffington made a great hit as Farquhar's 'Sir Harry Wildair', though the role – very far from epicene – had been made to measure for its creator, the dashing Wilks. Occasionally a whole play would be performed by women – Pepys relished Killigrew's 'bawdy loose play' *The Parson's Wedding* done like this in 1664,[3] and there are several instances of the novelty in the early eighteenth century. The converse of this process was less widespread, but regularly occurred in some plays and for some types of role: the part of Sir John Brute in Vanbrugh's *Provoked Wife*, and that of Smuggler in Farquhar's *Constant Couple*, gave male leads opportunities to clown in petticoats, as did the coarse old women of comedy and farce. Glumdalca the giantess in the expanded version of *Tom Thumb* was often taken by a man, and the tiny hero by a child actress. A few performances by companies of children or 'Lilliputians' are recorded, and a number

[1] Garrick, *Letters*, I, p. 152.
[2] Pepys, *Diary*, 2 March 1666–7; there is a useful analysis of this whole fashion in Wilson, *All the King's Ladies*, pp. 73–86.
[3] Pepys, *Diary*, 4 and 11 October 1664.

of indecent prologues and epilogues devised to be spoken by little girls survive to attest the immorality and profanity of the English audience.[1]

## (x) Stage orations and interpolations

Prologues and epilogues exploiting incongruity, transvestite or lisped, form
only one group of a great body of stage orations, mostly in verse, composed
and delivered to induce a propitious actor–audience relationship, and a sense
of significant occasion, in the intimate playhouses of this period. Their style
and subject-matter exploit every variety of appeal that can be derived from a
wide range of tone and a feverish insistence on topicality and novelty: to
write them became an art, to speak them an honour. As a method of impress-
ing his personality upon the audience, these miscellany items in the evening's
entertainment were welcomed by the actor, though successful tricks of delivery like wearing an outsize hat or riding an ass upon the stage (see Plate 30)
had little enough to do with the intrinsic merit of the oration or the play that
served as its pretext.[2]

A practice well received from certain actors but infuriating for colleagues
and playwrights was would-be comic ad-libbing and playing to the gallery.
William Pinkethman (d. 1725) was notorious for this: it may be significant
that he was also noted as an ass-epilogue speaker, a boothsman at Bartholomew Fair and a Harlequin.[3] The Italian *commedia dell'arte* methods of improvisation had their own discipline, but when misunderstood were an unlucky
influence on English players. Another kind of ad-libbing was more dangerous
to its exponents: when to the king's face John Lacy (1622–81) introduced
satirical comment on court matters into James Howard's *Change of Crowns*
(1667), he was imprisoned, and the company silenced.[4]

## (xi) Political considerations in repertory planning

Political considerations affected both actors and their repertory throughout
this period – the fortunes of the Vicar of Bray indeed provide a rough index

[1] 'Lilliputians' played at Lincoln's Inn Fields on 1 January 1729, and at the Tennis Court,
James Street, on 22 and 29 April, 23 and 24 May 1734. For risqué stage orations by little
girls, see Nicoll, *HED*, I, pp. 265 f., and II, p. 160.
[2] See Autrey N. Wiley's edition of *Rare Prologues and Epilogues 1642–1700* (London, 1940),
especially pp. xxxvi ff., 199–203. Nell Gwyn in a broad-brimmed hat and waist-belt spoke
Dryden's prologue to *The Conquest of Granada* (1670), mocking the stage-hat joke at the
other house: see W. B. Gardner's edition of *The Prologues and Epilogues of John Dryden*
(New York, 1951), pp. 33 f., 207–8.
[3] See Cibber, *Apology*, I, pp. 150–3.
[4] Pepys, *Diary*, 15, 16 and 20 April 1667; documents cited Nicoll, *HED*, I, p. 287.

to the changes of front in English theatre as the Merry Monarch wore out his mirth, his brother ate sour grapes, the granddaughters of Clarendon put England before Rome, and the Princes of Hanover put the Electorate before England. Staunchly royalist as a profession during the early Restoration period, though there was a painful spate of polemical banned plays at the time of the 'Popish Plot',[1] theatre allied itself with the Tory interest. Not till after the 1688 Revolution did Whig ideas get a firm foothold on stage. Dryden remained belligerently Tory, and drew Government fire with his *Cleomenes* in 1692; but other playwrights soon showed themselves fiercely anti-Jacobite. Rowe's *Tamerlane*, produced in 1701 as the War of the Spanish Succession was getting under way, was ostentatiously an allegory of King William's struggle with Louis XIV and became a regular Whig party piece, in the repertory only when Whigs were uppermost. Under Queen Anne 'another face of things was seen', and in the welter of clashing allegiances and shifting factions the stage temporized, at least not openly attacking the High Church Tory position. Cibber indeed claimed to have been a Whig at heart all the time, but no such thing showed in his repertory policy at Drury Lane. The startling success of Addison's *Cato* in 1713 seems to have rested in part on the fact that both parties considered its treatment of political liberty good party propaganda. When George in pudding-time came o'er, Drury Lane became overtly Whig and noisily loyal to the Hanoverian cause. Cibber's heavy-handed version of Molière's *Tartuffe*, *The Non-Juror* (1717), was a virulent attack on the Jacobites. Lincoln's Inn Fields remained neutral and was accused (by the rival house) of Tory sympathies. During the 1720s the Tory party lost ground, and the division between Walpole Whigs and Opposition Whigs became significant. It was perhaps for political reasons that Cibber refused the offer of Gay's *Beggar's Opera* with its cheerful digs at Walpole in 1728. Rich of course snapped it up, and would have brought out its sequel, *Polly*, the following year if Walpole (acting through the Lord Chamberlain) had not suppressed the production. Cibber was popularly held responsible for this intervention, and as a consequence his own ballad opera, *Love is a Riddle*, was damned by the Town. Cibber's vociferous support of authority was rewarded in 1730 with the Laureateship, a significant step in his progress towards the throne of Dullness in Pope's *Dunciad*.[2] Earlier in 1730 Fielding had jumped into the political arena, and his Haymarket pieces grew more blatantly anti-Walpole each year. By contrast, Lillo's *London*

[1] See Allardyce Nicoll, 'Political Plays of the Restoration', *Modern Language Review*, XVI (July–October 1921), pp. 224–42.
[2] A full account of the Cibber–Pope feud is given by Barker, op. cit. pp. 204–20.

*Merchant* in 1731 was written without polemic, in the same serious social vein as Steele's mercantile comedy, *The Conscious Lovers* (1722). They both became establishment pieces, supporting the political and social orthodoxy of the ruling class as a whole, an orthodoxy that was more and more closely identified with a patriotic 'Whig' philosophy. Though diehard factions did lift their voices in the audiences, there were many less committed theatre-goers who enjoyed the theatre of conformity and also the theatre of opposition. The reason that the Little Theatre in the Haymarket was able to keep playing and earning its nickname of 'Fielding's Scandal Shop' until its temerity provoked the Licensing Act of 1737 was that its repertory of satire, song, knockabout and shameless gossip exactly suited its patrons.[1]

## (xii) Size of companies

Companies grew larger, programmes longer and more varied after the turn of the century. About two dozen players, of whom only about a third were women, had been enough for a London playhouse giving a single five-act play with prologue and epilogue as an evening's entertainment in the Restoration period; but Garrick had over eighty people on the strength of Drury Lane in the season 1748–9, with singers, dancers and speciality turns to plump out his long programme of major play, afterpiece and assorted entr'-actes. Outside London things were often very different. The company a Mr Jones took round South Wales in 1741 set out with half a dozen players and was once down to three, but contrived to play Farquhar's *Beaux' Stratagem* – no doubt by extensive cutting and doubling.[2] A more prosperous venture, John Hippisley's summer vacation company at Jacob's Wells, Bristol, during the years 1741–8 varied from fifteen to twenty-one in strength, including six to eleven actresses. Its repertory included fifteen plays by Shakespeare, with fifteen comedies and six tragedies by Restoration and eighteenth-century favourites, notably Farquhar and Rowe.[3]

## (xiii) The repertory pattern

A great deal of modern scholarship has been devoted to assembling precise information about the day-by-day choice of entertainment in London during

[1] The whole subject of this paragraph is well treated by John Loftis, *Politics of Drama*.
[2] See F. T. Wood, 'Strolling Actors in the Eighteenth Century', *Englische Studien*, LXVI (August 1931), pp. 16–53, especially pp. 29–31.
[3] See Rosenfeld, 'Actors in Bristol'.

the theatrical seasons from 1660–1 onwards. The volumes of *The London Stage* contain much material on which to base box-office statistics, and are indexed in such a way that the fortunes of any play or author can be followed at will through the repertory pattern.[1] It is the detail of such investigations which compels interest: summaries of popularity trends can be both dull and misleading, partly because much work still remains to be done in collecting facts, and partly because the insidious implication of any general statement about what was actually staged is that the people concerned in the events recorded knew clearly what the sum of their separate actions would amount to, and shared, as they went along, a set of critical assumptions by which they promoted one thing or rejected another. Some of them sometimes were as determined and dogmatic as a summary of their actions suggests, and if they said so at the time their testimony is valuable. But much of the surface pattern of repertory lists is like the eddies and ripples of flowing water – explicable in terms of current, undercurrent hazards below the surface, accidental percussions; but not the result of concerted planning and not revealing very much about the nature of the river itself. Only with this in mind is it worth indicating a few general trends.

There are three main choices for repertory programming: (1) new plays, never staged before; (2) straight revivals; (3) translations and adaptations freshly prepared. After the theatrical interregnum, managers were obliged to base their programmes on revivals, drawing freely on Beaumont and Fletcher, Jonson, Shakespeare and other popular pre-war dramatists; soon followed reworkings of this English heritage; versions of continental material, mainly French and Spanish; and a small but gradually increasing number of brand-new plays.[2] Both the versions and the new plays themselves entered the revivals class as the century wore on, tending to be staged in preference to newer versions or untried new pieces, even by playwrights who had made a breakthrough. Some managers throughout the period fought shy of new work, and established successes were preferred by the players for their benefit performances. Long runs were rare before 1700 – *Oedipus*, by Dryden and Lee, 'took prodigiously, being acted 10 days together' in 1679[3] – but were more frequent and longer in the eighteenth century. Of the immediate suc-

---

[1] *The London Stage 1660–1800* (Carbondale, Ill., 1960–8). Part 1, 1660–1700, ed. W. Van Lennep; Part 2, 1700–1729, 2 vols, ed. E. L. Avery; Part 3, 1729–1747, 2 vols, ed. A. H. Scouten; Part 4, 1747–1776, 3 vols, ed. G. W. Stone; Part 5, 1776–1800, 3 vols, ed. C. B. Hogan.

[2] See A. L. Woehl, 'Some Plays in the Repertories of the Patent Houses', in *Studies in Speech and Drama in Honor of A. M. Drummond* (Ithaca, N.Y., 1944), pp. 105–22.

[3] Downes, *Roscius Anglicanus*, p. 37.

cesses, Otway's *Venice Preserved* (1682),[1] Congreve's *Old Bachelor* (1693) and *The Beggar's Opera* (1728) occasion a modern theatregoer no surprise, while to be told that the rest of Congreve's plays,[2] the comedies of Farquhar and a number of other 'manners' comedies proved their worth as popular revivals, and held the stage throughout the period, seems only natural. It is salutary to look at the less hallowed successes – Thomas Shadwell's *Lancashire Witches* (1681), Samuel Johnson of Cheshire's *Hurlothrumbo* (1729) or Henry Carey's *Dragon of Wantley* (1737), with sixty-seven performances in its opening season. These pieces took and held, whether we can see why or not. The eminence in our own day of Addison, Fielding and Dryden as literary figures makes it easier to accept the fact that *Cato*, many Haymarket skits, and pieces as diverse as *Sir Martin Mar-All* (1667) and *King Arthur* (1691), let alone *The Spanish Friar* (1680), appealed more to their first public than a casual reading seems to explain today. That the blazing rants of Lee's *Rival Queens* (1677), the heroic pathos of Southerne's *Oroonoko* (1695, based on Mrs Behn's novel), the morbid sensuality of Rowe's *Fair Penitent* (1703) and the awe-inspiring bourgeois morality of Lillo's *London Merchant* (1731) earned these plays and others by the same authors a safe and honoured place in repertory is a fact that the modern reader blinks at, unless by some lucky chance he has seen any of them played. The truth is that neither these nor any other stage successes of the period were judged on their literary pretensions alone. Given anything like the original acting style and the same intimate relationship of stage and auditorium, these pieces still have power to cast their old spell, and to prove once again that success in repertory is rarely in proportion to intrinsic literary excellence.

The repertory pattern in this period can be analysed from different points of view, and every special study illumines in its own way the vogues and vagaries of a public taste manifested in far wider fields than that of theatre. The fortunes of individual English playwrights, which have been traced in much detail, reflect fashions of thought: Beaumont and Fletcher enjoyed an enormous post-Restoration prestige, which waned after the turn of the century,[3] while Jonson held his own[4] and Shakespeare became an increasingly

---

[1] See A. M. Taylor, *Next to Shakespeare: Otway's Venice Preserv'd and The Orphan and their History on the London Stage* (Durham, N.C., 1950).
[2] See E. L. Avery, *Congreve's Plays on the Eighteenth Century Stage* (London, 1951).
[3] A. C. Sprague's *Beaumont and Fletcher on the Restoration Stage* was cited on p. 134, n. 6; see also J. H. Wilson, *The Influence of Beaumont and Fletcher on Restoration Drama* (Columbus, Ohio, 1928).
[4] See R. G. Noyes, *Ben Jonson on the English Stage 1660–1776* (Cambridge, Mass., 1935).

national and patriotic favourite.[1] French influence came in waves, strong in heroic and neoclassical tragedy, strong also in fashionable comedy: Molière was a continual stimulus and quarry throughout the period.[2] Spanish sources had a vogue, fostered by the king himself, in the Restoration years, but lost attraction after the turn of the century.[3] Certain themes became popular and were used with success in several rival pieces: Jewish history and tales from the East, the great treasure-house of classical literature and annals, the records of ancient and modern foreign affairs, the legends of Ancient Britain and chronicles of England from her Anglo-Saxon origins, all offered material for ambitious writing and evanescent hack-work that rode the tide of repertory together and appealed irrespective of their literary merit to the particular political and philosophical interests of a nation that took itself very seriously beneath the pleasure-seeking surface. Wherever the thread is teased out, it leads to a phenomenon outside theatre: the success of *Oroonoko*, for example, has something to do with the dawning respect for the 'noble savage', as well as with the personal attraction of Barton Booth in the leading role. Two placing procedures should be adopted by students of stage history who are faced with evidence that a given play or theme was a repertory favourite: the first is to look across at the poetry, belles-lettres and fiction of the same date, to see whether any general conclusion about current taste is suggested; the second is to check surviving cast-lists for premières and revivals of the given play, or plays on the given theme, to see whether the popularity of an actor is affecting the success of his vehicle. Until James Nokes retired, for example,

[1] Among the wealth of Shakespeare material, the study by Hazelton Spencer, *Shakespeare Improved* (cited on p. 134, n. 7), and the articles by A. H. Scouten, cited on p. 134, n. 1, and p. 134, n. 3, are of special value: reference should also be made to G. C. D. Odell, *Shakespeare from Betterton to Irving*, 2 vols (New York, 1920; London, 1921), and to G. C. Branam, *Eighteenth Century Adaptations of Shakespearean Tragedy* (Berkeley and Los Angeles, 1956). Good accounts of individual plays are Max Schulz, '*King Lear*: a Box-Office Maverick among Shakespearian Tragedies on the London Stage 1700–01 to 1749–50', *Tulane Studies in English*, VII (1957), pp. 83–90, and A. H. Scouten and Leo Hughes, 'A Calendar of Performances of *1 Henry IV* and *2 Henry IV* during the First Half of the Eighteenth Century', *Journal of English and Germanic Philology*, XLIII (January 1944), pp. 23–41. See also C. B. Hogan's calendar of eighteenth-century performances of Shakespeare (*Shakespeare in the Theatre 1701–1800*).

[2] Nicoll reviews the pattern of borrowing from French sources and gives references to further studies in *HED*, I, pp. 95–9, 186–91, and II, pp. 71–3, 143–6, 417, 419. A valuable study of Molière's influence is J. Wilcox, *The Relation of Molière to Restoration Comedy* (New York, 1938).

[3] Sir Samuel Tuke's *Adventures of Five Hours* (1663) and Crowne's *Sir Courtly Nice* (1685) were both worked from Spanish sources at Charles II's personal request, and both highly successful. Nicoll reviews Spanish influence on the comedy of this period in *HED*, I, pp. 191 f., and II, p. 146.

the public which flocked to *Sir Martin Mar-All* was saying 'yes' to Nokes as much as to Dryden – or to Molière and Quinault, Dryden's sources.

A very significant section of repertory in this period, and indeed in the next, includes plays about the theatre and dramatic fashions, of which Buckingham's *Rehearsal* (first staged in 1671) and Fielding's *Tom Thumb*, expanded in 1731 as *The Tragedy of Tragedies*, are only the most famous examples. Familiarity bred affection as well as contempt, and the spectacle of playwrights and players pulling each other to pieces never failed to divert the society in which they normally tried to shine.[1]

Another interesting topic to trace through the repertory pattern is the fate of pieces by actor-dramatists, intended as star-vehicles for their authors. John Lacy's *Sauny the Scot* (1667), a racy version of Shakespeare's *Taming of the Shrew*, was superseded in 1716 by two rival afterpieces, both taken from Shakespeare's comedy, both entitled *The Cobbler of Preston*: the first, by the lawyer Charles Johnson, was advertised well in advance of its opening at Drury Lane in February 1716 with Pinkethman as Kit Sly; it did good business that season in spite of its rival at Lincoln's Inn Fields – slapped together by the comic actor Christopher Bullock (*c.* 1690–1722) with himself in the lead, the work of a single weekend, rehearsed on the Monday and played on the Tuesday, 24 January, ten happy days before its too much advertised namesake. Shakespeare's play next appeared as a ballad farce in two acts by James Worsdale, *A Cure for a Scold* (Dublin and Drury Lane, 1735), which prevailed until yet another actor, Garrick, brought out his *Catherine and Petruchio* in 1756.

## (xiv) A model repertory

Perhaps the clearest comment on the established standard repertory of this period is provided by the list of plays which the emigrating company headed by Lewis Hallam (1714–56) prepared for the New World in 1752.[2] The 'twenty-four plays and their attendant farces' had been 'selected, cast and put in study before embarkation; and during the passage they were regularly rehearsed'. The quarterdeck of the *Charming Sally* in fact rang with lines that were utterly familiar to English audiences of the mid-century. Besides one pantomime, *Harlequin Collector, or, The Miller Outwitted*, which had first appeared at William Hallam's New Wells Theatre, Goodman's Fields, in May 1748, the afterpieces included Garrick's three current hits, *Lethe* (1740),

[1] See Dane F. Smith, op. cit.
[2] See William Dunlap, *History of the American Theatre* (1832), 2 vols (London, 1833), pp. 5–18, 26, 29.

*The Lying Valet* (1741) and *Miss in Her Teens* (1747), the last from a French source of 1691 (see Plate 32); Fielding's *Mock Doctor* (1732), which is from Molière; Cibber's ballad opera *Damon and Phillida* (1729); Hippisley's ballad opera *Flora* (1729), which is a version of Cibber's musical entertainment *Hob in the Well* (1711), itself based on a farce by Doggett (1696); Charles Coffey's musical farce *The Devil to Pay* (1731), which is based on the very popular *Devil of a Wife* by the actor Thomas Jevon (1652–88); and Edward Ravenscroft's musical piece *The Anatomist* (1697), in which the low comedian Cave Underhill (*c.* 1634–1710) had scored such a hit. The twenty-four major pieces comprised sixteen comedies and eight tragedies. Shakespeare contributed *Hamlet, Othello* and *Richard III* (this last no doubt in Cibber's recension of 1700), together with *The Merry Wives of Windsor, Henry IV* (perhaps in Betterton's version, *Part 1* (1700) or *Part 2* (1709)) and *The Merchant of Venice* – in its original form as arranged by Macklin, not *The Jew of Venice*, Granville's adaptation of 1700. Of other playwrights, Farquhar is the best represented, providing *The Constant Couple* (1699), *The Twin Rivals* (1702), *The Recruiting Officer* (1706) and *The Beaux' Stratagem* (1707), as well as *The Inconstant* (1702), which is a version of Fletcher's *Wild Goose Chase*. Rowe offers three tragedies – *The Fair Penitent* (1703), which is a version of Massinger's *Fatal Dowry*; *Jane Shore* (1714), a self-styled imitation of Shakespeare by his first serious editor; and the sublimely Whig *Tamerlane* (1701). Here too are the companion Whig pieces, Lillo's *London Merchant* (1731), which represents bourgeois sentiment, and Steele's *Conscious Lovers* (1722), which happily adapts the *Andria* of Terence and so illustrates the pervasive influence of classical authors. The comedy of humours provides Sir Robert Howard's *The Committee* (1662), a politically geared piece which survived for its one superb part, Teague the Irish footman, created by John Lacy. Congreve's *Love for Love* (1695) and Vanbrugh's *Provoked Husband* (1697) stand for the Restoration comedy of manners; Cibber's *Careless Husband* (1704) represents genteel comedy, and also the parts-written-for-players tradition, as Lady Betty Modish was made for Oldfield, and Lord Foppington for Cibber himself. There remain one heroic tragedy, Lee's *Theodosius* (1680), with the splendid part of Pulcheria, created by Mrs Betterton; one belated specimen of Spanish influence on comedy, *Woman is a Riddle* (1716), made over from Calderón's *La Dama Duende* by its star, Christopher Bullock; one recent London success, *The Suspicious Husband* (1747), by the king's physician Benjamin Hoadly, in which Garrick had created the great part of Ranger (see Plate 33); and the smash-hit of the century, Gay's *Beggar's Opera*.

With this repertory, the small company of eight men, four women and three children set out to take the New World by storm. The list reveals that Hallam's judgement was substantially that of a whole generation of theatre-goers. An actors' repertory, conventional and conservative, but lively, varied, and throwing in literary excellence as a bonus, the choice illustrates very neatly both aspects of the playwright–player relationship Dryden had pin-pointed, as near the end of his own working life in the theatre he looked forward to the new age:

> Thus they jog on; still tricking, never thriving;
> And Murd'ring Plays, which they miscal Reviving . . .
> With length of Time, much Judgment, and more Toil,
> Not ill they Acted, what they cou'd not spoil.[1]

[1] 'To Mr Granville, on his Excellent Tragedy, call'd Heroick Love' (1698), ll. 23–4, 33–4.

# III Plays and playwrights

*A. H. Scouten*

# 1 The emergence and development of restoration comedy

## (a) EARLY TRENDS AND CHARACTERISTICS

### (i) The new drama and the old

In the forty years after the monarchy was restored the playwrights created a remarkable body of dramatic literature, especially in comedy, which has been a subject of controversy ever since. The new comedy dominated the stage until the middle of the eighteenth century and then began to disappear. In the next century, Macaulay rejected it, and the critics regarded it as immoral or foreign, sometimes both. However, in modern times the Restoration plays have come back into favour. Man's grimmer re-estimate of the human condition, evident since the First World War, may be a factor in the modern reconsideration of these plays. The three-year run of *The Beggar's Opera* in London in the 1920s apparently led to the revival of Restoration comedies on the stage. The audiences responded with delight and excitement; thus a new vogue developed, and interest now seems to be increasing rather than diminishing.

In order to relate the new plays after 1660 to the dramatic traditions of the previous age and to indicate the nature of the new drama which was emerging, several matters must be dealt with immediately. Some misconceptions still prevail. The fame of *The Country Wife* and *The Way of the World* created the popular impression that Restoration comedy consists of only one type, variously termed high comedy, wit comedy, sex comedy or the comedy of manners, and that this kind of play appeared, full-blown, with the arrival of Charles II in 1660. Actually, the period saw the development of several highly distinct genres, among which the comedies of manners were relatively late in emerging.[1] About 440 new plays (or old plays substantially revised) were produced between 1660 and 1700, and the first thing to be said about them is that they are quite varied, from Christopher Fishbourne's pornographic *Sodom* to Purcell and Tate's charming *Dido and Aeneas*. There is so much variety that it is difficult to see how Allardyce Nicoll could have given a coherent picture of such a diverse body of drama in his valuable *History of Restoration Drama, 1660–1700* in 1923 without resorting to categories and classifications.[2] Since this informative pioneer work, critics have been too anxious to emphasize the category of 'comedy of manners'. Clifford Leech has pointed out the dangers in reducing the comedies to such categories as the intrigue play and the comedy of manners, particularly when there is rarely a pure example of the type.[3] Some plays with obvious similarities may conveniently be discussed together; otherwise, a more accurate and less biased picture may be given by proceeding chronologically by author through a number of representative plays.

Another problem is the relation of the new plays to the dramatic conventions of the previous age; explaining this relationship will also indicate the dangers of broad generalizations about Restoration drama. Older authors – Davenant, Thomas Killigrew and the Duke of Newcastle – had written plays before 1660; their styles were established, and their new plays naturally reflect a connection with the older drama. Then there were new playwrights like John Wilson, Edward Revet and Thomas Shadwell who deliberately carried on older traditions: in this case, Jonsonian humours. A most significant factor was the change in language. The characteristic that Restoration poets asserted was their refinement of the language. They felt that previous writers lacked ease and grace in both poetry and prose. For example, the reader who approaches the Restoration period after a study of drama from 1576 to 1642 might well expect James Shirley's comedies to be popular, especially *The*

---

[1] See Robert D. Hume, 'Diversity and Development in Restoration Comedy, 1660–1679', *Eighteenth-Century Studies*, V (1972), pp. 365–97.
[2] Now Vol. I of Allardyce Nicoll, *History of English Drama 1660–1900*, 6 vols (Cambridge, 1952–9) (Nicoll, *HED*).
[3] Clifford Leech, 'Restoration Comedy: The Earlier Phase', *Essays in Criticism*, I (1951), pp. 165–84.

*Lady of Pleasure* and *Hyde Park*. Yet the performance records in *The London Stage* show only one production for the latter and none at all for the former during the years 1660–1700.[1] In explanation, Bernard Harris states 'that the comparative neglect of Shirley's best social comedies . . . is a sharp corrective to many easy assumptions about the essential continuity' of the two periods, and he provides an analysis of Shirley's dialogues to demonstrate how far they fell short of Restoration prose.[2] The ease and grace of conversation in the new period Dryden called 'the last and greatest advantage of our writing'.

That Restoration comedy was indeed new and different may be shown by examining some of the changes made in adaptations of the older drama. Until new works were composed, Killigrew and Davenant, proprietors of the two patent companies, had to offer old ones, many of them in an altered form. In fact, it is curious that Davenant was under the obligation of revising Shakespeare's plays to be permitted to stage them.[3] Among the most popular of these was *The Tempest* (1667), prepared for the stage by Dryden and Davenant. Dryden's high praise of Davenant's structural changes is on record:

> *But Sir* William Davenant, *as he was a Man of quick and piercing imagination, soon found that somewhat might be added to the Design of* Shakespear . . . *he design'd the Counterpart to* Shakespear's *Plot, namely, that of a Man who had never seen a Woman; that by this means those two Characters of Innocence and Love might the more illustrate and commend each other.*[4]

For this new character, Hippolito, who has never seen a woman, Davenant has supplied a woman, Dorinda, who has seen no man but her father. With the spontaneity of the primitive, Hippolito decides that he wants Miranda as well (if one woman is good, two are better). This social deviation leads to a duel with the angry Ferdinand. Dissimulation and fighting did not exist before sexual knowledge, and Hippolito complains, 'We have no swords growing in our World.' The adaptation, says Norman Holland, is based on one continued joke: the contrast between the 'enchanted island' and the real

[1] E. L. Avery *et al.*, *The London Stage, 1660–1800*, 11 vols (Carbondale, Ill., 1960–8). All dates of performance and undocumented references to the theatre and stage history are taken from this work.

[2] Bernard Harris, 'The Dialect of those Fanatic Times', in J. R. Brown and B. Harris (eds), *Restoration Theatre*, Stratford-upon-Avon Studies 6 (London, 1965), pp. 19–22.

[3] John Freehafer, 'The Formation of the London Patent Companies in 1660', *Theatre Notebook*, XX (1965), pp. 6–30.

[4] Preface to *The Tempest*, in *Dryden: The Dramatic Works*, ed. M. Summers, 6 vols (London, 1931–2), II, p. 152.

world of 'the Town'.[1] When Dorinda tells Prospero she would be gentle to men so that they would not hurt her, he warns her:

> You must not trust them, Child:
> No Woman can come neer 'em but she feels
> A pain full nine months.

Davenant's design is to show the effect of knowledge, particularly sexual knowledge. Society is hostile, and the rake who has learned how to deal with the facts of an imperfect world is the final hero. Shakespeare's analogies, affirmations and final harmonies are rejected and replaced by the world of fallen man. In 1667 Milton told the story of what some modern critics like to call 'the Fortunate Fall', while Restoration dramatists showed the result.

Professor Holland calls attention to a similar pattern in the Duke of Buckingham's revision of Beaumont and Fletcher's *The Chances* (1667). Antonio is changed into an impotent lecher, the second Constantia into a blackmailing whore on one-night stands, and the Bawd to her mother:

> The change perfectly exemplifies the Restoration comic idea of the relation of parents to children. Their influence is never beneficial: in this play it is corrupting; in others repressive. Those who appear to be guides are in nature not. The use of a girl's mother for her bawd also sets a tone of universal social corruption surrounding the action, and this is an axiom of Restoration comedy – that one operates in a very fallen age indeed.[2]

I quote Holland at length here partly because his analysis helps account for modern interest in the comedy of this age but also because his remarks bring up the problem of the dangers of generalizations about literary periods. Many Restoration plays are marked by bitterness of tone, and parents and other older characters are treated with contempt or hostility in most early Restoration comedies, but not in all. The plays, as in other literary periods, were written under different circumstances and for different ends; it follows then, as in every art form, that they display irreconcilable diversity, even though literary historians are reluctant to face this fact and try to implant a single rubric.

In the recently discovered comedy *The Country Gentleman*, written by Sir Robert Howard and George Villiers, second Duke of Buckingham, for an intended production in February 1669, the tone is not bitter, and the leading

---

[1] Norman Holland, *The First Modern Comedies* (Cambridge, Mass., 1959), pp. 217–21.
[2] Ibid. pp. 214–15.

character – 'The Country Gentleman' – is an older man, a father who is treated with great respect and sympathy.[1] *The Country Gentleman* is a festive comedy somewhat like *As You Like It* or Brome's *The Jovial Crew*, lacking even the temporary hardships in those plays for the principal characters. Sir Richard Plainbred, the leading character, is a vehement partisan of the West of England and plain country living, an upholder of English linguistic purity, and an opponent of French foods and customs. Far from being the heavy father usual in Restoration comedy, he is lenient, good-humoured and sensible; he thoroughly relishes his daughters' tricks on the two fops, and looks with warm approval on the suitors Worthy and Lovetruth, themselves country gentlemen from the West of England. Throughout the play, Sir Richard extols the plain, old-fashioned English country virtues. A modern reader, who had read too many generalizations about Restoration drama, might suppose Sir Richard the butt of raillery and satire, yet he is constantly endorsed and held up for admiration. At the same time, within this largely genial play there is such savage personal satire of a member of the King's Privy Council, Sir William Coventry, that the victim challenged the Duke of Buckingham to a duel, eliciting the intervention of the ambassador from France, and final action from Charles II, who sent Coventry to the Tower and interdicted the play. Thus the personal satire in *The Country Gentlemen* places this comedy in the current vogue of plays with personal satire, Shadwell's *The Sullen Lovers* (1668), the Duke of Newcastle's *The Heiress* (1669) and the Duke of Buckingham's later play, *The Rehearsal* (1671), but the air of 'festive comedy' diverges sharply from the bitterness of tone that characterizes other contemporary plays, notably those of Etherege and Wycherley.

Returning to the adaptations, we shall find still further problems in the categorizing of Restoration drama. It is the well-known thesis of Bonamy Dobrée, in his study of this period, that satirists are conservatives, protectors of the traditions of society. Attacks on the rising class of former Puritans and defences of the old order are prevalent in the new plays, as we shall soon see, yet some of the comedies are marked by an iconoclasm which again makes generalizations about the period difficult. Here, an adaptation from Molière deserves special notice. The actor-manager Thomas Betterton drew upon *George Dandin* for his popular and influential comedy *The Amorous Widow; or, The Wanton Wife*, *c.* 1669 (a play that, in other respects, is properly considered by some critics to have led towards the development of 'sex comedy').

[1] The MS of this play was found in 1973 by A. H. Scouten and R. D. Hume and reported in *TLS*, 28 September 1973, pp. 1105–6. It has now been edited by them (Philadelphia, 1976).

Molière includes some gentle ridicule of an elderly couple belonging to the rural petty nobility who put on airs above their proper status in rebuking their son-in-law, a rich farmer. Betterton transforms Dandin into a rich London tradesman, Barnaby Brittle, who has caught a young rake carrying on an affair with Mrs Brittle, 'the wanton wife'. Brittle complains to her parents, the Prides (as he has had to finance the old couple to save their estate). Instead of being sympathetic, the aged parents boast of their old and honourable lineage, prating about honour, the proper titles of respect and the differences between the Prides and the Brittles until one realizes that the concepts of social hierarchy and rank are being criticized, concepts that Molière never dreamed of questioning. Consequently, as we survey plays dealing with the class war, we must remember that there are also examples of iconoclasm, as in *The Amorous Widow* and Wycherley's *The Plain Dealer*.

## (ii) Political plays against the Puritans

The comedy of manners was by no means the first kind of new drama to appear at the reopening of the theatres. Such precedence belongs to a group of topical, political comedies, to musical drama or the heroic play, and to the comedy of Spanish romance. It is not surprising that a cluster of topical satires should constitute the first group of new plays, for one characteristic of much Restoration drama (including the tragedies) is recognition of the class war. The older élite had lost much of their wealth, both in land and investments, while a multitude of industrious merchants were raising England into a commercial empire and forming a *nouveau riche* class superseding the Tudor establishment. ('I was not born to ease or Acres,' says the rogue Wheadle, in a fine irony from Etherege's *The Comical Revenge*; 'Industry is all my stock of living.') The expatriates swarming or straggling back into England in 1660 were well aware of the upward thrust from the lower classes and were determined to beat them down, even as they borrowed money from the new merchants and married their children off to these purveyors of ready cash. The animosity was virulent: Teague (in *The Committee*) responds with incredulous laughter and Careless and Blunt with rage on learning that the former kitchen maid Mrs Day owns a coach. In 1660, the Commonwealth had ended, the king had come into his own again, and the royalist writers were itching to ridicule the deposed saints.

While many plays contain jeers at the Puritans, the early group consists of John Tatham's *The Rump* (1660); the poet Abraham Cowley's *Cutter of Coleman Street* (1661), a revision of his earlier work *The Guardian*; Sir Robert

Howard's *The Committee* (1662); John Wilson's *The Cheats* (1663); and John Lacy's *The Old Troop* (1663). Much of Tatham's political allegory in *The Rump* is crude propaganda. However, the portrayal of Lady Bertlam's social pretensions is skilfully done, comic tension being generated by the audience's knowledge, in the spring of 1660, that these pretensions would never be realized. Tatham creates a vivid satire at the end in a vindictive and grotesque scene where Cromwell's lieutenants burst out into the street like frenzied hucksters, offering turnips, oranges and 'geodly ballads', while a mob of boys taunt Dame Cromwell.

Abraham Cowley's *Cutter of Coleman Street* continues the ridicule of the Commonwealth state, but with some differences. Where Howard shows only a simple dichotomy of staunch royalists in the hands of hypocritical Puritans, and where Tatham, Lacy and Wilson see only unrelieved greed and opportunism, Cowley, as a metaphysical poet, was capable of seeing multiple points of view, and he presented more complex situations. Unfortunately, since he was not a professional dramatist, his conception is often better than his execution. Still, he has some good episodes. Jolly suffered for the king at Oxford, but he blames himself for having got involved there. Jolly also regains his sequestered property by marrying one of the saints, Mistress Barebottle, whose deceased husband had bought Jolly's estate from the committee of sequestration. This stroke of realism, which only portrayed what was going on all over England, drew sharp criticism from the initial audience.

Cowley moves immediately into a study of appearance and reality with his dramatis personae. The role-playing begins with Cutter and Worm pretending to be royalist army officers ruined by Cromwell's triumphs, and Cutter mourns over his escape from the *débâcle* at Worcester in disguise. Jolly sardonically expresses a desire to see Cutter disguised as a gentleman. Cutter's desire lies elsewhere, for he makes a new entry as Abednego, a newly converted independent preacher ready to exhort the faithful on Coleman Street. Worm now pretends to be Jolly's long-lost (and deceased) merchant brother just returned from the 'Tartar' tribes in Africa, accompanied by Puny, who pretends to be his servant Remembrancer John (so called because he must always refresh his master's memory). Jolly detects the ruse and counters by dressing two of his servants (one having had real thespian training as the bear in *Mucedorus*) as the merchant brother and Remembrancer John.

Another of these political plays, Howard's *The Committee*, has had only brief notice and needs to be examined more closely. Indeed its meaning is so clear that no critical explication is required, but the play is significant in that the central conflict is maintained rather than resolved. On one side are the Puritans, exemplified by a sequestration committee under the chairmanship of Mr Day, whose wife, a former kitchen maid, is a dictatorial, arrogant and loudmouthed upstart. Against them are two orphaned daughters of royalist gentry and two young colonels from the king's army, back in England to compound for their estates. The Days have secured the deeds to the estate of one orphan, Ruth, and they intend to acquire the land of the other, Arabella, by arranging for her to marry their son Abel. The most bitter animosity exists between the two groups. The colonels hate the Puritan conquerors so much that, in a bitter scene, they refuse to take the covenant (prerequisite to a consideration of compounding for their land), denounce the committee and stalk out of court. Yet the quickwitted Ruth manages a fortunate solution wherein the royalists will regain their estates and the two plucky young women will marry the two Cavaliers.

How this is done merits some attention. The time of the action must be close to 1660, as Mrs Day forges a letter addressed to Mr Day, supposedly from the absent Charles II, in order to strengthen her husband's standing with his committee. The implication is that the minor Puritan leaders are not unaware that Charles may return to power and they wish to hedge against this contingency. But the baulking of the committee is not achieved by the king's coming into his own again; the Commonwealth regime is still entrenched in power as the play ends. What happens is that the innocent orphan, Ruth, uses theft and blackmail. Mr Day, greedily excited to learn that he is to be the executor of a colleague's will, forgetfully puts down the keys to his closet as he rushes off to visit the dying friend. Ruth takes the keys and rifles the cabinet to discover not only the deed to her father's estate but some incriminating letters to Mr Day from two women. One requests additional money for a bastard child fathered by the committee chairman, and the other rejects a suggestion for an abortion. Ruth also comes upon the letter Mrs Day had forged. Hence, when the Days intend to have soldiers imprison the two colonels, Ruth blocks the plan and states her terms: she and Arabella will retain their property; Arabella need not marry young Abel Day; and the two colonels will have their land restored. To soften the blow, she promises a £500 bribe to the Days. Irked by the information about her husband's wenches, Mrs Day remains stubborn and wants to summon the soldiers. Wait, interposes Ruth, do you want your husband turned out of office as chairman of the committee? Here is the letter from the king; it might cause you worse trouble. At this point, Mrs Day capitulates, but the significant aspect to notice is that the original conflict is not resolved. The two young women and their colonels have regained their property, but the country continues under the Commonwealth, and the committee will continue with bribery and extortion. The young couples yearn for the return of the king; the committee want the Puritan regime to endure. Earlier in the play, in a great farcical scene perpetuated by eighteenth-century engravings, the loyalist Teague had cajoled Obadiah, clerk of the committee, into overimbibing and had persuaded him to drink the king's health. In the final scene, the Irishman again brings the clerk on stage, at dagger's point, but the tenacious Obadiah refuses to drink to the Stuarts even if Teague uses the dagger.

Here is a situation much different from those at the end of most Elizabethan comedies. We can see the difference if we look at the resolution of Act IV of an older play which contains much bitterness, *The Merchant of Venice*. The bond is invalidated, Bassanio can marry Portia, and a favour is done to Shylock by making him a Christian. Moral lessons have been taught: hate breeds hate, but love breeds love; and thereafter (also invoking other Shakespearian comedies) there is a universal harmony. All will go well if people can hear the music and follow the rhythms. But though the young lovers in *The Committee* are going to marry, the conflict between Puritan and loyalist remains at the end of the play. The kitchen maids want to come up in the world and own their own coach; the royalists want to regain their prerogatives and put the lower classes back in their place, but they lack the power to execute their will. Control changes several times during the course of the action. When Colonel Blunt puts down the constables with his sword, the clerk Obadiah brings in regular army troops to capture and imprison Blunt. To be sure, once he reaches the gaol former soldiers from the king's regiments help him out, but the scene is one of protracted conflict. By theft, blackmail and bribery, the young couples extricate themselves, but there is no harmony.

If we turn from Howard's play to later Restoration comedies, we shall see the same patterns. Those social and economic conflicts that are presented at the beginning of the plays remain at the end. This is not to say that these dramatists discovered evil in the world or that they could achieve the brilliant psychological analysis of an evil character in the way that Middleton, Marston or Webster could do. For one thing, the new playwrights were not trying to portray any one specific individual; instead, they dealt with fops, fools, avaricious widows, sexual perverts and other types. In contrast to Molière, 'They set out to amuse by pointing out the deficiencies of life, he by pointing out those of men and women'.[1]

[1] Norman Suckling, 'Molière and English Restoration Comedy', in Brown and Harris (eds), *Restoration Theatre*, p. 102.

That is to say, of the different types of comedy in world literature, Restoration comedy more closely resembles the plays of Plautus in classical comedy and Ben Jonson in earlier English drama than it resembles the comedies of Shakespeare, Dekker or Chapman before them or the sentimental drama after them.[1] The new playwrights generally stand with Ben Jonson in a cold, unflinching view of man's hostility towards his fellow man, in contrast to the resolutions provided by Shakespearian harmony or to the optimistic ideology of benevolence which emerged in the next century. In retrospect, we can observe that Howard, offering his play in 1662 to a partisan audience, could easily have invoked poetic justice and solved the young couples' problems by announcing the return of Charles II; instead, he constructed a plot in which there is no such sweeping reversal.

### (iii) The comedy of Spanish romance

Another aspect of the new drama can be found in those plays influenced by Spanish literature.[2] The works in this group are characterized by complicated intrigue plots, high-spirited women and a rigid code of ethics. The fathers or guardians are choleric and headstrong; the young heroes are proud and idealistic; the women are witty, resourceful and honourable – but they want their own way. These heroines object to arranged marriages, but they are virtuous in the extreme. The most important was *The Adventures of Five Hours* (1663). Complications arise from mistaken identity, and Antonio, the hero, is placed in circumstances that cause a conflict of love against his code of honour. (In such situations, rhymed couplets replace blank verse.) The two pairs of young lovers have idealistic attitudes, and their language is free from any indecency. The vivacious young ladies are not the losers in any duel of wits, but no *double entendre* or indecorous remarks appear in their talk. Against this serious plot are set the low-comedy scenes of the gossiping servants, whose cowardice affects the progress of the main plot.

Turning to the history of this influential piece, we find that its composition was urged by Charles II, that fashionable society attended rehearsals and that the production was an outstanding success, acted for thirteen consecutive performances. Praise came from several sources. Pepys for example found the play 'without one word of ribaldry, and the house, by its frequent plaudits, did show their sufficient approbation'. Thus the nature and the

---

[1] This view is set forth in detail in Howard L. Koonce's unpublished University of Pennsylvania Ph.D. dissertation, *Comic Values and Comic Form* (1969).
[2] See John Loftis, *The Spanish Plays of Neoclassical England* (New Haven, Conn., 1973).

reception of Tuke's dramatic effort proves, significantly, that a play did not have to contain 'bawdy' to be popular, and, for those who like archetypes, it contains the essence of both the heroic drama and social comedy.

The author was the royalist Sir Samuel Tuke, though some contemporaries name George Digby, the second Earl of Bristol, as author or collaborator. Digby had been brought up in Spain, where his father had been ambassador for James I, and he showed his acquaintance with Spanish drama in a series of pieces similar to *The Adventures*. Two titles are recorded as being performed between 1662 and 1665, and Downes names a third, but only one survives, *Elvira*. Its plot relies on a sequence of mistakes, the characters are idealistic, and there is no indecency whatever. In the same year as *The Adventures* and based upon some as yet unidentified Spanish source is Thomas Porter's *The Carnival*. Again we find the conflict of love and honour, and the leading characters are affected by the generosity and goodness of other characters. A serious complication in the main plot is balanced by the comic capers of the servants; in addition, a subplot concerns the youthful members of a Spanish aristocratic family. Here, 'in the irresponsible Don Felices and Miranda', James Sutherland finds 'an early example of the gay couple'.[1]

Thomas St Serfe's *Tarugo's Wiles; or, The Coffee House* (1667) has little merit as a drama, but it has the same interest for the literary historian that a transition layer among the strata has for the archaeologist, and it has an important position in the evolution of the new comedy. The setting is in Spain, the source is from Spanish drama, and the characters and plot have the same characteristics as in the comedies that have just been mentioned. However, in the third act, the setting is changed to that of a London coffeehouse, where the speakers ridicule the virtuosi, blood transfusions, various projects of the Royal Society and the Puritans. The violation of unity from this structural flaw puts emphasis on the different components, and the pure state of the form of Spanish romance is at an end. When the Spanish material is drawn upon in the future, as in Wycherley's *The Gentleman Dancing-Master*, the earlier tone of the importation will disappear, and the material will be used for realistic, topical comedy.

### (iv) The development of social comedy

A vivacious couple had already appeared in Richard Rhodes's offering, *Flora's Vagaries* (1663), a work based on an Italian rather than a Spanish

---

[1] James Sutherland, *English Literature of the Late Seventeenth Century*, Vol. VI of *The Oxford History of English Literature* (Oxford, 1969), p. 95.

source. The chief character is a sprightly, uninhibited and talkative young woman named Flora, the ward of a stupid lout, old Grimaldi, who tries to keep both Flora and his beautiful but timid daughter Otrante shut up in his house. The villain Francisco asks a shy young man, Lodovico, to accompany him on a supposed venture to elope with Otrante. Actually, Francisco is trying to abduct the girl, and when Lodovico learns the true situation from Otrante's protests and Flora's gibes he quickly protects Otrante and wounds Francisco in the ensuing brawl. Her awareness being aroused by falling in love with Lodovico, Otrante correctly interprets his shyness as insecurity, and she resorts to a trick (told in the Third Tale of the Third Day in the *Decameron*, and repeated in Dryden's *The Spanish Friar* and Otway's *The Soldier's Fortune*), complaining to the friar that Lodovico has accosted her and requesting that an expensive bracelet be 'returned' to him. By carrying out her scheme, Otrante gets up enough courage to talk back to her father and Lodovico enough courage to propose. Meanwhile, Flora's suitor, Alberto, ambushes old Grimaldi and takes his clothes in a farcical episode which ends with the irate guardian locked out of his house by Flora. All four young lovers plan an elopement, but Alberto gets drunk and innocently reveals the scheme. At this juncture, the villain bursts in with his gang of cut-throats, only to be beaten off by Lodovico, and the young couples all get married.

Early in the play, Alberto, who is genuinely fond of Flora, makes the mistake of relating an anecdote at her expense where she can overhear him. She tongue-lashes him in no uncertain way and warns him that she isn't a trull because she talks freely. The result is that she elicits his respect and a more serious interest. Rhodes's comedy marks a transition point in the development of the new drama. A witty, railing actress can make the part of Flora intensely exciting, and when Nell Gwyn took the role the audience must have been greatly entertained. Consequently, the introduction of actresses on the London stage changed the medium. When the dramatists contrived plays containing vivacious young women who engage in a duel of the sexes and the managers cast the parts with sprightly and attractive actresses (as opposed to having women's roles acted by young boys as was previously done), the nature of the drama was bound to change. The playwrights now indulge in presenting the spirited love-game, with the famous encounters of Dorimant and Harriet, Mirabel and Millamant, to follow in due course.

The place of James Howard's works in the development of the new comedy was formerly overlooked: until new dates of performance were determined, he was regarded as a writer who was imitating his betters. But a Scandinavian visitor saw *The English Monsieur* (traditionally dated December 1666) in July

1663, so that we must consider Howard as an experimenter rather than a follower. The play contains a Frenchified fop and a duel of the sexes, this time between Welbred, a fashionable young man addicted to gambling, and the widow Lady Wealthy, whom he courts every time his losses run deep. She is well aware of the financial motivation and refuses to marry him until he can fee the clergyman ten gold pieces. As Welbred lacks 'the ready', he is denied admission to her house for the ceremony until he can produce a hundred pounds in gold. There are of course lively duels of wit between the two. Trick follows trick until the young rake at last has a run of luck at the gambling table. Then he loses again; however, the marriage does take place. Howard also has an amusing scene where another young rake is interrupted in his planned departure from London by the appearance of a fresh young country girl. The interruption and consequent indecision were parodied later in *The Rehearsal*. Howard adds to the mirth by having the rural miss reject the London sophisticate.

The new date of 1665 for Howard's *All Mistaken; or, The Mad Couple* gives added significance to this double-plot drama, assumed in the past to be derived from Dryden's *Secret Love*.[1] An incest motif, so frequently used by Dryden, appears in the main plot. The story is quite intricate, but in the end we learn that the hero and heroine are not after all brother and sister. Howard could have been influenced by Fletcher's *A King and No King*, very popular on the stage in these years. The other plot is farcical, containing a 'Mad Couple', Philidor and Mirida. They protest against marriage though they are in love with each other. Later, Philidor is followed by six other women who assert he has promised them marriage and by three nurses who escort bastard children of his. The author moves down another level to present a purge scene on stage, which was adversely commented upon at the time.

From the repartee of this 'Mad Couple', we can observe the direction in which the playwrights are taking drama. The earliest plays based on the Spanish are without any objectionable incidents or language. The ladies are high-spirited, but their speech is free from innuendo or vulgarity. Rhodes has Flora use a frank and lively vocabulary, with more invective and less decorum, though nothing is salacious. Thus it is James Howard, with Dryden and Etherege (as we shall see), who begin to use the racy language that can be found throughout the rest of the period, descending at times to the salacious. The heroines taken from the comedy of Spanish romance remained virtuous,

[1] See James Sutherland, 'The Date of James Howard's *All Mistaken or The Mad Couple*', *Notes and Queries*, CCIX (1964), pp. 339–40, and Robert D. Hume, 'Dryden, James Howard, and the Date of *All Mistaken*', *Philological Quarterly*, LI (1972), pp. 422–9.

however. They were also heiresses; young women without fortune and virtue never play the leading roles in Restoration comedy. A woman who lacks wealth is forced to be predatory and catch a rich but stupid husband. Lacking virtue, a young woman has no chance at all and is discarded like Bellinda or scorned like Mrs Loveit in *The Man of Mode*.

Given the variety of comic effort in the early years of the Restoration, comedy could have gone in several directions. It might have continued the Caroline mode or it could have followed the patterns of French drama, since so many members of the court had been in Paris during the Interregnum. Nevertheless, from the plays that we have been describing it can rightly be inferred that social comedy was to be dominant.

## (b) THE NEW DRAMATISTS

### (i) John Dryden

Dryden's comedies cannot be placed in any one category; instead, they reflect the general diversity. His fondness for double-plot structure led him to work chiefly in tragicomedy. He seems to pursue a zigzag course, experimenting with different types of drama. His early pieces, *The Wild Gallant* and *Secret Love*, are sex comedies of the kind that developed into the comedy of manners, but he proceeded to write heroic plays and tragicomedies; in fact, his best specimen of the comedy of manners is the subplot to *Marriage à la Mode*. His first compositions show the influence of Jonsonian humours, but he went on to write intrigue comedies in a very different style. Furthermore, he appeared diffident about his talent in comic drama and wrote, or affected to write, as if driven by necessity.

He is generally credited with helping to develop the lively young male and female leads termed the 'gay couple' by John Harrington Smith.[1] Still, the record is not clear, for his first play, *The Wild Gallant*, failed in 1663, was revised for a production in 1667 and was not printed until 1669. Hence we do not know exactly what the audience of 1663 saw. Pepys himself could not identify among the characters the 'wild gallant' of the title. Dryden does present a lively, outspoken young woman in Isabella, but she marries Sir Timorous, a stupid oaf, for his money, whereas the juvenile lead, Loveby, is paired with Lady Constance, a woman who is pleasant and cheerful rather than exuberant.

Dryden next followed the vogue of tragicomedy based on the Spanish

[1] J. H. Smith, *The Gay Couple in Restoration Comedy* (Cambridge, Mass., 1948).

romance by writing *The Rival Ladies* (1664), a work filled with intrigue and sudden reversals. Here he uses an incest motif for the first time. The hero's sister (unaware of his identity) is one of the two rival ladies who disguise themselves as pages to follow their man, vying for his favour. Montague Summers, who helped to revive interest in Restoration drama even though he discredited himself with unreliable editions and unnecessary quarrels, writes warmly and colourfully of this play:

> It is remarkable how admirably Dryden has achieved his atmosphere in *The Rival Ladies*, for, setting on one side the locale, Alicant, the swift incidents, the bandits on land and picaroons at sea, the masques and disguises, the twilight street, the duels, the ornate gallantry and brocaded honour, the thrust and riposte of clinquant dialogue, are all extremely Spanish in character and taste.[1]

Of his tragicomedy *Secret Love* (1667), Dryden complimented himself on the regularity and the 'symmetry of parts', a claim likely to elicit cynical amusement, for the 'symmetry' of the final scene portrays an idealistic queen giving up her throne and the man she loves in a situation where seven young women hover about two young men, with explicit references to the physical appearance of the original actresses. No wonder Charles II called it 'His Play'. This titillating device reminds us again that the institutional change of permitting women on the stage was to affect the nature of the works being presented. Dryden has now gone past his apprentice period, for his creation of Celadon and Florimel gives us the wittiest gay couple who have yet appeared.

The next piece with which Dryden is associated is *Sir Martin Mar-All* (1667), for which he provided corrections and alterations. The play itself was written by the elderly William Cavendish, Duke of Newcastle. The duke had made an adaptation of Quinault's *L'Amant indiscret* and needed to have a professional dramatist prepare it for the stage. Dryden was also required to devise a bigger role for the low comedian James Nokes, in the part of the stupid Sir Martin. The work is built around the farcical episodes of Sir Martin, who accidentally gives away everyone's schemes. Working with farcical material led Dryden to write a play which he labelled farce, *An Evening's Love* (1668). The play sets forth an uncompromising thesis: life and the world are for the young. There are two sets of young couples, Wildblood and Jacintha, Bellamy and Theodosia, but Theodosia is also being courted by Don Melchior de Guzman, described in the dramatis personae as

[1] In his edition of Dryden's plays, I, p. 131.

'of a Great Family, but decay'd Fortune'. Too bad for him: he is old and has lost his money. The young blade Bellamy, aided by a clever servant, upsets all of Melchior's affairs, and in the end Melchior is disgraced. This conclusion would not have been permissible in eighteenth-century drama, where sentiment would have required Melchior's restoration at the end.

In *Marriage à la Mode* (1671) Dryden attained artistic success by presenting 'a witty, realistic sexual intrigue which makes a philosophical and melancholy dissection of marriage and lust'.[1] It is indeed a thoughtful treatment of sex and marriage, and Dryden's comedy reaches its most adult level.[2] 'Every argument in favour of extra-marital relationships is brought forward with extraordinary wit,' writes Bonamy Dobrée.[3] Here is the situation Dryden contrived: tired of his beautiful wife, Doralice, the newly married Rhodophil flirts with Palamede's fiancée, Melantha, while Doralice yearns to be a wandering lady as she was before marriage. Palamede is very much attracted by her, but she finally chooses to remain constant. John Harrington Smith's description well illustrates Dryden's emphasis:

> The situation now works up exquisitely, each man wanting to have both women, especially the one he has no right to, and the two being mighty polite to each other, for each wants access to the other's female property. ... Sensing that Palamede is interested in Doralice, Rhodophil finds himself not so indifferent to his wife as he had supposed. Palamede makes a similar discovery (about Melantha).[4]

Moreover, Doralice learns more about herself, discovering that her attitudes are not what she thought they were.

It must be remembered that *Marriage à la Mode* is a tragicomedy and that Dryden brings his lofty concepts of the heroic into the same play with earthy realism of the comic in his deliberate counterpointing of lust and love, cuckoldry and honour, rake and hero. Despite the most severe tests, the lovers in the main plot are faithful to each other; in the comic plot, they are promiscuous, or, as F. H. Moore puts it, 'The serious lovers are forever indicating their heroic willingness to die for love, while the comic lovers are un-

---

[1] John Traugott, 'The Rake's Progress from Court to Comedy', *Studies in English Literature*, VI (1966), p. 392; grounds for the new date are given by Robert D. Hume, 'The Date of Dryden's *Marriage A-la-Mode*', *Harvard Library Bulletin*, XXI (1973), pp. 161–6.

[2] Sutherland, *Late Seventeenth Century*, p. 101.

[3] Bonamy Dobrée, *Restoration Comedy, 1660–1700* (London, 1924), p. 108.

[4] Smith, *The Gay Couple*, pp. 70–1.

heroically busy trying to die of it.'[1] The most delicate balance is being maintained neither to accept idealism nor to reject it. To admit such a view of the human condition requires a strong stomach indeed, especially with the conclusion that marriage should be founded upon an entirely honest intellectual analysis. It is no wonder, concludes Traugott, that 'sentimentalists have taken this comedy as a personal affront'.[2]

Dryden tried to combine these elements again in *The Assignation; or, Love in a Nunnery* (1672), but he was unable to reach the necessary balance, and the work fails on artistic grounds. In the next few years came *All for Love* and the heroic plays, so that it was 1678 before he returned to writing comedy with *The Kind Keeper; or, Mr Limberham*. The play was rejected by the audience, evidence perhaps that the playgoers did not take kindly to having their cosy practices ridiculed. It was also officially interdicted after the third performance, a strange ruling in view of Dryden's assertion that Charles II had assisted in designing the plot.[3] For the main action, the rake Woodall spends all of his time trying to seduce four different women, all of whom are willing, but they get in each other's way. The story is an exemplum of the built-in defects of complete libertinage: the lesson of Restoration comedy is that you can't satisfy two women in bed at the same time, let alone four.

Returning to his favourite double-plot structure, Dryden brought out *The Spanish Friar* in 1680. He was able to secure dramatic tension, as G. Wilson Knight points out, in that 'complexities of plot support and draw excitement from the central guilt, nemesis and recognition'.[4] The hero finds himself married to an accomplice in the intended murder of his father; he has also fought against the man he believes to be his father. Further, as Bruce King explains, 'Raymond, who began as a noble patriot hoping to defend the legitimacy of the throne, has, in judging by his own reason, become a rebel involved in a Machiavellian intrigue against the real monarch'.[5] The extreme ridicule of the title character, Father Dominick, appropriate to anti-Catholic sentiments of the moment, later led to embarrassment for Dryden and, still later, for his modern defenders.

The entertaining wit comedy *Amphitryon* appeared in 1690. The work is based on both Plautus and Molière, though the parting scene between Jupiter and Alcmena is original and contains some of Dryden's best blank verse,

[1] F. H. Moore, *The Nobler Pleasure: Dryden's Comedy in Theory and Practice* (Chapel Hill, N.C., 1963), p. 104.
[2] Traugott, op. cit. pp. 393–5.
[3] *The Letters of John Dryden*, ed. C. E. Ward (Durham, N.C., 1942), p. 11.
[4] G. Wilson Knight, *The Golden Labyrinth* (London, 1962), p. 147.
[5] Bruce King, *Dryden's Major Plays* (London, 1966), p. 155.

tender and moving. The depiction of the avaricious servant Phaedra, wooed
by the deity Mercury, is quite good. She has no morals at all; her only
characteristic is greed. This stroke is also of Dryden's own invention. His
last play, *Love Triumphant* (1694), a tragicomedy, should be mentioned only
to complete the record. The main plot is overcomplicated, and the comic
scenes are weak. Again the incest motif is included. No matter; Dryden had
already established a place for himself in the nation's drama. In comedy
proper, he never reaches the heights attained by some of his contemporaries,
but he is the one writer in this period who works with considerable success in
all of the dramatic genres. He became the supreme practitioner of the heroic
play. More to the point here, he made double-plot tragicomedy a speciality,
playing off superficially alien elements with consummate skill, as in *Marriage
à la Mode* and *The Spanish Friar*. So thoroughly professional a playwright
was Dryden that he was able to work with remarkable success in distinctly
uncongenial forms. Thus *An Evening's Love* was a profitable exercise in
enlightened Spanish romance, and *Amphitryon* is the greatest farce of the
period, Ravenscroft's *The London Cuckolds* notwithstanding. In addition, he
built up a body of dramatic theory in his prefaces to the plays. In spite of
Congreve's brilliance, Dryden remains the major dramatist of his age.

## (ii) Sir George Etherege

*The Comical Revenge; or, Love in a Tub* (1664) is an ambitious exercise, for
Etherege, in an effort to show all levels of London society, attempts to cram
a Balzacian *comédie humaine* into five acts. The achievement was impossible,
but this is not to say that Etherege lacked control over his material. The
reader will find four distinct plots, but he will find them tightly interwoven
with reduplicating episodes and imagery.[1]

Etherege creates a multifaceted study of the relationship of the sexes, in
which different characters are affected by various social conventions. The
chief story-line presents the wooing of the Widow Rich by the young man
about town, Sir Frederick Frollick, a complete extrovert who moves on all
levels of city life. The Widow delays her acceptance of Sir Frederick until
circumstances suggest the possibility of equality in a marital state. A heightened love-and-honour plot embroils the aristocracy. The heroine Graciana
must repress her love for Lord Beaufort because another suitor, Colonel
Bruce, has attempted to kill himself after being disarmed by Beaufort in a

[1] Some of the parallels in this section are noticed by V. O. Birdsall, *Wild Civility: The
English Comic Spirit on the Restoration Stage* (Bloomington, Indiana, 1970), pp. 43–55.

duel; and the impossibly idealistic codes that prevail keep Graciana in suspense until Bruce recovers – to be loved by Aurelia. Another plot shows the fleecing of a country booby (knighted by Oliver Cromwell) by the two confidence men, Wheadle and Palmer. In this section, marriage is regarded only as a device for getting money and rising to a higher social class. The final complication (which provides the title and subtitle) concerns a crude practical joke played on Sir Frederick's valet, Dufoy. The English women-servants resent Dufoy's arrogant, domineering ways and place him in a tub to advertise his affliction with a venereal disease.

In connecting these plots, Etherege uses the technique of repetitive situations. The real duel between Beaufort and Bruce is preceded by a 'faked' duel between Cully and the sharper Palmer, where the 'seconds' make a show of fencing to work upon Cully's fears and compel him to pay his gambling debt of a thousand pounds to Palmer or face death in the duello. Sir Frederick, who had risked death fighting as a second to Lord Beaufort, has himself carried in a funeral procession to the Widow's, with the news given out that he has been killed in a duel. After this, Lord Bevil, misinformed, tells his daughter Graciana that Colonel Bruce died after the encounter.

There are two brawls in front of the Widow's door: one is staged by Sir Frederick, attended by musicians, who perform a masque; the other is produced by Wheadle and Palmer, when they send the drunken Cully in the role of a roisterer to impress the rich widow, who will, the rogues assure him, admire him to the point of marrying him. The maid, Betty, achieves a 'comical revenge' by gathering a number of other servants who overpower Dufoy and thrust him into the 'tub', an episode which is paralleled by a grim revenge scene in which the brother of a man killed by Colonel Bruce at the battle of Naseby assembles a gang of ruffians to ambush the brave officer on his way to the duel with Lord Beaufort. (Fortunately, Beaufort and Sir Frederick arrive in the nick of time to drive off the villains.)

But the most striking situational parallel comes at the end of the play. Earlier, Wheadle had gained the confidence of Cully and proceeded to introduce his own whore, Grace, as the wealthy sister of Lord Bevil, ready to marry Cully. Sir Frederick finds Cully drunk at the Widow's; suspecting a plot, he breaks up Wheadle's elaborate schemes and recovers the thousand-pound judgement. Thus far there is no surprise, either to the reader or for the contemporary audience, as a 'cross-biting' plot of this sort is familiar to both Elizabethan drama and prose fiction. However, after the rescue, Sir Frederick tells the grateful Cully that he will permit him to marry his sister, and that he should go and do so at once. The beaming Cully returns with his bride and calls Sir Frederick 'Brother', only to learn that he has married the rake's cast-off mistress. The incident recalls the class war, for Betty had commented earlier, ' 'Tis one of Oliver's Knights, Madam, Sir Nicholas Cully; his Mother was my Grandmother's Dairy maid' (V. i).

Plots and characters are also connected through disguises. Cully dresses as Sir Frederick; Grace as the Widow. Palmer first wears the garb of a cattle farmer, then dresses like Lord Bevil. As the play draws nearer the end, the pace becomes faster: first dancing masters, then musicians disguise as link-boys; musicians disguise as bailiffs and then as pall-bearers in mourning. The author calls attention to the disguises with the stage direction: '*Four Fidlers carry the Corps, with their Instruments tuck'd under their Cloaks*'. Consequently, we find the paradox wherein we see realism (the Battle of Naseby) in the artificial love-and-honour scenes contrasted with fantasy in the realistic, comic episodes.

The situational parallels are duplicated and stressed by language and linguistic styles. Early in the work, it appears that the author is careful about decorum, with the love-and-honour characters speaking in rhymed couplets and the comic scenes written in prose. Eventually we notice, against this pattern of order, that Sir Frederick, who appears in each of the four plots speaking prose, approaches the Widow once 'in a Canting Tone', talking in rhymed couplets:

> Alas, what pains I take thus to unclose
> Those pretty eye-lids which lock'd up my Foes!

Etherege underscores the parody by having the Widow comment on Sir Frederick's speech: 'What pitiful rhyming Fellow is that?' In telling Graciana of the supposed death of Bruce, Lord Bevil speaks in blank verse; so too does the chief mourner in telling the Widow that Sir Frederick was killed in a duel. When Wheadle and Palmer reflect on their criminal careers they do so, incongruously, in blank verse. When the two sharpers have laid their plans for fleecing Cully, the victim enters and the three men sing an intricate part-song, as if they were leagued in a common cause.

Connections are made through the imagery. In consecutive scenes we find fire-and-light images in the speeches of Graciana and Aurelia, followed by the same imagery in a conversation between Sir Frederick and the Widow. Near the close of a scene, in loose talk about the Widow, Sir Frederick uses an angler–bait–hook metaphor; Wheadle's last speech in the following scene contains the same metaphor. Various other connections are made. At the beginning, as characters are being introduced or identified, there is purposeful confusion between the names Grace (for Wheadle's woman) and Graciana (the love-and-honour heroine). Sir Frederick comments harshly on the adulation of women, associated with the *précieuse* tradition, and tells Lord Beaufort, 'I mistrust your Mistresses Divinity; you'l find her Attributes but Mortal: Women, like Juglers Tricks, appear Miracles to the ignorant: but in themselves th'are meer cheats' (I. ii). Here we can observe that subjects praised in the serious drama are topics of derision in the comedies.

Etherege's use of the dance is of considerable aesthetic interest. Much dancing occurs, from a prepared masque by professional dancing masters to wild jigging by the French valet Dufoy. 'Dance is a very subjective medium,' writes Jocelyn Powell:

> It draws you inside an experience through the compulsive effect of rhythm working directly upon the emotions. .... By his use of dance Etherege gives what is fundamentally a critical structure a new dimension. .... The images of the play are complementary in that they provide different facets of the same subject, but because they are danced rather than enacted one finds oneself simply experiencing the same idea in different ways, rather than appreciating different attitudes to it. .... The diversity of moods is fused and the ugly and vulgar made to take their part in a pattern of experience.[1]

Meanwhile, the audience cannot escape the exuberance and gusto of the drama, which falls into the long tradition of 'festive' comedy. Certainly *Love in a Tub*, as the piece was generally advertised, was very popular in the theatre and admired by contemporary commentators. We may well believe that its popularity affected Dryden and that he may have had this work in mind (as well as *All Mistaken* and *Secret Love*) when he made his defence of the multi-plot play in the *Essay of Dramatic Poesy*.

In his second play, *She Would If She Could* (1668), Etherege continues his study of folly in London life but narrows his scope. The two male leads, Courtall and Freeman, make a brief tour of the shops and engage in a certain amount of social criticism, but the focus of the work is restricted to a survey of a few representatives of upper-middle-class society, a focus which has generally been maintained in the comedy of manners ever since. One plot replaces the four complications of Etherege's previous play. Here he deals with the triumph of experience over hope, and consequently is quite satirical. Sir Oliver, old and impotent, dashes about day and night busily chasing

[1] Jocelyn Powell, 'George Etherege and the Form of a Comedy', in Brown and Harris (eds), *Restoration Theatre*, p. 50.

wenches. His wife is a nymphomaniac, and consequently almost too extreme a type for present-day comedy, whose conventions would require her to visit a psychiatrist. She spends her time trying to go to bed with any available man, but is continually frustrated by a series of accidents and plot turns. Ariana and Gatty share the same motivations, but will venture flirtations only, for they sense the consequences of flouting the mores of their society. Courtall and Freeman are still more sophisticated: they seek intrigue simply as a diversion to pass the time. They don't expect anything meaningful to happen. It is a wonder that Marxist critics have never noticed this play. Kathleen Lynch did notice it and built a thesis in *The Social Mode of Restoration Comedy*,[1] from which it appears that knowledge of etiquette is the main criterion for judging conduct in the comedies of the time. However, like some of the characters in the drama, she took the vehicle for the tenor, and did not see that Etherege, and other dramatists, used this means to show that the natural drives of the individual were in conflict with the customs of society, and that the way of the world would not permit self-fulfilment.[2] Not that Etherege resembled William Blake; the genial dramatist would have been horrified by the conduct of humanity untrammelled. Etherege was no philosopher: he was engaged in showing the tension that arose under present circumstances.

The artistry of *The Man of Mode* (1676) makes it a masterpiece of drama, though some modern readers are repelled by seeing a triumph of art over nature. The play is so complex that the commentator must stifle a desire for Jamesian sentences, carefully qualifying and modifying each statement. All can agree that it is a comedy about a group of self-centred people engaged in passing time by role-playing. ('Where is the mirror?' asks Sir Fopling Flutter on a visit to Dorimant's lodgings.) We are shown a young man, Dorimant, and his efforts to dominate a number of women: the passionate Loveit, who cannot control her emotions; the indiscreet Bellinda, who surrenders too easily; the heiress Harriet, who retains complete control of herself; and a whore, Molly, who wants opera tickets. The plot-lines are slight, though minor events early in the action yield important results, and the chief forward motion comes through character confrontation. Consequently, the author's main reliance is upon tone and social *ambiance*. The older characters are treated as fools, and we are regaled with the tricks of the knaves. Hence, the play bears no relation to exemplary drama, since fools and knaves are

---

[1] (London and New York, 1926).
[2] See Dale Underwood, *Etherege and the Seventeenth-Century Comedy of Manners* (New Haven, Conn., 1957).

alike the object of ridicule. Because of critical controversy over the nature of Restoration comedy, *The Man of Mode* may be used as a focal point in a discussion of the satiric nature of the drama of this period.[1]

In 1711, those two skilful politicians, Joseph Addison, high in Whig councils, and Sir Richard Steele, active pamphleteer and zealous advocate of the Hanoverian succession, began their oblique and covert repudiation of the Tory position with a presentation of the befuddled yet lovable Sir Roger de Coverley in the second issue of their new journal, *The Spectator*. Nos. 55–70 are a carefully organized, sequential group of essays in which Addison and Steele attempt to subvert established critical assumptions by praising 'Chevy Chace'[2] and continue their opposition to the Stuart dynasty by exposing what they considered a vulnerable weakness: the immorality of Stuart-sponsored drama. Steele wrote from both critical conviction and political fervour; in both his own practice and in literary theory he espoused exemplary drama. Thus in *The Spectator*, No. 65, he attacked Etherege's play as immoral on the ground that the 'man of mode' (whom he identified as Dorimant instead of Sir Fopling Flutter) was a corrupt person held up as a model to be imitated. The sturdy critic John Dennis chose to reply in 1722, at a time when everybody in the theatrical world knew that Steele's *magnum opus*, *The Conscious Lovers*, was in rehearsal.[3] Since this work (tentatively called 'The Fine Gentleman') was going to present a model hero for emulation, 'Dennis was taking issue with Steele on a point of fundamental importance in literary theory'[4] by thus defending Etherege.

Dennis begins by appealing to classical precedent:

> Has not *Aristotle* told us . . . that Comedy is an Imitation of the very worst of Men? And has not *Horace* . . . reminded us, that the old *Athenian* Comick Poets made it their Business to bring all Sorts of Villains upon the Stage, Adulterers, Cheats . . . ? (II, 243)

Then he makes his point:

---

[1] See Robert D. Hume, 'Reading and Misreading *The Man of Mode*', *Criticism*, XIV (1972), pp. 1–11, and 'Theory of Comedy in the Restoration', *Modern Philology*, LXX (1973), pp. 302–18.

[2] C. S. Lewis, 'Addison', in *Essays on the Eighteenth Century Presented to D. Nichol Smith* (Oxford, 1945), pp. 2–4; B. A. Goldgar, *The Curse of Party* (Lincoln, Nebraska, 1961), pp. 65 ff.

[3] See pp. 56–60.

[4] *The Critical Works of John Dennis*, ed. E. N. Hooker, 2 vols (Baltimore, Md., 1943), II, p. 496. Quotations from Dennis are taken from this edition.

> How little do they know of the Nature of true Comedy, who believe that
> its proper Business is to set us Patterns for Imitation: for all such Pat-
> terns are serious Things, and Laughter is the Life, and the very Soul of
> Comedy. (II, 245)

Dennis explains that Dorimant was an 'admirable Picture of a Courtier in the
Court of King *Charles* the Second', that otherwise the portrait would not
have been accepted by that original audience; however, it was so recognized,
so much so that people considered Dorimant to be modelled on Lord
Rochester, and that audiences for fifty years had been accepting the play as
depicting the type. What kind of person then was Dorimant? asks Dennis,
and he proceeds with his analysis:

> *Dorimont* [*sic*] is a young Courtier, haughty, vain, and prone to Anger,
> amorous, false, and inconstant. He debauches *Loveit*, and betrays her;
> loves *Belinda*, and as soon as he enjoys her is false to her. (II, 247)

Dennis then returns to the doctrine of genres: 'Thus Comedy instructs and
pleases most powerfully by the Ridicule, because that is the Quality which
distinguishes it from every other Poem' (II, 249). He also invokes the practice of Molière and cites play titles to show that Molière's 'principal Characters are ridiculous'.[1]

   Dennis's account of Dorimant is exactly right. Etherege had to depict
Dorimant as he did, or an audience of 1676 would never have accepted him
as a young man about town. The portrayal is satiric because Dorimant is
shown acting in a ridiculous way. The sharpest stroke comes at the close,
when he is being teased about his prospective trip to Harriet's rural residence
in Hampshire. Furthermore, Dorimant is shown to have a vicious streak in
that he feels he must dominate his women. His treatment of Mrs Loveit is
barbarous. Very revealing is the episode in which he thinks she is showing
some attachment to Sir Fopling Flutter. Though he must have known that
Mrs Loveit despised Sir Fopling, he trumps up a quarrel to reassert his
dominance over her.

   Since the text of the play so well supports Dennis's description and his
character sketch of Dorimant, there must be some other reason for the dispute over the interpretation. The difficulty may arise because Etherege is so
detached from the scene; there are no moral signboards posted, no interpretative chorus. Here is a real rather than a specious reason for some confusion on

---

[1] For an extended discussion, see C. O. McDonald, 'Restoration Comedy as Drama of
Satire', *Studies in Philology*, LXI (1964), pp. 522–44.

the part of critics conditioned by nineteenth- and twentieth-century exemplary drama. Two kinds of explanation can be provided in the hope of ending the confusion. If we consult the authors themselves, we find that the poet Cowley replied to some criticism of Colonel Jolly, in *Cutter of Coleman Street*, for having some faults by saying: '*I did not intend the Character of a Hero, one of exemplary virtue.... If I had designed here the celebration of the Virtues of our Friends ... they should have stood in Odes, and Tragedies, and Epique Poems ...*'[1] It is difficult to see how an author could be more explicit; furthermore, Cowley invokes decorum of genre, a powerful criterion in late seventeenth-century literary criticism.

That contemporary audiences recognized the presence of satire in Restoration comedies can be documented at large. Here is an unambiguous commentary on Dryden:

> What is either wicked or silly in modish colours he has ... well painted ... more particularly this of shunning Marriage, and being entred perfidiously to break a vow so easy to be kept, in his Play of *Marriage-a-la-Mode*: a more gentile Satyre against this sort of folly, no Pen can write, where he brings the very assignations that are commonly used about Town upon the Stage; and to see both Boxes and Pitt so damnably crouded, in order to see themselves abused ...[2]

It was the 'modish colours', we recall, against which Sir Richard Steele took exception; yet without the 'modish colours' the audience would not recognize an imitation from life.

The other explanation is that Etherege expected the audience to have a value system; hence none had to be posted within the play itself. Earl Miner states this succinctly:

> The most elementary fact to be understood about Restoration comedy is one which the critics have had most difficulty in setting forth: that to it we must bring normal human assumptions to be shared with the dramatists and, at a distance of three centuries, with the original audience; and that the judgment shared is based upon ethical and even social norms common to us and the Restoration.[3]

Whatever Hobbes and Rochester may have thought, the audience is assumed to bring to bear standards of common decency. This brings us to the central

[1] Cowley, *Essays, Plays and Sundry Verses*, ed. A. R. Waller (Cambridge, 1906), p. 263.
[2] *Marriage Asserted* (1674), quoted by Harold Brooks, 'Some Notes on Dryden, Cowley and Shadwell', *Notes and Queries*, CLXVIII (1935), p. 94.
[3] Earl Miner, *Restoration Dramatists* (Englewood Cliffs, N.J., 1966), Introduction, pp. 7–8.

problem of interpreting the plays written by Etherege and other authors who contribute to the sex-comedy boom of the 1670s. If the spectator is going to identify with Dorimant or with Horner, in *The Country Wife*, the place for him is a burlesque house or a private club in Soho – unless we are to consider *The Man of Mode* and other similar plays as pornographic drama. Wycherley addresses himself precisely to this point (following the technique of Molière's *Critique de l'École des femmes*) by making Olivia (in *The Plain Dealer*) complain about the lasciviousness of the 'china scene' from *The Country Wife*. Olivia dilates on 'the clandestine obscenity in the very name of Horner', whereupon Eliza replies,

> What then? I can think of a goat, a bull, or satyr, without any hurt.
> OLIVIA: Ay; but, cousin, one cannot stop there.
> ELIZA: I can, cousin.
> OLIVIA: Oh, no! for when you have those filthy creatures in your head once, the next thing you think, is what they do; as their defiling of honest men's beds and couches, rapes upon sleeping and waking virgins, under hedges, and on haycocks, nay further . . . (II.i)

If one is to agree with her response, he might as well identify with the characters in Pinter's *The Homecoming*, in which case he needs a psychiatrist rather than a drama critic to explain the play to him.

## (iii) Sir Charles Sedley

Unlike the professional dramatists, the noble Sir Charles Sedley could compose a play whenever he jolly well felt like it, and did not need to concern himself with current vogues in the theatre. Whatever the reason, both of his comedies are out of line with the dominant trends in the years when they were first produced. *The Mulberry Garden* (1668), his first effort, is of uneven texture, and slight dramatic merit, but it is of interest to the literary historian. It is written by the scene, as in Elizabethan drama. It is the first of several plays to be based upon Molière's *L'École des maris* and on Terence's *Adelphi*. One of its plots, set at the close of the Commonwealth period, has a *deus ex machina* ending, written in rhymed couplets, in which General Monck declares for the king. In this story, Old Forecast forbids his daughters to have anything to do with two young Cavaliers in hiding; nevertheless, he is wrongly charged with concealing these two royalists and is arrested and imprisoned. Learning that the king is returning, the old hypocrite elects to remain in gaol in order to be counted on the winning side. However, several scenes in the other plot-line clearly take place well after the Restoration, wherein we see two young women go out on the town for flirtatious adventures – Sedley's early title was 'The Wandering Ladies'. Finally, there is a gay couple, Wildish and Olivia, properly equipped with witty dialogues. V. de Sola Pinto conjectures that the romantic story was written quite early, possibly around 1660, and that Sedley composed the rest of the work on the model of *She Would If She Could*.[1]

*Bellamira; or, The Mistress* (1687) is a much superior work. Sedley has improved his dialogues and achieved a harsh, raucous sex comedy, a court wit play. Ten years earlier, it would have been a stage hit, but in 1687 it was scandalous. The action contains a successful rape and several 'cross-biting' plots. Remarks about sex are quite explicit, and there is a good deal of prurient talk. The attitude throughout is extremely cynical, as expressed in the following judgement: 'A Husband is a good Bit to Close ones Stomach with, when Love's Feast is over' (I. iii. 116–17). All in all, it gives a vivid picture of fashionable London life in the early days of the Restoration.

## (iv) Thomas Shadwell and humours comedy

Revered as Ben Jonson was, the humours style was not dominant in the late seventeenth century; furthermore, concepts had changed. What appears to be an imitation of Jonsonian humours on the dramatis personae page of a Restoration play quarto often turns out to be something else entirely in the text. The new playwrights were concerned with types, not with what Jonson meant by 'humours'. Hence, when a work seems to be in the mode of the older drama, for example, John Wilson's *The Cheats*, we are likely to suspect that it was composed before 1660. Wilson has a play filled with incident, where the satirist's lash is laid on nonconformist preachers, astrologers, street ruffians, aldermen and constables, all plying their trade of cheating. Among the works that attempt to follow Jonson are those by William Cavendish, Duke of Newcastle: *The Humourous Lovers* (1667) and *The Triumphant Widow; or, The Medley of Humours* (1674). If these pieces continue an old mode, they also form a link with new ones, for the structure of the first work is that of comic opera, and the second approaches ballad opera.

Another play in the tradition of older comedy is Edward Revet's *The Town Shifts* (c. 1671), a work which has incorrectly been labelled 'sentimental' in recent years. The elements that have elicited this categorization are its

[1] *The Poetical and Dramatic Works of Sir Charles Sedley*, ed. V. de Sola Pinto, 2 vols (London, 1928), I, pp. 101–3.

Elizabethan aspects. The characters Goody Fells, Clowt the Constable and Mold the Sexton indicate the relation to the previous age. The female lead is not sentimental; instead, she is, as Montague Summers says, like a heroine in the comedies of Thomas Heywood.[1] Besides, there are none of the moralistic preachments that we find in sentimental comedy.[2]

Thomas Shadwell was, however, a professed follower of Ben Jonson who asserted his discipleship and praised the master in prefaces, prologues and epilogues. He should not be taken altogether at his word, as five of his earliest plays were adapted from Molière, with two others drawing upon Molière.[3] Unfortunately, neither apprenticeship yielded much return. Shadwell became adept at revealing an eccentricity in individual sketches, but he generally experienced difficulty with the overall control of a work. According to John Harold Wilson, Shadwell 'presented a wide variety of fops, fools, bumpkins, lechers, sharpers, knaves, whores, and cowards, but his attitude toward them was narrowly moralistic; he never organized them into a rounded interpretation of human experience.'[4] During his early career, he opposed the kind of comedy that was dominant, yet he called *She Would If She Could* the best play written since the Restoration and wrote two comedies in its mode. Later, he began to introduce characters who rebuke the errors of others and broke from the usual practice of holding all persons up to a greater or lesser degree of ridicule.

His first piece, *The Sullen Lovers; or, The Curious Impertinents* (1668), based upon Molière's *Les Fâcheux*, contains a group of odd characters, the chief of whom is Sir Positive-At-All, a parody of Sir Robert Howard. This attack was quite skilfully done, but one can observe that Shadwell is mocking the faults of an eccentric individual rather than dealing with weaknesses of human nature. He shows his opposition to the 'gay couple' by presenting young lovers who are serious and have no searching doubts about matrimony, and by a direct attack in the preface, where he scorns 'a Swearing, Drinking, Whoring Ruffian for a Lover, and an impudent ill-bred *tomrig* for a Mistress'.

In 1669 he revised John Fountain's pastoral, *The Rewards of Virtue*, to become *The Royal Shepherdess*, and adapted *Tartuffe*, offering it as *The Hypocrite*. In *The Humorists* (1670) Shadwell presented two serious young lovers in the leading roles; they spout wisdom and are pure in heart. He includes a preface in which he returns to his attack on contemporary comedy (except for

[1] Montague Summers, *The Playhouse of Pepys* (London, 1935), pp. 387–8.
[2] J. H. Smith (*The Gay Couple*, pp. 122–3) emphasizes this point.
[3] John Wilcox, *The Relation of Molière to Restoration Comedy* (New York, 1938), pp. 27–8, 117–26, 180–1.
[4] J. H. Wilson, *A Preface to Restoration Drama* (Boston, 1965), p. 154.

his praise of Etherege), and Jonson again is endorsed. In presenting his own theory of comedy, he shows himself much too inflexible and doctrinaire. His next work was *The Miser* (1672), where he added numerous characters to provide more action than was in his source (*L'Avare*). Such an increase in both characters and plot complication was frequently true of adaptations from the French dramatist. Shadwell lowers the status of the two young men, Rant and Hazard, to sharpers and bullies, so that the serious lover, Theodore, can put forward encomiums on women, modesty and virtue.

One could say that in *Epsom Wells* (1672) Shadwell joined the opposition, for he now inserts wild rakes, two gay young couples and citizens who get cuckolded. After composing libretti for two operas and helping the Duke of Newcastle revise a play, Shadwell wrote his best comedy, *The Virtuoso* (1676). This is a highly satiric work, with some fine strokes of ridicule on sexual irregularity and hypocrisy in the place of didactic pronouncements as in his other plays. The action moves at a good pace, marked by energy and gusto, and the dialogue is much improved. The best section is the satiric treatment of the would-be scientists. *A True Widow* (1678) has mixed elements. In his secondary pair of young lovers, Shadwell has a creditable example of the gay couple, for the girl, Theodosia, is quite witty. Unfortunately, the comic effect engendered by the wit is marred by the emphasis placed on moralizing in the main plot. As the story unfolds, Lady Busy attempts to persuade Isabella to become a kept woman. Isabella refuses, so that the play ends with virtue triumphant and the rake Bellmour repentant. In Act IV there is a lively play within the play, with a vivid scene of bullies and hectors breaking up a performance.

*The Woman Captain* (1679) is a strange work, unlike anything else being currently done. Though it is not a humours play, Shadwell may be working from the precedent of Mistress Otter in *The Silent Woman* in creating the part of Mrs Gripe, a usurer's wife, who dominates her husband, swears the tavern bullies into her 'army' and drills them up and down the hall. In one scene, Shadwell introduces lesbian characters, and it is difficult to say whether the episode is presented for its titillating effect or whether Shadwell intended a satire. In other sections more and more commentary is inserted; a prodigal appears, and his follies are described in chorus-like explanations by the steward. The most comic scene parodies gay-couple comedies by having a rake engage in a proviso scene with a courtesan. This farcical work represents a retreat from Shadwell's more serious satire, as shown in his earlier and unsuccessful *The True Widow*.

In 1681 Shadwell got into trouble with his play *The Lancashire Witches* by ridiculing an Anglican clergyman. The entire comedy was Whig political propaganda, and large sections were deleted by the censor. Shadwell was now in real difficulty and stopped writing plays for a seven-year period. When he resumed, it was with *The Squire of Alsatia* (1688), a comedy which became immediately popular because of the presentation of gangsters and inclusion of their slang.

In this play the intention of the author seems highly problematical.[1] Drawn from Terence's *Adelphi*, it presents a comparison of two educational systems: a strict rural training against a liberal one in town, to be illustrated in the effects of the two methods upon the Belfond boys and to be debated by their father, Sir William Belfond, and their uncle, Sir Edward Belfond.[2] During the argument, the country ignoramus, Belfond Senior, comes to London, where he feels that he is enjoying himself splendidly in the company of the rogues and bullies he has met and is fascinated by the argot of the London underworld. He has never had such a good time in his life.

From the course of the debate between the father and the uncle, we learn that Belfond Junior is a model of goodness and that our sympathies should be with the liberal theory, but Shadwell proceeds to make a ridiculously defective case for it. We learn that Belfond Junior has a child by Termagant, a woman whom he has cast off. Next, we see him immediately after his seduction of Lucia, the naïve and very young daughter of a lawyer. Then we hear him lie to her and then to the uncle who has been supporting him. However, Belfond Junior does provide support for Termagant and the child, and his uncle pays a large sum to Lucia's father. Thus 'Belfond Junior is left with all the odor of sanctity that money can buy'.[3] Shadwell failed to keep his play under control. Although Belfond Junior reforms for practical rather than moral reasons, Shadwell trumpets the exemplary nature of the reform and evidently believed that he was fulfilling a serious didactic purpose with his presentation. Consequently, *The Squire of Alsatia* is a landmark in the direction of exemplary drama.

In *Bury Fair* (1689) Shadwell again offers the combination of ridiculous conduct and 'model behaviour'. The work is satiric when Mrs Fantast and her mother enthusiastically accept a barber disguised as a French count; it is exemplary when Lord Bellamy, a 'man of sense', displays ideal conduct and lectures the young rake Wildish on the evils of debauchery and uncontrolled

[1] See the severe comments in Nicoll, *HED*, I, p. 200.

[2] On Shadwell's use of his source material, see the unpublished University of Pennsylvania dissertation by John Freehafer, *The Emergence of Sentimental Comedy, 1660–1707* (1950).

[3] Robert D. Hume, 'Formal Intention in *The Brothers* and *The Squire of Alsatia*', *English Language Notes*, VI (1969), pp. 176–84.

appetite. Numerous barbs are directed against French culture and Italian music. In *The Man of Mode*, years earlier, Sir Fopling Flutter was ridiculed for affecting French styles and manners, for such affectation revealed that he did not have a developed taste; in Shadwell's later works, the ridicule proceeds from provincialism and chauvinism. Unlike the majority of Restoration comedies, the action is located outside London.

*The Scowrers* (1690) is of uneven construction, with much reliance upon farce. Again we find an older person taken seriously, when the young rake William Rant is emotionally affected by his father's serious advice, and again we have a fifth-act repentance, demanded by a virtuous heroine. The second lead, Wildfire, also reforms, overcome by pure love, to marry Clara. Meanwhile, Shadwell has been giving much space to the old 'scowrer' Tope, who has taken the role of chorus at several points, once warning the young men against early-morning drinking (but not for moral reasons). When young Rant repents, greatly pleasing his father and the heroine, Tope comments again:

> Ha, ha, ha, fine Fools, turn sober Scots, give over all Vanities, as you call 'em, for the greatest Vanity on the Earth, Matrimony! you may leave any other Vanities when you please, but that will stick to you with a vengeance. Matrimony ha, ha, ha, there's nothing in the world worth being in earnest, I am sure not being sober, 'tis all a *Farce*.

Shadwell's last effort, *The Volunteers* (1692), has serious dramatic weaknesses, for it embraces too much material and has no semblance of unity. It does have matter for the historian, and at the end of his career Shadwell may be developing a sense of irony. Otherwise, his playwriting moves from humours to eccentrics to stereotypes. In this piece, we are introduced to two pure young damsels, one of them cast out of her home, an example of virtue in distress. In contrast, we are then presented with an affected, frivolous girl, Teresia, and a downright 'bad' girl, Winifred, duly frowned upon and eventually awarded to a dancing master. In addition, there are a faithful servant and a wicked stepmother.

Along with this prelude to melodrama, Shadwell achieves some laughable scenes in his presentation of the fantastic beau, Sir Nicholas Dainty. The circumstances are that the old Cavalier Colonel Blount has invited Colonel Hackwell, 'an Anabaptist Colonel' under Cromwell, to dinner in order to arrange a reconciliation between Hackwell and his children. (Hackwell is an old scoundrel who is busy selling fraudulent stock; as long as he doesn't handle illegal commodities himself, he sees no sin in unloading them on an ungodly public.) At dinner, these ancient political enemies unbend to fight the Civil War all over again with genial fervour. Then the fop Dainty appears, and amazes the elderly battle-veterans by telling them of the fine garments, velvet bed, 'service of Plate', eight wagons of supplies, including troughs for fresh vegetables, that he is going to take with him for the ensuing campaign against France in Flanders. This amusing situation gave Macaulay just the kind of paradox he sought, and in his *History of England* he told how Dainty was anxious to cross swords with the best French fighters, but was dejected about whether his servants could secure ice to cool his wine.[1] In due course, a ranting bully concludes that Dainty is effeminate and insults him. This move turns out to be the bully's great mistake, for Dainty challenges him; at the place of the intended duel, the fellow won't fight, whereupon Dainty kicks and beats him. The inclusion of two duels brings up another problem in interpreting Shadwell. In a previous work, *Bury Fair*, a moral lesson had been taught in showing that duelling was wrong and, as Steele was to argue later, not the sign of a gentleman. But here, in composing a different play, Shadwell uses a duel to demonstrate that Dainty is a gentleman. The reader is thus given cause to have doubts about Shadwell's own position: whether he was a new moralist, or an opportunist, or simply a recorder of life as he observed it.

Dryden's picture in 'MacFlecknoe' has damaged Shadwell for us, and it is difficult to make a just evaluation of his uneven contribution to English drama. Possibly the most valid one comes from Saintsbury, who calls attention to the accurate observation, the exuberant stock of situations, the keen eye for contemporary manners, and yet the coarseness, tediousness and the flatness of dialogue.[2] Then Saintsbury exclaims, 'How absolutely alive', in speaking of the play within the play in *A True Widow*.

Shadwell's comedies are marked by exuberance, energy and gusto, and the most striking is the 'mirror' scene which elicited Saintsbury's praise. Here, the character Carlos has bespoken a performance at the theatre, and we see people gather inside the playhouse. One rowdy fellow gets off an excellent line: 'What Play do they play? Some confounded Play or other.' Three other bullies refuse to pay the doorkeeper, and yet another wants credit. The playlet begins, showing two lovers, a wife and a husband, with the first lover and the wife talking in platonic language (the *précieux* vocabulary). Now a member of the fictive audience starts some crude, schoolboy jokes, whereupon the bullies begin fighting with the main characters of the 'real' play. Thus the

---

[1] Macaulay, *The History of England from the Accession of James the Second*, ed. C. H. Firth, 6 vols (London, 1914), IV, p. 2030.
[2] *Thomas Shadwell*, ed. George Saintsbury (London, n.d.).

1 Interior of the Haymarket Theatre (1720–1820), in 1807

W. Dolle. fc

**2-6** Engravings by W. Dolle for Settle's *The Empress of Morocco* (Dorset Garden Theatre, 1673)

W. Dolle fc

W. Dolle. sc

**7** Dolle engraving from *The Empress of Morocco*, showing the exterior of Dorset Garden Theatre

8 Wren's drawing for the interior of a playhouse (possibly Drury Lane)

9 Model by Richard Southern reconstructing Wren's drawing

10 Thornhill's design for *Arsinoe* (1705): 'Garden by moonlight'

Act IV Sc. 3
A Room of State, w.th Seating & Buffet

Arsinoe on a Couch

D 28 g.

11 Thornhill's design for *Arsinoe*: 'A room of state'

12 Thornhill's design for *Arsinoe*: 'A great hall looking out on a garden'

13 Thornhill's design for *Arsinoe*: 'Arsinoe in a fine garden'

14 John Rich as Lun, imitating a dog (1731)

15 John Rich as Lun, helping Punch kick Apollo (1735)

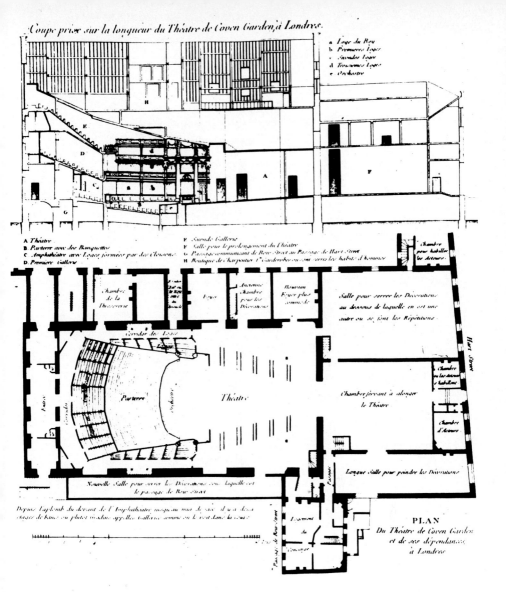

16 Dumont's engraving (1763) of Covent Garden interior

18 Hogarth's engraving ridiculing *The Beggar's Opera* (1728), showing Rich's Lincoln's Inn Fields Theatre

19 John Lacy

20 Henry Harris

21 Edward Kynaston

22 Hogarth's engraving of John Rich's entry into Covent Garden (1732)

23 Theophilus Cibber's revolt (1733)

24 Rowe's frontispiece (1709) to *Hamlet*, showing Betterton [?] and the overturned chair

**25** Rowe's frontispiece (1709) to *King Lear*

26 Rowe's frontispiece (1709) to *Cymbeline*

27 Anne Bracegirdle as Semernia in *The Widow Ranter* (1689)

28 James Quin as Coriolanus

29 Benefit ticket for William Milward, showing *The Beggar's Opera* (1728)

30 Joe Haines delivering an epilogue on an ass

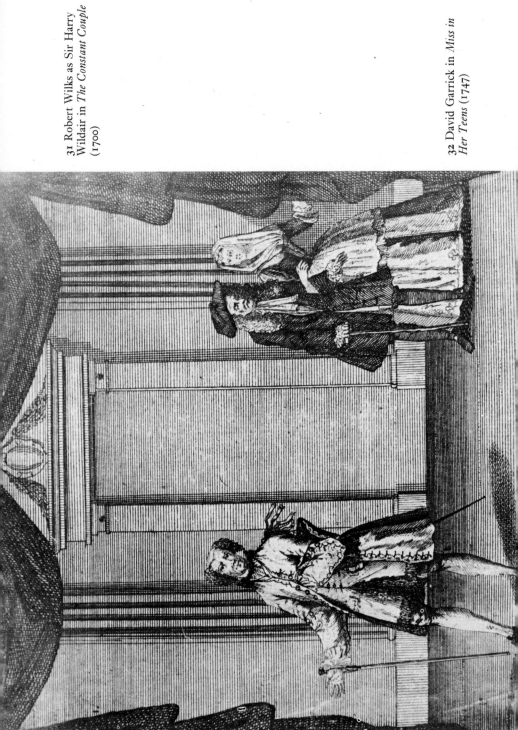

31 Robert Wilks as Sir Harry Wildair in *The Constant Couple* (1700)

32 David Garrick in *Miss in Her Teens* (1747)

**34** Colley Cibber as
Lord Foppington in
*The Relapse*

# THE
# Blind Beggar

## OF
## BETHNAL GREEN.

35 Title page of Dodsley's version of *The Blind Beggar of Bethnal Green* (1741)

episode goes from boisterous raillery to pushing and elbowing, from fisticuffs to hard fighting with swords, so that the production is abruptly broken off, the actors running off the 'stage' while the women go out screaming. Shadwell does deserve praise for the construction of this scene. Nevertheless, the work as a whole becomes tiresome as the play continues. Both Lady Busy and Lady Cheatly attempt to talk the virtuous Isabella into being a kept mistress, when all that was dramatically needed was to have the suggestion made. The accuracy of the individual character sketches is not sufficient to make the entire work a satisfactory dramatic conflict, with the result that these plays become of more interest to the social historian than to the student of literature. Thus we cannot really improve upon George Saintsbury's summation, in which he balances accurate observation and exuberance against coarseness and lack of control. The coarseness came from lack of selectivity, as Lord Rochester saw long ago:

> Shadwell's Unfinish'd Works, do yet impart
> Great Proofs of Force of Nature, none of Art.[1]

In rereading and studying the plays, one can see that Shadwell was not a creative artist who could select; all he could do was photograph life.

## (v) William Wycherley

In Wycherley we come to a master dramatist, a major writer of English comedy. In fact, he was so truly a dramatist that his plays were misunderstood once they ceased to be acted. His comedies must be seen in the theatre, for as literary texts they are open to misinterpretation. He was such a consummate artist that generalizations become dangerous. In one sense, his comedies are static (a characteristic they share with others of his time) in that they do not argue theses or provide any philosophy of life. When an estimate is made of a person like Freeman in *The Plain Dealer* (1676) or Alithea in *The Country Wife* (1675), Wycherley lets the character split his ship on the rock of another experience. His works, writes Ian Donaldson, have a 'strong back and forth movement, in which the actions and motives of all characters are shown in different lights'.[2] Hence, one must avoid simplistic responses. It is instructive to note that Manly (in *The Plain Dealer*) and Swift's Lemuel Gulliver are eliciting similar interpretations and controversies from modern critics.

   The ideas in Wycherley's comedies do not seem difficult. All four of them

[1] From 'Horace's 10th Satyr of the First Book Imitated', *Works* (London, 1709).
[2] In a review in *Review of English Studies*, XVIII (1967), p. 79.

continuously expose the hypocritical rationale of conduct in a society that encourages people to a show of virtue, not to its practice. Obviously, Wycherley had observed that facts of conduct do not always square with theories of conduct. Such observation was, of course, not original. His problem – as Swift was to discuss later, in one of his few notes on literary criticism – was how the satirist could keep the beholder watching his reflection in the glass. Wycherley, like Swift, had a measure of success, but like Swift again he has been abused ever since by those who did not like what they saw. Over the years, past and present, the main charges against Wycherley are (1) that he was rebelling against society, (2) that Manly represents the author's own views, and (3) that the plays are blatantly immoral. Macaulay also called him a skunk.

Answers will have to come from the plays. It is unfortunate that some modern defenders attempt to aid Wycherley by insinuating that he presented model characters. Teachers of the drama should perhaps sue for libel, on grounds of denigration of Wycherley's artistic reputation. One critic calls Alithea the representative of true honour.[1] Let us examine *The Country Wife* on this point. A rake named Horner has announced his impotence in the demonstrably successful hope that feminine responses will guide him to those who are seeking sex. In an angry scene at the end, with both Sparkish and Pinchwife demanding information, Pinchwife suspects the truth, that he has been cuckolded by Horner. At this point, the representative of true honour, Alithea, interposes (after Margery has testified to Horner's virility – 'to my certain knowledge'). Alithea says, 'Come Brother, Your Wife is yet Innocent.' As Wycherley's editor, Gerald Weales, points out, Alithea has now joined Dorilant and the Quack in lying and covering for Horner.[2] One may excuse her conduct by arguing that she is attempting to protect Margery Pinchwife, but even so, to the extent that Alithea is defended, the defender is implicitly protecting Horner and his machinations.

Modern revivals of these comedies should lead to a better understanding of them, since Wycherley's plays are designed entirely for production. T. W. Craik observes that Wycherley's interest is in theatrical effectiveness,[3] and he does have a fondness for providing comic turns for the players. Weales calls attention to the extended comic turn between Katherine Corey (playing the bawd Mrs Joyner) and Lacy (playing Gripe), when they both compliment

[1] Rose Zimbardo, *Wycherley's Drama* (New Haven, Conn., 1965), pp. 161–5.
[2] *The Complete Plays of William Wycherley*, ed. Gerald Weales (New York, 1966), Introduction.
[3] T. W. Craik, 'Some Aspects of Satire in Wycherley's Plays', *English Studies*, XLI (1960), pp. 168–79.

each other in the opening scene of Wycherley's first play, *Love in a Wood* (1671). The numerous allusions to actors and actresses, dramatists and plays, show that Wycherley was closely studying the contemporary theatre and was using it for a functional purpose in his own works. We can observe that he held the mirror up to the audience by constant reminders that the play was about them. He uses many devices towards this end. In *Love in a Wood*, Lucy says that Dapperwit 'wou'd have brought me into the Playhouse, where I might have had as good luck as others'. The first intention was to draw a laugh, but the line interweaves literature and life, and prevents audience withdrawal. Later, when a professional singer comes on stage to sing the lyric in Act IV, the speaker says, 'She comes as if she came expressly to sing the new Song.' Thus Wycherley controls the satiric thrust of his work more carefully than the plot structure.

Wycherley's use of a multiplot structure in *Love in a Wood* shows his knowledge of Etherege's *Love in a Tub*; it was not his source (that was Calderón's *Mañanas de abril y mayo*), but he follows Etherege's pattern of interlocking plots. The leading characters are two fashionable young men of the leisured class, Ranger and Valentine, so suspicious and distrustful of women that one wonders why these men go to the trouble of pursuing them. However, Ranger is courting Lydia, and Valentine is paired with the virtuous Christina, much too good for him. Act II contains a lively night scene in St James's Park, complete with music, dancing and masking with the consequent mistakes in identification, as the men search for women and Lady Flippant looks for a husband. As the action continues, Wycherley keeps devising new situations to disconcert the anticipations of the characters in their devious and greedy quest for money and sex.

The poet Dapperwit has been riding high, having found a Lolita in Miss Lucy and being able to use Sir Simon as a cover or blind under which he can court Martha, the daughter of the rich Puritan usurer Gripe. Sir Simon is the gull, who has taken a job as clerk to Gripe in order to court Martha and get the old man's estate. But Gripe wants a young girl himself, and the bawd Mrs Joyner provides Miss Lucy for him. Through Sir Simon's aid, Martha escapes from her house, only to jilt him for Dapperwit, whom she immediately marries. Dashed, Sir Simon informs Gripe, who hastens to the scene and learns that his daughter has indeed married Dapperwit, thus making him Gripe's heir. However, Dapperwit learns that Martha is six months pregnant by some other man and that Gripe has taken Lucy, whom he supposed carefully concealed. Gripe now arranges to marry Lucy: if she bears him a son, Dapperwit will never see a penny of Gripe's estate.

Here we can repeat the point about Restoration plays being static in that the characters move around the room as at a dance but don't get anywhere. The same hostilities remain that existed at the opening of the play. There isn't going to be any resolution, let alone a 'happy ending'. The characters in *Love in a Wood* are all in search of money and sex. Some are successful and some are not. Those who work the hardest at it, Lady Flippant and Sir Simon, get the least. Neither has any money, and they get each other. Sir Simon's money was spent in bribing a laundress at court to get himself knighted; he had taken a job to get near the heiress, Martha, and was pledged to pay the bawd, Mrs Joyner. The resultant situation is a refinement on *The Alchemist*, or else we could say, with Harold Love, that the two plays illuminate each other.[1] In Jonson's comedy, the cleverest rogue gets off free; in *Love in a Wood*, Dapperwit becomes an accidental overreacher. He too is the cleverest of the group, and, as such, might be expected to succeed in his design. Things have been quite cosy, with two women supposedly under his control. Then he gets the prize, only to realize that he has been left at the post. Both Dapperwit and the audience have been betrayed. Gripe, not Dapperwit, is triumphant at the close of the action. One must note that a Restoration playwright does not necessarily ask us to approve the character to whom he awards success. No viewer finds Gripe attractive at any point. In this respect, Wycherley's practice resembles that of Ben Jonson.

Wycherley was fond of showing fluctuating relationships among characters. Lucy's mother first portrays Dapperwit as a friend who has sustained their household financially, and she states her gratitude. However, when she learns that Gripe will pay all of her bills, she repudiates Dapperwit. Later, after Lucy and her mother had been defending him, Dapperwit turns pimp and extracts money from Ranger to bring him to Lucy. But Gripe has never been put in a sympathetic light. Throughout the drama, he has revealed his objectionable characteristics: greed, unctuousness, hypocrisy, self-deception. Wycherley describes him as a 'covetous, leacherous, old Usurer of the City'. He is victorious at the end of the play because Mrs Joyner, though despising him, has been paid for her labours as a bawd (whereas Sir Simon had only promised payment). Her business is to provide service, and she duly delivers the young wench to Gripe. What moral lessons can be learned here? The only moral that the evidence will yield is to be sure to pay procuresses in cash. As Mae West said on another occasion, 'Goodness had nothing to do with it.'

*The Gentleman Dancing-Master* (1672), Wycherley's second work, has a more unified construction than do his other plays, but this factor is not

[1] In a review in *AUMLA*, XXVII (1967), p. 108.

enough to save it from being his weakest production. He employs many of the same devices as in his other comedies, but they are not always successful. Again we see the changing estimates of the characters. Early in the action, we are made to feel sympathetic towards the heroine; later, as her growing independence turns her into a virago, our sympathy is for the suitor. When Wycherley has the two actors Nokes and Angel discuss their relative merits, he gives an impression of merely performing a clever trick rather than achieving a successful blending of literature and life. He also tends to labour the study of appearance and reality, so brilliantly done elsewhere. Early in the story, Monsieur is presented as an Englishman who dresses in French garb and speaks with an atrocious French accent. Then he is ordered to wear Spanish costume or lose the heiress, so he reappears in Spanish clothes, the father placing the Golilia (collar) on him. Monsieur now speaks English, the language he had ridiculed earlier. Another character comments: 'What a strange Metamorphosis is this? you look like a *Spaniard* and talk like an *English*-man.'

All dramatic elements come together to make *The Country Wife* (1675) a comic masterpiece. Wycherley achieves his wittiest dialogue, as Horner saunters through London in his quest for sexual triumphs. This brilliant comedy was a stage success in its own day, and with *The Way of the World* it is more frequently revived by professional companies in modern times than any other Restoration plays. The pervasive hypocrisy of the various characters, emerging from the conflict of natural desires against established social mores, keeps the action 'relevant', I suppose, though one might argue that audiences may simply appreciate the artistic skill of the presentation. Watching a modern production reminds us that drama is a reduplicating art form: the sets, costumes, music, lighting, the actors' voices and gestures repeat, restate, parallel and intensify the text of the play. *The Country Wife* shows Wycherley's awareness of the cumulative impact of drama. In the beginning, Sir Jasper says, 'My pleasure, business; your business, pleasure', and this phrase is repeated and restated thereafter. To connect the audience with the action on the stage, there are numerous topical references to playhouses, actors, actresses, role-playing, seating locations and costumes.[1]

Another device is that of having characters watching or overhearing other characters, and then making interpretative comments. There are over a hundred asides in *The Country Wife*. Wycherley expands on this device by placing some characters where they are concealed from the other players but

[1] A full account is given by Cynthia S. Matlack in her unpublished University of Pennsylvania dissertation, *Dramatic Techniques in the Plays of William Wycherley* (1967).

are visible to the audience. Anne Righter makes the perceptive comment that 'All the characters of the comedy reveal their true selves in front of Horner';[1] actually, the revelation is even more comprehensive. In Act IV Quack has stated his doubts regarding the efficacy of Horner's scheme and consequently is invited to watch it in operation. What he sees is the famous 'china scene'. Horner sends Quack behind a screen when Lady Fidget enters; now the audience can watch Quack watch Horner and Lady Fidget. On her husband's arrival, Lady Fidget disappears into another room, with Horner leaving by another exit. The husband announces that Horner has gone in to Lady Fidget 'the back way', as Sir Jasper, Lady Squeamish and Mrs Squeamish intently eye the door through which Lady Fidget had departed, with Quack still observing them. Nor is Quack silent, for he comments from time to time, making speeches which indicate that Wycherley wants the audience to notice Quack, as in Shakespeare's use of the same device in *Troilus and Cressida* (V. ii).

It is unfortunate to have this satiric portrayal of self-deception and hypocrisy muffled by some recent attempts to divide the characters into groups representing 'Right-way' and 'Wrong-way', a division which seems simplistic and unsound. The notion may have arisen because of the sharp contrast between the decent Alithea and Lady Fidget and her corrupt gang of nymphomaniacs. In fact, Norman Holland is so repelled by this obnoxious group that he persuades himself that Harcourt and Alithea are the leading characters of the play.[2] One may miss in the reading what is so clear in a production, but Wycherley has arranged matters to have Alithea engage in self-deception and entangle herself in a ridiculous position. She is engaged to Sparkish, a silly fop, though she does not love him. Taxed on this point, she explicitly states that she will hold firm and marry Sparkish only because the marriage has been arranged, with Pinchwife putting up the dowry, and she is going to go through with it. In the next plot turn, she finds herself in an awkward position: Sparkish encourages Harcourt to court her. Sparkish is a fool, and at several points in the play, especially when Alithea is being questioned by her maid, she twists and turns to avoid recognizing his folly. As a result, at the end of the action, Sparkish accuses her of being a fallen woman. She would not have suffered this unhappy incident if she had faced up to the situation and told Sparkish off in Act II. In holding desperately to appearances, Alithea appears somewhat ridiculous. She is not the butt of Wycherley's

[1] Anne Righter, 'William Wycherley', in Brown and Harris (eds), *Restoration Theatre*, p. 80.
[2] Holland, op. cit. pp. 93–107.

satiric attack on female hypocrisy, yet the fact that he treats her more gently than the Fidget tribe does not make her the heroine of the play (as Norman Holland insists). The leading woman in this comedy is Margery Pinchwife, 'the Country Wife'.

When we reach Wycherley's last play, *The Plain Dealer* (1676), all the critics seem to disagree in their judgements. The actions lack unity, there seems to be a shift of emphasis during the play, and there may be some 'blurring of artistic purpose'.[1] The ending of the work seems to be on a different basis from the beginning. Wycherley starts *The Plain Dealer* with great irony. In the opening speeches, Manly takes an impossible stance, insisting on the rejection of all social courtesy, while the cowardly fop, Lord Plausible, defends conventions and argues for the *via media* in man's relations with his fellow man. Manly becomes much too extreme, yet as the plot unfolds he engages in the kind of conduct which he had previously denounced. However, an audience loves to see a downright rebel, so that Wycherley achieves strong dramatic tension.

After his clash with Lord Plausible, Manly plunges into his war with society and becomes a richly comic figure. His character deteriorates as the plot continues, and he engages in dishonest and sordid actions; ultimately, he is dragged through the mire he despises. Nevertheless, he is rewarded at the end, wins his revenge, exposes Olivia, recovers his money and marries his faithful page, Fidelia. As we have seen in the previous comedies, Wycherley is fond of contriving matters to change our evaluation of the characters. Here, he may have been inconsistent in making Manly both a ruggedly independent but ridiculous misanthrope and a straight character as in a tragedy. Wycherley may have changed his own mind during the composition of the play.[2] The result is a drama with much raw power but lacking in the polish and control of *The Country Wife*.

Wycherley is the dramatist who stands highest currently, but curiously enough, critics rate him highly for different and contradictory reasons. V. O. Birdsall thinks he is a free spirit; Rose Zimbardo sees only a serious, moral satirist; Norman Holland believes that Wycherley is artfully didactic; Bonamy Dobrée, who founded the vogue for Wycherley, sees in him a near-tragic intensity; and Gerald Weales identifies him as a burlesque *farceur*. The conclusion one would have to reach from these contrary views is that Wycherley is a complex enough writer to allow not only such disagreements but also

---

[1] Katherine M. Rogers, 'Fatal Inconsistency: Wycherley and *The Plain Dealer*', *ELH, A Journal of English Literary History*, XXVIII (1961), pp. 148–62.
[2] Ibid.

a radical variety of basic misunderstandings. Every man to his own Rorschach, says Gerald Weales. Can a historical interpretation help us see Wycherley as some of his contemporaries saw him? An understanding of his context undermines many of the modern views. One cannot ignore the heavily formulaic element in these plays, especially in the first two, but even working within the conventions of Restoration drama, Wycherley is increasingly able to communicate a dark but ultimately comic view of human experience.

## (vi) Summation of trends

Comedy reached a peak and a dividing point in 1676, the year in which *The Man of Mode*, *The Plain Dealer* and *The Virtuoso* appeared. Biographical fact assumes importance here in the history of the drama, for 'gentle George' Etherege and 'Manly' Wycherley had each written his last play. It is doubtful whether either dramatist was aware of this situation, and certainly no one else was. A dozen years later, James II was expecting another comedy from Etherege, and Wycherley was only thirty-five years old in 1676. Few periods in the history of drama could stand the simultaneous loss of two such able practitioners, certainly not the newly emerging Restoration movement. Had these two men continued, it is only reasonable to expect that they would have contributed more of the urbane, sophisticated comedies which they had already offered. But their absence left a vacuum which the repertory system of the time required to be filled. Furthermore, another prominent writer, Thomas Shadwell, ceased dramatic activity for many years, blocked because of his political affiliation, and when he resumed he composed works in the sphere of exemplary drama. His change of stance is a signal to prepare us for further changes. The vacuum needed to be filled, and new playwrights would meet the need, but their works would be of a somewhat different nature from those of the early Restoration.

# 2 The later comic dramatists

## (a) PROFESSIONAL PLAYWRIGHTS AFTER THE RETIREMENT OF ETHEREGE AND WYCHERLEY

### (i) Introduction

After 1676, the vogue for comedy of manners diminished for some years, yielding to the intrigue plays and sombre tragicomedies of Aphra Behn and relatively bitter comedies by Otway, to political drama and to farce. The production of sex comedy also declined. *Sir Patient Fancy* (1678) and *A True Widow* failed, and Dryden's boisterous *Mr Limberham* was banned. The collapse of the King's Company in the spring of 1682, with the players combined into only one acting troupe, led to a considerable decrease in the number of new offerings each year. Meanwhile, the troubled political situation led to topical plays on the controversies. The new form to emerge was the full-length farce. Edward Ravenscroft was the chief agent, joined by Tom D'Urfey, Nahum Tate, Aphra Behn, Tom Jevon and others. The list even includes Dryden, who had been a leader in denouncing farce. A movement in the direction of sentimental drama got under way in the didactic pieces by Shadwell and in D'Urfey's experiments with serious emotion.

## (ii) Aphra Behn

Aphra Behn contributed a great many plays, though not nearly so many as Dryden. Like him, she catered for prevailing tastes and preferred tragicomedy. In the preface to her third play, *The Dutch Lover*, she explicitly disclaimed the existence of theme or moral in her writings; nevertheless, broken or loveless marriages and the distress caused by arranged marriages appear in a majority of her works. Like Otway, she was concerned with tracing the effects of broken friendship. It is as if both authors were so shocked and appalled by a breach of friendship that they were fascinated by this form of evil and felt required to portray and analyse it. Her first offering, *The Forced Marriage; or, The Jealous Bridegroom* (1670), is a tragicomedy dealing with a breach in the platonic code of friendship. Its plot shows a court favourite, Alcippus, using his influence with the king to marry a woman whom he knows his friend loves.

Mrs Behn also followed the vogue of the Spanish romance, and *The Dutch Lover* (1673) is a comedy of intrigue from the Spanish. The charm and innocence of the earlier plays of this type have yielded here to a titillating sex chase. After her only tragedy, *Abdelazar* (1676), an adaptation from *Lust's Dominion* (1600), she returned in *The Town Fop* (1676) to the topic indicated in the title of her source, George Wilkins's *The Miseries of Enforced Marriage* (c. 1606). The execution is faulty, as the author reveals lack of craftsmanship in her laudable attempt to show the effect of the forced marriage upon the husband, the woman he was required to marry and the woman he loved, followed by a happy ending with the promise of a divorce – pure wish-fulfilment under current law.[1] With a cowardly fop strutting in and out of these episodes, the injury to tone is as bad as the insult to probability. Nevertheless, Mrs Behn constructs one scene that shows her grasp of human psychology. In it, the hero, Bellmour, leaves his unwanted bride on the wedding night and hurries to a bordello, where he drinks and gambles heavily. Here appears Betty Flauntit, showing up for a night's employment. The intoxicated Bellmour harangues the group about his emotional distress. As he denounces lust at the expense of spiritual satisfaction, the streetwalker Betty misunderstands his apostrophe and assumes she has a certain customer for the evening.

Experience in playwriting gradually improved Mrs Behn's craftsmanship, and she shows much skill in managing a large number of characters in the

[1] See Gellert S. Alleman, *Matrimonial Law and the Materials of Restoration Drama* (Wallingford, Pa., 1942).

most popular comedy she ever wrote, *The Rover* (1677). She drew heavily upon Killigrew's narrative *Thomaso* to create a lively comedy of intrigue, set in Naples at carnival time. From the group of expatriates, she provides a spirited pair of young lovers, Willmore and Hellena, and achieves a witty dialogue. Unfortunately, the sequel, *The Rover, Part 2* (*c.* 1681), again violates both tone and unity of action, being a conglomerate of episodes rather than a structured drama, and unity is broken rather than supported by the insertion of a scene between Harlequin and Scaramouch.

*Sir Patient Fancy* (1678) is another treatment of her favourite topic, though here the unhappy marriage comes from economic necessity which forces the heroine to marry an old man. Although drawn from several different pieces by Molière, the work illustrates Mrs Behn's skill in character delineation. This is especially true in the presentation of Sir Patient, 'the typical Whiggish merchant seen from the high Tory point of view, a pious Puritan who is only too happy to shift his devotions to liquor and sex when nightly prayers are called off'.[1] Opinionated and stubborn as he appears, Mrs Behn never makes him contemptible or pathetic.

A great plunderer of old plays, Mrs Behn now drew upon John Marston's sombre psychological drama *The Dutch Courtesan* to adapt it (anonymously) as *The Revenge: or, A Match in Newgate* (1680). The strain upon friendship, developed in the plot of this work, is one of the reasons Mrs Behn has been suggested as the reviser. It was followed by *The False Count* (1681), another story of parents arranging a marriage against the lovers' wishes.

The heated political situation in the winter of 1681 elicited two plays for Tory propaganda needs, *The Roundheads*, a refurbishing of Tatham's *The Rump*, and *The City Heiress*. In the latter work, propaganda did not result in bad art, for this comedy is very well constructed, and the dialogue is as good as in *The Rover*. F. M. Link calls it 'racy, suited to the characters, full of the rhythms of speech, and, above all, plain and natural'.[2]

Arrested in 1682 for criticism of the Duke of Monmouth, Mrs Behn was forced out of the theatre until 1686, when she returned to her favourite subject in *The Lucky Chance* (entered in the Stationers' Register as *The Disappointed Marriage*). Here Leticia, informed that her lover is dead, is tricked into marriage with an old man. Another character, Julia, is shown as already married to an alderman, Sir Cautious Fulbank, a very greedy person, so avaricious, in fact, that he gambles with his wife's lover, using Julia as table stakes, one might say. As to whether the play is primarily concerned with

[1] F. M. Link, *Aphra Behn* (New York, 1968), pp. 54–5.
[2] Ibid. p. 71.

showing the strong emotions of the young lovers or simply with being bawdy, the critics disagree.[1]

Mrs Behn makes a splendidly representative dramatist for this period. She starts out with old-fashioned romantic tragicomedy, experiments with revenge tragedy, and moves with time into the sex comedy of the 1670s. During the Popish Plot, she turns political with her revision of *The Rump* and anti-Whig city comedy, and in one of her last comedies, *The Widow Ranter* (1689), we find her experimenting with an almost Drydenesque split tragicomedy. She never reached any heights of originality, but she eventually became a highly competent technician, turning out skilful exercises in contemporary drama.

## (iii) Thomas Otway

Otway's ventures into comic drama provide further testimony to the wide variety of work produced during the age. His comedies do ridicule the self-centred individual and various kinds of pretence, yet even when he is dealing with the same material as his fellow dramatists – arranged marriages and wedlock for economic security – his treatment is quite different. Many individual episodes are genuinely funny and he was able to create amusing characters, but the tone of his plays is one of profound pessimism. The affectations of his characters are at a tangent from those of the familiar comic creatures of the other playwrights: Etherege's Sir Fopling Flutter dances in the drawing room in order to show off; Melantha, in *Marriage à la Mode*, insists on a vocabulary from French; and Congreve's Petulant arranges to have himself paged in coffee-houses, but Otway's Malagene (in *Friendship in Fashion*, 1678) trips up a wooden-legged cripple to boast of it. This, the first of his comedies, is a strange and bitter study of broken and subverted friendship. A newly married rake tries to marry a cast-off mistress to one friend and dashes off in pursuit of a woman whom he knows to be adored by another friend.

His most successful effort is *The Soldier's Fortune* (1680). Where Ravenscroft makes a lark of the young rakes enjoying the wives of busy aldermen in *The London Cuckolds*, Otway seems more vindictive, constructing a scene in which the cuckold is obliged openly to yield his wife to the rake Beaugard. Otway has been credited with introducing a new type in the pervert, Sir Jolly Jumble, but the dramatist changes the character during the course of the action. At first Sir Jolly is a voyeur, a pimp with homosexual tendencies, and is held up to ridicule. Later he is presented as a pleasant, good-humoured

[1] Nicoll, *HED*, I, p. 268; Sutherland, *Late Seventeenth Century*, pp. 135–6.

fellow who protects whores. The play ends with an amusing proviso dialogue between Courtine, the second lead, and Sylvia. Its favourable reception led Otway to compose a sequel, *The Atheist ; or, the Second Part of the Soldier's Fortune* (1683). Like the other two works, it is a boisterous study of London life, far from being a drawing-room set piece. Otway shows inventiveness, creating a fop who pretends to atheism and is exposed as a coward, and broad comedy in the episode where a father sponges off his son. Nevertheless, it is a depressing play, as we follow the sordid outcome of what had seemed such a promising alliance between Courtine and Sylvia after their proviso scene. So strong are the implications here that one hastens to leave the famous comedies of the age just where their authors terminated them. After noticing the corrosive vision in this sequel, the reader can visualize Dorimant back in London with dingier Bellindas and Loveits while Harriet (securely placed in society) runs with her new gallants, and Horner treated by Quack for a real case of the pox. Otway's comic works have been sadly neglected. Critics have found them revolting, but we should not fail to appreciate the toughness and strength Otway achieved in them.

## (iv) John Crowne

Though Crowne wrote both tragedies and comedies, his talent lay in his comic vein, and he contributed a number of well-constructed dramatic productions. His first work, *The Country Wit* (1676), contains a lively picture of a country squire, Sir Mannerly Shallow, as he wanders around London. A firm royalist, Crowne concocted a propaganda play, *City Politiques* (1683), to ridicule Titus Oates and his Whig backers. It had been licensed in 1682, but permission had been withdrawn until the political crisis was over and the Whigs were in full retreat. Since we are now less concerned with the topical satire, we are better able than the original audience to see that Crowne achieved a light-hearted tone, marked by sudden whimsies, and a colloquial dialogue.[1] As an enjoyably farcical romp, this work deservedly lived on many years after the Popish Plot.

Crowne's reputation as a dramatist rests upon his stage success, *Sir Courtly Nice*, in 1685. Like *Tarugo's Wiles*, it is based upon Moreto's *No puedo ser*, and it is another (and the last) of the plays of Spanish origin suggested for the English stage by Charles II. It is also a transition piece, containing elements of both older and current trends. Unlike earlier Restoration

---

[1] See John Harold Wilson's excellent preface to his edition of Crowne, *City Politiques* (Lincoln, Nebraska, 1967).

comedies, it includes a considerable amount of moralizing; marriage is held to be superior to flirtations and a good wife to young prostitutes. Yet this aspect is overshadowed by the sharply satiric scenes and Crowne's character delineations. The servant Crack, pretending to be the demented Indian prince, Sir Thomas Callico, is very well sketched, but the character best remembered is the fop, Sir Courtly Nice. When making a marriage proposal, he is so conceited that he looks in the mirror to admire himself, giving the young lady a chance to slip unobserved from the room. Sir Fopling Flutter is a self-centred but innocent figure. In comparison, Sir Courtly Nice is seriously and fully consecrated to being a professional fop. His entire time and energy are expended in the effort, and he is more than a match for any contestants. Crowne makes a technical innovation here in having Sir Courtly do some patter-singing in one lyric.

In *The English Friar* (1690) a new attitude is shown in the treatment of the gay young couple, for Laura, the witty and wild juvenile heroine of the kind seen in the 1660s, is disciplined by events and by the wisdom of two young 'men of sense'. Her flirtatious behaviour has been misunderstood, and a young rake attempts to assault her. She then realizes that marriage to the reformed hero, Wiseman, is superior to flirtation.[1]

In his last comedy, *The Married Beau* (1694), Crowne turns to the presentation of a married couple as the leading characters, and deals with marital incompatibility, like so many of his fellow playwrights in the 1690s. What follows is a problem play in which a vain husband is cuckolded as a result of persuading a friend to tempt his wife's virtue, with blank verse being employed in the appropriate passages. The wife repents, but her repentance is not the point of the play, for Crowne keeps the emphasis on the problem of marital maladjustment.[2] Overall, Crowne must be accounted a minor writer. Nevertheless, in *Sir Courtly Nice* he did achieve a significant contribution both to the company of memorable Restoration fops and to the rising tide of essentially moralizing comedy.

## (v) Thomas D'Urfey

Tom D'Urfey was a prolific author, turning out twenty-four comedies, four tragedies and two dramatic operas in thirty-four years of playwriting, apart from composing, collecting and singing songs, which was his main interest. Although many of his plays are imitations of contemporary successes, he took

---

[1] Smith, *The Gay Couple*, pp. 142–4.
[2] Sutherland, *Late Seventeenth Century*, pp. 127–8.

the lead in introducing elements of exemplary drama. He started playwriting with a rush, bringing out two comedies and a tragedy in the autumn of 1676, but his first work of literary merit was *A Fond Husband* (1677), a fast-moving presentation of sexual intrigue. It drew royal favour: Charles II attended three of the first five performances and urged Dryden into imitating it in his *Mr Limberham*. This beginning is a microcosm of his career in drama: in most of his plays he was drawing upon and following older or recent works; then he would take one step ahead of the pack.

In *Squire Oldsapp* (1678), he incorporates a *mélange* of dramatic traditions in having a dramatis personae of humours characters and a plot-line similar to that of *The Merry Wives of Windsor* and Ravenscroft's *The London Cuck-olds*. The first trace of his sentimentality appears in his next offering, *The Virtuous Wife; or, Good Luck at Last* (1679). Here D'Urfey has a serious situation in which the rake Beverly marries Olivia, a good woman, by deceit; later, caught in infidelity, Beverly repents and promises to reform. The rest of the action is given over to slapstick farce, with rakes at assignations getting surprised and cudgelled. The comedian Jevon, playing Whimsey, complains about the physical defects of his 'wife', old Lady Beardly, played by Nokes. Actually, most of D'Urfey's comedies were vehicles for the low comedians Nokes and Leigh. There is also an amusing induction scene in which the notorious Elizabeth Barry refuses to act the part of a virtuous woman (she had recently borne Lord Rochester an illegitimate child).

A staunch royalist, D'Urfey turned to propaganda during the time of the Popish Plot in *Sir Barnaby Whigg* (1681) and *The Royalist* (1682), the latter set at the end of the Commonwealth period, dealing with a sequestration committee as in Howard's *The Committee*. After two adaptations from Fletcher and one from Shakespeare, D'Urfey stepped forward in introducing local colour and a serious treatment of marriage in a significant work for the literary historian, *Love for Money; or, The Boarding School* (1691). The inclusion of these elements represents a considerable change in both D'Urfey's style and prevailing practices in the drama of that time. After sex comedies to feature Elizabeth Barry and farce for Nokes and Leigh, *Love for Money* presented the beautiful young actress Anne Bracegirdle, an *ingénue*, playing the distressed heroine, with William Mountfort in the leading role as a 'man of sense', not as a young rake. In addition, the external characteristics of sentimental comedy and even melodrama appear: obscure birth, the settlement 'Papers' and the cruel uncle who bribes a man to kidnap the heroine. Because the hero, Merriton, has scruples about marrying Myrtilla after he learns of her large inheritance, some critics have labelled the play sentimental; however, the text shows that after the heroine leaves the stage, Merriton tells the audience that he had to act coy in order to hold the upper hand over Myrtilla, and that he had no intention of losing the money but did not want her to taunt him after their marriage with allusions to her wealth. D'Urfey also has some brisk but coarse dialogue in the local-colour scenes of the girls in the boarding school.[1]

*The Richmond Heiress; or, A Woman Once in the Right* (1693) is a satire on fortune hunters. All of them are rejected by the heroine, so that the action ends without a marriage of the principal characters. For Jack not to have his Jill is a change from previous theatrical tradition. Yet D'Urfey, again, has other innovations. Both the serious treatment of the morality of the characters and the heroine's refusal to marry, together with the significance placed on the 'Papers' to the estate, are in line with drama of a much later date. D'Urfey purposely breaks the theatrical illusion at one point to name many of the leading actors of the time and designate their type of role.

D'Urfey hastened in another direction with Parts 1, 2 and 3 of *The Comical History of Don Quixote* (1693 and 1694). He stuffed all three pieces not only with charming and wistful songs set by Purcell and Eccles but also with situations and language so licentious that they became a chief object of Jeremy Collier's wrath.

*The Bath* (1701) is an ambitious but uneven play. It is in accord with the contemporary trend of having a main plot dealing with marital incompatibility. The wedding takes place early in the action, but both principals seek another mate. At a crucial point in the intrigue, the heroine's brother, Colonel Philip, and the young rake have a serious conversation. It is evident that the colonel cares little about his sister or her husband. All he wants is to save appearances, so he asks the young rake to disappear. The colonel then tells a lie about the affair to the husband, and the couple are preserved in the golden chains of matrimony. When the rake agrees to depart and give up his pursuit of Sophronia, the colonel becomes quite complimentary and says that only brave men can be touched by rational argument; others would have drawn a sword. (Sir Richard Steele's dramatic career was devoted to this crux.) There are two subplots, one concerning a country girl with a broad Somerset accent. Ridiculed by all and tricked into marrying the loutish Crab, who is a nobody, she coolly states that with money she will make him into somebody. On her trip to London, she sees a production of Lee's *Sophonisba*

---

[1] See Arthur Sherbo, *English Sentimental Drama* (East Lansing, Mich., 1957), p. 170; K. M. Lynch in *Philological Quarterly*, IX (1930), p. 49; Nicoll, *HED*, I, p. 276; Smith, *The Gay Couple*, pp. 131–9.

and gives a description of it. The entire play is very long, and from newspaper advertisements we know that it had to be cut considerably for production. It is closer to the eighteenth-century novel than either Rowe's *Fair Penitent* and *Jane Shore* or the *Spectator* papers (which have been hailed as precursors of the novel). Despite D'Urfey's bad reputation as a dismal hack, he was a thoroughly professional playwright, and he made successful and historically significant contributions to the drama of his age.

### (vi) Summation of trends

In the 1680s we have seen a shift from both the harsh sex comedy and the comedy of manners of the earlier Restoration traditions towards the sentimental drama of the next century. During these years the older dramatists die, withdraw or grow less active, though Shadwell, Dryden and D'Urfey continue into the next decade. The troubled times of the Popish Plot discourage new writers from breaking into the theatre. Old plays are plundered for use again, while new plays are marked by both moralizing and a growing licentiousness.

## (b) THE LAST RESTORATION DRAMATISTS

### (i) Introduction

The last decade of the century was notable for the strong revival of the satiric comedy which had flourished during the middle of Charles II's reign and, according to most histories of drama, for the emergence of sentimental comedy. Both trends require some explanation to provide an adequate context in which to examine the plays. A new group of playwrights – Southerne, Congreve, Vanbrugh, Farquhar – appeared and contributed a body of satiric comedies of dramatic and literary excellence. Congreve, whose plays unite all elements of the genre,[1] was chief among the group; however, Southerne not only began the revival in 1691 with his play *The Wives Excuse* but also changed the focus of interest from the pursuit of the witty heiress to the study of marital incompatibility. Since Congreve was the outstanding dramatist of the time and since his plays are generally in the former pattern, literary historians have not usually perceived the shift in comedy to the problems of the married couple. But a shift took place, and it should be obvious because

[1] Clifford Leech, 'Congreve and the Century's End', *Philological Quarterly*, XLI (1962), pp. 275–93.

comedies for the past hundred years had usually ended with the marriage of the hero and heroine. The change in subject and theme is found not only in better-known plays such as *The Relapse, The Provoked Wife* and *The Beaux' Stratagem* but also in a large number of lesser-known and badly written new comedies. It is present in plays of both the new writers just mentioned, together with other newcomers – Cibber, Burnaby, Mrs Manley, Mrs Pix, Doggett and Lord Lansdowne – and in the late offerings of the older authors Crowne and D'Urfey. Furthermore, it is found whether the plays are in the older satiric vein, such as *The Wives Excuse* or *The Double Dealer*, or whether they are in the group considered sentimental, such as *Love's Last Shift* and *The Careless Husband*.

This tangled situation will not permit a simple cyclical theory wherein one trend runs its course until it is superseded by another. Cyclical changes were in operation, but the movement was erratic rather than regular. Continuance of the comedy of manners tradition, the dominant type of the 1670s, was halted by the unexpected retirement of Etherege and Wycherley and possibly by the political turmoil begun by Titus Oates, but it did not cease entirely. Instead, as we have just noted, it came on with a rush in the 1690s, being manifested in some of the best comedies in the language. However, before this revival of high comedy, other plays were exhibiting major or minor changes in another direction.

These changes have been called sentimental; nevertheless, the term 'sentimental' should be avoided in references to late seventeenth-century drama. The word had not acquired its present meaning of a response exaggerated beyond the stimulus. When the term came to be used, it meant capacity for feeling, and it is an eighteenth-century phenomenon. As Arthur Sherbo has shown, use of the term 'sentimental' for Restoration drama leads to confusion. From the many definitions that Sherbo lists, every play in the period can be called sentimental, so obviously nothing is gained by this application.[1] We ought also to avoid the temptation of seeing the doctrine of natural goodness in plays before 1700, and probably for some time after that. It is not a concept of the time: orthodox theology was too firm on this matter, even among the deists, and it is unlikely that any dramatist before Richard Cumberland held this doctrine. Fifth-act reformations are uncertain stigmata; some may even represent a cynical gesture. Last-minute reformations

---

[1] Sherbo, op. cit. pp. 1–31. John Loftis provides a detailed analysis showing the impropriety of using the term 'sentimental' for comedy even as late as *The Conscious Lovers*, and he advocates the term 'exemplary' instead; see his *Steele at Drury Lane* (Berkeley, California, 1952), pp. 183–213.

before Steele usually reveal only weak dramaturgy on the part of the author. Until a changed attitude towards the nature of man has been assimilated by the playwrights, these sudden repentances represent a plot device rather than a serious ideological manifesto.

Nevertheless, changes from the 'illusionless outlook' of the satiric dramatists did occur, and they can be recognized and identified. First is the increasingly favourable treatment of older characters. In most Restoration comedies, anyone over thirty was suspect, though *The Country Gentleman* remains an exception. Older people were into something only for their 'interest'. Besides, they had got England into a mess and they were hypocrites; both Lacy and Cowley present this view. Worst of all, older people acted as if they were founts of wisdom. Such was the treatment in the earlier comedies. Therefore, when we find an older person treated sympathetically and his remarks not sneered at or rejected, a change has taken place. Shadwell was probably the first writer to make this shift to a favourable treatment of older people. The second change was the introduction of ethical advice, as opposed to the detachment of the earlier writers. Such edifying instruction may be called *sententiae* (to avoid the word 'sentiments' because of the referential objections to it). Authors began to insert them as signposts for the audience or reader. Thus the uncle, Sir Edward Belfond, in *The Squire of Alsatia*, utters wise advice to the young hero, who listens respectfully. The third change came when playwrights began to treat one of the main characters sympathetically, to secure audience identification. Other characters would be ridiculed for their follies, as formerly, but one person would be treated as a model. Many examples of this mixed type can be found as we move towards the close of the century. Finally, the dramatists began to present some matters as actual problems for society instead of using the levity, for example, with which Horner and his friends responded to Pinchwife's complaints in *The Country Wife*. Consequently, the significance of Cibber's *Love's Last Shift* is not that Loveless is portrayed as basically 'good' or that he repents at the end but that he can respond to 'reason' and can express his feeling. Satiric drama was waning and was being replaced by experiments and makeshifts until its successor, exemplary drama, was established. The term 'exemplary' provides us with a genuine distinction. In satiric comedy, the follies of all the characters are held up for laughter; in exemplary drama, instructive models appear, characters whose words and conduct permit positive emotional responses.

Another complicating factor at the end of the century is that some dramatists turned to pornography after Jeremy Collier's attack on the stage, odd as this may sound. The writers and managers announced, in reply to Collier, that they were writing moral works, but their offerings after 1698, especially the prologues and epilogues, are noticeably marked by prurience and innuendo. Allardyce Nicoll is quite right in saying that a few writers issued moralizing statements as a screen to cover vicious and titillating material.[1]

### (ii) Thomas Southerne

Southerne is a much neglected dramatist, and it is regrettable that no modern edition of his works is available.[2] If his plays were revived on the stage, the producers might find them congenial to the modern temper. Those who have read them bestow high praise. James Sutherland speaks of the 'unusually acute observation of human behaviour and human motives'. John Harrington Smith terms *The Wives Excuse* (1691) 'one of the five most considerable comedies written between 1660 and 1700'. More recently, Kenneth Muir has called attention to this play as an outstanding illustration of the comedy of manners, quoting extensively to document this point.[3] It was Dryden who noticed at the time the comedy appeared that Southerne was following the tradition of Wycherley by writing satiric drama. Like Wycherley, Southerne took great pains to write special turns for the players in the company, and tested the physical capacity of the Drury Lane stage to the limit with his alternating scenes and special effects, as well as relying heavily on music. The dialogue of his first comedy, *Sir Anthony Love* (1690), is certainly intended only for the stage, and Allardyce Nicoll directs attention to the 'overuse of theatrical broken sentences, wherein the meaning of one speaker is continued or subverted by another'.[4] *Sir Anthony Love* is a 'breeches' play, with the heroine, Lucia, disguised as a man. The part was written for the attractive comedienne Susanna Percival Mountfort. Instead of the labels 'sentimental' and 'manners', critics might discover more reliable terms if they noticed that Congreve was writing comic parts for Anne Bracegirdle, Southerne for Mrs Mountfort, and Cibber and Farquhar for Anne Oldfield.[5]

---

[1] Nicoll, *HED*, I, pp. 265–6.

[2] Harold Love and Robert Jordan are currently preparing an edition, under the auspices of the Clarendon Press; meanwhile, a scholarly edition of *The Wives Excuse* has now been done by Ralph Thornton (Philadelphia, 1973).

[3] Sutherland, *Late Seventeenth Century*, p. 145; Smith, *The Gay Couple*, p. 144; Kenneth Muir, *The Comedy of Manners* (London, 1970).

[4] Nicoll, *HED*, I, p. 240.

[5] Bernard Harris makes some valuable observations on this point in Brown and Harris (eds), *Restoration Theatre*, pp. 11–40.

The harshest satire in the work occurs when the homosexual abbot tries to make advances to Lucia (dressed as Sir Anthony).

*The Wives Excuse* presents the story of a marriage that is ruined almost as soon as it is made. The young, newly married wife, Mrs Friendall, immediately finds that her husband is a coward and a philanderer. Friendall acts as the leader of a social set, entertaining the members of his group with sponsored concerts and continual open house in his home, where his wife is expected to be entertaining the guests while he openly pursues different women. Upon observing this nasty situation, one man is quick to offer Mrs Friendall the opportunity of revenging herself upon her husband, with the result that she has to concern herself not only with achieving emotional balance over the problem of her husband's errant conduct but also over the importuning of her new friend. Meanwhile, the remaining members of the large cast move with surface courtesy through the scenes, showing strong hostility towards the rest, each one seeking a bedfellow. The opening scene is a dramatic gem. A large group of servants await the end of a concert where their masters are in attendance. The servants gamble, talk lewdly and gossip. The concert doors open, the servants depart for the carriages, and the society set move downstage, to begin talking and acting in just the same way that their servants had done.[1] The final episode is no less dramatic. Utilizing the resources of the Drury Lane stage, Southerne presents four successive receding 'discovery' scenes, from the apron to the back of the stage, opening these scenes until, in the last one, the faithless husband and a town flirt are exposed, as the characters in the play and the audience see 'Friendall *and* [Mrs] Wittwoud *upon a Couch*'.

The real action of *The Wives Excuse*, writes Harold Love, 'consists in a step-by-step enrichment of our sense of the moral predicament of the central character, Mrs Friendall', trapped in a society built around an inadequate definition of human nature. Southerne, he concludes, is 'as close as a Restoration dramatist could be to the dramatic method of Chekhov'.[2] The satire must have been too severe for an audience of the 1690s, and the play failed.

Southerne persevered to write one more harshly satiric comedy, *The Maid's Last Prayer; or, Any Rather than Fail* (1693), in which he departs from the customary procedure of having a young woman as the heroine to present instead a spinster, an older person, as the main character.

[1] A. H. Scouten, 'Notes toward a History of Restoration Comedy', *Philological Quarterly*, XLV (1966), pp. 62–70. I am obliged to the editors for allowing me to reprint this paragraph.

[2] Harold Love, 'Dryden, Durfey, and the Standards of Comedy', *Studies in English Literature*, XIII (1973), pp. 422–36.

Disappointed by its unfavourable reception, Southerne turned to tragedy and abandoned comic drama, save for his late and indifferent *Money the Mistress* of 1726. Obviously, the theatrical climate was hostile to his comic vision and consequently his work had little effect on the direction taken by the drama in the 1690s except for his noteworthy innovation of choosing a married couple to be the leading characters in a comedy, a striking deviation from the customary formula. This change was employed, in one way or another, by most of his contemporary dramatists down through Farquhar's *The Beaux' Stratagem* in 1707. Southerne's failure with the London audience should not blind us to the power and subtlety of his dramaturgy. His acute psychological perception and his coldly realistic analyses of social and marital relationships make him one of the most artistic dramatists of the seventeenth century.

### (iii) William Congreve

Congreve's genius flowered early; his first work, *The Old Bachelor* (1693), appeared when he was twenty-three, and all five of his plays were produced before he was thirty. The young Irishman created a sensation with the manuscript of *The Old Bachelor* when he brought it to London. Dryden, Southerne and Arthur Mainwayring studied and polished the text, with Dryden arranging the order of the scenes. The production on 9 March 1693 was an instant success; on the 11th the Earl of Cork wrote to the poet's father: 'Your sons Play was Acted on Thursday last & was by all the hearers applauded to bee the best that has been Acted for many yeares.'[1]

It was an ambitious effort in that Congreve filled the stage with a large cast of characters and several subplots. From a technical view, Congreve demonstrated his ability in making the several actions and numerous characters functional to the main design. He also passed the real test of dramatic artistry in showing that he could organize experience. 'Each character', writes Norman Holland, 'is created from a single factor, his reaction to the central problem of appearance contradicting nature.'[2]

Restoration gallants, whether in leading or minor roles, prided themselves on easy conquests of the fair sex; it was an article of faith. Congreve drew upon this convention and invented a new character from it, Vainlove, who is irresistible to the opposite sex. However, as soon as a woman indicates a

---

[1] The National Library of Ireland, MS 13, 226 (18) fol. 2a; from this letter comes the new date of the première. Also see *The Complete Works of William Congreve*, ed. Herbert Davis (Chicago, 1967), pp. 2–5.
[2] Holland, op. cit. p. 138.

favourable response, Vainlove hands her over to Bellmour for the final chase and seduction. Congreve is satirizing the attitude in the duel of the sexes whereby the conquered one is despised so that the victor forfeits the satisfaction of the triumph. Other implications of Vainlove's behaviour were later developed by Richardson and Laclos in the characters Lovelace and Valmont.[1] Thus this comedy ends without promise of marriage between Vainlove and Araminta, since Araminta dares not consent lest Vainlove leave her.

In other episodes, we find some ludicrous scenes in which three humours characters are involved: the misanthrope Heartwell, the complete fool Sir Joseph Wittol and the 'religious' Fondlewife. At first, Heartwell is trapped by Sylvia (who has been through the Vainlove–Bellmour dance) because she acts the role that he idealizes. Congreve later extricates Heartwell and assigns the unchaste Sylvia to the bumbling Sir Joseph, an absurd character who talks mysteriously about 'his Back', by which he means his crony, the boaster (and coward) Captain Bluffe. Old Fondlewife, the suspicious husband, is also zealous, much given to biblical analogy, larding his speech with religious terms. His young wife, Laetitia, is beginning an affair with Bellmour. Sir Joseph Wittol calls at Fondlewife's house to borrow some money and arrives at a time when Bellmour is calling with a less innocent reason. Laetitia attempts to use Sir Joseph's presence to advantage by denouncing him as an assailant when her husband unexpectedly arrives. Fondlewife acts as if a mild oath by Sir Joseph was of equal gravity with Laetitia's charge:

> Oh, how the blasphemous Wretch swears! Out of my House, thou Son of the Whore of Babylon; Offspring of Bell and the Dragon – Bless us! Ravish my Wife! my Dinah! Oh Shechemite! (IV. xviii)

Sir Joseph's departure does not resolve the unpleasant situation of Fondlewife's catching his wife with Bellmour. Now Fondlewife has to struggle with the problem of whether to accept self-deception or the harsh reality of the situation; the former triumphs when he says, 'I won't believe my own Eyes.' Congreve ends this excellent scene by using Bellmour to turn on Fondlewife's 'religiosity' in saying: 'See the great Blessing of an easy Faith; Opinion cannot err' (IV. xxii).

The other sign of the arrival of a major playwright was the sparkle of the dialogue. The witty exchanges in this play were praised by contemporaries, by Samuel Johnson and by almost every critic since. 'Could'st thou be content to marry *Araminta*?' asks Bellmour:

[1] Kenneth Muir, 'The Comedies of William Congreve', in Brown and Harris (eds), *Restoration Theatre*, p. 223.

VAINLOVE: Could you be content to go to Heav'n?

BELLMOUR: Hum, not immediately, in my Conscience not heartily? I'd do a little more Good in my Generation first, in order to deserve it. (III. iii)

The dialogue is also marked by striking and vivid metaphor. So effective is the impact that the dialogue occasionally gives the impression of containing more tropes than an actual count supports, as illustrated in the following speech by Heartwell:

> Yet it is oftentimes too late with some of you young, termagant, flashy Sinners – you have all the Guilt of the Intention, and none of the Pleasure of the Practice – 'tis true you are so eager in Pursuit of the Temptation, that you save the Devil the Trouble of leading you into it. (I. iv)

Satire of a much more bitter nature appears in *The Double Dealer* (1693) with the characters Lady Touchwood and Maskwell, who would normally be placed in tragedy or tragicomedy. The plot complication is tight. The leading couple, Mellefont and Cynthia, are in love with each other. Lady Touchwood, who is infatuated with Mellefont, is having an affair with Maskwell, a cold-blooded scoundrel carefully scheming to marry Cynthia. However, there is a technical flaw in that there seems to be a violation of unity of tone in the scenes ridiculing the Froths and the Plyants, empty-headed fools that they are. There may be an explanation for these contrasting scenes (in addition to the fact that these characters are so hilariously funny that we couldn't do without them). Congreve has elevated Cynthia into a perceptive, intelligent woman who entertains doubts about marriage because of the intrigues of the villains on one side and the folly of some married couples on the other. To show the latter, Congreve had to introduce the frivolous Froths and Plyants. This concern over achieving a successful marriage will reappear in his remaining comedies, for Congreve was as involved in the study of marital incompatibility as his fellow playwrights who elected to begin their plots with the leading couple already married.

*Love for Love* has been the most popular of the four comedies on the stage. The première was the occasion for opening the new Lincoln's Inn Fields Theatre on 30 April 1695, where *Love for Love* enjoyed a thirteen-night run, and it was a successful play throughout the next century. The title means that the heroine Angelica will not give her true love to Valentine until she has his. Marriage must not be entered without it. Valentine plays Proteus, twisting and turning in different directions, feigning madness and engaging in various schemes to no avail. Angelica also engages in some unbecoming behaviour to affect complete indifference. She wants assurance of Valentine's love, but she also wants to make sure that Valentine's inheritance of the Legend money and property will not be lost to his brother, the sailor Ben. 'Let me consult my lawyer,' responds Angelica to Sir Sampson Legend at one point in the negotiations. (Penelope Gilliatt calls the play 'Love for Loot'.) The emphasis on financial security will be repeated in *The Way of the World*, where the disposition of Millamant's inheritance is so crucial that some critics call the play a legacy hunt.[1] If Valentine, Angelica, Mirabell and Millamant had been willing to leave London to work in a factory or, better yet, a Welsh coal mine, L. C. Knights might have seen some merit in Congreve's writings.[2] But the desire to have true love, a successful marriage, and yet live in London society is too much for the social critics.

Congreve displays increased technical skill in the juxtaposition of groups of characters in contrasting scenes. Valentine and Angelica are highly sophisticated members of upper-middle-class society. Against them are posed the innocents – sailor-boy Ben and the *ingénue* Miss Prue. In between are the parasites, Scandal and Tattle, and the 'would-bes', Mrs Frail and Mrs Foresight, in a series of entertaining encounters. The episode in which Tattle teaches the innocent Prue the way of the world is delightful satiric comedy and has been highly commended.[3] The control of dialogue seems to increase in each successive work. Congreve not only achieves the rhythms of colloquial speech, but also a vocabulary and idiom appropriate to the speaker. Kenneth Muir stresses this achievement:

> Many dramatists succeed in distinguishing some of their characters by giving them tricks of speech; but Congreve is unique among dramatists since the Restoration in his ability to distinguish all his characters in his last two plays by their manner of speech.[4]

The increased control of language becomes one of the factors that make *The Way of the World* such an artistic success. It was not a success in 1700,

---

[1] Paul and Miriam Mueschke, *A New View of Congreve's Way of the World* (Ann Arbor, Mich., 1958).

[2] See L. C. Knights, 'Restoration Comedy: The Reality and the Myth', *Scrutiny*, VI (1937), pp. 122–43. Knights found Congreve 'dull'. A controversy developed in the 1957 volume of F. W. Bateson's journal, *Essays in Criticism*.

[3] See F. W. Bateson, 'L. C. Knights and Restoration Comedy', *Essays in Criticism*, VII (1957), pp. 56–7.

[4] Muir, 'Comedies of William Congreve', p. 228.

but the numerous performances in the second quarter of the eighteenth century and the favourable reception in modern revivals demonstrate that the play's complex intrigue can be understood in the theatre. Command of language enabled Congreve to achieve mastery of tone, the unmistakable feature of this work. Important as the plot is, we learn less from it than from the tone created by the speech, manner and attitudes of the characters.[1]

Congreve assumes that the audience can distinguish between good and bad, even when the distinctions are not obvious. The characters are not divided into heroes and villains; instead, Congreve gives the different persons due play for their motives, their insight into others and their separate abilities. We are not asked to choose between raw, uninhibited emotions on one hand and insincere manners on the other, though both are depicted. When Mirabell complains of Millamant, in the opening scene, that 'She is more mistress of herself than to be under the necessity' (of flattering her aunt), we learn that the play deals with values achieved by discipline. Mirabell insists on self-control, balance, order and the rejection of extremes. Fainall takes on the aspect of a villain only when he loses his temper; elsewhere through the play he is the same suave, intelligent observer of London life that Mirabell is. Marwood, who engages in villainous acts, is the only person who shows common courtesy to Sir Wilfull Witwoud, the country booby, when he enters the drawing room in his filthy boots. It is this booby who has the fast reflexes to interpose his sword to protect Mrs Fainall after Fainall has already drawn a sword. Against this effete group in the drawing room, not used to real swords and real fighting, Sir Wilfull makes a favourable contrast. Yet when placed in a situation which requires emotional maturity – the encounter with Millamant – he is rude, insensitive and coarse. Fast reflexes help him save Mrs Fainall but they are not an adequate substitute for sense and refinement.

Nor is Mirabell a perfect hero.[2] We learn of his affair with Arabella, terminated by a cold-blooded, practical decision to marry her off to Fainall when she thought she was pregnant. Mirabell arranges to have his servant disguise as Sir Rowland and court Lady Wishfort, but to prevent treachery Mirabell makes certain that the servant (Waitwell) marries Foible, and he inspects the wedding certificate himself. He also has small flaws, for which Millamant teases him – sententiousness and gravity. The charming Millamant, who

[1] Cleanth Brooks and R. B. Heilman, *Understanding Drama* (New York, 1945), pp. 441–50. Though a commercial textbook, this work contains one of the best analyses yet made of this play.
[2] See Jean Gagen, 'Congreve's Mirabell and the Ideal Gentleman', *PMLA*, LXXIX (1964), pp. 422–7.

affects a vapid manner, is intelligent enough to recognize that Mirabell is far too serious to make a gay companion.

The great irony develops from the marriage proposals in the fourth act when Congreve exercises his talent in contrasted episodes. The first shows Sir Wilfull approaching Millamant with all the rural embarrassment of the natural man. Unequal to the occasion, he cannot get to the subject and departs. Mirabell enters, and there follows the long proviso scene with Millamant which romanticists have denounced. Upon Mirabell's departure, Petulant enters, drunk, and makes an address marked by vulgarity and indecency: 'Look you, Mrs Millamant – if you love me, dear nymph – say it – and that's the conclusion – pass on, or pass off, – that's all.' He concludes, after this disgraceful exhibition, 'I'll go to bed with my maid.' Now Lady Wishfort brings Sir Wilfull back to propose to Millamant. He disposes of it shortly: 'But if you have a mind to be married, say the word, and send for the piper; Wilfull will do't' – but shortly afterwards he will echo Petulant by saying 'Wenches, where are the wenches?' At this point, one might ask whether there is any place for romance. The answer is supplied by the final proposal – that of the servant Waitwell (disguised as Lord Rowland) to Lady Wishfort: 'My impatience, madam, is the effect of my transport; – till I have the possession of your adorable person, I am tantalized on a rack.' When Lady Wishfort replies, 'If you think the least scruple of carnality was an ingredient', Waitwell says, 'Dear Madam, no. You are all camphire and frankincense, all chastity and odor.' The vocabulary of romance has appeared, but it hardly seems satisfactory either. If we re-examine the supposedly artificial proviso scene in the light of the other proposals, its impact is considerably enhanced. Millamant doesn't want to dwindle into the kind of wife that Mrs Fainall is. Both Mirabell and Millamant want to retain their essential dignity, which the stereotyped marriage removes.

Congreve's attitude is not one of cynicism and indifference. The characters who conform to the way of the world are censured.[1] Mirabell and Millamant's whole struggle is to achieve the self-discipline that will enable them to reject the appearances of life without the reality. They want a marriage based on mutual respect. Waitwell's proposal is a parody of romantic courtship, with the devastating implication that it appears only when it is pretended. Yet to say this is not to be cynical. What this sequence of proposal scenes does is to make us less willing to accept appearances and yet more tolerant of human nature.[2]

[1] T. J. Fujimura, *The Restoration Comedy of Wit* (Princeton, N.J., 1952), p. 200.
[2] Louis Kronenberger, *The Thread of Laughter* (New York, 1952).

The proviso scene is often charged with being removed from life though it is actually based upon harsh realism. A witty and charming heiress like Millamant naturally wishes 'to prolong and increase the prenuptial glamour'.[1] The excitement of the agreeable attentions of a flock of admirers ends with the wedding ceremony, as the bride adjusts to life with one man. It is not an artificial view of life which portrays Millamant as enjoying coquetry, for Congreve has very well caught the dilemma of the popular young débutante who finally gives her hand in marriage, when the game of flirtation must end. Today, a woman can obtain a divorce and resume the old dance, but this recourse was not available to Millamant.

In *The Way of the World*, William Congreve achieved his most perfectly wrought drama. It lacks the boisterous, if imitative vitality of *The Old Bachelor*, the harsh satire of *The Double Dealer*, the blithe high spirits of *Love for Love*. But responding in part, at least, to Collier's attack on the stage, Congreve was able to create a work which was both serious and dazzlingly witty. He covered himself against obvious moral reproach, but without moving into exemplary drama. Presumably his decision to abandon the stage was public knowledge by 1702. We may surmise that, like Southerne, he found the theatrical climate hostile. His failure to write any original plays after the age of thirty constitutes a major loss to the English theatre.

### (iv) Colley Cibber

The actor-manager Colley Cibber was very much a professional dramatist and he wrote a number of comedies that show the transition between Restoration and Augustan drama. His output can be conveniently divided into two groups: his own inventions and his revisions or adaptations. As F. W. Bateson pointed out long ago, Cibber's original work dealt with a problem: the reconciliation of a married couple who have drifted apart.[2] Cibber, then, joins Southerne, Vanbrugh, Burnaby, Farquhar and others in the study of marital incompatibility. The plays in this group are *Love's Last Shift* (1696), *The Careless Husband* (1704) and *The Lady's Last Stake* (1707), together with one later revision, *The Provoked Husband* (1728). Such a grouping leads to a better understanding of his plays and their relation to the work of his contemporaries than isolating *Love's Last Shift* and calling it the first sentimental drama.

*Love's Last Shift* does contain more than one element of the new exemplary

---

[1] Mueschke, op. cit. p. 30.
[2] F. W. Bateson, *English Comic Drama, 1700–1750* (Oxford, 1929), p. 36.

comedy. While discussion usually centres on the fifth-act repentance of the long-absent rake who is lured into moral consciousness by sexual gratification and achieves, as John Harold Wilson cynically observes, the remarkable feat of cuckolding himself,[1] Cibber includes other features. He presents a talkative young woman, Hillaria, of the vivacious type seen in many an earlier comedy; but here she is treated as a coquette and is instructed by others to desist from frivolity and marry the Elder Worthy, a man of sense. Thus in one plot a virtuous woman converts a rake and in the other plot an older man disciplines or corrects a coquette. Meanwhile, we find many grave *sententiae* in the dialogue, and we have clearly reached exemplary drama. The combination of witty, sardonic dialogue with gratuitous moral instruction and the titillating bedroom scene of the last act constitute a real offence against unity of tone. As far as comedy is concerned, Cibber contributed a more stylized fop, Sir Novelty Fashion.

*The Careless Husband* (1704) is a mixture of divergent features. Cibber includes bawdy talk for its own sake; the male lead, Sir Charles Easy, is enjoying not one but two women in addition to his wife; and Lady Betty Modish is represented as a Restoration heroine. Yet Cibber inserts heavy *sententiae* into the dialogue and provides a truly sentimental ending. When Easy's wife returns to the house and finds her husband asleep with the maid, she places a neckcloth over his head, ostensibly to prevent his catching cold; when he awakes, he repents, though modern readers may wonder whether he was fully awake. This 'steinkirk' episode was much discussed, and the play was frequently acted.

*The Lady's Last Stake; or, The Wife's Resentment* again shows marital disharmony, and reconciliation seems impossible because of the proud, unyielding personality of the wife, Lady Wronglove. The genuine dramatic tension engendered by the conflict is lost when Cibber contrives an implausible solution by bringing in a sententious old man, Sir Friendly Moral, whose grave advice stops the hostilities. F. W. Bateson tries to justify the false ending by arguing that through it Cibber was demonstrating that life was not a matter of great moments, 'but a daily round of nervous irritation, petty quarrels, and insignificant injuries'.[2]

In 1728, Cibber produced *The Provoked Husband; or, A Journey to London*, a comedy which enjoyed the longest run of any of his plays, and this against the competition of the first run of *The Beggar's Opera*. Cibber knew that he had written a good play, and when credit was denied him he contemptuously

[1] Wilson, *A Preface*, p. 192.
[2] *English Comic Drama*, p. 33.

printed Vanbrugh's manuscript so that 'the Town' could learn that the broad, farcical episodes were by Vanbrugh, leaving Cibber as the inventor of the drawing-room scenes. In this play, which belongs in the marriage group, a flirtatious wife has to be chastened – Vanbrugh intended to have her turned out of the house – by her husband, Lord Townly. The work abounds in apophthegms, and three of the main characters are sober, thoughtful persons. The wife is reclaimed, and the couple become reconciled. The play is announced as exemplary comedy in the prologue:

> Plays should let you see
> Not only, what you Are but Ought to be.

The great majority of Cibber's plays are revisions and adaptations. Cibber was a skilful play-doctor, often bringing material together from two or three different works rather than adapting one. Such an amalgamation is *Woman's Wit* (1697). Here he secures a real conflict wherein Lovemore is loved by a virtuous woman, Emilia, while he is fascinated by a flirt, Leonora. When a kindly friend, Longville, attempts to bring Emilia and Lovemore together, he arouses the wrath of Leonora, whose attempt to baulk his plan and get vengeance takes the work towards tragedy. The tone is serious throughout, and the audience sees an insincere and affected woman lose out to a woman of virtue.

The next comedy, *Love Makes a Man* (1700), is long and broken-backed. The first two acts are from Fletcher's *The Elder Brother*, and the last three from Fletcher's *The Custom of the Country*, including the triple romances from the latter, one of the coarsest Jacobean sex dramas. Where Fletcher has Carlos reach manhood by falling in love, Cibber uses the device of a duel instead. The popularity of this hotchpotch is inexplicable; it was acted every season for about fifty years, and was one of the most popular comedies of the century, gaining even more showings than *The Careless Husband*. Cibber continued refurbishing old plays until 1745, turning out comedies, farces, pastorals, tragedies and ballad operas.

Cibber remains something of a joke, and as the object of the Scriblerians' derision he is hard to resurrect. *Love's Last Shift*, the work which has gained him attention from literary historians, is basically a dishonest work,[1] and it is hard to find any higher praise than 'clever' for his best comedies. Little can be said for his many late adaptations, but he cannot be denied some importance as a trend-setter around the turn of the century. Though he was not the

---

[1] The view of Alan Roper, 'Language and Action in *The Way of the World, Love's Last Shift*, and *The Relapse*', *ELH*, XL (1973), pp. 44–69.

harbinger of sentimental comedy that older critics once called him, he capitalized successfully on audience taste for improbable sentimental reform, developing the trend started by Shadwell and D'Urfey.

## (v) Sir John Vanbrugh

The rank improbability of Colley Cibber's touching finale to *Love's Last Shift* led to Vanbrugh's mirthful protest, *The Relapse*, and brought a new dramatist into the theatre ahead of his intention. Vanbrugh has been compared unfavourably with Congreve; however, though Vanbrugh is at a disadvantage in such a comparison, he brought to the drama a robust vigour lacking in many of his contemporaries, as well as real inventiveness in his plots and character sketches.[1] Modern revivals have helped Vanbrugh's reputation, for the wit still sparkles and the characters still have vitality.

*The Relapse* shows the young rake in hot pursuit of the first woman he meets, but this is only one of the developments which Vanbrugh builds from Cibber's play, for he alters and expands the character delineation of the two brothers, Tom and Sir Novelty Fashion. The latter was ennobled to 'Lord Foppington', the most professional fop of the entire period (see Plate 34). Lord Foppington possesses a resilient inner core of absolute self-confidence. He never acknowledges himself the object of contempt, even after the farcical trick perpetrated on him at the close of the play. Instead he preserves the glacial exterior with which he meets all circumstances, and with a 'stap my vitals' he is ready to strut into another adventure. Vanbrugh's other change concerns the social and economic inferiority that primogeniture enforced on younger brothers, sarcastically alluded to by numerous playwrights. Cibber had shown the two brothers as congenial, ready to aid each other, but Vanbrugh introduces bitter animosity so that he can deal seriously with the predicament of younger brothers. There is no heavy didacticism, for the episodes are so constructed that Lord Foppington's frigid indifference and Tom's hatred produce laughter. Vanbrugh has lively sketches of rural scenes as Tom goes to the country to gain ascendancy over his brother and win a fortune by marrying the country girl, Hoyden. In another plot complication, Worthy attempts to seduce the mistreated and abused Amanda. She rebuffs him, and he temporarily accepts her verdict in an encounter which has been called sentimental, possibly because Vanbrugh shifts from prose to blank verse for Worthy's oration.

[1] Bonamy Dobrée, *English Literature in the Early Eighteenth Century, 1700–1740* (Oxford, 1959), p. 231.

The success of *The Relapse* encouraged Vanbrugh to complete *The Provoked Wife* (1697). In this comedy he follows Southerne's lead in using a married couple as his main characters, and he successfully presents 'a sustained and rational treatment of marital incompatibility, which exploits to the full both the comic and the critical aspects of his theme'.[1] Sir John Brute is a cowardly and vulgar scoundrel, and Vanbrugh's creation was highly praised, especially in the interpretation later given by David Garrick. Vanbrugh takes pains to avoid building sympathy for the abused wife, Lady Brute. In a long soliloquy after the first quarrel in the play, we can note with amusement the attempts of Lady Brute to find arguments justifying the adultery which she lacks courage to translate into action. Sir John's drunken rambles about London add more comic incident. Unfortunately, the rest of Vanbrugh's plays are adaptations, heavily derived from Dancourt and other French writers, and are as well forgotten. His involvement in architecture, landscape gardening and Italian opera filled his time, thus depriving the theatre of an excellent comic playwright.

### (vi) George Farquhar

In 1697 George Farquhar came to London ready to take on the Establishment, a lively member of the series of Irish dramatists who have for several centuries provided London audiences with entertaining comedies. His opening piece, *Love and a Bottle* (1698), was far from revolutionary; it is in fact much like other new plays of the time. Efforts at cynicism in the dialogue only sound flippant – perhaps a clue to the organization of the play. The action begins as if the piece would be extremely bawdy, with a good deal of railing at the sins of society as a justification for unprincipled conduct, and the characters supposedly dominated by self-interest; however, as the plot unfolds we find exemplary persons in Lovewell and Leanthe. The young author is at the old dodge of simultaneously offering themes of wit and disillusion while presenting models to show virtue and good sense. Society is corrupt, the play suggests, but a person can be virtuous and a rake can reform. The only good thing that can be said for this first effort is that it has the verve and gusto, the 'life force' or energy present in all of Farquhar's work.

*The Constant Couple* (1699) was an improvement. It was also a tremendous success, enjoying some fifty-five performances the first season, the author claimed (in his preface to *The Inconstant*). He has something for everyone

---

[1] P. Mueschke and J. Fleischer, 'A Re-Evaluation of Vanbrugh', *PMLA*, XLIX (1934), pp. 848–9.

here. The curtain goes up on an emotional scene with humanitarian implications, a tableau of disbanded soldiers in distress and a woman wronged. A licentious rake, Sir Harry Wildair, tries to sow some wild oats but is reformed by the love of a virtuous woman. A prevailing gaiety informs the work, its various episodes marked by vivacity and good humour. Festive comedy makes its reappearance with Farquhar. Unfortunately, he sought easy profit in adding a sequel, *Sir Harry Wildair* (1701), but this jumbled extravaganza deservedly failed. *The Inconstant* (1702), his adaptation of Fletcher's *The Wild Goose Chase*, was initially a failure, though it recovered (too late to profit Farquhar) to be a stock piece for many years. A similar fate befell *The Twin Rivals* (1702), an exemplary drama showing men of sense and virtuous women, with a young rake held up for ridicule. The première was a failure, and though his play was revived years later, when this type of comedy became more fashionable, and was acted on into the nineteenth century, Farquhar's poverty forced him to leave London temporarily.

Three years of vicissitudes provided added material and experience. Moreover, he had personally discovered the actress he needed in Anne Oldfield. For this sprightly wench, he designed the effervescent *The Recruiting Officer* (1706). The first act is one of the most rollicking opening acts in English comedy; the dash and verve remind one of Dekker's *The Shoemakers' Holiday* or the opening tavern scene in *1 Henry IV*. As the scene opens, the setting is rural, the characters bourgeois, and the tone is one of infectious optimism (a word seldom found in treatises on Restoration drama). The entire action is dominated by Anne Oldfield, playing Sylvia, disguised as a man. No one is spared by her wit, as she controls the scene, costumed in a uniform of white trimmed with silver, and is the centre of homosexual innuendo.[1] The author's method is to gain early sympathy for the two main characters, Silvia and Plume; then if he wishes to venture into satire he is safe in doing so. In a perceptive essay John Traugott asserts that sentimentalism by no means constituted the death of comedy; instead, it gave authors like Farquhar and Goldsmith opportunity for invention.[2]

During his final illness, the highspirited playwright completed his masterpiece, *The Beaux' Stratagem* (1707), the protagonist Archer to be played by Wilks and the heroine, Mrs Sullen, by Anne Oldfield. The work is 'a consideration of the state of marriage', writes Bonamy Dobrée.[3] It is that and many other things as well. Again set in the country, the play offers two

[1] Detected by G. Wilson Knight, op. cit. p. 172.
[2] Traugott, op. cit. p. 406.
[3] From a review in *Études anglaises*, XX (1967), pp. 89-91.

penniless rakes (one disguised as master, the other as valet) who must, between them, marry an heiress or join the army. Farquhar invents a large cast of characters. Instead of stereotypes, he moves towards naturalism in charting a predatory innkeeper, his wealthy and luscious daughter Cherry, highwaymen who know their legal rights on the scaffold, Lady Bountiful and Squire Sullen whose head aches consumedly. That Farquhar's treatment of the social problem of marital maladjustment is not accidental is demonstrated by his repeated quotations from the tract in which John Milton argued for divorce on grounds of incompatibility.

Character delineation is not simplified. Where Farquhar had used atrocious French in previous works for propaganda and ridicule, he now makes Count Bellair observe about Mrs Sullen's essential nature: 'Begar, madam, your virtue be vera great, but garzoon, your honesty be vere little' (III. iii. 468–9). This stroke was cut from the otherwise excellent and successful revival in London in 1970. Its deletion makes the modern viewer consider Farquhar only an amusing writer from an older period instead of seeing him as a powerful dramatist. Farquhar treats the 'good' girl Dorinda to a similarly searching examination. Throughout the action, she has been held up as the virtuous and reasonable woman, frequently attempting to restrain Mrs Sullen from wild talk and conduct. Yet at one point we discover that Dorinda yearns for the social life of London, and imagines herself leaving a London theatre in fashionable attire, with the linkboys crying 'Lights for Lady Aimwell'.

Farquhar balances Aimwell against Archer, in the search of the two young rakes for financial security. Aimwell turns soft, confesses the plan to the virtuous Dorinda, and shows that he has feelings and has attained sensibility. Archer remains a wild rake, without scruples. When Mrs Sullen evinces gratitude at his saving her from robbers, Archer is ready to fling her on the bed instantly. Since the Church did not countenance divorce, Farquhar has to end the play with a *deus ex machina* trick, so that the lovers can climb into bed. From the sharp contrast between the conduct of the two male leads, we can observe that the play points two ways, Archer backwards to the older sex comedies of the Restoration and Aimwell towards the drama of sensibility of the future. It is clear that George Farquhar took English comedy out of the London drawing room, and that he also took the road towards naturalism; it is even clearer that he wrote two comedies of enduring fame, *The Recruiting Officer* and *The Beaux' Stratagem*. A month after the première of his last work, Farquhar was dead, and the comic tradition of energy and amiable humour which he had so ably carried on died with him. There was to be a long wait for Sheridan and a longer one for Shaw and Wilde.

## (vii) Minor dramatists

Late in December 1695, at the première of George Granville, Lord Lansdowne's *The She Gallants* (a comedy in the manners style written a dozen years earlier), the characters engage in a symposium on the problem of marital discord. It seems more than coincidence that seven of the next ten comedies to appear dealt with this subject, beginning with *Love's Last Shift* in January 1696. Of these, Mrs Mary Pix has three works in which one or more of the leading characters is married; in two of them the plot complications include adultery, treated sympathetically, though not endorsed: *The Spanish Wives* (1696) and *The Deceiver Deceived* (1697). In the third, *The Innocent Mistress* (1697), the hero is married; hence he and his true love, Marianne, can have only a platonic attachment – until the end of the play, when there is a *deus ex machina* turn. Mrs Delariviere Manley's *The Lost Lover* (1696) deals with the unhappiness resulting from a forced marriage. Olivia, in love with Wildman, has been married to a rich merchant through her father's insistence. We are moving further from the Restoration as we listen to Olivia spurning Wildman on ethical grounds, 'so that her Virtue can be cherished'.

Satiric comedy in the older style was continued by William Burnaby. His first play, *The Reformed Wife* (1700), contains a cynical approach to 'reform'. For fear of discovery, the young wife Astrea covers her intrigue with Freeman by letting him court Clarinda. The complications of this arrangement get out of hand, not proving as convenient a device as Astrea had hoped, for Freeman and Clarinda proceed to marry. Unable to continue the illicit affair, Astrea is left as a reformed wife, but through circumstance rather than surface morality or inner conscience. Burnaby includes an amusing character in Lady Dainty, who affects illness as a fad: 'No Woman of Quality is, or should be in perfect health,' she says. Later, she grieves because poor people are permitted to complain of the same ailments. The tone of the entire work is that found in earlier Restoration comedy. Burnaby has a talent for building repartee in the numerous dialogues.

Satire and cynicism abound in his next offering, *The Ladies' Visiting Day* (1701), by mocking scandalmongers at their soirées, where fashionable society gather to mention visits to Mrs Phillips (to get contraceptives) and to affect the mode of approving only what comes from another country.[1] To win Lady Lovetoy, Courtine has to dress like a Russian and promise to lie in the sun for a month to gain an 'Olive' complexion. It will be noted that Burnaby avoids

[1] See F. E. Budd's introduction to *The Dramatic Works of William Burnaby* (London, 1931).

the stale device of using French customs as the sole object of satire. In his final original piece, *The Modish Husband* (1702), the affectation ridiculed is that of pretending interest only in something other than the real object of concern. Again Burnaby uses married people as his principal characters, showing two unhappy or at least restless couples whose several intrigues all collapse in failure. Burnaby stocks his comedies with figures resembling Zimri in Dryden's *Absalom and Achitophel*, who sincerely desire the path of wickedness but are of means bereft. The tone is skilfully controlled, for the biting repartee very well renders the animosity and self-preoccupation of Burnaby's representatives from the social world. The play might have succeeded twenty years earlier, but it failed and was severely condemned by the Rev. Arthur Bedford. Clerical condemnation was superfluous, because the mode of witty sex comedy had come to an end. If the more restrained and polished *Way of the World* did not gain popularity, one need not suppose that the changing London audience would accept the harsh ridicule of their way of life in the satiric comedies of William Burnaby.

An imitation of Jonsonian humours comedy appears in the four plays by Thomas Baker, though only *Tunbridge Walks; or, The Yeoman of Kent* was successful. It is a wartime piece, after Shadwell's *The Volunteers* (1703), with praises lavished on old English hospitality and attacks upon French culture. The young hero is a spokesman for 'Economic Man'. 'No more hereditary honour,' he declares; 'money will be the Protector.' He predicts that peerages will be for sale and suggests 'the Earl of Stockmarket' as one title. The humours character Hillaria is well drawn and was acted to perfection by Susanna Mountfort Verbruggen, we are told. Garrick used this work in his *Miss in Her Teens*.

## (viii) Summation of trends

Lack of success for *The Way of the World* and dwindling attendance at both playhouses led to desperate expedients. For a few years after 1700, theatre programmes resembled vaudeville more than anything else. Stock plays were reduced in length, celebrated parts from Purcell operas were extracted and offered alone, French dancers and Italian singers were imported to offer solos, and even jugglers and rope-dancers made their way to the legitimate stage. The experiment of presenting a double feature led to a market for one-act farces and initiated the tradition of the double bill. No one seemed to know in which direction to turn. Collier's attack and the failure of Burnaby's satiric offerings probably persuaded the young dramatists to abandon manners comedy. Nevertheless, performance records indicate only slight support for the newer exemplary drama, especially when we note the failure and criticism of Steele's entirely didactic piece *The Lying Lover*. To call the exemplary mode dominant at the turn of the century would be inaccurate. If any one type found acceptance, it was a formula comedy of four acts of intrigue and flippant dialogue followed by a fifth-act repentance and reformation. Cibber's *The Careless Husband* is the best example. For this type of comedy, Allardyce Nicoll used the term 'genteel comedy'.

# 3 Comic dramatists of the Augustan Age

## (i) Introduction

The chaotic state of the theatrical world at the turn of the century was slowly but eventually settled by more competent managers, leading to steady production and a more favourable financial situation. An increase in the number of theatrical companies after 1714 led to a modest demand for new works, and in the first half of the century a large number of writers offered dramatic pieces of one kind or another. From this motley group, only a few of the more representative playwrights will be selected for mention. The period between the death of Farquhar and the appearance of *The Beggar's Opera* in 1728 was a relatively quiet one. The managers who had brought stability and achieved a measure of prosperity were more concerned with improving the quality of acting and staging than in introducing new dramatists. For such new plays as were needed, authors were content to turn out formulaic farces and intrigue comedies. Cibber and Mrs Centlivre were the most prominent of the professional hacks early in the period. The influence of Steele's *The Conscious Lovers* was far-reaching but not immediate. The outstanding success of Gay's ballad opera began a tremendous revival of theatrical activity, and the 1730s were a time of great potential, with an expansion of the number of acting troupes and the appearance of new types of plays. The upsurge was soon ended by Walpole's ruthless imposition of the Stage Licensing Act of 1737. Pantomime then dominated the playbills, and the most promising newcomer, Henry Fielding, abandoned the London stage for a different arena.

## (ii) Sir Richard Steele

Steele is a figure of prime importance in the history of drama because he repudiated the inherited satiric and comic tradition to formulate a narrowly didactic and exemplary mode of representation. Shadwell had supported the exemplary in theory, and some other playwrights had rejected the orthodox view of the frailty of human nature, but Steele consciously introduced model behaviour as the mainspring of his dramatic structure. Hence his works need to be examined to observe the characteristics he introduced.

'*The Funeral* (1701) is hardly a satire on anything,' writes Calhoun Winton; 'there are satirical touches on marital duplicity, on gossips, on hypocritical mourners, but the play is a thoroughly good-humoured comedy.'[1] Suspicious of his wife, Lord Brumpton pretends to die; aided by his faithful servant, Trusty, he hides in a closet where he learns of his wife's true nature and the lawyers' dishonesty. Finally, he becomes aware of the goodness of his dis-inherited son, Lord Hardy. The reunion of father and son follows, and some farfetched plot turns bring happiness all around. *Sententiae* abound. The ending 'is difficult to take seriously,' writes F. W. Bateson, 'as the writing collapses as the emotions are intensified.'[2]

Unrelieved didacticism marks *The Lying Lover* (1703), a lugubrious work in which Steele attacks the practice of duelling. His own synopsis tells us all we need to know: the hero, Bookwit, 'makes false Love, gets drunk and kills his Man; but in the fifth Act awakes from his Debauch, with the Compunction and Remorse which is suitable to a Man's finding himself in a Gaol for the Death of his Friend, without His knowing why.'[3]

*The Tender Husband* (1705) is much different, since it is less of a thesis drama and contains more of the comic. How much of the change is due to Addison is a matter for conjecture, but the shift of emphasis is noticeable. The two separate plots are unified by the theme of fortune-hunting. Cleri-mont Senior is a brutal and domineering man ('tender husband' is ironical),

---

[1] Calhoun Winton, *Captain Steele* (Baltimore, Md., 1964), p. 62.
[2] *English Comic Drama*, p. 48.
[3] From the preface to *The Lying Lover*, *The Plays of Richard Steele*, ed. Shirley Strum Kenney (Oxford, 1971), p. 115.

who is using his cast-off mistress, Lucy Fainlove, disguised as a man, to involve his extravagant wife so that Clerimont can humiliate her. While executing this sordid plan, Lucy is able to catch the booby, wealthy young Humphry Gubbin, in marriage and escape old Clerimont's control over her. Meanwhile, the old rogue's son, Captain Clerimont, woos and wins the romantic heiress, Biddy Tipkin, whose person and fortune Gubbin had been planning for his son Humphry. This résumé suggests the cynical tone of the work, for our sympathies are at all times with the young fortune hunters and against the old folks. Captain Clerimont uses deception to disguise himself as an artist to win the affected, novel-reading Biddy, and the presentation is arranged to make us sympathize with the trickery. The humiliation of Mrs Clerimont is handled in a severe manner, and there is more realism in this work than in Steele's other plays.

The 'sentimental mask'[1] which young Bevil, the hero of *The Conscious Lovers* (1722), exhibits to the beholder was not hastily constructed. Though Steele had engaged in a busy career of politics and of essay-writing in the seventeen years since his last play, John Loftis has shown that Steele was composing *The Conscious Lovers* by 1713 and that there are numerous references to it in the ensuing years. In 1717, he hoped to produce the work in the coming season, and the intended title had changed from 'Sir John Edgar' to 'The Fine Gentleman'. The concepts set forth in the work had been stated again and again in issues of *The Tatler*, *The Spectator* and *The Guardian*.[2] Repudiation of duelling as a code of behaviour and the supposedly exemplary conduct of young Bevil are the two main concerns of the work.

Young Bevil thinks of himself as continuously virtuous, but he also wants to get what he wants. He secretly maintains Indiana, a beautiful and penniless maiden (and compliments himself on his charity). However, obedience to his father leads him to propose marriage to Lucinda, who is loved by his friend Myrtle. On the wedding day, young Bevil, dressed for the ceremony, decides he wishes to see Indiana, a reckless move which might lead to suspicion and detection. His mask now puts on a demonstration:

> We must often . . . go on in our good offices, even under the displeasure of those to whom we do them, in compassion to their weaknesses and mistakes. – But all this while poor Indiana is tortured with the doubt of me. She has no support or comfort but in my fidelity, yet sees me daily

[1] This apt term comes from Paul E. Parnell, 'The Sentimental Mask', *PMLA*, LXXVIII (1963), pp. 529–35.
[2] Loftis, *Steele at Drury Lane*, pp. 183–92.

pressed to marriage with another. . . . The religious vow to my father restrains me from ever marrying without his approbation, yet that confines me not from seeing a virtuous woman . . . the pure delight of my eyes and the guiltless joy of my heart.

He cites only those aspects of his actions which are favourable to himself, but he refuses to notice the imprudence of his conduct. Furthermore, Indiana cannot really be tortured with doubt over his impending marriage because he has carefully concealed this news from her, and she has no other means of learning it. He devotes his time to reinterpreting his motives. When Myrtle challenges him, young Bevil gets out of a nasty predicament by committing the impropriety of showing him Lucinda's letter, when a little frankness earlier would have prevented the crisis from arising. Bevil now announces his own humanitarianism in offering to assist in a match between Lucinda and Myrtle; actually, Bevil will not be free to marry Indiana until Lucinda is taken off his hands. The mock-humility and secret superiority is really contrary to Christian doctrine, in spite of Steele's protestations to the contrary.[1] A recently discovered letter provides a clear statement of authorial intent: on 16 January 1722, Steele wrote to Daniel Finch, Earl of Nottingham: 'I have written a Comedy, not only consonant to the rules of Religion and Virtue, in Generall, but also in [word deleted] analogy even to the Christian religion.'[2] The reader can now understand why some time was required for the author to invent this elaborate psychological state represented in young Bevil. Had Steele shown any awareness of the pose or treated it with irony, he might be ranked with Stendhal today.

Sir Richard Steele's lifelong task was to repudiate the tradition of Restoration comedy. The history of English drama after his time testifies to his success. His projection of the criterion of 'sensibility' was most influential upon later eighteenth-century dramatists, and 'the sentimental mask' was to reappear in many later plays. The method by which he structured *The Conscious Lovers* was to lead to the full development of sentimental comedy. Holding up 'The Fine Gentleman' as a model for emulation shattered the pattern of satiric Restoration comedy, in which the weaknesses and folly of man were held up to ridicule. Steele is important, then, because of his part in deflecting the course of English comedy. We should also notice the significance of his political basis for rejecting Restoration comedy. The nature (and influence) of his bias reveals that much of the eighteenth- and perhaps even

[1] The above material is abstracted from Professor Parnell's article, pp. 529–35.
[2] Pat Rogers, 'A New Letter by Steele', *English Language Notes*, VII (1969), pp. 105–7.

of the nineteenth-century assault on the alleged immorality of Restoration drama proceeds from political grounds. This situation has been obscured by the extensive publicity received by Collier's attack on the stage. Since Jeremy Collier, a 'Non-Juror', was politically 'sound', historians of the drama have been slow to detect the political motivation behind later attacks. Steele's onslaught on Etherege's *The Man of Mode* reveals an instructive syllogism which may be stated as follows: presenting a debauchee (Dorimant) as hero is immoral; therefore, Restoration drama is immoral; this immoral drama was sponsored by and flourished under Charles II; conclusion – the bad Stuarts gave us immorality and, presumably, should be replaced by another dynasty. If we re-examine other Whiggish eighteenth-century attacks on Restoration comedy and look closely at the tenor of Macaulay's scornful diatribe, we shall see this curious logic and political bias again.

### (iii) Susannah Carroll Centlivre

Mrs Centlivre began her career with a tragicomedy, and later composed one tragedy, but her chief work was in comic form. Between 1702 and 1722 she wrote a total of seventeen comedies or farces. Much of her work was derivative. Her earliest pieces are taken from French drama; then she turned to Spanish sources; in her final productions, she went back to Ben Jonson for a model, though not for a plot source. In *Love's Contrivance; or, Le Médecin malgré lui* (1703), she draws upon two plays by Molière (*Le Mariage forcé* is the other) to build up a five-act drama. In this adaptation, she presents a detailed background explanation for the affected dumbness of Lucinda, whereas Molière simply makes a single expository statement when he reaches that point in the episode. The French audience was apparently satisfied; for the English, 'causes' had to be given. In Molière the servants are main characters; here, they are not even named.

She then plundered Regnard's *Le Joueur* to write *The Gamester* (1705), a serious treatise on the evils of gambling, and again changed her source to provide a sentimental ending. Moral lessons are taught in both plots. In one, the young rake is disinherited by his father, but, on a promise to abjure gambling, the heroine agrees to marry the supposedly reformed rake. In the subplot, the conceited Lady Wealthy has been rebuffing her serious lover, Lovewell. When she incautiously sends an indiscreet note and money as well to the young rake, Lovewell recovers the incriminating evidence, whereupon Lady Wealthy is so overcome by honest emotion that she changes her ways and marries Lovewell. The only good scenes are at the gambling house. The loser's rages, the attempts to pick quarrels, the continual call to hasten and roll the dice – all give verisimilitude.

Mrs Centlivre now moves into the type of drama in which she did her best-known work – intrigue comedy from the Spanish. In 1709 appeared her greatest success, *The Busy Body*. The chief source of mirth is the character Marplot, possibly suggested by Sir Martin Mar-All. His naïve questions collapse one intrigue after another. He is on the side of the angels, but unfortunately his meddling also demolishes the schemes of his friends, as his innocent curiosity keeps tearing down a mountain of complication. This lively piece became a stage favourite at once. Another intrigue drama, *The Wonder : A Woman Keeps a Secret* (1717), has the usual plot of highly strung young women whose fathers wish to send them to nunneries or loveless marriages. The play was just successful enough to go into repertory, without being acted very frequently until mid-century; then the performances increased, and it was acted well into the nineteenth century. This type of play disappeared but was drawn upon later by writers plotting melodramas.

In striking contrast to the procedure in which other dramatists had begun writing in the Restoration mode and then moved into farce or the drama of sensibility, Mrs Centlivre did just the reverse. She had started with farce and heavy, serious drama, but at the very end of her career, in her last two plays, she dropped the exemplary mode for the satiric. The first, *A Bold Stroke for a Wife* (1718), was successful; *The Artifice* (1722) was not. Both in dialogue and situation, Mrs Centlivre was writing vigorous and satiric comedy. She also seemed to have developed an interest in Ben Jonson, with her 'Simon Pure' and with the guardians in *A Bold Stroke*. Unfortunately, by the end of her career, what the managers wanted was farce and pantomime.

### (iv) John Gay and the ballad opera

Gay wrote a number of dramatic compositions, most of them defying classification, as he intended. His output included two ballad operas in addition to *The Beggar's Opera*, three regular comedies, three irregular ones and a tragedy. His first offering, *The Mohocks*, is a whimsy and defies description. Neither version of *The Wife of Bath* (1713, 1730) has any real dramatic merit. In 1715 came *The What D'Ye Call It : A Tragi-Comical Pastoral Farce*. In spite of Gay's precautions against literary historians, there is an appropriate recognized category for it – burlesque. Gay constructs both a rehearsal and a play within a play. He created such a far-reaching contrast between the 'seriousness' of the plot and the ludicrous tone of the language and presentation that audiences did not know how to respond; in fact, Alexander Pope's deaf friend Cromwell was astonished when the audience laughed.[1] The work includes parody of *Richard III*, *Macbeth*, *Venice Preserved* and other old favourites.

With the assistance of Pope and Arbuthnot came the farcical *Three Hours after Marriage* (1717). It goes along without much plot or organization, though many of the individual episodes are ludicrous, even absurd. There is ridicule of Dr Woodward of Gresham College, amid other topical hits. All in all, the treatment is somewhat coarse, with sexual innuendo and scatological jokes, really beneath the dignity of the three authors. However, it is a useful antidote to the boring clichés about the placid nature of 'The Age of Reason'.

On 29 January 1728 appeared the perennially entertaining *Beggar's Opera*, an ironical masterpiece. Gay must be given credit for his originality in both the form and the execution. The work is called a ballad opera because Gay used ballads (in the early eighteenth-century meaning of 'a popular song') in a three-act (hence operatic) production. The sixty-nine airs represent music familiar to an audience of the time; the songs mainly come from or are parodies of those in Tom D'Urfey's *Pills to Purge Melancholy*, but Gay purposely creates a discrepancy between words and music which was a surprise and source of delight to the contemporary audiences, though it is lost for us. That is, Gay would use a tune associated in the minds of the hearers with a ribald or erotic song and compose for it a tender or pathetic lyric, and vice versa. The original impact was irresistible.

Years later the notion grew that Italian opera was the main butt of Gay's ridicule, but this seems unlikely. Gay was fond of music, he attended the opera, he collaborated with Handel both before and after the production of *The Beggar's Opera*. Certain absurdities are mocked, and the childish quarrel between the two sopranos Faustina and Cuzzoni in 1727 is ridiculed, but the main satiric thrust was elsewhere. Tory poets had lost their best symbol – divine right of kings. The only way to use the heroic tradition was to turn it into mock-epic or pastoral and reject the possibility of heroes in the modern world. Under a Whig triumph, the only resource left to the poets was to portray the commercial and ruling classes as rogues.[2] Gay presents two kinds of rogues: the thieves and prostitutes, who parody the aristocratic ideal; and the managers, Lockit the warden, Peachum the 'fence', and their families, who parody the bourgeois ideal. The rise of the bourgeois causes the conflict, for the pleasure of the thieves and prostitutes is dependent on the decisions of

[1] *The Correspondence of Alexander Pope*, ed. George Sherburn, 5 vols (Oxford, 1956), I, p. 282.

[2] William Empson, *Some Versions of Pastoral* (London, 1935), pp. 195–250.

Lockit and Peachum, the Whig leaders. Yet Gay avoids sentiment. The lesson of *The Beggar's Opera* is that 'the World is all alike' – everyone is motivated by self-interest. The two betrayals of Macheath are by Jenny Diver and by Jemmy Twitcher, to show that the rogues and drabs are operating on the same bases as Lockit and Peachum. All of us pay lip-service to one set of principles, but in practice are motivated by another set. 'The institutions of society, which we pretend are so solidly established, rest upon a fiction that has no external actuality.'[1] Private interest is the sole criterion. Sir Robert Walpole may have been no literary critic, but he understood this play well enough: he banned Gay's sequel.

The wit of the dialogue is charming and delightful; in fact, it is so charming that powerful ironies are passed over by many auditors. Bitterness is entirely missing, and its absence may explain why the satire has lost its sting for some people today. If Jonathan Swift, who suggested the plan of the work to Gay, had written it, we should not have to bear with simplistic social critics who assert the superiority of Brecht's *Threepenny Opera* in irony and satiric protest. However, the Dean did not relish music, and we would have lost the entertainment which Gay provides.

A few words may be said about analogues, sources or possible influences.[2] Thomas D'Urfey used an increasing number of songs in his last plays; his *Wonders in the Sun* (1706) approaches comic opera. Much of Gay's musical material comes from D'Urfey's *Pills to Purge Melancholy*. In his burlesque *The Mock Tempest* (1674) Duffett employed numerous lyrics of various metrical types, and varied musical scores. Richard Estcourt's *Prunella* (1708) contains fifteen songs set to airs from the operas *Camilla* and *Arsinoe*. In 1724, John Thurmond's pantomime *Harlequin Sheppard* deals with the career of the juvenile delinquent, Jack Sheppard, and with Jonathan Wild, who is more commonly termed a prototype of Peachum. A song in this work contrasts the 'Fellows of Newgate' who rob and steal with public officials who embezzle public funds. Meanwhile, in Paris, entrepreneurs at the Fairs had developed a genre very similar to ballad opera, the *comédies en vaudevilles*, pieces which had comic scenes in dialogue, songs to known tunes, and ridicule of bourgeois types (lawyers, judges, financiers, coquettes). Such pieces had recently been played in London. Lesage and Fuzelier's *Le Tableau de mariage* had been performed at the Little Haymarket in both 1725 and 1726.

The remarkable success of *The Beggar's Opera* launched an immediate

---

[1] Bertrand H. Bronson, 'The Beggar's Opera', in *Studies in the Comic* (Berkeley, California, 1941), pp. 197–231.
[2] For a detailed account, see Edmond Gagey, *Ballad Opera* (New York, 1937).

vogue, as anyone can see by looking at Nicoll's handlists or *The London Stage*. The considerable number of ballad operas appearing in the twenty-odd years until mid-century may be categorized by the different aspects of Gay's play which they followed: scenes and characters from low life, pastorals, farces, parodies and burlesques. Of the first group, the most noteworthy is Thomas Walker's *The Quaker's Opera* (1728). Walker took his ballad opera from the anonymous and unacted farce *The Prison Breaker; or, The Adventures of John Sheppard*, published in 1725 as designed for the theatre in Lincoln's Inn Fields. Modern scholars have wondered whether Gay read this farce. It deals with Sheppard's capture by Wild and contains a good deal of satire. The anonymous *The Jew Decoyed; or, The Progress of a Harlot* (1733) includes a scene of grim realism. Allan Ramsay's charming pastoral, *The Gentle Shepherd*, was reworked into a ballad opera in 1729; in London Theophilus Cibber presented it under the title *Patie and Peggie* in 1730. The most popular of all the ballad opera farces was Cibber's *The Devil to Pay*. Fielding wrote several, of which *The Mock Doctor* (1732) and *The Intriguing Chambermaid* (1734) held the stage for many years. Carey's *The Dragon of Wantley* was the most popular of the burlesques.

## (v) Henry Fielding

The lively and experimental work of Fielding in drama has been much neglected. Numerous essays appear on oft-studied cruces in *Tom Jones* while the plays are largely ignored. Yet his *Pasquin* (1736) had as long an initial run as *The Beggar's Opera*, and the story of Fielding's management and productions at the Little Theatre in the Haymarket in 1736 and 1737 provides one of the most exciting episodes in the history of English drama. Fielding wrote some two dozen pieces for the theatre, several of which contain hilarious comic scenes and display remarkable innovations in dramaturgy. The works may be roughly divided into regular comedies, farces (many of which were adaptations from Molière and Regnard) and burlesques.

It is true that the quality of his work is uneven, and he started slowly, evidently trying to imitate the Restoration comic masters, whereas his best plays marched to the sound of a different drum. The early comedies – *Love in Several Masques* (1728) and *The Temple Beau* (1730) – are apprentice work, marked by heavy and complicated plots. *The Modern Husband* (1732) also contains an involved plot with interlocking complications, but the treatment has much improved. A great deal of ground is covered, and there are seventeen named characters. The result is a panorama of upper-middle-class

London life, showing place-seeking at levees, heavy losses at the gambling tables, blackmail, bribery, unpaid bills and the consequent swarm of creditors, and desperate shuffles to secure ready money. The £100 note which Bellamant dispatches in answer to an urgent call of distress from his inamorata turns up in the hands of his wife, to his great surprise, a short time later. In another plot, Modern and his wife have been living beyond their means. To recoup, Modern attempts vicious expedients. He bribes a footman to testify he had seen Bellamant in intimacy with Mrs Modern. The charge is false, but Bellamant had previously had an affair with her. Modern persuades his wife to yield herself to Lord Richly for £1500. The money spent, Modern plans litigation against Richly for adultery. The hopelessness of the situations and dilemmas of the various characters is very well rendered.

The most interesting aspect of *The Universal Gallant: or, the Different Husbands* (1735) is the manner in which Fielding carefully alters the initial impression made by the principal women characters. Lady Raffler is presented as a virtuous woman, put in a natural state of distress by her husband's excessive jealousy. However, as the play continues, she speaks and acts in such an extremely prudish way that the reader is alienated. Still more ambiguity marks the delineation of Mrs Raffler. Not as strict as Lady Raffler, she has had an extramarital affair. She now respects her trusting husband and wishes to avoid any further impropriety, yet when she is in a room alone with a male admirer she cannot restrain herself from heavy flirtation.

*The Wedding Day* (1743) begins with a long prologue in the metre and style of Swift's 'Humble Petition of Frances Harris', couplets with nine or ten beats to the line. Fielding also uses his favourite device of blending literature and life. Parson Abraham Adams (from *Joseph Andrews*) is mentioned, and the actor Macklin, who is speaking the prologue, addresses the author directly: 'O there he sits: / Smoke him.' Much of the satire is directed against a social climber, who becomes frantic in alternating between choosing the daughter of a wealthy merchant or the sister of a (supposed) noble lord as a match for his son. The main plot turns on the formula of 'obscure birth', the disclosure of which prevents a man from marrying his daughter. The two bawds or procuresses in the play are very well depicted. The tone is pretty cynical, as can be guessed, yet the play is an exemplary comedy, in which a man of sense is able to counsel and change a heartless rake into a more benevolent creature.

Fielding's remaining comedies are much lighter. For example, in *Eurydice* (1737), his treatment of classical myth is quite amusing, for he makes Eurydice trick Orpheus into looking back, in order to get rid of him. The Devil is shown as hen-pecked by his shrewish wife – that's why it's Hell. The emphasis given here on Fielding's elaborate character delineation should not obscure the fact that his comedies contain a good deal of humour, and are generally entertaining. His greatest talent in dramaturgy, however, lay in the burlesque mode.

### (vi) Minor dramatists

A few remaining writers need to be mentioned. Charles Shadwell, son of the Restoration dramatist, imitated Jonsonian humours comedy with his lively piece, *The Fair Quaker of Deal; or, The Humours of the Navy* (1710). The heroine is well drawn, an independent, talkative woman who is neither a coquette nor a passive sufferer. There is much local colour and nautical diction.

Charles Johnson had a long career as a playwright, composing nine comedies, six tragedies, two farces and two ballad operas from 1701 to 1732, without ever having a smash-hit or moving himself into the category of well-known dramatists. What makes him noteworthy is that he wrote at least one play in each of the new styles or types of drama that were current in his time. For the vogue of the matrimonial dilemma, he revised Shirley's *The Gamester* into a very sombre tragicomedy, *The Wife's Relief*, in 1711, which may have been his most popular play. Oddly enough, of the many ballad operas put together in the hope of riding the success of Gay's play, Johnson seems to have written the best. It is called *The Village Opera* (1729) and it enjoyed moderate success until Bickerstaff revised it as *Love in a Village* in 1762, after which it became a fixture in the repertory. One other ballad opera, *Silvia; or, The Country Burial* (1730), by George Lillo, has some curious aspects. It is a long play, with seventy-one songs and a grotesque episode about a woman being buried alive. The characters are Elizabethan (Goody Gabble, Goody Costive, Lettice Stitch); the language is coarse and realistic; and the plot has the elements of a late eighteenth-century melodrama: the virtuous heroine, the illicit proposal, the aged father, the threat to evict the aged father from the farm for the girl's refusal of the illicit proposal and the obscure birth of both the main characters of the play.

As a matter of record, the last playwright to compose works in the style of Restoration manners comedy was William Popple. His offerings were *The Lady's Revenge* (1734) and *The Double Deceit* (1735). The best-known comedies of Etherege, Wycherley and Congreve were flourishing on the stage in the 1730s, so that it is not surprising that at least one writer should have tried to emulate them. Popple himself was the victim of a claque, and his productions were not judged on their merits.

Edward Moore tried to continue the trend in domestic tragedy with *The Foundling* (1748), a comedy which is not comic. It was produced at Drury Lane with great *éclat*, using the chief players of the time: Garrick, Barry, Sparks, Macklin, Mrs Woffington and Mrs Cibber. Appearances are all against the heroine: she emerges from a brothel pure as a lily. Realism on one side; romance on the other. Nicoll calls it the connecting link between early and late eighteenth-century sentimentality.[1]

Nicoll's remark about a 'link' should remind us of the two traditions in the development of sentimental comedy. One is found in exemplary comedy, of which Steele's *The Conscious Lovers* is the apex. The other is the convention imported from French *comédie larmoyante*. The first example of this latter type to appear in English was John Kelly's *The Married Philosopher* (1732), a translation from *Le Mari honteux de l'être, ou le Philosophe marié*, by Destouches. It is Kelly's *drame* which provides authentic sentimentality (if I may be permitted a contradiction in terms). The action in this work shows the young hero, Bellefleur, devoting the entire five acts to talking about his feelings.

Robert Dodsley, the publisher who reprinted so much Tudor and Elizabethan drama, introduces a different and novel thematic line in his own compositions: sentimental royalism. In *The King and the Miller of Mansfield* (1737), Dodsley exploits the notion (later used by John Wesley to help hold people in support of George III) that the king is a surrogate father who protects the people from the vicious nobility.[2] The plot is taken from the ballad of Henry II, who is lost in the forest and entertained incognito by the merry miller. Dodsley inserts further complication by a subplot in which a courtier seduces the sweetheart of the miller's son. The nobleman tries to brazen out everything by alluding to his own rank, whereupon the king replies:

> What makes your Lordship Great? Is it your gilded Equipage and Dress? Then put it on your meanest Slave, and he's as great as you. Is it your Riches or Estate? The Villain that should plunder you of all, would then be as great as you. No, my Lord, he that acts greatly, is the true Great Man.

While there were immediate protests that Dodsley was trying to overthrow the ministry,[3] there is really nothing revolutionary here. Dodsley was not

[1] Nicoll, *HED*, II, p. 207.
[2] See F. C. Green, *Minuet* (London, 1935), p. 168.
[3] See Nicoll, *HED*, II, p. 181.

attacking the system; he was providing a scapegoat for overflowing animosities. His playlet went on to become one of the most frequently acted afterpieces of the age.

His ballad opera in one act, *The Blind Beggar of Bethnal Green* (1741), is a true drama of sensibility. It is based on Day's *Blind Beggar*, but Dodsley (of dissenting stock) adds a Puritan, a lascivious hypocrite. There is no regular plot, as Genest would seem to indicate by his synopsis; instead, there is something like a tableau, whereby Bessy (Virtue), the daughter of the blind beggar, meets each suitor in turn. The text overflows with moral sentiments. When the father (the beggar) decides that the hero truly loves Bessy, he gives his blessing and £5000, meanwhile revealing that he is Sir Simon Montford, living in retreat from the vengeance of the Earl of Essex. Thus we have the obscure birth formula again. Note the engraving on the frontispiece of the 1745 edition, showing the blind beggar with flowing white hair accompanied by a collie dog (Plate 35).

### (vii) Trends in eighteenth-century comedy

If we regard the drama between 1700 and 1750 as an isolated unit, without looking ahead to the pervasive effect of *comédie larmoyante* in one direction and the revival of comic form by Goldsmith and Sheridan in another, we shall see that these fifty years encompass a transition period of sharp fluctuation rather than a steady movement towards late eighteenth-century sentimental comedy and melodrama. At the beginning appeared the 'genteel' comedy exemplified by Cibber's *The Careless Husband*, together with the spontaneous gaiety of Farquhar's comedies, but the first type diminished into insignificance and Farquhar died in his early prime.

The next event of importance was *The Conscious Lovers*, the peak and culminating point of exemplary drama. Didacticism had triumphed over the comic, for there was to be no return to Southerne or Wycherley; yet the records do not include any considerable number of authors immediately patterning their works upon Steele's achievement. The impact of the French *drame* was needed before the sentimental drama displayed in Cumberland's *The West Indian* (1767) was to evolve. Instead, satiric laughter returned with the première of *The Beggar's Opera*. This comic form spawned parasitic rather than generative growth, and these numerous ballad operas yielded no advance in comedy. However, the larger potential audience revealed by Gay's smash-hit led to an increase in the number of theatrical troupes in London, a magnet to attract young dramatists to compose the new plays needed in a period of expansion. For a brief time in the 1730s, then, we can observe the signs of a tremendous revival in English drama. With Henry Fielding setting the pace, a variety of experimental works were produced. Diverse kinds of non-representational drama appeared in the topical satires or revues and innovative burlesques of Fielding, Henry Carey, Samuel Johnson of Cheshire, Theophilus Cibber and others. What we see is promise rather than fulfilment, as many of these new pieces are marked by clumsiness and lack of control side by side with inventiveness and verve. The new young playwrights needed to learn their trade as in the 1580s and the 1660s. The entire revival was crushed by the artificial limitation to only two theatres meted out by the Stage Licensing Act in 1737. This restriction prompted a conservative and non-competitive management policy, in which the chief demand for new works was supplied by pantomimes. To recapitulate, the reduction of theatres halted the innovative drive for new forms, and regular comedy had been deteriorating since Farquhar. Contemporaries were well aware of the decline: when Hoadly's intrigue comedy, *The Suspicious Husband*, was launched in 1747 it was hailed in the newspapers as the first regular comedy of merit since *The Beaux' Stratagem*. The young creative writers who were being attracted by the theatre and were coming from the provinces to London with a comedy in hand, like Tobias Smollett, were to turn as Henry Fielding did to the new and challenging artistic form of the novel. Progress in comedy had to await the momentum of the French drama of sensibility and a later generation of new dramatists – Foote, Murphy and Goldsmith.

# 4 The farce and burlesque tradition

## (a) FARCE

Spanning the entire period under consideration is a convention of lighter drama which should not be ignored. In full-length plays and in afterpieces, in literary spoofs and in personal attacks, authors produced an extensive and popular, if often ephemeral, body of literature. The earliest regular Elizabethan comedies were farcical in nature, but the prevailing practice was to use farce for comic relief and in subplots, and some early Restoration pieces such as Boyle's *Guzman* and *Mr Anthony* continue this method. In time, however, both full-length and one- or two-act farces were constructed as separate works. Objections were soon raised against the form by the critics, who classified it as too 'low' for the legitimate stage and lacking classical sanction. Dryden and Shadwell were among the early opponents, but the popularity of farces with the London audiences was an endorsement of the new fashion which led both of these protesting dramatists to engage in writing farces. After producing one farce, Nahum Tate even attempted to discover classical precedent, in a long essay tracing farce through Ben Jonson's *Silent Woman*, Renaissance Italian popular comedy and eventually Aristophanes. All this discussion was of no consequence in an actual situation where the appearance of those gifted low comedians Nokes, Leigh and Jevon cried out for the utilization of their talents. It is as if Will Kemp had stayed with the Lord Chamberlain's Company in the 1590s, and Shakespeare had been forced to keep building parts for him instead of for Robert Armin. A variety of comic actors were to appear in the eighteenth century, but in the Restoration period the outstanding comedians were naturally cast for farcical roles.

An examination of the origin and sources of Restoration farces reveals much the same background as for the serious drama. There were native elements as exemplified in the Interregnum skit of *Simpleton the Smith*, the constables in *Much Ado about Nothing*, and the mock-shaving and robbery of Grim the Collier in Richard Edwards's *Damon and Pythias*. The other source was the Italian improvised comedy. This comic tradition was encountered by Englishmen on the Grand Tour, like Sir Aston Cokain, watching *commedia dell'arte* in some Italian city, or by expatriates in Paris during the 1650s, or absorbed through the *petites comédies* of Molière and other French writers who were using *commedia dell'arte* techniques and materials. Later, such productions could be viewed directly when the Italian or French troupes came to London, as they did frequently in the 1670s, especially the troupe of the famous Scaramuccio, Tiberio Fiorelli. Among the earliest farces were the actor John Lacy's *The Old Troop* and *Sauny the Scot* (1667), the latter an adaptation of *The Taming of the Shrew*. The former shows the influence of Italian popular comedy by its numerous *lazzi* (such as the theft and sale of a cheese), the rapid changes of costume for disguises and extravagant stage properties.

The chief popularizer of farces was Edward Ravenscroft, a playwright who utilized the main sources of farce in his different plays. In *Mamamouchi* (1672) the low comedian Nokes pleased Charles II and the rest of the audience so much that it was acted about thirty times in its first season. Ravenscroft domesticated his importation, as Professor Sutherland explains:

> Sir Simon Softhead in this play (Molière's Monsieur de Pourceaugnac) is a Suffolk knight born and bred at Bury St Edmunds, where he used to romp with little Peggy, George Goodale's daughter at the Rose, a 'witty little baggage' that he would 'run after to kiss from one room to another'. There is no equivalent in Molière . . .[1]

Ravenscroft next brought in the *commedia dell'arte* undiluted, as the title of his play shows: *Scaramouch a Philosopher, Harlequin a School-Boy, Bravo, Merchant and Magician. A Comedy after the Italian Manner* (1677).

---

[1] *Late Seventeenth Century*, p. 129. Its first printed title was *The Citizen Turn'd Gentleman*, but the play was advertised and later published as *Mamamouchi*.

In 1681 came Ravenscroft's notorious and highly successful production, *The London Cuckolds*. It was quickly established as an institution, to be acted on Lord Mayor's Day until Garrick stopped the practice in 1751. This hilarious farce draws both on earlier English drama and on European folk-lore. One of the several plots is that told in a bowdlerized way by Hans Christian Andersen as the Great Claus and Little Claus story. There are other plots as well, for the play contains *lazzi* of disguise, substitution and decep-tion, complete with chamber pots, stupid constables and a young gallant trapped in the cellar (from Middleton's *Blurt, Master Constable*).[1] *The London Cuckolds* and *Mamamouchi* made Ravenscroft the leading farce writer of the age and attracted other dramatists towards low comedy. In 1696, Ravenscroft gave up his method of concocting a farce from a number of different sources and contented himself with adapting Hauteroche's *Crispin médecin* as *The Anatomist; or, The Sham Doctor*. After a dissection scene and a lecture on anatomy by the doctor, the scamp Crispin stages a mock-dissection on his father. Naturally, the father gets beaten.

Sir Aston Cokain had watched two performances in Italy by a *commedia dell'arte* troupe and set down the contents in a five-act play, *Trappolin Supposed a Prince*, before the Civil War. Nahum Tate shortened the piece to three acts, deleting its egalitarian or 'levelling' sentiments, and brought it out in 1685. Filled with amusing *lazzi*, it had a favourable reception and held the stage through the next century. Tate's reduced version is close to a one-man show, dealing with the escapades of the rogue Trappolin. Another piece taken entirely from the Italian improvised comedy was Aphra Behn's *The Emperor of the Moon* (1687). It is a full work, including slapstick farce, a love-intrigue plot and an elaborate masque, the production of which must have tested even the resources of the Dorset Garden Theatre. There is also an amusing duel when Harlequin and Scaramouch, dressed as great heroes, 'fight at barriers'.

Yet some of the most popular eighteenth-century farces were derived from native sources. An account of a cluster of farces on the 'cheater cheated' motif might serve as a brief history of the development of eighteenth-century farce in general. In the sombre, psychological portrayal of hatred which marks *The Dutch Courtesan*, John Marston had employed for comic relief some farce scenes. He probably did not know that one of the farcical episodes had been used fifteen years earlier by William Percy in the play *Cuck-Queanes and Cuckolds Errants*, an incident borrowed from a tale in Masuccio. During the Interregnum, the farcical scenes from Marston's work were culled out for

[1] Leo Hughes, *A Century of English Farce* (Princeton, N.J., 1956), pp. 118–20.

presentation. A rogue swindles a vintner's wife out of a punchbowl by bringing her a salmon; to purchase a new punchbowl, the vintner gets a bag of money, but the rogue enters disguised as a barber, lathers the vintner and steals the money. In 1680 Marston's play was revived in adapted form, designed for Jevon to enact the rogue. An additional scene is included in which the rogue gambles away the stolen money and wanders the streets, where he steals a blind harper's cloak. The victim raises the watch, who close in on the rogue, but he evades them by giving the cloak to the pursuing vintner (chasing his bag of money), who is arrested and taken to gaol, where the rogue makes a formal visitation in the garb of a Presbyterian clergyman. The play continued to be acted into the next century, but in 1715 Christopher Bullock trimmed it down to three acts, *The Woman's Revenge; or, a Match in Newgate*, as a vehicle for his talents as a low comedian. While reducing Marston's plot, Bullock expanded the farce by having the rogue beguile the vintner in the mock-shaving episode with a series of extravagant adventures, one of which tells of a white fox as large as a Flanders mare. In the 1740s, several different entrepreneurs took this work, stripped it down to one or two acts by removing all traces of the main plot, and used it as ballad opera, pantomime or farce. It was played at Bartholomew Fair as *The Bilker Bilked* (1742). In the same year, Thomas Yarrow brought it out as *Trick Upon Trick; or, The Vintner Outwitted* for Henry Ward to play the rogue. Then Ward (grandfather to Sarah Siddons, and a veteran manager of strolling companies) produced it in 1753 as *The Vintner Tricked; or, The White Fox Chased*. From the subtitle, we can see that the episode of the 'tall tale' is increasing in importance. Thomas Este later employed the farce as an anti-Methodist polemic in a production denounced by John Wesley himself. In the early nineteenth century, the amusing tricks from this farce were still being seen in the London theatres.[1]

Still another illustration of a farcical subplot surviving the main action can be found in the history of *The Country Wake* (1696), a comedy by the comedian Thomas Doggett. The central plot-complication deals with the seduction of a married woman, with a poignant ending; against this picture of conflict in high life, the rest of the work presents the farcical episodes of a young lout, Hob, who can outcudgel all comers. Doggett reduced the piece to a one-act farce, *Hob; or, The Country Wake* (1711). After several adventures, Hob gets revenge by beating the squire at cudgel play. At the end, the squire retains his obstinacy and refuses to be reconciled with Hob. This crux is resolved by

[1] See Leo Hughes and A. H. Scouten, 'Some Theatrical Adaptations of a Picaresque Tale', *University of Texas Studies in English* (1946), pp. 98–114.

another character, Dick, who says, 'Won't you? Why then, Mr Pack give out the play, and Mr Newman the prompter let down the curtain.'

By far the most popular of all eighteenth-century farces was *The Devil to Pay*. The actor Jevon had written *The Devil of a Wife* in 1686 (possibly assisted by Shadwell), a comedy in which by magic transformation a psalm-singing cobbler tames an arrogant lady. In 1731 Charles Coffey and John Mottley revised the piece into a ballad opera. Further changes were made by Theophilus Cibber. *The Devil of a Wife* did not have the double-plot structure of *The Country Wake*, but was made up of a ridiculous story combining slapstick with the supernatural. Young Cibber deleted the religious denominational conflict and shortened the entire story into a one-act farce. In this form, it was acted in England and America until the middle of the nineteenth century, attained over forty printings and was adapted into French and German.[1]

A variety of sources provide material for additional farces. The actor Mountfort borrowed episodes from Marlowe together with *lazzi* from Italian comedy to make an opus called *The Life and Death of Doctor Faustus Made Into a Farce, with the Humours of Harlequin and Scaramouche* (c. 1685). In 1698 Vanbrugh translated Dancourt's *La Maison de campagne* into *The Country House*, and in 1704 Farquhar used La Chapelle's *Carosses d'Orléans* for *The Stage Coach*. A late borrowing from Italian improvised comedy is Aaron Hill's *The Walking Statue; or, The Devil in the Wine Cellar* (1710); after this time, the chief influence was pantomime rather than legitimate drama. After the Jacobite revolt of 1715, Christopher Bullock used the induction from *The Taming of the Shrew* to make the afterpiece named *The Cobbler of Preston* (1716). It will be noted that Doggett and Bullock had succeeded Nokes, Leigh and Jevon as the leading low comedians.

Clever use of the naïve buffoon appears in John Hippisley's farce comedy *A Journey to Bristol* (1731). Not all afterpieces were borrowed from French and Italian sources, and the material in this work is original except for one episode taken from Haughton's *Englishmen for my Money*. A thoroughly professional piece, it presents a native Welshman, delineated as a distinct individual. The action is lively; the sequence of events is natural, not forced or improbable; and the jokes are witty rather than coarse. The dialogue is notable in both the verbal quips and the structure. When an official releases Sanguin, the rogue says, 'You are the Mirror of Modern Magistracy'; when

[1] See Leo Hughes and A. H. Scouten, *Ten English Farces* (Austin, Texas, 1948), pp. 173–200, and '*The Devil to Pay*: A Preliminary Check List', *University of Pennsylvania Library Chronicle*, XV (1948), pp. 15–24.

the drunken Tipple mistakes Sanguin's voice for a high wind, he mutters, 'Sad work at Sea now.' Sections of the dialogue are arranged like the interlocutor and end-man colloquies of nineteenth-century American minstrel shows. Curiously enough, while *A Journey to Bristol* was frequently selected by actors for their benefit night, the play never entered into any company's repertory. Audiences evidently preferred the stereotyped Welshman, Irishman or Scot to the individualized protagonist of *A Journey to Bristol*.

Henry Fielding wrote several farces, even though his first offering, *The Letterwriters* (1731), was a failure. *The Lottery* (1732) is a farce in ballad-opera form and was more successful. Several authors had plundered Molière's *Le Médecin malgré lui*, but Fielding's *Mock Doctor* (1732) was the best adaptation, with the vigorous physical clowning of traditional farce, the character sketches and the sharp commentary. Still more lively was *The Intriguing Chambermaid* (1734), an adaptation of Regnard's *Retour imprévu* designed for the popular comedienne Kitty Clive. To arrange the piece for her, Fielding substituted a soubrette for Regnard's clever valet.[1] This matter is mentioned also because of the dominant vogue of clever-valet farces from French drama. A popular specimen is David Garrick's afterpiece *The Lying Valet* (1741), drawn from Hauteroche's *Le Souper mal apprêté*. The importance of this piece in an account of the trends in farce is that it illustrates the movement away from rough slapstick and pratfall to rapid action and skilful dialogue. Garrick followed this initial stage success with *Miss in Her Teens* (1747), an afterpiece based on Dancourt's *La Parisienne*. Garrick gave himself several good farce turns, and he and the low comedian Woodward carried it to success at Drury Lane.

On the whole, there were very few pure farces like *Hob* or *The Bilker Bilked*. Writers tended to insert farcical episodes in other forms such as the ballad opera or mix them with salacious plot complications of the woman-almost-seduced-but-rescued-in-time, with a moral lesson gratuitously added. In fact, the latter type, with sticky emotions, was so prevalent as to lead Allardyce Nicoll to group farces with sentimental plays in his history of the drama.

## (b) BURLESQUE

In an age of satire, it would be surprising if someone had not contrived a successful burlesque, and *The Rehearsal* (1671) justifies the expectation. This famous work was a long time in the making, for it was begun in 1663 as a satire on Sir Robert Howard and Sir William Davenant. Closing of the

[1] Hughes, *A Century of English Farce*, pp. 261-2.

theatres because of a cholera epidemic stopped production in 1665, and it was not acted until 1671, by which time it had been thoroughly reworked. The text we now possess is a collaborative project by George Villiers, second Duke of Buckingham, Samuel Butler, Thomas Sprat and Martin Clifford. Revision and the passing of time led to the elevation of Dryden as the chief butt but also to the evolving of a composite type in the central figure, Bayes. *The Rehearsal* is not a burlesque of the heroic drama alone; at least half of the plays ridiculed are in other genres of dramatic form, and perennial faults of the theatre are included. Still, the best satiric hits happen to be those directed against the heroic play, such as the inspired ending, where the protagonist Drawcansir comes on stage and kills everybody. The duke chose to use the structure of a play within a play and handled this framework very professionally. The work begins with the author of the play to be rehearsed, Bayes, talking with two men before the rehearsal starts. In the next scene, we hear three of the actors talking among themselves before they start the rehearsal of the play within the play, so that Buckingham is moving on two levels.

If it were not for our knowledge that the royalist Butler aided the duke, we might put a different interpretation on the whole work. With the duke's malice and Martin Clifford's known political views, there might have been 'miching mallecho' in such an assault on the heroic drama which Charles II had suggested, sponsored and endorsed. By 1671 Buckingham may have been deliberately satirizing Dryden's reverential praise of monarchy. In the first version, however, he may well have been nursing a private grudge against the Howards. He had barely escaped injury in a riot at a performance of Henry Howard's *The United Kingdoms* in 1662, and he may have seen Molière's *L'Impromptu de Versailles* in Paris in 1663 and decided to use the technique shown in it.[1]

*The Rehearsal* did not, however, 'kill' the heroic drama. Buckingham threw the playwrights on the defensive, but a look at *The London Stage* will show that after 1671 older heroic dramas were revived and more new ones were being composed. The travesty was acted for at least a century, but by the 1740s it had changed to become a vehicle for take-offs on contemporary actors.

Modern literary historians are fond of scoffing at Restoration adaptations of Shakespeare, yet were we to have more diaries and personal correspondence from that period we might learn that men of taste held as low an opinion of these adaptations as we do. The operatic productions of *The Tempest* and *Macbeth* elicited the ridicule of Thomas Duffett in travesties which

[1] D. F. Smith, *Plays about the Theatre in England* (London, 1936), pp. 9–11.

presumably entertained the audiences. Duffett's first attempt was a burlesque of Elkanah Settle's *The Empress of Morocco* under the same title in 1673, in which he used a conventional neoclassical technique by reducing Settle's heroes to corn-cutters, draymen and a 'scinder-Wench'. He parodies the love-and-honour conflict of the plot and the inverted word order of Settle's verse. Ridicule of the operatic version of *Macbeth* is shorter and in an entirely different mode – an epilogue. A lengthy epilogue to *The Empress of Morocco* achieves burlesque by using flying witches and 'The most renowned and melodious Song of John Dory'. Fuller structure and more skilful techniques of burlesque characterize *The Mock Tempest; or, The Enchanted Castle* (1674). Duffett locates the scene in Bridewell, where Prospero appears as the keeper, and assaults the dramatically weak device of introductory background exposition by having Prospero tell Miranda:

> Thy father, Miranda, was 50 years ago a man of great power, Duke of my Lord Mayors Dogg-Kennel.
>
> MIRANDA: O lo, why Father, Father, and are not I Miranda Whiffe, sooth, and arn't you Prospero Whiffe, sooth, Keeper of Bridewell, my Father?

According to J. H. Wilson, Duffett increased the travesty by having an orange-woman play Ariel, rather than an actress.[1] Duffett introduces seventeen lyrics, of various metrical types (two verses are close to the Skeltonic metre), and varied musical scores.[2] *Psyche Debauched* (1675), Duffett's final travesty, is unfortunately rather feeble, the intended satire becoming quite tedious.

Many other plays include burlesque scenes. In the newly discovered comedy, *The Country Gentleman*, the Duke of Buckingham inserted a devastating parody of the methodical habits of Sir William Coventry by having two large tables with holes in the centre brought on stage. Two actors, impersonating Coventry and his companion Sir John Duncombe, stationed themselves in these holes, covered the tables with papers (representing state documents), and then engaged in an amusing game of shouting out English and European place-names, in *bouts-rimés*, while frantically scrambling the documents to find the papers supposedly thus labelled. In *The Reformation* (1673) Joseph Arrowsmith includes an episode ridiculing the heroic drama, with a personal mocking of Dryden. Previously mentioned is the parody of an audience assembling before the beginning of a play, in Shadwell's *A True Widow*. In 1697 the anonymous burlesque *The Female Wits; or, The*

---

[1] *A Preface*, p. 139.
[2] *Three Burlesque Plays of Thomas Duffett*, ed. Ronald E. DiLorenzo (Iowa City, 1972).

*Triumvirate of Poets at Rehearsal* is an attack on the female dramatists Mrs Manley, Mrs Pix and Mrs Trotter. The three authors are shown attending the rehearsal of a play which turns out to be a travesty of Mrs Manley's own drama, *The Royal Mischief*. The incest story in that work is mocked by having a character fall in love with his mother-in-law.

Samuel Johnson of Cheshire, whom all agree to have been insane, wrote several irregular and curious pieces, of which the most interesting is *Hurlothrumbo ; or, The Super Natural* (1729). In one section the vehicle for travesty is Miltonic diction; thus we see ridicule of Miltonic imitation even before one supposes that the vogue of adulation had really got under way. The piece also contains ridicule of the formulas of exemplary comedy and of the third Lord Shaftesbury, whose ideas underlay the new didactic comedy. The popularity of *Hurlothrumbo* is difficult to understand. The piece was played twenty-nine times in the spring of 1729, and members of the nobility heavily subscribed to the printed edition, Walpole himself taking thirty copies.

A successful practitioner in both farce and burlesque was the minor poet Henry Carey. Much of his work is occasional and limited in appeal, but he wrote two burlesques which were not only immediately successful but made a sufficient impact to hold the stage for a long time. In the first, a burlesque of Restoration tragedy called *The Tragedy of Chrononhotonthologos* (1734), pantomime and opera are attacked with gusto. Like Fielding, Carey mocks the language of the older drama, suggesting that the poets of a new generation were more offended by the imagery and style of Restoration verse than by the plot or content of Restoration tragedy. In 1737 came his real triumph in the burlesque manner, *The Dragon of Wantley*. This parody of the absurdities of Italian opera became the talk of the town. The music (composed by J. F. Lampe) was in keeping with the mood of the work. The speeches are in rhymed couplets, for which Carey supplied delightful nonsense rhymes.

The great master of burlesque was of course the irrepressible Henry Fielding.[1] His originality can be seen in the techniques of satire that he employed. For *Tom Thumb*, he contrived a burlesque without the cumbersome machinery of a play within a play. This innovation has not always been noticed, since critics prefer to praise the hilarious annotations of H. Scriblerus Secundus which appeared in the printed text of 1731, when Fielding lengthened the work from two acts to three and changed the title to *The Tragedy of Tragedies ; or, The Life and Death of Tom Thumb the Great*. However, there is scarcely any way for a director to introduce these satirical

---

[1] For a full account of Fielding's career in the theatre, see W. L. Cross, *The History of Henry Fielding*, 3 vols (New Haven, Conn., 1918).

textual notes in the theatre, unless he wants to send commentators on stage to read these footnotes. Consequently, the secret of Fielding's art must be sought elsewhere. What Fielding did was to mock the figurative language of Restoration and early eighteenth-century tragedy as well as to satirize the plot and ideas. To do this, he drew on parody, a method Swift, Pope and others were employing in non-dramatic literature. Fielding's technique was to parody the rhetorical form of the heroic drama as exemplified by the epic simile, so frequently found in those plays. Fielding begins the parody with brief similes: 'Thy pouting breasts, like kettle-drums of brass' (II. v. 2). Then he constructs full Homeric similes, which get longer as the play continues:

> So, when two dogs are fighting in the streets,
> With a third dog one of the two dogs meets,
> With angry teeth he bites him to the bone,
> And this dog smarts for what that dog had done. (I. v. 54–7)

After several more 'low' similes of five and six lines in length, Fielding extends the trope into an eight-line passage of parallel verse, beginning 'So have I seen the bees in clusters swarm'. Even before this ludicrous climax is reached, the audience is alerted by the signal of 'like' or 'so' and can begin laughing as the lines are spoken. Other flaws in the rhetoric of earlier tragedies are also parodied, such as mixed metaphors:

QUEEN: He is, indeed, a helmet to us all,
   While he supports, we need not fear to fall. (III. vi. 14–15)

Absurdities in plot are ridiculed, but Fielding's chief object of attack was the language of tragedy.

Fielding continued his experiments with dramatic form until he reached a species of burlesque which might properly be distinguished as the revue, parodic commentary on current, topical matters. This form, long known in the French drama, and popular in London today, is differentiated because a burlesque assumes disapproval of the object of the attack, whereas a revue must be played straight. Fielding began this technique in *The Author's Farce* (1730), in which he deals with a large number of contemporary subjects, not only pantomimes and bad plays but also inept, tasteless and extravagant language in these works. Fielding also breaks the dramatic illusion in a variety of ways throughout the play. The main character, Luckless, badly in debt, wishes to produce a puppet show, the profits of which would meet his obligations and permit him to marry his sweetheart. This puppet show, called

'The Pleasures of the Town', is played by live actors. Luckless calls upon the composer Seedo (who provided the music for three of Fielding's dramas) to conduct the orchestra. After a survey of various contemporary follies, Italian opera is chosen as the worst offender. Now the 'shew' is interrupted by the intrusion of a magistrate with constables to arrest Luckless for debts. He is saved by the plot turn of 'obscure birth' which reveals him to be the King of Bantam. In the general mirth, the performers in the puppet show mix with the intruders from the real world and the actors of the main play. Colley Cibber and Orator Henley are mocked. The epilogue is a full dramatic scene. The participants are 'four Poets', the author (Luckless, the King of Bantam) and a cat. The cat (which was to give the epilogue) walks off, and in replaced by the actress who impersonated it. The continuous juxtaposition of realistic and non-realistic elements produces a remarkable satiric effect and shows Fielding working towards non-representational drama.

In *The Covent Garden Tragedy* (1732) Fielding attacks the doctrine of poetic justice by a burlesque of 'Namby-Pamby' Philips's pseudo-classical tragedy *The Distressed Mother* (1712), with a probable glance at its source, Racine's *Andromaque*. Neoclassical tragic diction is also ridiculed by having low-life characters speak in blank verse with elevated vocabulary, some of it taken directly from John Banks's tragedy *The Unhappy Favourite*. The dialogues continue with various mock-heroic similes and a long metaphor on 'sugar-plums'.

Fielding's chief box-office success was *Pasquin, A Dramatick Satire on the Times : being the Rehearsal of Two Plays, viz. A Comedy called, The Election ; and a Tragedy, called The Life and Death of Common-Sense* (1736). The first play within the play begins with a scene in which a candidate from the Court Party (for Fielding uses 'Court and Country' instead of 'Whig and Tory') is seated at a table giving out cash bribes to the mayor and aldermen. The author (Trapwit) is quite dissatisfied with the staging and complains that the audience can't see the money being passed. To make everything perfectly clear (as modern politicians put it), Trapwit moves the entire group forward to the apron of the stage, where they all stand while the candidate passes the money down the line. Small wonder that the play went into a run and that Walpole determined to force Fielding out of the theatre. There are numerous telling strokes. The 'Country' candidates bribe by purchasing merchandise from the alderman. One candidate offers to make a drunkard a poet laureate, so that he can write odes. The electors make their choice, but the mayor's wife persuades him to certify the losing side as the winner. Next, a *danseuse* argues with the prompter, insisting that she enact the 'First Goddess' and refusing to follow another actress. 'I am sure I shew more to the audience than any lady upon the stage,' she says, and then observes that the theatres would play Shakespeare to empty benches if it were not for the dances. Troubles harass the rehearsal of the tragedy. One actor gets arrested when he steps outside the playhouse; the barber disappears to shave 'the Sultan' at the other theatre; and the ghost of Common-Sense improperly appears before the catastrophe in which her death is to occur.

*The Historical Register for the Year 1736* (1737) includes much the same sort of topical raillery, achieving devastating political satire. Fielding also works in some fine attacks on current adaptations of Shakespeare. More interweaving of disparate elements can be seen: during the auction in the rehearsal section of the play, one of the bystanders, Lord Dapper, gets so excited by the auctioneer that he joins the bidding. At the end, the 'Patriots' are openly bribed, while an actor on stage laughs at them, an episode of very harsh political satire. Meanwhile, Walpole was hastening his bill through Parliament, and by the end of the season the Stage Licensing Act ended Fielding's interesting experiments in dramaturgy.

Surveying these light comic forms, one has to admit that the farces do not hold up as literature, while even the best of the burlesques lose most of their force and amusement for readers unfamiliar with the objects of the satire. It is important, however, to note, in following the shifts in technique during this period, that we find a parallel with the direction noticeable in the major works of the time: the parody and satire of *A Tale of a Tub* and *The Rape of the Lock*.

# 5 Tragedy

## (a) THE HEROIC PLAY

Soon after the reopening of the theatres, there appeared the quasi-tragic drama which is called the heroic play. In contrast to the slow development of Elizabethan tragedy through Tudor interludes, chronicle plays and crude revenge dramas, the heroic play was designed or projected *a priori*. The drift of critical theory led to the establishment of heroic drama on the model of the epic, the apex of classical literary forms.[1] Hobbes and Davenant made specific suggestions in this direction. Therefore, while the new efforts in the tragic mode showed an affinity with Caroline drama and their language was affected by the decorum of Fletcher's diction and by the couplets of French tragedy, an understanding of the new form is more likely to come from a study of the theory than from concentrating solely on sources and influences in the older drama.

The plan was to elevate the drama by patterning it after the epic. With the recent civil strife in mind, the prevailing subject-matter became the vicissitudes of the nobility. The action would be set against a background of war

[1] J. H. Smith and D. MacMillan, in the notes to the California edition of Dryden's *Works* (Berkeley, California, 1962), VIII, pp. 284–6; they give an excellent survey of the trends in scholarship in estimating the native and foreign elements of the heroic drama.

and presented in a heightened style. Heroic virtue would be apotheosized to inculcate the admiration of the beholders. Since *admiration* was the object sought, the death of the protagonist would not be necessary. The vocabulary would be kept pure from improper diction; similes would be used instead of the metaphors that characterized Jacobean tragedy. The locale would be distant and exotic; the production would stress various sensational stage effects; painted scenes, songs and instrumental music would enhance the action and dialogue.

What made this farrago at all plausible was that both the history-reading middle class and the aristocratic members of the audience were very much attracted by the conflicts between a prince's public role and his private life. Furthermore, as Morse Peckham suggests, seventeenth-century audiences were more interested in problem-raising than in problem-solving.[1] Consequently, we have a set of circumstances where the position and function of a king was still regarded with high respect, courtiers were attracted by stories which dealt with the problems of rulership and responsibility, and extensive discussion about models to emulate in Renaissance romances and courtesy books had created an intellectual milieu in which playwrights were encouraged to put such models on the stage.[2]

It is important to observe that the rhymed couplet is not an ornament but is highly functional to the new heroic drama. To understand this point, we must try to appreciate the attitudes of the new creative writers in the 1660s. For them, a large number of pre-Restoration tragedies were an object of praise and a cause of national pride; nevertheless, these modern dramatists set themselves higher ideals of dramatic *propriety*, as well as wanting to surpass their predecessors in merit.[3] Creative writers instinctively knew that they must not imitate the styles of a previous generation; consequently, they needed to find a new style and felt proud when they had done so. Denham and Waller suddenly became the heroes and standard-bearers of English poetry because of their achievement in the iambic pentameter couplet. We can note that Sir Robert Howard, with Dryden's collaboration, wrote *The Indian Queen* in rhymed couplets. If we group with this practice Dryden's dedication of *The Rival Ladies* and his assertions in his *Essay of Dramatic Poesy*, we shall find that this young poet, aware of his talent with the rhymed couplet, was 'trying to parley his instinct for rhyme into a full-fledged theory

[1] Morse Peckham, *Man's Rage for Chaos* (Philadelphia, Pa., 1965).
[2] See Erich Auerbach on Racine's tragedies in *Mimesis* (Princeton, N.J., 1953), pp. 316–46.
[3] See Dryden's *Essay of Dramatic Poesy*; see also G. Sorelius, *The Giant Race before the Flood* (Uppsala, 1966), pp. 22–116.

of drama'[1] and endorsing a style which would lead to his own fame. In his dedication of *The Rival Ladies* to the Earl of Orrery, Dryden writes that by means of rhyme Waller made 'Writing . . . an Art', that Denham used it for the 'Epick', and that Davenant 'brought it upon the Stage, and made it perfect, in the *Siege of Rhodes*'. Actually, Davenant's couplets are not regular or complete, but what we should notice is that Dryden is setting up a manifesto for the new poets. Rhymed heroic verse, *the last perfection of Art*, is clearly the vital centre of Dryden's theory of the heroic play.[2]

Against the immediate objection that rhymed couplets were not a natural or realistic mode of expression, Dryden shifts to relativism and insists that the different elements in the staging of a play were all conventions: 'So that the street, the window, the houses, and the closet, are made to walk about, and the persons to stand still,' says Neander. Which artificiality does one prefer?[3] People under emotional stress do not talk in blank verse either. What is achieved in the rhymed couplet is 'Nature wrought up to a higher pitch'. Having established artifice as the governing factor, Dryden could then justify on the same basis the use of spectacle, scenery and the extravagant rhetoric of the characters, all in order to make the heroic drama more remote from everyday life rather than closer to it. As Sarup Singh points out, 'Rhyme, thus, was an inevitable outcome of the theory of the heroic play.'[4]

In describing the heroic drama, one should take pains to avoid the terms 'neoclassic' or 'neoclassical', as they are quite misleading. The rubric of neoclassicism fails to explain the non-classical elements which every reader will observe in these plays.[5] The works are more properly placed in the baroque mode; and the pervasive French influence is not classicism but *préciosité*, from which come the adulation of women, the distilled language, the moralism and the intricate code of behaviour, as the English comic playwrights very well knew.[6]

Finally, it is well to remember that there is nothing of the alienated artist in the development of the heroic drama. Some modern critics, living in an

[1] A. C. Kirsch, 'The Significance of Dryden's *Aureng-Zebe*', *ELH*, XXIX (1962), pp. 160–75.

[2] A. C. Kirsch, *Dryden's Heroic Drama* (Princeton, N.J., 1965), p. 27.

[3] David Daiches, *Critical Approaches to Literature* (Englewood Cliffs, N.J., 1956), pp. 188–215.

[4] Sarup Singh, *The Theory of Drama in the Restoration Period* (Bombay, 1963), pp. 93–122.

[5] Sorelius, op. cit. pp. 116–18.

[6] For fuller treatment, see the excellent introduction by W. S. Clark to his edition of *The Dramatic Works of Roger Boyle, Earl of Orrery* (Cambridge, Mass., 1937); also K. M. Lynch's *Roger Boyle, First Earl of Orrery* (Knoxville, Tenn., 1965); and numerous articles by David S. Berkeley.

age of democracies, assert that the plays could not be taken seriously and that Dryden mocked the heroic play in his own works in this form.[1] Dryden's enemies (who were numerous) failed to detect such mockery, and when an attack on heroic drama was made in *The Rehearsal* Dryden was ridiculed for his affirmation of the new genre. In fact, Dryden never gave up on the analogy with the epic, as can be seen by his Preface to a late work, *The Parallel of Poetry and Painting*. Recent talk of 'satirical debunking' overlooks the Renaissance theory of genres. Restoration authors were masters of satirical debunking, as we can observe from the verse satires 'Last Instructions to a Painter' or 'Macflecknoe'. They were also ready to affirm the values of a hierarchical society. The dramatists composed the earliest heroic dramas on the suggestions of Charles II himself, the plays were shown before large crowds of fashionable audiences, produced with great care (including costumes provided by royalty) and eulogized by the diarists. It is impossible to believe that the plays were completely misunderstood.

The widespread interest in preparing Corneille's tragedies for theatres in London and Dublin yields a striking indication of audience response towards the new genre. One translation, *The Valiant Cid*, was presented at court on 1 December 1662. Katherine Phillips's translation of *Pompée* was produced in Dublin in February 1663 and apparently again in London later that spring; another version by Edmund Waller, Sir Charles Sedley, Charles Sackville, Earl of Dorset, Edward Filmer and Sidney, Earl Godolphin was shown at court on 1 January 1664. A different group of translators then prepared *Heraclius*, much to the disappointment of Lodowick Carlell because their version was acted instead of his, and still another translation was made by Sir Thomas Clarges. Of the acted version, Pepys writes:

> But at the beginning, at the drawing up of the curtain, there was the finest scene of the Emperor and his people about him, standing in their fixed and different postures in their Roman habits, above all that ever I saw at any of the theatres (8 May 1664).

---

[1] Particularly Bruce King, in his *Dryden's Major Plays* (London and New York, 1966), who extends the more tentative views of D. W. Jefferson, 'The Significance of Dryden's Heroic Plays', *Proceedings of the Leeds Philosophical and Literary Society*, V (1940), pp. 125–39.

## (b) THE DRAMATISTS

### (i) Roger Boyle, Earl of Orrery

The earliest works to be composed in the new style were those of the first Earl of Orrery. Starting in 1661, he wrote eight specimens of the new genre, although only five of these were acted immediately. The first was *The General*, a work which had been suggested by the king. Its première was in Dublin on 18 October 1662, under the title of *Altemera*. Meanwhile, Charles II had sent his own copy to Killigrew for a performance by the King's Company. However, Orrery had completed another one, *The History of Henry the Fifth*, which Davenant produced in August 1664 by the Duke's Company before Killigrew was able to stage *The General*. These facts need to be kept in mind when giving the date of the 'first heroic play'.

These works are highly artificial. *The General* is not so much a drama as a collection of various heightened scenes contrasting love against duty, or revenge, or honour, passion against friendship. Orrery emphasizes the internal struggle and offers lofty, idealistic notions, together with much strained logic in the debates between the characters. Consequently, his works are probably closer to French drama than to previous English plays, despite the similarities between *The General* and Suckling's *Brenoralt* and *The Sad One*. The villain is killed, but there is no reason for death to overtake the 'good' characters. The hero gallantly resigns his pretensions to the heroine and leaves to gain more glory in yet other wars, leaving the heroine, Altemera, free to marry the second lead, Lucidor.

Both *Henry V* and *The Black Prince* treat their historical subject-matter as in the French romances, presenting the emotions of the main characters, everyone trying to outdo the rest in delicacy and generosity. *Mustapha* turns from the mood of these plays to show episodes of scheming and revenge. The good characters, who wish to repudiate malice and treachery, are trapped in an imperfect world by the schemers and plotters. There are long debates on the topic of dissimulation by rulers. Poetic justice requires that the villains be killed after the death of the two heroes, Mustapha and Zanger, but Roxalana, who participated in the fatal conspiracy, is forgiven after her prolix statements of grief and repentance, guilt and sorrow. It was the plays of Orrery that incorrectly led some historians to consider the heroic drama entirely a French import. All eight are in rhymed couplets.

## (ii) Sir Robert Howard

The first heroic drama staged in London was the *Indian Queen* (25 January 1664) by Sir Robert Howard and John Dryden.[1] It presents the story of the warrior-hero Montezuma, so courageous that he must be admired, and his love for the beautiful and highminded Orazia. Complications arise because he is loved by Zempoalla (the usurping Indian Queen of Mexico) and because both the idealistic Acacis (the second lead) and the villain Traxalla are in love with Orazia. Finally, Acacis and Zempoalla commit suicide, and Montezuma, now discovered to be the true heir to the throne, kills the villain, so that the true and pure lovers are alive at the end.

Howard later wrote another love-and-honour drama, *The Vestal Virgin; or, the Roman Ladies* (1665) which is notable only because the author wrote an alternative fifth act with a happy ending, instead of the blood-bath with which the initial draft ended. *The Great Favourite; or, the Duke of Lerma* (1668) is a much better composition, close to genuine tragedy. Alfred Harbage's explanation is that the work represents Howard's redaction of a manuscript play by Henry Shirley, *The Spanish Duke of Lerma*.[2]

## (iii) John Dryden

In April 1665 the two companies edified 'the Town' with specimens of the new heroic play, the Duke's Company presenting Orrery's *Mustapha* and the King's Company offering Dryden's first solo effort in this genre, *The Indian Emperor*. This play has a full plot, with a variety of reversals of situation and complicated emotional relationships. These complications illustrate a number of themes – libertinism, cultural relativity, the need for *gloire*, the code of friendship – but the dominant one seems to be the opposition between public and private roles. In conflicts that carefully parallel one another, Montezuma sacrifices personal integrity, Cortez demonstrates his worthiness; Odmar follows his personal inclinations, Guyomar chooses duty.[3] With the spirited action, there is one very interesting scene when the captured Montezuma, tortured by Pizarro and a Jesuit priest to discover the location of gold, enters into a debate on cultural relativism. The sceptical rationalism which

---

[1] On the controversy over the respective shares of Howard and Dryden in the composition of this work, see H. J. Oliver, *Sir Robert Howard* (Durham, N.C., 1963).

[2] Alfred Harbage, 'Elizabethan-Restoration Palimpsest', *Modern Language Review*, XXXV (1940), pp. 287–304.

[3] Kirsch, *Dryden's Heroic Drama*, pp. 89–96.

pervades this scene is highly characteristic of the author and makes a good starting point for the study of his heroic plays. When we see this view shared with a fascination for the epic, we find truly unusual drama. The central situation in Dryden's serious drama, writes R. J. Kaufman, 'is a dying emperor in the midst of a dying empire – Montezuma, Boabdelin, Maximin, the Old Emperor, Cleopatra and Antony, Muley Moloch, Cleomenes. The images are of sunsets, twilight, entropy, extinction, and exhaustion.'[1]

In his next work, *Tyrannic Love; or, The Royal Martyr* (1669), Dryden changes the formula to make the leading character, Maximin, the villain and gives him the extreme tirades and exaggerated diction which were becoming associated with heroic drama in the public eye. The libertine views of Maximin have led critics to assume incorrectly that Dryden's characters are walking spokesmen for Hobbes. However, when all of his plays are studied, we can observe that only the villains are endowed with Hobbesian attitudes.[2] The baroque nature of this production is brought out by the witty and mischievous speech for Nell Gwyn that Dryden wrote:

EPILOGUE
Spoken by Mrs Ellen, when she was to be carried off dead by the Bearers.
To the Bearer. *Hold, are you mad? you damn'd confounded Dog,*
*I am to rise and speak the Epilogue.*

*Aureng-Zebe* and *Don Sebastian* may be more artistic achievements, but Dryden's best example of the heroic drama is the two-part, ten-act *The Conquest of Granada* (1670). Its hero is a warrior named Almanzor, brought over to Spain from Africa by Abdalla, younger brother to Boabdelin, the Moorish king, to aid the Moors against Spanish attacks. The opening scene reveals internecine strife arising between two factions of the Moors, the Zegrys and the Abencerrages. Dryden is being didactic here: the internal broils foreshadow the loss of Granada to the Spaniards. Furthermore, Boabdelin is not a true monarch since he cannot make the leaders of the factions obey him. To this scene enters the warrior-visitor Almanzor. The ideal hero, he arrays himself on the side of the smaller group, kills one of the opposing chieftains and, after Boabdelin's ineffectual appeal for obedience, dominates both fac-

---

[1] R. J. Kaufman, 'On the Poetics of Terminal Tragedy', in B. N. Schilling (ed.), *Dryden: A Collection of Critical Essays* (Englewood Cliffs, N.J., 1963), p. 89.
[2] Louis Teeter, 'The Dramatic Use of Hobbes' Political Ideas', *ELH*, III (1936), pp. 140–69.

tions and forces them to cheer the king. Almanzor then leads them into a victorious battle against the Spaniards.

As the complications develop, Dryden presents carefully balanced groups of characters. The virtuous and self-controlled Almahide, an ideal heroine, is contrasted with the completely selfish and vicious but beautiful Lyndaraxa, whose actions are motivated by ambition. Engaged to the brave Abdelmelech, Lyndaraxa plays on the emotions of Abdalla, taunting him because he is not a king and promising to give herself to him if he attains supreme monarchy (or to any other man who rises to kingship, she coolly adds). She stirs his passions until he leads the Zegry faction into a palace revolution against his brother. Now Abdelmelech is overcome with jealousy over Lyndaraxa's conduct. Motivated by the code of friendship, Almanzor joins Abdalla and in conquering the city comes upon the virtuous Almahide with whom he instantly falls in love. Zulema, the Zegry chief, also claims her, leading to a strong presentation of pure versus impure love:

ALMANZOR: I have receded to the utmost line,
    When, by my free consent, she is not mine:
    Then let him equally recede with me,
    And both of us will join to set her free.
ZULEMA: If you will free your part of her, you may;
    But, sir, I love not your romantic way.
    Dream on, enjoy her soul, and set that free;
    I'm pleased her person should be left for me. (III. i. 483–90)

Fearful of losing Zegry support, Abdalla bestows Almahide on Zulema. The fearless Almanzor instantly changes sides to rescue Boabdelin and conquer Abdalla. The defeated prince hastens to Lyndaraxa, who knows his rebellion has failed and spurns him. 'I love a king, but a poor rebel hate,' is the response Abdalla receives from the haughty Lyndaraxa.

Against the self-centred conduct of this wretched pair, Dryden introduces an example of pure love in the persons of the gentle Benzayda, daughter of a Zegry leader, and the brave Ozmyn, an Abencerrage chieftain. Here we have love at first sight, followed by unselfish devotion. As the action continues, each saves the other's life; both have real reasons for respecting each other.

From these contrary situations, the author is unfolding a range of conduct and character. Almahide represents perfection, Zulema is entirely evil, Abdalla becomes evil, Ozmyn remains pure. Abdelmelech has the admirable quality of bravery and is concerned about the fate of others; these favourable signs are cancelled out by his strong jealousy, which he cannot control.

Almanzor can master his emotions, he has not let his will be overcome by his reason, and thus will eventually win Almahide. Nor is he a libertine, for he subordinates his natural desires to Almahide's moralizings. By the end, we can see an extensive number of topics or motifs: pure versus profane love, ideal kings and false leaders, the dangers of the mob and of internal feuds, and the private stresses affecting public figures.

From statements in the dedication and the prologue to *Aureng-Zebe* (1675), it is clear that Dryden has lost confidence in the heroic couplet, even though this drama contains some of his best flights in rhymed verse. Genuine dramatic conflict is engendered by 'the complex interrelation of opposing wills, trying dilemmas, and desperate passions'.[1] The hero Aureng-Zebe, his father (the Old Emperor), his brother, the villain Morat, and the general Arimant are all in love with Indamora, but the empress Nourmahal is in love with her stepson, Aureng-Zebe. The frequent debates between these characters lend themselves to the rhetorical potential of the couplet.

There are some changes in emphasis from the previous heroic plays. The passions become more important, and scenes of personal distress, such as the tribulations of Morat's wife, Melesinda, are presented. However, to make these observations is not to suggest that Dryden had turned soft or was writing pathetic tragedy but rather to indicate the variety of his dramaturgy. He would not be a major writer if his vision were limited to Almanzors. Instead, we learn more about Dryden's skill when we notice that *Aureng-Zebe* contains the same subject-matter as *The Conquest of Granada*: rebellion and chaos, the problems accompanying the succession of a new prince and personal triumphs in love with public triumph in war; yet all is done with very different types of characters and patterns of relationship.[2] For example, Indamora holds a strong ethical position and is able to conquer the blood-thirsty Morat. Yet in a contiguous episode we observe her timidity and fear of death when confronted by the enraged Nourmahal.[3] Almanzor and Maximin may lead critics to generalize about the 'flamboyant hysterics of heroic tragedy',[4] but we should not overlook the pious and virtuous hero Aureng-Zebe.

*All for Love* (1677) is a deceptive play and appears weaker than it is. Furthermore, it is wrongly approached as an adaptation. Dryden did not take the text of *Antony and Cleopatra* and alter the plot and revise the imagery as

[1] Moody Prior, *The Language of Tragedy* (New York, 1947), p. 158.
[2] W. W. Alssid, 'The Design of Dryden's *Aureng-Zebe*', *Journal of English and Germanic Philology*, LXIV (1965), pp. 452–69.
[3] Eugene M. Waith, *The Herculean Hero* (London and New York, 1962), pp. 184–6.
[4] C. D. Cecil, in a review in *Modern Language Review*, LXIII (1968), p. 193.

he did the following year with *Troilus and Cressida*. Instead, as he explains in the preface to *All for Love*, he attempts to draw the bow of Ulysses and compete against all the poets who had previously told this story. Returning to the historical sources, Dryden wrote his own blank-verse drama (rejecting rhymed couplets), sometimes deliberately paralleling a Shakespearian effect, such as the alliteration in the River Cydnus passage, where Cleopatra is described. Shakespeare spreads out a panorama over several countries and many years, but Dryden restricts the action to one day and offers a series of close-up shots. The awkward consequence of the time limit is that forward movement is prevented, and not much is left for the lovers to talk about save past events or present emotions.[1] Thus Dryden was in a structural trap – unless he wrote a drama of introspection and self-analysis like Racine. Unfortunately, Antony's introspection seems to resemble self-pity.

The first act, however, is well constructed: the quarrel between Antony and Ventidius shows a dramatic conflict, Antony regains his 'noble eagerness' for war, and he decides to abandon Cleopatra. In Act II, in a dialogue about their past relationship so lengthy that immediacy of scene is lost, Cleopatra persuades him to cancel his plan. His yielding to her makes his second reversal, giving the impression that he wears down too easily. This impression is heightened in the third act, as Dryden employs sensational theatrics by introducing Octavia and the little ones, so that Antony is quickly subdued again into agreeing to leave Egypt. The reader should not be startled to learn that the next reversal, in Act IV, will show Antony rescinding this decision and turning again to Cleopatra. Each time, a pathetic motivation was used. The play could have been saved by rigorous character analysis, but the author creates new difficulties here. 'Nature meant me a Wife,' Cleopatra reveals, 'a silly, harmless, household dove.' Had Nature carried out this intention, Pompey, Julius Caesar and Antony would have stayed scarce the running of an Egyptian hour-glass. We can only conclude that the play has very little to say to a modern audience. Nevertheless, *All for Love* held the stage for a century, and if we probe more deeply we may find why it continued to please its audiences two hundred years ago.

Comparison of this play with *Antony and Cleopatra* is most helpful in revealing the way in which tragedy has changed. In Elizabethan tragedy the emphasis is on the individual. Marlowe, Chapman, Webster and Shakespeare focus on the tragic protagonist. When John Fletcher wrote his tragicomedies, he shifted the emphasis to a study of the passions. He examined human nature in the abstract, the type rather than the personality. When we watch

[1] Brooks and Heilman, op. cit.

the quarrel between Brutus and Cassius in *Julius Caesar*, we are struck by the difference in their personalities; in Dryden's presentation of the quarrel between Antony and Ventidius, we see two men who are alike but who hold different views. In the light of the rising theory that human nature is the same at all times and in all places, the thing to do is to search the mind to learn why people act in different ways. The method is to study the passions. Marco Mincoff contributes a significant distinction when he suggests that Shakespeare shows us other people as they look to us, but that Fletcher and Dryden show us how we look to ourselves.[1] If we re-examine *All for Love* from this point of view, we may note that Dryden is trying to go inside the mind to reveal principles of human behaviour through a study of decision-making. If so, precarious balance becomes a structural principle. Since Dryden is concerned with the type rather than with the personality, he organizes his material to show cross-currents and fluctuation of emotions.

Seen in such a light, *All for Love* may reveal its secrets, and we can better understand the changes Antony makes. Thus we can observe the play of emotions as Antony weeps on seeing Ventidius weep, then laughs at being told Ventidius wishes to heal his fortunes, and shows military spirit in hearing of twelve legions marching from Parthia. An apparent trifle of this sort is enough to make Antony believe in himself again, writes Eugene Waith.[2] A sudden change comes and he calls Ventidius a traitor. Later in the play, he learns that Octavia plans, after arranging for his freedom, to send him to Athens. This thoughtfulness elicits a generous response from Antony. All of these reactions could be convincing to audiences before Rousseau announced that everyone possessed a unique personality.

Dryden had one more important drama to contribute in *Don Sebastian* (1689). It is a carefully constructed, double-plot tragedy in blank verse. Self-conscious as ever, Dryden informs the reader how functional the comic sub-plot is:

> You see Dorax giving the Character of *Antonio*, in the beginning of the Play, upon his first sight of him at the Lottery; and to make the dependence, *Antonio* is ingag'd in the Fourth Act, for the deliverance of *Almeyda*; which is also prepar'd for by his being first made a Slave to the Captain of the Rabble.

In a drama concerned with the topics of justice, reward and the will, Dryden

---

[1] Marco Mincoff, 'Shakespeare, Fletcher, and Baroque Tragedy', *Shakespeare Survey*, XX (Cambridge, 1967), pp. 1–15.
[2] Waith, op. cit. pp. 191–2.

tries through the subplot for a sharper focus. Eric Rothstein summarizes the organization:

> The tragic incest of Sebastian and Almeyda can perhaps be seen fore-shadowed in Antonio's fruitless affair with the Mufti's wife and daughter, and later in Morayma's mistaking her father for her lover; the elements of a father's will, an alien court, and cuckoldry are common to both plots. In both plots we have characters taking turns in captivity – Antonio, Johayma, and the Mufti in the comedy – and plans to ravish women. . . . In both plots, we find themes of loyalty, tyranny, reward, kindred, disguise for reasons of love-jealousy (Dorax', the Mufti's), and the metaphoric conversion of religion and love into power or money. Finally, both plots use similar metaphors, such as those of animality or of clay . . .[1]

Dryden had employed his favourite motif – incest – to prepare for a tragedy. Throughout the work, he has carried along a theme of inherited guilt, though it seems muted when Don Sebastian has married Almeyda and established a reconciliation with the fierce Dorax. Then the blow falls when Don Sebastian learns that Almeyda is his sister. Still, the tone seems sad rather than tragic at the end. One more serious work was left, *Cleomenes* (1692), in which he was aided by Southerne. It lacked both development and credibility, and can well be forgotten.

Nevertheless, his best efforts should be remembered. He led the parade of the heroic play, and his *Conquest of Granada* is certainly the most outstanding example of the new genre. His organization of the double-plot play displays considerable technical skill. *Aureng-Zebe*, *Don Sebastian* and *The Indian Emperor* remain the highpoints in the uneven attempt of the Restoration playwrights to create a new type of tragedy. Finally, his achievement in the rhymed couplet places him among the major dramatic poets.

## (iv) Elkanah Settle

Settle wrote nine tragedies before he became City poet and applied himself to designing pageants for Lord Mayor's Day. These dramas will seem pre-posterous to a modern reader, yet in his time he had strong backing at court and was considered a prominent poet by some admirers, though these did not include Dryden, Crowne, Shadwell or Roger North (who called him a 'thick-sculd poetaster').[2] North's animosity sprang from a badly presented masque

[1] Eric Rothstein, *Restoration Tragedy* (Madison, Wisconsin, 1967), pp. 148–9.
[2] *Roger North on Music*, ed. John Wilson (London, 1959), p. 306.

which Settle had inserted into his popular heroic play *The Empress of Morocco* (1673). Settle was indeed a promoter of spectacle. His dramas are noted for elaborate backdrops, prisons, torture-chambers, ghosts and other special effects.[1] A look at a few of them may show what appealed to his contemporaries.

As Allardyce Nicoll points out, Settle's first work, *Cambyses, King of Persia* (1671), contains 'all the formulae for a popular heroic play' much as if Settle had carefully inserted each ingredient from an inventory.[2] In *The Empress of Morocco*, the scene opens in the second act to a large backdrop showing a river with a fleet of ships; trumpets and guns are heard. In Act III the hero, Muly Hamet, enters to find the Empress and her favourite, Crimalhaz, sleeping on a couch. He reports this news to the young Emperor her son, but the Empress extricates herself in the manner of Potiphar's wife. She manages to have the Emperor stabbed during the masque which drew North's criticism. Then her luck runs out: she is killed and the second villain turns honest, delivering up Crimalhaz to the hero, who marries Mariamne, and all ends happily, after the villain's tortured body has been exposed on stage. The ending is important, for poetic justice has been carried out. The Empress and her lover are wicked and deserve suffering and death; the young lovers, who emerge triumphant, represent innocence in a world of corruption. The justice of Providence has been vindicated, and this was the kind of drama that Thomas Rymer liked.[3] 'For the *Drama*, the World has nothing to be compared with us,' Rymer had said; and Curt Zimansky has shown that this statement refers to the heroic play.[4]

Settle's next play, *Love and Revenge* (1674), is in blank verse, but he returned to the rhymed couplet and an exotic setting with *The Conquest of China by the Tartars* (1675). In 1680, Settle abandoned rhyme again for blank verse in *The Female Prelate*, a violently anti-Catholic propaganda exercise. In March 1682 appeared his final effort in the heroic line, *The Heir of Morocco, with the Death of Gayland*. During the action, the hero, Altomar, is promised the king's daughter, Artemira, in marriage. However, when the king learns that a favourable alliance could be secured through the marriage of his daughter to Gayland, he revokes his pledge. Such action was policy, wherein private wishes had to be subordinated to national interest. Altomar

---

[1] See pp. 95–108.
[2] Nicoll, *HED*, I, p. 117.
[3] Sorelius, op. cit. p. 128.
[4] *The Critical Works of Thomas Rymer*, ed. Curt A. Zimansky (New Haven, Conn., and London, 1956), pp. xx–xxi, 10.

personally objects to the policy and kills Gayland, but he is captured and tortured on stage in the concluding scene of the play.

## (v) John Crowne

Crowne supplied the theatres with a dozen tragedies and is conspicuous for adhering to the heroic drama long after other dramatists had turned to different types of tragedy. In 1698 he wrote *Caligula* in rhyme much on the pattern of the early heroic plays.

His only significant work was the two-part drama, *The Destruction of Jerusalem by Titus Vespasian*, both parts appearing in January 1677. The conflict of private and community interests, common to the heroic drama, is very well developed; in fact, it is expanded because there are two national interests, the Roman and the Jewish. The tension is further heightened by conflict over religion. The emperor Titus, in love with Berenice, has laid siege to the holy city, his soldiers led by the barbarous general Tiberius. The defenders are divided, with Matthias as their leader, and the villain John leading a faction against him. Much use is made of the supernatural: the revengeful ghost of Herod and numerous omens of disaster. Into this lurid scene comes a stranger, as in *The Conquest of Granada*, the military hero, Phraartes, in love with the virgin Clarona. Thus far, all could have been predicted; the new element is Phraartes' rationalism, if not downright atheism. He scoffs at the omens and warns the spirits not to try any of their tricks on him. Rhymed couplets had been used by Dryden for philosophic argument, and Crowne follows this tradition very well, letting Phraartes present numerous critical evaluations of priestcraft and religion. In fact, Crowne achieves both dramatic tension and intellectual vigour in his portrayal of this character. The death of Clarona drives Phraartes into madness and insane vision, in heroic opposition to the cosmos, so that there is a tragic fall. This drama of Crowne's should not be overlooked, for Phraartes is one of the most interesting and authentic tragic heroes in Restoration drama. The rest of Crowne's tragedies are uneven and make no particular contribution. The reason for the patronage he enjoyed from Charles II and Rochester was the exaggerated praise of royalty in his early works, *The History of Charles VIII of France* (1671) and *The Ambitious Statesman* (1679).

## (vi) Nathaniel Lee

The tragedies that display the highest intensity of passion are those of Nathaniel Lee, a nervous, self-conscious poet, who wrote a dozen plays before his mental disorders in 1684. Unfortunately, he did not learn the art of increasing and diminishing intensity, or any method of changing his pace, until very late in his career.

His first three plays were rhymed heroic dramas, beginning with *The Tragedy of Nero* (1674), a work marked by his dependence upon Elizabethan models for his verse as well as by his efforts to maintain an emotional peak. *Sophonisba; or, Hannibal's Overthrow*, a year later, was more successful. The emphasis given to the characters Rosalinda and Sophonisba and continued in his extravagant account of the death of Narcissa in *Gloriana* (1676), his third play, would suggest that Lee was the leader in the shift towards pathetic tragedy, especially when we observe the popularity of *Sophonisba*. Nevertheless, 'pathetic' is not quite the proper label for Lee's highly strung and feverish dramas, as we can see by looking more closely at the first play he composed after giving up rhymed couplets: *The Rival Queens; or, The Death of Alexander the Great* (1677). Neither title nor subtitle is appropriate, as this tragedy is about the personality of the great military genius, not his women or his death. Eighteenth-century playbills reflect the chief interest in listing the work simply as *Alexander*. The great popularity of this tragedy, and contemporary remarks about it, such as the statement that the actor Charles Hart (playing Alexander) 'might Teach any King on Earth how to Comport himself',[1] are reasons for believing that audiences were fascinated by a drama which revealed the conflicts emerging from the private difficulties of a public figure.

In this story, Alexander has turned towards a young woman, Statira, and promised sexual abstinence from his queen, Roxana. His return to Roxana leads Statira to vow never to see him. Alexander does come to Babylon to visit Statira, and she is persuaded to break her vow. Roxana, urged by Cassander, stabs Statira, as she awaits the great general, whereupon Cassander poisons Alexander. What we have here is the traditional love triangle, in which three persons are involved: one destroys the happiness of another; on the death of one lover, all three must perish. It was this stereotyped plot that was to have bad effects on the plays that followed.

Lee assumes the audience's knowledge of the fame of Alexander and moves directly into a severe analysis of his inner nature. In addition to Roxana and Statira, we are shown Alexander's male favourite – the handsome young Hephaestion. Alexander's actions indicate insecurity. He orders Philotas to be tortured. Then he is torn between natural admiration for his brave

[1] Attributed by John Downes to a member of Charles II's court, *Roscius Anglicanus* (1708), p. 16.

lieutenant Lysimachus and his own vanity. When Lysimachus tactlessly requests the hand of the beautiful Paristatis (though the old soldier Clytus tries to restrain him), Alexander has him thrown to the lions.

The tension increases at the great banquet. When the veteran Clytus refuses to wear a Persian robe, Hephaestion and Eumenes try to pull him forcibly from the hall; drunk, he remains and becomes obnoxious. From the heated dialogue, trouble looms because Clytus cannot subscribe to Alexander's demands for deification. Your father Philip was a better soldier, argues Clytus, too inebriated to recognize any danger signals, whereupon Alexander responds with violence, hurling a javelin into the faithful retainer's breast. Horrified, Alexander regrets his brutal action, but we have learned that passion has overcome his will. The clash of honesty and flattery, pettiness and glory is very well presented.[1]

In *Mithridates* (1678) Lee does seem to be striving for pathos in his treatment of the beautiful but ruined Semandra; the play is about her and could have been named after her, as the prologue states: 'In the first Draught, 'twas meant the Lady's Play.' The pathetic mode is avoided in *Caesar Borgia* (1679), Lee's next unaided work after the collaboration with Dryden in adapting *Oedipus* (1678). Lee appears to be showing gradual degradation in the character of Borgia. On the surface, *Caesar Borgia* looks like crude, anti-Catholic propaganda, but a closer study indicates that Lee was making a psychological examination of both Machiavel and Borgia. A woman is the main character of *Theodosius* (1680), but authorial emphasis is on delineation of the heroine, Pulcheria, and pathos is only incidental.

The production of *Lucius Junius Brutus* just three months after *Theodosius* shows that Lee was not only working at top speed but also achieving what some critics term his best tragedy.[2] However, not many Londoners had an opportunity to see it, as the Lord Chamberlain banned it on 11 December (after its third or sixth performance), for its 'Scandalous Expressions and Reflections'. The censor made no error in appraisal, 'for the play is a reflection of the Whig constitutional position during the Exclusion controversy' and is a celebration of constitutionalism.[3] The story shows a protagonist who must die because his passions have overruled duty and obedience. The inclusion of scenes in which the low comedian Nokes plays Vinditius (Titus Oates) indicates that the author has learned to alternate tense situations with comic relief.

---

[1] G. Wilson Knight bestows high praise on this scene, op. cit. pp. 161–3.

[2] A survey of the criticism is in *The Works of Nathaniel Lee*, ed. T. B. Stroup and A. L. Cooke, 2 vols (New Brunswick, N.J., 1955), II, pp. 318–20.

[3] See the introduction to John Loftis's edition of *Lucius Junius Brutus* (Lincoln, Nebraska, 1967), pp. xiii–xiv.

Unfortunately, mental instability was leading to a breakdown just as Lee was mastering dramatic techniques. He abandoned his own political views to join Dryden in the Tory tract *The Duke of Guise* (1682). After *Constantine the Great* in 1683, his career was over, as he was confined for insanity. *The Massacre of Paris*, first acted in 1689, had been composed many years earlier.

More perhaps should be said about his verse. Figurative language came easily to him, and the images cluster throughout the dialogues, as may be seen in the following excerpts from *Lucius Junius Brutus*:

> Throw thy abandon'd body on the ground,
> With thy bare brest lye wedded to the Dew. (III. iii. 23–4)

> As in that glass of nature thou shalt view
> Thy swoln drown'd eyes with the inverted banks,
> The tops of Willows and their blossoms turn'd,
> With all the under Sky ten fathom down,
> Wish that the shaddow of the swimming Globe
> Were so indeed, that thou migh'st leap at Fate. (III. iii. 33–8)

He uses run-on lines, half-lines and even prose to get aural discontinuity. In his early, rhymed plays, he used quatrains for the same purpose. In *Gloriana*, at a scene change, he slows down his tempo with a dialogue written entirely in quatrains. His dramas contain some fine poetry, but he often spoiled the effect by extending the expression too much. To label his work pathetic is to confuse the man with his compositions and to overlook the possibility that he may have been designing emotional speeches for the special histrionic style of the actress Elizabeth Barry.

### (vii) Thomas Otway

While Lee's compositions, taken together, may illustrate the emphasis on passion, Otway is a more significant dramatist. This importance comes from the prestige achieved by *Venice Preserved* and from the fact that his plays set the direction towards the pathetic which later tragedy was to take. He started slowly. *Alcibiades* (1675), his first offering, has little merit; *Don Carlos*, in the following year, exhibits a certain amount of power and drive, but lacks control and polish. Both are conventional heroic dramas, built on stock characters and situations, and the verse is marred by awkward or forced rhymes. However, he avoided the extravagant rhetoric that appears in so many contemporary dramas. The derivative nature of his early work is seen in his adaptations: *Titus and Berenice* (1676) is taken from Racine, and *Caius Marius* (1680) combines *Romeo and Juliet* with an episode from Roman history. In the latter alteration, Otway shows dramatic originality in changing his source to let the lady awaken before her lover's death, in the burial-vault scene.

In March 1680 appeared *The Orphan*, in which the emphasis on pathos engendered a new type of serious drama. In spite of its great influence, *The Orphan* is no model of dramaturgy. The clumsy and contradictory situations throughout the piece are certainly exasperating. 'Why does Acasto grow ill . . . and then recover?' asks Clifford Leech; 'neither illness nor recovery is linked to the main happenings of the play. Why is the marriage of Castalio and Monimia kept secret? Why does Castalio assure his brother so vehemently . . . that he has no intention of marrying Monimia?'[1] But theatregoers would have taken these objections to be cavils; the tender poet had provided an object for pity, and audiences wept with Elizabeth Barry, with later audiences weeping (with other actresses) for almost two centuries, not only in London but also in Baltimore, Philadelphia and New Orleans.

The play is deceptive. In spite of the serious dramatic faults, it begins well, with a pastoral setting which provides the needed tone. The use of the supernatural as a foreshadowing device and the precociousness of the six-year-old page all lull the critical senses. To us, Chamont, the heroine Monimia's brother, seems a crude, stuffy fellow, yet this was the role that both Garrick and Charles Kemble chose to enact. Letting all these matters rest as insoluble, one can turn to observe the historical significance of Otway's delineation of Castalio as a moral weakling, much like Clyde Griffith in Theodore Dreiser's *American Tragedy*. The long tradition of a strong or valiant hero was crumbling.

On 9 February 1682 the Duke's Company produced Otway's masterpiece, *Venice Preserved*, with the role of Belvidera as a vehicle for the great tragedienne Elizabeth Barry. What is surprising in the history of the production of this drama over the next two centuries is the substitution of Pierre for Jaffeir as the male lead: in the Restoration and early eighteenth century, the leading tragic player of the company (Betterton, Quin) acted Jaffeir; thereafter, he played Pierre (Garrick, J. P. Kemble, Macready). Such a shift can hardly represent an actor's whim; there may have been a popular reinterpretation of the play before the academic critics set up their literary dictatorship.

A plot synopsis makes the work appear a more heightened melodrama than

[1] Clifford Leech, 'Restoration Tragedy: A Reconsideration', *Durham University Journal*, XI (1950), pp. 106–15.

*The Orphan*: the beautiful Belvidera is cast out into the street by an order from her father, Priuli; Jaffeir, her husband, joins a conspiracy and agrees to put up Belvidera as a hostage, but she later persuades him to betray the plotters, including his friend Pierre. Yet Otway was able to transcend these melodramatic elements and achieve a tragic condition instead. He took his story from the Abbé de Saint-Réal's fictional work *La Conjuration des Espagnolles contre la République de Venise*. In his source Otway found the account of a Spanish conspiracy by the Marquis de Bedmar, who planned the destruction of Venice to increase the power of Spain.[1] Bedmar's hired soldiers of fortune were led by a Nicholas Renault and included Captain Jean Pierre, a Norman, and his friend Antonio Jaffeir, a Provençal. A Venetian senator named Antonio Priuli is mentioned. Most of the conspirators are lodged in the house of a Greek courtesan.

Otway was composing his play at a time of great commotion and unrest after the Titus Oates plot but before anyone could surely predict the outcome of the turbulence. That Otway was a monarchial absolutist would be no protection, for the authorities would be unlikely to sanction any work showing conspiracy against the state, much less a justification of such a conspiracy. In fact, Lee's *Lucius Junius Brutus* had been banned fourteen months earlier, as we have seen. Otway, then, had the problem of avoiding a justification of rebellion or a presentation of his leading characters as only hired bullies, motivated by bribes. He solved this dilemma by providing new characters. He invented a woman (Belvidera) married to Jaffeir who could provide the needed motivation. Antonio Priuli was split into two persons: Priuli would be the Venetian senator, father to Belvidera and incensed at her marriage to a man who was not bringing wealth into the family; Antonio would be an unscrupulous senator, and interpreted as a rich London alderman by the coterie audience at the Dorset Garden theatre. Such characters could engender conflict. Priuli's harshness to Jaffeir would lead to the heroic concept of revenge for indignity to personal honour.[2] In this way Jaffeir becomes a Cavalier gentleman with a Texas motto: 'Don't push me around'. Nevertheless, great pains would have to be taken in sketching the nature of the man who would lead Jaffeir into the conspiracy. For this, Otway uses sound dramatic creativity in portraying Pierre as a man who confuses personal injury – Antonio took his girlfriend Aquilina away – with universal justice.[3]

[1] J. H. Wilson, *A Preface*, pp. 96–8.
[2] See the excellent account by Aline M. Taylor, *Next to Shakespeare: Otway's Venice Preserv'd and The Orphan* (Durham, N.C., 1950), pp. 39–72.
[3] D. R. Hauser, 'Otway Preserved: Theme and Form in *Venice Preserv'd*', *Studies in Philology*, LV (1958), pp. 481–93.

This delineation is an excellent stroke and by itself puts the play on tragic ground. After this confusion is presented, the author can move towards rendering a dramatic situation in the notable 'Nicky-Nacky' scenes between Aquilina and Antonio, where several ends will be served: (1) they justify Pierre for wanting revenge; (2) we see, in the words of Goethe, 'How utterly unfit for government the senate had become'; and (3) they exhibit the masochistic Antonio, with his 'patter' speeches, allowing Otway to contrast profane love with the pure love of Belvidera and Jaffeir. However, Otway was not writing a play to attack parliament; consequently, he set up a pathetic situation to show Jaffeir caught between the wicked revolutionaries and a vicious senate. It is not tragic because Jaffeir is a weakling, incapable of heroism.

Consequently, it does not matter whether we accept John Harold Wilson's view that Otway wanted to build a play for Mrs Barry and incorporate some scenes for the popular low comedian Anthony Leigh (who played an alderman in other plays for satiric effects); or whether we follow a theoretical view that Otway had a new concept of tragedy in which the protagonist would be a moral weakling; or whether we use the history-of-ideas approach and label Jaffeir an early example of a creature of sensibility, over-susceptible to emotional appeals and consequently a canvas for Otway to paint the passions; or whether the drama is a variant on a favourite theme from French romance, a love versus friendship plot – all interpretations complement rather than contradict one another in explanation of this very popular tragedy.

The view that Antonio represents the first Lord Shaftesbury is supported by the epilogue and by some earlier works in which a character representing Shaftesbury is shown chasing whores. However, an epilogue was usually composed at the time of the première; by 9 February 1682 both Otway and the man in the street knew that the king had achieved control and Shaftesbury had lost. But the play itself must have been written over a period of time, and in 1681 the outcome of the political struggle was not certain. What is more significant is that Otway's previous play, *The Soldier's Fortune*, had already included the actor Anthony Leigh playing the role of a sexual pervert of a different kind.

Otway maintains a delicate balance in his presentation of human nature. The conspirators talk of the common good and of disposing of a corrupt government, yet their fright at an unidentified sound betrays their fears and disunity. Their speeches reveal much self-deception, and Renault attempts to rape Belvidera. Nor is Belvidera perfect. She lacks the Roman constancy of which she boasts in alluding to Portia; she misunderstands Jaffeir; her report to her father is far from the truth, as she conceals her reason for wanting to spare Pierre's life and acts as if Jaffeir would harm her. Everybody makes solemn oaths, all of which will be broken, both by the members of the conspiracy and the senate. Yet the conspirators die bravely enough, and Jaffeir attains a measure of redemption in protecting Pierre against shame and torture. Belvidera goes mad, too weak to endure both her husband's sins and her own emotional pressures. What comes out of all this is a feeling of truth or universality because the different persons are depicted as complex, as mixtures of strength and weakness, of good and evil. This achievement establishes *Venice Preserved* as the chief Restoration tragedy.

The work displays tragic structure in that the opponents Priuli and Pierre are inflexible. Priuli will not act like a father and he completely rejects his daughter's husband; Pierre's method for protecting his wounded ego against injustice is to plunge the whole city into distress. It is from such absolutes that tragedy can develop. Yet Otway does not keep the drama under complete control. Towards the end, 'the external appeal of suffering becomes more significant than its quality'.[1] Instead of a strong character being overwhelmed, it is the unstable Jaffeir who falls, evoking pity without fear or terror. The influence of this play and *The Orphan* will be strong; we shall see that later dramatists become concerned with presenting a beautiful woman in distress and with securing the pity of the audience. Genuine tragedy will not appear unless a fresh start is made upon different principles.

## (viii) John Banks

Whatever difficulties blocked Dryden and Lee from achieving tragic drama, they were genuine poets. The playwright John Banks laboured under the handicap of being a turgid versifier; it would strain definition to call him a poet. Nevertheless, Banks is of prime importance in any account of Restoration and eighteenth-century drama because he turned to English history as a source for his later plays and set the trend for using women as the central characters in tragedy.

His early work showed little promise, marked as it was by its imitative and derivative aspects. He began with a heroic drama, *The Rival Kings* (1677), slavishly patterned after Lee's *The Rival Queens*, with the result that he was pigeonholed in one category by literary historians before Allardyce Nicoll, who first recognized the significance of Banks's later plays.

[1] Rothstein, op. cit. p. 108.

When Dryden abandoned the rhymed couplet, he caused no little confusion among the playwrights. Some followed his change to blank verse, and some held to rhyme. John Banks's solution in *The Destruction of Troy* (1678) was to write partly in couplets and partly in blank verse. Unlike most heroic drama of the time, this piece has no villain, as the Homeric figures encounter love and honour. Some time before May 1681 Banks composed a third offering in this genre, *Cyrus the Great; or, The Tragedy of Love*, taken from *Le Grand Cyrus* by Madeleine de Scudéry. The intended production was interdicted, being the first of three of his plays to be so treated, and approval was delayed until 1695.[1]

At this point, Banks ceased being an imitator and proceeded to compose four melodramatic works on episodes from English history in the lifetime of Queen Elizabeth I; in fact, she appears as a major or minor character in three of them. For the first, *The Unhappy Favourite; or, The Earl of Essex* (1681), Banks picked up the romantic legend of Queen Elizabeth and the ring, to secure an emotional impact. Women dominate the action. The chief villain is the Countess of Nottingham, the heroine is the Countess of Rutland, but the most important person is the Queen herself. She vacillates, conceals her views, dilates on the defeat of the Spanish Armada and browbeats her counsellors as if the author were a twentieth-century historian instead of a Restoration playwright. *The Unhappy Favourite* was generally well received, being frequently acted and reprinted, although we may note Sir Richard Steele's observation in *The Tatler* that there was not one good line of poetry in the entire play.

In March 1682, Banks offered another pathetic, historical tragedy, *Virtue Betrayed; or, Anna Bullen*. Here Cardinal Wolsey is the villain and more male characters appear than in the previous work, but the play is mainly concerned with pathetic scenes: between Lady Diana Talbot and Anna Bullen, Diana and Piercy, Anna and Piercy, together with a fine scene between the young Princess Elizabeth and Henry VIII. Instead of the extravagant language of love and honour, we find the extravagant language of the maiden in distress; and in a suppressed epilogue Banks refers to his play as a 'Domestick Tale'. It was very popular and held the stage for many years.

For the following season, Banks prepared the story of another maiden in distress, *The Innocent Usurper; or, The Death of the Lady Jane Gray*. The execution of a Protestant damsel in distress by a (wicked) Catholic queen had

[1] A. F. White, 'The Office of Revels and Dramatic Censorship during the Restoration Period', *Western Reserve Bulletin*, XXXIV (1931), pp. 5–45; Nicoll, *HED*, I, p. 389.

no chance to reach the stage; the play was banned by the censor. Undaunted, Banks offered for the ensuing season the pathetic story of a Catholic queen executed by a Protestant one: *The Island Queens; or, The Death of Mary, Queen of Scotland*. The times were not yet favourable for this situation either; the play was banned, and harshly vilified as well. Twenty years and three sovereigns later it was finally produced at Drury Lane in a revised version, *The Albion Queens*. That Banks was an innovator cannot be disputed. The Earl of Orrery had drawn characters from English history, but they were only ornaments and adjunct to the 'moral' he was presenting. He was not concerned with the historicity of Owen Tudor, for he was concentrating on the artifice of his imitation of the epic. Banks has shifted from artifice to illusion, and the historicity is part of the illusion.

### (ix) Thomas Southerne

Southerne began with a political allegory on behalf of the Duke of York, *The Loyal Brother* (1682), in which the hero survives all sorts of atrocious plots by the villains Ismael (Lord Shaftesbury) and Arbanes (Monmouth), as well as the ingratitude of his brother, Seliman (Charles II). After this clumsy apprenticeship, Southerne composed a very curious drama, *The Disappointment; or, The Mother in Fashion* (1684), in which he creates a strong, aggressive villain, the libertine Alberto. However, Alberto does not at all resemble the young rakes of Restoration comedy chasing women in St James's Park. Instead, he wants to engross all women. Erminia, the chaste wife of an eccentric, Alphonso, particularly whets his appetite. Southerne employs the *Measure for Measure* bed trick twice, with Juliana substituting freely, as in American football, but the tone is always foreboding, never comic. The best parts of the work are the dialogues between Alphonso (who affects madness) and the bluff, sceptical and impoverished Rogero. The author shifts from verse to prose for these discussions. This strangely serious work is not at all in the heroic tradition, nor is there any indecency or innuendo in action or language. Alphonso and Erminia survive, yet the villain Alberto does not die, so that we cannot label the piece a tragedy. Southerne called it 'A Play'.

After writing his brilliant comedies, Southerne returned ten years later to tragic form in *The Fatal Marriage; or, Innocent Adultery*. The plot is like that of Tennyson's poem 'Enoch Arden'. The heroine Isabella is shown in circumstances of great distress, her husband missing for nearly seven years. An older man, Villeroy, characterized by emotional stability, has aided the afflicted heroine, but has steadily sought to marry her. The early action is very well done, Southerne writing with skill and restraint to render Isabella's final yielding to the importunings of Villeroy. After their marriage, catastrophe appears with the return of the missing husband. At this point, Southerne appears to lose his previous control of language and tone, so that rhetoric takes over as Isabella is defeated and crushed. However, Southerne does employ a comic subplot to great advantage. Instead of trying to sustain the same high level of emotional intensity, as Lee tried to do, Southerne inserts his comic scenes functionally, and by relief and contrast is able to heighten his sad story. The work was immediately popular and survived for over 150 years, first in Garrick's revision, *Isabella*, and later in J. P. Kemble's alteration.

Southerne had taken his plot from a novella by Aphra Behn, and in 1695 he drew upon her popular account of the noble slave Oroonoko for still another success. He tried for some realism in his satirical portrayal of the colonial merchants, again to provide relief from the pathetic scenes. *Oroonoko* is sometimes misinterpreted as a humanitarian and pathetic play. However, it must be remembered that the influence of the heroic drama was still strong and its best examples were still being produced in the theatre. Consequently, Oroonoko is not so much the noble savage as a heroic figure trapped by fate, and the conflict of love and honour is still present.[1]

Neither *Oroonoko* nor *The Fatal Marriage* is an entirely successful tragedy. Both are weakened by an overemphasis on the display of emotion. However, Southerne showed in *The Disappointment* that he was capable of innovation and experiment, and the grim realism of the comic subplots displays his dramatic talents.

## (c) SUMMATION OF TRENDS

The rhymed heroic play only briefly held its position as the dominant convention in tragedy. With royal sponsorship, it was the most fashionable serious drama for a dozen years, but it never received full acceptance. Strong enough to withstand the satiric attack of *The Rehearsal*, it was not sufficiently established to hold the allegiance of the leading playwrights in the next generation. Nathaniel Lee led the revolution by using blank verse for his tragedy *The Rival Queens* (17 March 1677). Dryden, the staunchest defender of rhyme, followed in December with *All for Love* in blank verse.

[1] See Moody Prior, op. cit. pp. 178–9.

Subversion of the heroic aspects came more slowly and required more time. It was done by introducing weak, unstable and indecisive characters like Lee's Theodosius, Otway's Castalio (*The Orphan*) and Jaffeir (*Venice Preserved*) in the place of Almanzor and Solyman as the leading characters, and by shifting the emphasis from the bold hero to distressed heroine. There is a modulation in the depiction of the heroines, from sympathetic roles like Statira in *The Rival Queens*, Pulcheria in *Theodosius*, and Belvidera in *Venice Preserved*, to distressed maidens like Monimia in *The Orphan*, to women whose misfortunes dominate the entire works, as in the plays of John Banks, to women who just suffer, like Isabella in *The Fatal Marriage*. As a consequence, the criterion of 'pity' replaces that of 'admiration', and the nomenclature shifts from 'the heroic play' to 'pathetic tragedy'.

Dryden was not a participant in these trends towards the sentimental and the pathetic, in spite of recent efforts to enrol him in the movement. The refutation for such attempts is the nature and the late dates of his *Don Sebastian* (1689) and *Cleomenes* (1692), both of which continue in the heroic mode. Dryden had a fondness for the grotesque and the extravagant, but his knowledge of human nature normally prevented him from the falsified character delineations we find in much late Restoration drama. Besides, his critical writings show his opposition to what we would term sentimentalism.[1] As for the assertion that the presentation of Melisinda in *Aureng-Zebe* reveals Dryden moving towards the pathetic, it is more plausible to appraise the episode within its context and say that Dryden was representing her as too soft to be an emperor's wife, should her husband Morat succeed.[2]

A few other varieties of tragic drama need to be mentioned. There were a number of political plays. These works, while retaining the externals of a remote setting and exotic situations from the heroic play, were political allegories. *The Usurper* (1664) of Edward Howard deals with Cromwell, Hugh Peters and General Monck. In 1674 Henry Nevil Payne brought out *The Siege of Constantinople*, a work in which the emperor represents Charles II and Thomazo is the Duke of York. The treacherous chancellor who betrays the city to the Turks is Lord Shaftesbury. Payne includes a scene at the end of Act II showing the chancellor rioting with whores, an early example of this kind of attack on Shaftesbury. Nahum Tate, Crowne, Southerne and various other writers also indulged in this sort of dramatic allegory.

A curious eddy of authorial taste in serious drama was manifested towards the end of Charles's reign when a large number of Shakespeare's tragedies,

[1] See R. D. Hume, *Dryden's Criticism* (Ithaca, N.Y., 1970).
[2] Alssid, op. cit. pp. 452–69.

histories and tragicomedies were heavily revised and produced within a relatively short period of time.[1] From January 1678 to March 1682 ten of these plays were acted. The adaptations were staged by both companies, and seven different playwrights made the revisions. This upsurge did not coincide with any decline in the number of new tragedies being offered; in fact, this four-year interval marked the appearance of a number of new and successful tragedies, *The Orphan*, *Venice Preserved*, *Theodosius*, *The Unhappy Favourite*.

When Charles Booth, prompter for the defunct King's Company, relinquished the archives, a number of pre-Restoration play manuscripts fell into the hands of the actors. From these, several tragedies were refurbished and produced, in the hope of profits from a benefit on the third night. *King Edward III*, *with the Fall of Mortimer* (1690) and *Henry II*, *King of England*, *with the Death of Rosamond* (1692) are two examples from the total ascertained by Alfred Harbage's literary detective work.[2] Such opportunistic ventures must not be misinterpreted as an Elizabethan revival.

Meanwhile, offstage, the theorists were urging an entirely different style: classical tragedy on French principles. There was only minimal response, as the dramatists preferred their coarsely realistic scenes, violent deaths on stage, torture scenes, comic subplots and diction which was far from French neoclassical decorum. John Bancroft's *The Tragedy of Sertorius* (1679) seems to be the only drama after the French pattern until the 1690s. At the turn of the century, several playwrights became interested, and Addison's *Cato* was probably composed around 1700. In the early eighteenth century, however, French classical tragedy and the native pathetic drama will be the two most active influences upon writers of tragedy.

## (d) FORMS AND MOVEMENTS 1700–1750

Changes in the response of audiences at the turn of the century made for unsettled conditions. Authors experimented with different types of tragedy only to have their efforts damned in the playhouse. Congreve's *The Mourning Bride* (1697) was a mild success, but it was an exception. Furthermore, playwrights were lacking who could match the poetry which Samuel Johnson extolled in this work. Bad management of the theatres and a changing audience were only part of the impasse; the young dramatists were concerned

[1] A. H. Scouten, 'The Increase in Popularity of Shakespeare's Plays in the Eighteenth Century', *Shakespeare Quarterly*, VII (1956), pp. 189–202.
Harbage, op. cit. pp. 312–19.

with the problem of the language of tragedy. Thus we have the new playwrights experimenting unsuccessfully with both language and tragic form.

The trials of a group of women dramatists may be used for an illustration. In 1695 Mrs Catherine Trotter offered *Agnes de Castro*, but this and her three following tragedies all failed. Mrs Jane Wiseman's *Antiochus the Great* achieved a few performances in 1701. Mary Pix brought out five efforts at tragedy. The first, *Ibrahim, the 13th Emperor of the Turks*, was well received at its première in May 1696 but did not go into repertory. *Queen Catherine* failed in 1698 and *The False Friend* in 1699. These three works were somewhat imitative of the old heroic play, but were written in blank verse. In the spring of 1701 came *The Double Distress*, containing both heroic and pathetic elements and a reversion to rhymed couplets in various scenes. That too failed. The stress under which this writer was working is reflected by her unconventional use of prose in her next tragedy, *The Czar of Muscovy* (1701). She displays no other kind of innovation, and the plot complication about a wicked, usurping tyrant is banal. Mrs Pix was not the only writer experimenting with prose, for the veteran songster Thomas D'Urfey had brought out a two-part tragedy in prose, *The Famous History of the Rise and Fall of Massaniello* (1699). The plot contains much incident, and D'Urfey achieves a certain amount of vigour and speed, but the work was a failure none the less. 'Its historical importance,' writes Eric Rothstein, 'like that of *The Czar of Muscovy*, is as a symptom of the breakdown of decorum and the drive for mimesis.'[1]

From stage history we can see that audience approval would eventually be bestowed upon a more talented dramatist who would carry on and amplify the vogue of the 'pathetic' established by Otway and Banks. This person turned out to be the genial poet Nicholas Rowe. His initial work was of another kind, *The Ambitious Stepmother* (1700), and it attracted no interest. His second, *Tamerlane* (1701), an offering of no intrinsic worth as a tragedy, accidentally profited by the current political situation. Bajazet was read as Louis XIV and Tamerlane as William III, with the fantastic result that *Tamerlane* achieved a tremendous number of performances by being played throughout the eighteenth century on King William's birthday.

In 1703 Rowe finally got into the right groove in securing pathos in *The Fair Penitent*. This sentimental tearjerker was lifted from Massinger and Field's play *The Fatal Dowry*. Rowe condensed the first two acts of his source into an opening episode and reduced the number of characters, to show good

[1] Rothstein, op. cit. p. 172.

control over his design. A significant change was to convert the minor character Calista, who had been the willing paramour of Lothario, into a wronged and injured victim. In Lothario, Rowe hit upon a rich vein for dramatic use – the wicked seducer. Such a figure was no original invention, of course, but Rowe went into detailed analysis of the mentality of Lothario with the result that he created a personality which was at once evil and fascinating. The work did not succeed at its première, but later audiences were to be simultaneously repelled and attracted by Rowe's new villainous type. In prose fiction, where an author was not bound by a two-hour limit, creative writers might see even more possibilities, as Richardson did.

Two more tragedies were also to fail before Rowe followed Banks's lead by composing pathetic tragedy based on English history. Audiences were ready when Rowe offered *Jane Shore* in 1714. Not only was this tragedy instantly popular but *The Fair Penitent* was revived, and the two plays were acted almost every season for the rest of the century and were performed well into the Victorian era. Rowe added one more tragedy based on English history, *The Tragedy of Lady Jane Gray* (1715). It is a weak piece, but its anti-Catholic sentiments gave it a favourable reception in the theatre.

There is a notable resemblance between the consequences of Rowe's *Jane Shore* and of Steele's *The Conscious Lovers*. In these works, each author perfected and brought to culmination a form which had been developing over a long period, and which numerous previous playwrights had practised: Steele's play was the peak of the exemplary mode of comedy as Rowe's *Jane Shore* was of pathetic tragedy. Yet neither work drew immediate adherents of ability in the drama. Hence, one might say that pathetic tragedy realized itself in *The Fair Penitent* and *Jane Shore* and then ceased. That is, no other competent dramatists emerged after Rowe to continue writing pathetic tragedies of any merit. The long-range influence of these plays by Rowe and Steele was pervasive and strong, but it was delayed and may have affected the novel more than the drama. Since no new pathetic tragedies of any dramatic value appeared in the years following Rowe's contribution, the managers satisfied audience response by regularly offering Banks's 'she-tragedies', Otway's *The Orphan* and *Venice Preserved*, Southerne's *The Fatal Marriage* and Shakespeare's *Romeo and Juliet* (as revised by Otway and later by T. Cibber). Meanwhile, tragedy continued its decline.

Other Restoration modes occasionally reappeared. Rhymed heroic dramas came out sporadically throughout the period. Allardyce Nicoll highly praises Robert Gould's *The Rival Sisters* (1695).[1] The last one was Robert Ashton's

[1] Nicoll, *HED*, I, p. 153.

*The Battle of Aughrim* in 1728. Many more heroic dramas in blank verse were produced. In 1697 Lord Lansdowne's *Heroic Love* was a slight success, in a season when most plays did badly. Charles Gildon contributed a heroic play in *The Patriot* (1703). Colley Cibber, John Dennis and Lewis Theobald each wrote one play of this type. Of more merit was Dr Joseph Trapp's *Abra-Mule ; or, Love and Empire* (1704). The poet Edward Young wrote two heroic dramas in his customary monotonous and sententious blank verse, *Busiris* (1719) and *The Revenge* (1721). Elijah Fenton's *Mariamne* (1723), a blank-verse tragedy with heavy emphasis on the emotions, was well received. David Mallet composed two pieces in this mode, *Eurydice* (1731) and *Mustapha* (1739). One of the last was the actor William Havard's *Regulus*, produced at Drury Lane in 1744.

Meanwhile, the critics were encouraging a more formal kind of tragedy. Very popular with them was Edmund Smith's adaptation from Racine, *Phaedra and Hippolitus* (1707). Another adaptation from Racine, *The Distressed Mother* (1712) by Ambrose Philips, was popular with both critics and audiences. The chief work in this mode is Addison's *Cato* (1713), whose instant success appears far beyond its merits from a modern point of view. The production was well advertised in advance, and when the Whigs came to applaud the Tories cheered as loudly. What is interesting is that the work is a reflection of that society which filled Drury Lane for the première; the moral tenacity of the protagonist represented the goal the leaders of the aristocracy had set for themselves. To what extent any reached that objective, I leave to the historians and sociologists, but Cato's sense of duty struck a responsive chord in the breast of the ruling class. Addison must be credited with restoring the atmosphere of tragedy in presenting the spectacle of a great and noble individual going inevitably to destruction.[1] Thus the broad view. Examined more closely, *Cato* has the weaknesses of which John Dennis first complained – the absence of dramatic passion and the stiffness of language. The encomiums it received led to a number of weak imitations, not worth consideration today. It is doubtful whether the tradition of Racine and French neoclassical drama was viable for English playwrights in the next generation, who were more likely to look to Voltaire than to Racine.

Such an admirer was Aaron Hill, who fancied innovation. He had long called for a changed style of acting and held a low opinion of current types of tragedy. For many years he had laboured diligently over a play from early English history, offering it in 1710 as *Elfrid* and in 1731 as *Athelwold*. He was ready to welcome any method of repudiating contemporary patterns in

[1] Bonamy Dobrée, *Restoration Tragedy*, p. 175.

tragedy, so he turned to introducing plays by Voltaire to English audiences. Six months after the première of Voltaire's *Alzire* in Paris in January 1736, Hill had his adaptation, *Alzira*, produced in London. He had previously adapted *Zaïre* and followed with *Mérope* in 1749.

One additional author who might be mentioned is James Thomson, more because of his prestige than for the intrinsic merit of his tragedies. They were generally unsuccessful, though *Sophonisba* (1730) and *Tancred and Sigismunda* (1745) managed to get a few performances. The latter work has some dramatic force, generating a conflict between accepted civic virtues and the protagonist's staunchly held personal code. Unfortunately, the quality of the verse in his dramas is much lower than that of his well-known poems.

Tragedy was indeed deteriorating so completely that nothing could revive it except the appearance of a great dramatist or else a fresh start in tragic form. No outstanding playwright did appear, but a change in the nature of tragedy appeared in an abortive movement called 'domestic tragedy'. At least six domestic tragedies were acted, and three of them are of significance: George Lillo's *The London Merchant* and *Fatal Curiosity*, and Charles Johnson's *Caelia*. The remainder might be listed for the record: Osborne Sydney Wandesford, *Fatal Love* (1730); John Hewitt, *Fatal Falsehood* (1734); Thomas Cooke, *The Mournful Nuptials* (its published title in 1739, but billed at the theatre in 1743 as *Love the Cause and Cure of Grief; or, The Innocent Murderer*). Allardyce Nicoll also includes *The Fatal Extravagance* (1721) by Aaron Hill and Joseph Mitchell.[1] This work, a revision of the Elizabethan play *The Yorkshire Tragedy*, displays a refinement of sentiments associated with the trends in later sentimental comedy. From the titles of these six dramas, one can see a significant characteristic in the change of tragic concept: these are tragedies of fate. Unlike Brutus or Bussy d'Ambois, the male lead no longer chooses the way that brings on the catastrophe; he just goes through the motions, for the disaster has already been fated.

*The London Merchant*, or *George Barnwell*, as it was usually billed, made a sensational impact not only upon its first audiences at Drury Lane in 1731 but also upon writers and critics throughout Western Europe. To us the work presents a warped morality in its suggestion that an offence against commercial success is the greatest crime and in Barnwell's posturing with a sentimental mask when he speaks with horror at having murdered his 'dear' uncle.[2] At the end, the emphasis shifts from the dramatic conflict to pure didacticism. The turgid prose and the unequal conflict between Barnwell and

[1] Nicoll, *HED*, II, p. 119.
[2] Brooks and Heilman, op. cit. pp. 180–8.

the spirited, aggressive Millwood seem to be overwhelming disadvantages, but critics were demanding a play about the 'common man' (even though the common man turns out to be a George Barnwell or Willy Loman), and Lillo supplied that need.[1]

In the following year, Charles Johnson, a minor playwright who had attempted a truly unusual number of varying types of drama, and who had earlier approached domestic tragedy in *The Force of Friendship* (1710), offered a powerful but uneven tragedy in *Caelia; or, The Perjured Lover* (1732). A tender heroine, Caelia, is abducted and confined in a brothel, where she dies of a broken heart. The production failed, partly because of the remarkable realism of the brothel scenes and partly because of Johnson's violation of decorum in composing a tragedy in prose. A critic in the *Grub Street Journal* of 8 March 1733 praises the play but asserts that its weakness lies in the lack of poetic diction.

One observer who showed interest in this new type of tragedy was Henry Fielding, then manager of the Little Haymarket theatre. He staged the only domestic tragedy of genuine artistic merit, Lillo's *Fatal Curiosity* (1736), a three-act work based on a black-letter ballad.[2] From the memorialist Tom Davies, we learn that Fielding took great pains in conducting the rehearsals and composed a prologue for the opening night. The plot is simple, economical and overpowering in its implications: it is the 'You can't go home again' motif of Thomas Wolfe's novels and of Robert Penn Warren's 'Ballad of Billie Potts'. Into the home of his aged and poverty-stricken parents comes the long-lost son, disguised so that he can postpone and extend the emotional bath of observing the old folks' joy on eventual recognition. Meanwhile, the hero's sweetheart has a horrible dream which foreshadows the catastrophe. The destitute parents meditate on the casket of jewels the visitor has relinquished for safe-keeping, and they murder him in his sleep. On the discovery of the 'stranger's' identity, the father kills the mother and commits suicide. Lillo controls the play with a firm hand; moralizing and commentary are held to a minimum. Two brief 'recognition' scenes occur early to build an ironical effect. From the sweetheart's dream, we realize that all must happen as it does, yet the hero deliberately makes the fatal error of concealing his identity. The effectiveness of the structure overshadows Lillo's ineptness as a prose writer to the extent that we can credit the author with achieving tragic form even if he could not perfect it. What progress domestic tragedy would have

[1] See Bernbaum, op. cit. pp. 151–8.
[2] See C. F. Burgess, 'Lillo, Sans Barnwell, or the Playwright Revisited', *Modern Philology*, LXVI (1968), pp. 5–29.

had in the hands of more capable dramatists, we do not know; the experiment was no sooner begun than it was checked with the closing of the small theatres by the Stage Licensing Act. What did happen was that the drama yielded to the novel the dominant position it had so long held in English literature. There was nothing to do but stand around and wait for Ibsen.

# 6 Dramatic opera

From time to time throughout this period there appeared musical dramas of a varying nature which were referred to as operas. Much confusion has arisen because these productions differed so much from the contemporary French and Italian opera, there was no clearly defined evolution or development, and many regular plays contained considerable amounts of vocal and instrumental music. Contradictions and inconsistencies in nomenclature brought more difficulties. Nevertheless, a substantial amount of musical drama was performed, involving important poets and composers, so that an account of English opera needs to be given.[1]

If the musical drama of the early Restoration is closely examined, its affinity to the dramatic masques staged by professional actors at theatres in the Caroline period will be recognized. The development is not from the proper masques by Ben Jonson and Inigo Jones but from works offered at the theatres, of which Thomas Heywood's *Love's Mistress; or, The Queen's Masque* (1634) is the best illustration. In 1661, this work was so much in vogue that it was performed by both the Duke's and the King's companies,

---

[1] For a full survey, see F. E. Haun, *But Hark! More Harmony: The Libretti in English of the Restoration Opera* (Ypsilanti, Mich., 1971), and E. J. Dent, *Foundations of English Opera* (Cambridge, 1928).

and it stayed in repertory for a number of years. Heywood calls the work 'a drama' in both the dedication and the 'foreword', but it is described as a 'masque' on the title page. The plot is the story of Cupid and Psyche; the dancing, which is considerable, is extraneous to the plot.

The term *opera* had not come into use in the Caroline era, the first recorded use being by John Evelyn in describing a performance in Rome in 1644. Richard Flecknoe, who was acquainted with Italian opera and who wrote two operas himself, uses the word in his preface to *Love's Dominion* (1654), not to mean a musical entertainment but rather a particular kind of play. Thomas Blount, in his *Glossographia*, explained that in Italy an opera was a 'Tragedy, Tragi-comedy, Comedy or Pastoral ... performed by voices in that way, which the Italians term *Recitative*, being likewise adorned with scenes by Perspective, and extraordinary advantages by Musick.'[1] If Richard Flecknoe had been as influential as he hoped, he would undoubtedly have brought opera along in the Italian manner. In 1654 he published *Ariadne Deserted by Theseus and Found and Courted by Bacchus. A Dramatick Piece Adapted for Recitative Musick*. It is divided into sixteen musical numbers. The soloists are Ariadne and Bacchus, and there are both a male and a female chorus. From the stage directions we learn that scenery in perspective was to be used, and there are several interludes which are entirely instrumental.[2]

Various types of musical drama were being put before the public towards the end of the Interregnum. From Leslie Hotson's researches, we know that pieces with music such as *Oenone* and *Actaeon and Diana* were being surreptitiously performed,[3] as was Thomas Jordan's *Cupid his Coronation*.[4] Several masques brought out by professional actors were being published, together with new works, one of which was Flecknoe's *Love's Dominion*.[5]

Such activity prepared the way for Davenant's aims. Before the Civil War, he had wished to build a theatre entirely for musical productions. Now, towards the end of the Protectorate, and with the approval of Sir Bulstrode Whitelock (representative of wealthy London Puritans who were fond of music), he offered the experimental piece, *The First Dayes Entertainment at Rutland House* (1656).[6] It was an odd combination of musical interludes,

---

[1] (London, 1661).
[2] Haun, op. cit. pp. 24–49.
[3] Leslie Hotson, *The Commonwealth and Restoration Stage* (Cambridge, Mass., 1928), pp. 48–50.
[4] Clifford Leech, 'Jordan's Interregnum Masques', *TLS*, 12 April 1934, p. 262.
[5] G. E. Bentley, *The Jacobean and Caroline Stage*, 7 vols (Oxford, 1941–68), II, pp. 373–4; VI, p. 71.
[6] Montague Summers, *The Playhouse of Pepys*, pp. 34–8.

spoken dialogues and songs. Before the year had ended, he constructed a more unified work based upon a historical incident, *The Siege of Rhodes*, and produced it also at his London residence, Rutland House.

This première is often considered as a landmark, historically, wherein Davenant is credited with simultaneously introducing two new forms – opera and the heroic play. A number of distinctions erode this achievement, however. The stories in Italian opera were classical, and Davenant's plot comes from recent European history. Music and elaborate machinery characterize Renaissance Italian opera, whereas Davenant had no machinery at Rutland House, and it is unlikely that the singing approached the intensity of Italian productions. Later, when Davenant staged Part 1 of *The Siege of Rhodes* in July 1661 at the playhouse in Lincoln's Inn Fields, his artificer John Webb was able to use machines and painted scenery.[1] Yet on this occasion he was offering a play, a very different work from his musical drama of 1656.

Experimentation with opera was now put aside, and a dozen years passed before any more attempts were made. When operatic works appeared again, from 1673 to 1677, a new trend could be noted, in which old plays were revised and refurbished into musical productions – 'semioperas', Roger North called them.[2] The first was *Macbeth*, turned into a musical drama in 1673, with music by Locke, Channell and Priest. The roles of the witches were enlarged, and new scenery was designed. Next was *The Tempest* (1674), over which great pains were taken.[3] Shakespeare's comedy had been revised earlier by Dryden and Davenant, and from this text Shadwell wrote a libretto. Locke, Hart and Pietro Reggio composed the music, and Draghi arranged the dancing. Betterton was sent to Paris to observe the operas, and he was given charge of producing *The Tempest*. There are extended sections of almost continuous vocal music, and for the first time a terminal masque is included, *Neptune and Amphitrite*.

The most elaborate of all was Betterton's production of the French tragedy-ballet *Psyche*, with Shadwell supplying the libretto. The vocal music was by Locke, the instrumental music by Draghi and the choreography by St Andrée. The next was Charles Davenant's *Circe* (1677), with music by John Bannister, who was responsible for a development in form by having each act contain one major musical scene involving the whole apparatus of production.

[1] Ibid. pp. 40–6.
[2] *Roger North on Music*, p. 274.
[3] For the extensive scholarship dealing with the operatic version of *The Tempest*, see C. Spencer, *Five Adaptations of Shakespeare* (Urbana, Ill., 1965).

Actually, there is very little relation between this cluster of operas and Davenant's early productions.

A lull in the preparation of operas again occurred, broken after a few years when John Dryden turned his interest in the direction of opera. He began by rewriting *Paradise Lost* into an opera, *The State of Innocence*, which was never produced. From his remarks we know that he considered it a drama with incidental music. He was concerned with finding epic material for use in an opera, as we can see from his next work, *Albion and Albanius*. It was, however, one of the weakest pieces that Dryden ever wrote, and it was not helped by an indifferent composer, Louis Grabut.

Nevertheless, Dryden reached success in his next and final venture in this medium. For material he had gone to Arthurian legend; for a composer, he had found a musical genius, Henry Purcell. The co-operation between the two yielded the opera *King Arthur* (1691). Both Dryden and Purcell entertained hopes that they might create that 'apogee of patriotism linked with the arts' – a British National Opera.[1] It was his most enduring success, for it held the stage until 1842. In previous writings, Dryden had considered 'the Poem' of sole importance: the poet wrote the work; afterwards, a musician set it to music. In the Epistle Dedicatory, Dryden shows a changed position. He now concedes the pre-eminence of the music, and he shifts to being a collaborator in writing a libretto for a composer, saying:

> But the Numbers of Poetry and Vocal Musick are sometimes so contrary, that in many Places I have been oblig'd to cramp my Verses, and make them rugged to the Reader, that they may be harmonious to the Hearer.

Where Dryden had called *The Tempest* 'a mixt Opera', he now made a different identification and labelled *King Arthur* a dramatic opera, the first time this term was used. Similar pieces in the 1690s were generally called operas, but Dryden's term eventually became established and used by other writers.

Purcell had only recently brought out his own masterpiece, *Dido and Aeneas*, in 1689, with Nahum Tate as the librettist. It was not produced in London, or even at a theatre. It was sung at a girls' school, and Purcell's anxiety over the voices of his singers may have caused him to tone down some baroque excesses. It is the one Restoration work that has continued uninterrupted until the present day. In 1690 he set the music for Betterton's operatic revision of Fletcher and Massinger's *The Prophetess*. *Dioclesian*, as this work was usually billed, was not as completely an opera as *King Arthur*.

[1] R. E. Moore, *Henry Purcell and the Restoration Theatre* (Cambridge, Mass., 1961), p. 73.

Betterton and Purcell conceived of *Dioclesian* as a masque-like extravaganza, with magic as the pretext for spectacle; hence the new title – *The Prophetess*.[1] The emphasis remains on the play, and music is added to an existing work rather than being an integral part of the whole. Later, Purcell composed the music for Elkanah Settle's *The Fairy Queen* (1692), a work based on *A Midsummer Night's Dream* but actually far from Shakespeare. In 1695 he may have tried again for a national theme in setting the music for George Powell's operatic alteration of Fletcher's *Bonduca*. In fact, his music for *The Indian Queen* in 1695 may have propped up the heroic play a little longer.

For a brief time dramatic opera was flourishing. Even after Purcell's death, in 1695, his brother Daniel, John Blow, John Eccles and other composers continued to write operas. In 1696 Daniel Purcell composed the music for *Brutus of Alba*, and later in the same year achieved artistic success with the music for Thomas D'Urfey's *Cinthia and Endimion*. Though D'Urfey called his work a dramatic opera, it is really a pastoral, with a survival of the emblematic techniques of the early masques; in fact, F. E. Haun considers it to be more of a masque than an opera.[2]

Here, at the peak of activity, may be the place for a broad definition. Dramatic opera was a baroque form, combining the arts. The direction and shape it took was typically, almost comically, British in that the result was a practical expedient, part accident and part compromise, with a mixing of Italian styles and native traditions, and a refusal to accept a work that was entirely sung. Tension in balance is its baroque characteristic. Music and poetry together did not constitute dramatic opera; words and music can be heard at a concert. Instead, the ideal mode 'combined the arts of poetry and melody with those of the visual arts – of painting, architecture, costume, and the dance.'[3] In practice, a dramatic opera was a full-scale theatrical entertainment, organized as a five-act drama, including one production number to each act. The story was a romantic dream involving tragic occurrences but usually ending happily for the main character. The subject was frequently mythological. No indication is given for restricting the number of characters or casting the roles in terms of voices. All too often the music was unrelated to the main action of the drama, and production numbers seem to be inserted for their own sake.

Nomenclature remained confusing. For example, Elkanah Settle's *The World in the Moon* (1697) was termed an opera when it is really an exemplary

[1] Ibid. p. 145.
[2] Haun, op. cit. p. 161.
[3] Moore, op. cit. pp. 5, 32.

comedy in which music and dancing have been inserted. These have nothing to do with the story, and the individual pieces are more like song-and-dance numbers. That the confusion of terminology continues can be illustrated by Manfred Bukofzer's calling John Blow's three-act masque *Venus and Adonis* (*c*. 1682) 'a full-fledged opera'.[1] Bukofzer's view may arise from the fact that *Venus and Adonis* is in continuous music, with the arias set off from the choruses. However, in the Restoration period, *masque* was the name given to a short, compact entertainment, set to music and performed at court or in some nobleman's residence, or, in the theatre, as a part of a larger work.[2] When *Dido and Aeneas* was brought to the London stage it was inserted into Gildon's adaptation of *Measure for Measure* (1700) and later into some other play.[3] Hence Bukofzer's term 'court opera' does not fit the social situation of late seventeenth-century England. When the monarch wanted a musical drama at court, a masque was called for, such as John Crowne's *Calisto; or, The Chaste Nymph*, the extravaganza on 15 February 1675 which was the triumph of that social season.[4] In the theatre, P. A. Motteux's masque *The Loves of Mars and Venus* (1696) was interwoven between the acts of Ravenscroft's *The Anatomist*; Motteux's masque *The Four Seasons* was presented at the end of the operatic *Island Princess* in 1699; and Dryden's 'Secular Masque' was inserted into Vanbrugh's adaptation of Fletcher's *The Pilgrim* (1700). Probably the best of these masques, according to Professor Haun, is John Eccles's *The Rape of Europa* (*c*. 1694), in which Anne Bracegirdle sang Europa.[5] The arrangement of the singing and dancing is most graceful.

At the close of the century, two contradictory trends were under way, one increasing interest in the opera, and another undermining it. The ameliorative aspect was a general increase of interest in both vocal and instrumental music. The vogue for music showed itself in the innovation of public concerts and the favourable reception of entr'acte songs at the theatres. Composers and singers were very popular. This increase in musical interest augured well for the opera, but unfortunately the chaotic conditions in the theatre, where there was no strong leadership and the managers were resorting to a variety of temporary expedients, led to the vicious experiment of programmes made up of single acts, scenes or even favourite songs from different operas. In June 1697, Motteux presented a *mélange* of five parts

[1] Manfred Bukofzer, *Music in the Baroque Era* (New York, 1947), p. 189.
[2] Haun, op. cit. p. 121.
[3] Dent, op. cit. p. 177.
[4] For a full account, see Eleanore Boswell, *The Restoration Court Stage* (Cambridge, Mass., 1932).
[5] Haun, op. cit. pp. 145–8.

labelled *The Novelty*; one of these was a masque (Eccles's *Hercules*), and another was Oldmixon's one-act pastoral opera *Thyrsis*. After 1702, when we have increased information about the theatres from newspapers' bills, we learn that both companies began offering single acts from *King Arthur* and other favourite operas in conjunction with a play or some other short piece. Such programmes represent sheer desperation on the part of the entrepreneurs and could only have a damaging effect on the regular operas.

The flourishing activity of dramatic opera now began to diminish, leaving only sporadic offerings. In 1698, Motteux made an elaborate production of Fletcher's *Island Princess*. Daniel Purcell was the main composer, but the masque in the last act was set by Jeremiah Clarke. Three years later, Elkanah Settle brought out his scenic opera, *The Virgin Prophetess; or, The Fall of Troy*. The final upsurge came in 1706, with expensive productions of two musical dramas. The first was Lord Lansdowne's *The British Enchanters*, a dramatic opera somewhat reminiscent of the heroic play. The other was Thomas D'Urfey's *Wonders in the Sun; or, The Kingdom of the Birds*, a piece which Allardyce Nicoll classifies as comic opera.[1] It will be noted that three composers worked on this opera – Eccles, Draghi and Lully.

Finally came the invasion of Italian opera, against which the local product could not stand. In January 1710 appeared Buononcini's *Almahide* and a year later Handel's *Rinaldo*. Italian opera had the prestige, in a few years it would have the support of the new royal family from Hanover (accustomed to Italian opera), and it had the great composers. Lampoons appeared in the bookstalls, and Addison and Steele led the attack on opera in *The Spectator*, but to no avail. Addison and the composer Thomas Clayton put together *Rosamund* (1707), an opera sung in English though structured on the Italian mode, but it was unsuccessful. In 1712 John Hughes made another attempt to maintain English opera in his *Calypso and Telemachus*, but this also failed. The enterprising Lewis Theobald experimented in another direction by trying to combine opera with pantomime in *The Rape of Proserpine* (1727), with music by Galliard. This work did succeed but one suspects that the vogue for pantomime carried it.

Feeling remained strong on the subject of opera. The dramatists and the actors bitterly resented the success of Italian opera, and many voices clamoured for a return to native opera. Chief among these were Aaron Hill and the songwriter Henry Carey.

Their resolve became manifest in positive action when Carey and a group of composers – the Arnes (father and son), J. F. Lampe and J. C. Smith –

[1] Nicoll, *HED*, II, p. 233.

produced a series of seven English operas at the Little Theatre in the Hay-market from April 1732 until the spring of the following year. The first was Carey's *Amelia*, composed by J. F. Lampe, and the last was a burlesque opera, Eliza Haywood's *Opera of Operas*, with music by T. A. Arne. The project met with an indifferent response, even though the operas were very carefully got up, with remarkable advances in scenery in Thomas Lediard's *Britannia*. Aaron Hill, a sympathizer with the group, made an emotional appeal to Handel, asking him to compose English operas. There was no reply, and the era of dramatic opera had closed. Handel himself was to create a new form with his dramatic oratorios, such as *Semele* and *Hercules*, works which are perhaps better studied in a history of music.[1]

---

[1] See Winton Dean, *Handel's Dramatic Oratorios and Masques* (London, 1959). For a survey, see Roger Fiske, *English Theatre Music in the Eighteenth Century* (London, 1973).

# Bibliography

## Abbreviations

| | |
|---|---|
| ECS | Eighteenth-Century Studies |
| ELH | Journal of English Literary History |
| ELN | English Language Notes |
| HLQ | Huntington Library Quarterly |
| JEGP | Journal of English and Germanic Philology |
| MLR | Modern Language Review |
| MP | Modern Philology |
| N & Q | Notes and Queries |
| PMLA | Publications of the Modern Language Association |
| PQ | Philological Quarterly |
| SEL | Studies in English Literature |
| SP | Studies in Philology |
| SQ | Shakespeare Quarterly |
| TLS | The Times Literary Supplement |

## I The social and literary context

(a) GENERAL

Several modern works of scholarship are relevant to nearly all phases of serious study of English drama, 1660–1750. First in importance is *The London Stage, 1660–1800; a Calendar of Plays, Entertainments and After-pieces, together with Casts, Box-Receipts, and Contemporary Comment* in 5 parts (Carbondale, Ill., 1960–8), ed. W. B. van Lennep, E. L. Avery, A. H. Scouten, G. W. Stone, Jr, and C. B. Hogan, of which the first four parts deal with theatrical seasons within this period. Allardyce Nicoll, *A History of English Drama 1660–1900*, 6 vols (Cambridge, 1952–9), of which the first two volumes treat the years from the Restoration until the middle of the eighteenth century, is a standard work of reference. The lists of plays arranged alphabetically by author included at the end of each volume are especially valuable. Although replaced by *The London Stage* as an authoritative record of the plays performed, John Genest, *Some Account of the English Stage from the Restoration in 1660 to 1830*, 10 vols (Bath, 1832), of which the first four volumes are chronologically relevant, remains a valuable source for the research student because of the inclusion of anecdotal material and plot summaries of new plays. Percy Fitzgerald, *A New History of the English Stage*, 2 vols (London, 1882), must be used with caution and with attention to more recent scholarship, but it provides the most comprehensive narrative history available of the patent theatres in this period.

John Downes's *Roscius Anglicanus* (1708), the only important account of the Restoration theatres written by anyone with a close and personal knowledge of them, is especially valuable for the information it provides about repertories, actors and actresses, and cast lists of individual plays. It was edited by Montague Summers (London, 1928) with extensive commentary. More recently, since *The London Stage* has appeared with what is in effect the needed commentary, it has been published in photographic facsimile by the Augustan Reprint Society (Los Angeles, 1969), with an introduction by John Loftis and an analytical 'Index of Performers and Plays' by David Stuart Rodes.

The long span of theatrical and dramatic history from the 1690s until 1738, of which Colley Cibber was both a participant and a witness, is fully though not impartially related in his autobiography, *An Apology for the Life of Mr Colley Cibber*, published in 1740. The most fully annotated edition of it is that by R. W. Lowe, 2 vols (London, 1889); the most recent edition is that by B. R. S. Fone (Ann Arbor, Mich., 1968).

As Sir Walter Greg explained (see below, p. 303), English dramatic bibliography properly began in the late seventeenth century with the work of Gerard Langbaine, *Momus Triumphans* of [1687] 1688 and *An Account of the English Dramatick Poets* of 1691. The Augustan Reprint Society published the two works in photographic facsimile (Los Angeles, 1971), the earlier of them with an introduction by David Stuart Rodes, the later with an introduction by John Loftis. The Scolar Press also published *An Account of the English Dramatick Poets* in facsimile (Menston, Yorks., 1971).

The most comprehensive bibliography, for this as for other periods, is James F. Arnott and J. W. Robinson, *English Theatrical Literature, 1559–1900: A bibliography incorporating Lowe's 'A Bibliographical Account...'* (London, 1970). Useful bibliographies of plays are Alfred Harbage, revised by Samuel Schoenbaum, *Annals of English Drama, 975–1700* (London, 1964); Carl J. Stratman, *Bibliography of English Printed Tragedy, 1565–1900* (Carbondale, Ill., 1966); and Gertrude L. Woodward and James G. McManaway, *A Check List of English Plays, 1641–1700* (Chicago, 1945). Carl J. Stratman, David G. Spencer and Mary Elizabeth Devine, *Restoration and Eighteenth Century Theatre Research: A Bibliographical Guide, 1900–1968* (Carbondale, Ill., 1971), provides a convenient listing of relevant modern publications.

(b) THE COURT AND THE STAGE

For an understanding of theatrical history during the first two decades of the Restoration, some knowledge of the personality, intellectual achievements and influence of the sovereign is necessary. Many contemporary accounts of Charles II are available, of which Clarendon's *History of the Rebellion and Civil Wars* and his autobiography are perhaps most valuable. For a brief modern study of the subject, the reader can consult James Sutherland, 'The Impact of Charles II on Restoration Literature', in Carroll Camden (ed.), *Restoration and Eighteenth-Century Literature* (Chicago, 1963), pp. 251–63. The king's patronage of dramatists was primarily directed to the public theatres. But he and his successors frequently commanded performances at court, a subject treated by Eleanore Boswell, *The Restoration Court Stage 1660–1702* (Cambridge, Mass., 1932). The more prominent of the men of letters of high rank surrounding Charles II are the subjects of individual biographies; they are also considered collectively by John Harold Wilson, *The Court Wits of the Restoration* (Princeton, N.J., 1948). An account of the changing relationship between the court and the stage from the Restoration until the reign of George II is included in John Loftis, *The Politics of Drama in Augustan England* (Oxford, 1963).

## (c) THE AUDIENCE

For the first nine years of the Restoration, Samuel Pepys in his Diary provides insight into the composition of the audience as well as information about other aspects of the theatre. Until the new edition of it by Robert Latham and William Matthews (London and Berkeley, 1970–   ) has been published in full, the standard edition remains that by Henry B. Wheatley, 10 vols (London, 1893–9). Using Pepys as well as other sources, Emmett L. Avery has written a valuable analytical account of the audience during Charles II's reign: 'The Restoration Audience', *PQ*, XLV (1966), pp. 54–61. The nature of the audience at that time is the subject of a lively and informative debate between Harold Love and A. S. Bear: Love, 'The Myth of the Restoration Audience', *Komos*, I (1967), pp. 49–56; Bear, 'Criticism and Social Change: The Case of Restoration Drama', *Komos*, II (1969), pp. 23–31; and Love, 'Bear's Case Laid Open: Or, A Timely Warning to Literary Sociologists', *Komos* II (1969), pp. 72–80. On the audience during the closing decades of the seventeenth and the first three decades of the eighteenth centuries, essays by John Dennis are particularly informative: *Critical Works*, 2 vols, ed. Edward N. Hooker (Baltimore, Md., 1939–43). The eighteenth-century audience provides the subject of Leo Hughes, *The Drama's Patrons* (Austin, Tex., 1971). Although primarily concerned with the later period, Harry W. Pedicord, *The Theatrical Public in the Time of Garrick* (New York, 1954), has relevance as well to the first half of the century.

## (d) GOVERNMENTAL CONTROL OF THE THEATRES

Two modern works print contemporary documents that illuminate the early history of the patent companies: John Quincy Adams (ed.), *The Dramatic Records of Sir Henry Herbert* (New Haven, Conn., and London, 1917); and Leslie Hotson, *The Commonwealth and Restoration Stage* (Cambridge, Mass., 1928). Watson Nicholson, *The Struggle for a Free Stage in London* (Boston, 1906), takes as its focus the tensions generated by the establishment of theatrical monopoly and the long history of resistance to it. *The London Stage* provides the most comprehensive account of the relationship between the government and the theatres in the first half of the eighteenth century. P. J. Crean, 'The Stage Licensing Act of 1737', *MP*, XXXV (1938), pp. 239–55, is a detailed study of the events leading to the most important act of theatrical legislation of the century.


(e) DRAMA AND SOCIETY

It would not be profitable to attempt to list the large number of valuable works, both contemporary and modern, that are relevant to the social history of England, 1660–1750. Only a few of particular value to the student of drama can be mentioned. As an introduction to the voluminous recent publications on the causes of the mid-seventeenth-century civil wars – wars that deeply affected Restoration drama as well as much else in later English history – Lawrence Stone's *The Crisis of the Aristocracy, 1558–1641* (Oxford, 1965) is perhaps most informative. An article by Mr Stone, 'Social Mobility in England, 1500–1700', *Past and Present*, XXXIII (1966), pp. 16–55, provides an analysis based on non-literary sources of one of the principal subjects of the Restoration comedy of manners. In *The World We Have Lost* (London, 1965), Peter Laslett, using the results of recent research in demography, examines the social structure of England in the seventeenth and eighteenth centuries, reaching some conclusions relevant to the drama that are at variance with long-held opinions on the subject. Making use of the findings of Mr Laslett and Mr Stone, among others, John Loftis has examined 'The Limits of Historical Veracity in Neoclassical Drama', in H. T. Swedenberg, Jr (ed.), *England in the Restoration and Early Eighteenth Century* (Berkeley, 1972), pp. 27–50. Although devoted to non-dramatic poetry, the anthology in seven volumes under the general editorship of George DeF. Lord, *Poems on Affairs of State* (New Haven, Conn., and London, 1963–75), provides what is in effect a political and social history of England, 1660–1714, based on contemporary sources. With its full and precise annotation, it is consistently useful to the student of the drama.


(f) DRAMATIC THEORY

First to be mentioned are important modern editions of contemporary works that include essays in dramatic theory and criticism: J. E. Spingarn (ed.), *Critical Essays of the Seventeenth Century*, 3 vols (Oxford, 1908–9); Scott Elledge (ed.), *Eighteenth-Century Critical Essays*, 2 vols (Ithaca, N.Y., 1961); John Dryden, '*Of Dramatic Poesy' and Other Critical Essays*, 2 vols, ed. George Watson (London, 1962); Thomas Rymer, *Critical Works*, ed. Curt A. Zimansky (New Haven, Conn., 1956); John Dennis, *Critical Works*, 2 vols,

ed. Edward N. Hooker (Baltimore, Md., 1939–43); Joseph Addison, Richard
Steele and others, *The Spectator*, 5 vols, ed. Donald F. Bond (Oxford, 1965);
and Aaron Hill and William Popple, *The Prompter*, ed. William W. Appleton
and K. A. Burnim (New York, 1966).

The most satisfactory account of critical theory in the period, dramatic as
well as non-dramatic, is that in Edward N. Hooker's extensive commentary
on Dennis's *Critical Works*. In *Restoration Tragedy* (Madison, Wisc., 1967),
Eric Rothstein provides a new interpretation of the theory of tragedy at the
time, developing the useful conception of 'affective tragedy'. An account of
*The Theory of Drama in the Restoration Period* (Bombay, 1963), comic as well
as tragic, has been written by Sarup Singh. Robert D. Hume, in *Dryden's
Criticism* (Ithaca, N.Y., 1970), examines in detail the work of the most
important of the Restoration critics of drama.

### (g) THE REFORM MOVEMENT AND THE THEORY OF DRAMATIC GENRES

Much of the dramatic criticism of the first half of the eighteenth century is
all but inseparable from the Jeremy Collier controversy and the ensuing
reform movement, which influenced the drama and the theatres throughout
the century. An account of the Collier controversy, with a bibliography of the
critical writings it generated, is provided by Joseph Wood Krutch, *Comedy
and Conscience after the Restoration* (New York, 1924). John Harrington
Smith has written a more specialized study of the consequences for comedy
of the reform movement: 'Shadwell, the Ladies, and the Change in Comedy',
*MP*, XLVI (1948), pp. 22–33. John Loftis's *Steele at Drury Lane* (Berkeley,
1952) is a study of the career in the theatre of Collier's most influential
popularizer.

Tragedy was affected by the reform movement, though much less directly
than comedy. In any event, the emphasis on poetic justice was accentuated,
as is apparent in Clarence C. Green, *The Neo-Classic Theory of Tragedy in
England during the Eighteenth Century* (Cambridge, Mass., 1934). Innovation
in tragedy, notably by George Lillo, is examined in Fred O. Nolte, *The Early
Middle Class Drama, 1696–1774* (Lancaster, Pa., 1935).

### (h) 'SENTIMENTALISM'

Studies of the elusive subject of eighteenth-century 'sentimentalism' have in
the main taken two forms: examinations of the literary expressions of sentimentalism with reference to contemporary ethical theory; and descriptive or

inductive examinations of sentimental literature with minimal attention to the history of ideas. Notable studies concerned with ethical theory are Ernest Bernbaum, *The Drama of Sensibility* (Boston, 1915); Ronald S. Crane, 'Suggestions toward a Genealogy of "The Man of Feeling" ', *ELH*, I (1934), pp. 205–30;and Ernest L. Tuveson, 'The Importance of Shaftesbury', *ELH*, XX (1953), pp. 267–99. Although only peripherally concerned with sentimentalism, Maynard Mack's introduction to his edition of Pope's *An Essay on Man* (London, 1950) provides a lucid account of ethical theory relevant to it. Notable studies of sentimentalism that are largely restricted to the examination of literary expressions of it are Arthur Sherbo, *English Sentimental Drama* (East Lansing, Mich., 1957), and Paul E. Parnell, 'The Sentimental Mask', *PMLA*, LXXVIII (1963), pp. 529–35.

### (j) THE DRAMA AND THE NOVEL

Although Ian Watt's *The Rise of the Novel* (London, 1957) includes little direct comment on the drama, it is relevant here both for its contribution to the sociology of literature in the eighteenth century and for its analysis of changes in the theory of literature that had consequences for the drama as well as for the novel. Clifford Leech's 'Congreve and the Century's End', *PQ*, XLI (1962), pp. 275–93, describes modifications in the nature of comedy that can be interpreted as an anticipation of eighteenth-century developments in the novel. Ira Konigsberg describes similarities between Richardson's novels and eighteenth-century plays in *Samuel Richardson and the Dramatic Novel* (Lexington, Ky., 1968).

### (k) THEATRICAL RECORDS AND THE RISE OF THEATRICAL SCHOLARSHIP

René Wellek, in *The Rise of English Literary History* (Chapel Hill, N.C., 1941), provides a comprehensive account of the developing interest in the literary past of which theatrical scholarship is one expression. The importance of Gerard Langbaine's role, late in the seventeenth century, in bringing English dramatic bibliography to maturity is described by Sir Walter Greg, *The Malone Society, Collections*, Vol. I, Parts 4 and 5 (1911), pp. 324–40. Carl J. Stratman has compiled a bibliography of *Dramatic Play Lists, 1591–1963* (New York, 1966). As aids to the use of early newspapers, two works are especially valuable: Charles H. Gray, *Theatrical Criticism in London to 1795* (New York, 1931), and Sybil Rosenfeld, 'Dramatic Advertisements in the Burney Newspapers, 1660–1700', *PMLA*, LI (1936), pp. 123–52.

## II Theatres, actors and repertory

(a) BASIC REFERENCES

(i) A compendium of information on repertory in this period, arranged calendar-wise with extensive supporting quotation, full cross-reference by author and players, valuable introductions and useful illustrations, is *The London Stage* (Carbondale, Ill., 1960-8): Part 1, 1660-1700, was edited by W. van Lennep; Part 2, 1700-1729, in 2 vols, by E. L. Avery; Part 3, 1729-1747, in 2 vols, by A. H. Scouten; Part 4, 1747-1776, in 3 vols, by G. W. Stone; Part 5, 1776-1800, in 3 vols, by C. B. Hogan.

(ii) Allardyce Nicoll devotes the first two volumes of his *History of English Drama 1660-1900*, 6 vols (Cambridge, 1952-9), to this period, and his sixth volume contains an alphabetical hand-list of play titles: this closely documented and copiously annotated work is an essential reference tool for the study of theatre in England.

(iii) R. W. Lowe's *Bibliographical Account of English Theatrical Literature* (London, 1888) has never been superseded as a compact reference guide to persons and writings connected with the theatre in England, though it should be used in conjunction with the findings of more recent scholarship.

(iv) The Society for Theatre Research's pamphlet, J. F. Kerslake (ed.), *Catalogue of Theatrical Portraits in London Public Collections* (London, 1961), is a valuable guide to the visual material on players in this period.

(b) GUIDE TO SOURCE MATERIAL

(i) *Professional records*

J. Q. Adams has edited *The Dramatic Records of Sir Henry Herbert* (New Haven, Conn., and London, 1917) to throw light on the operation of the Revels Office in the Restoration period.

'Rich's Register', a manuscript record of plays and receipts at Lincoln's Inn Fields and plays at Drury Lane between 1714 and 1723, is preserved in the Folger Shakespeare Library, and the Lincoln's Inn Fields accounts between 1726 and 1728 in the Harvard Theatre Collection: both have been used in the compilation of *The London Stage* (see (a) (i) above), where references to modern work on them may be found.

(ii) *Early general surveys of companies and players*

*Historia Histrionica*, a lively dialogue which compares stage conditions before and after the Civil War, was written by the antiquary James Wright and published anonymously in 1699; perhaps the most accessible of its reprints is that prefixed to R. W. Lowe's edition of Colley Cibber's *An Apology for the Life of Mr Colley Cibber, Comedian*, 2 vols (London, 1889).

*A Comparison Between the Two Stages*, published anonymously in 1702, is a coarse piece of work sometimes implausibly assigned to Charles Gildon; it has been well edited by S. B. Wells (Princeton, N.J., 1942).

*Roscius Anglicanus*, by the veteran prompter John Downes, appeared anonymously in 1709, and has been edited with full notes by Montague Summers (London, n.d. [1928]).

*The History of the English Stage from the Restauration to the Present Time* (1741) was ascribed by its publisher, Edmund Curll, to Thomas Betterton, who died in 1710; though it is a gossipy ragbag, some of the famous actor's papers may have been used in its compilation.

The stage manager William Rufus Chetwood was responsible for two early surveys which are worth looking at: *A General History of the Stage* (1749) and *The British Theatre* (Dublin, 1750).

The *Dramatic Miscellanies* of Thomas Davies, actor and bookseller, have been a rich quarry of anecdote since their three volumes appeared in 1784.

By far the most complete and systematic of the early surveys is *Some Account of the English Stage . . . 1660 to 1830*, by the Bath clergyman John Genest, published in 10 vols (Bath, 1832).

(iii) *Early material on individual players*

The major autobiographical source for theatre in this period is Colley Cibber's *An Apology for the Life of Mr Colley Cibber, Comedian* (1740); there are useful modern editions by R. W. Lowe, 2 vols (London, 1889), and by B. R. S. Fone (Ann Arbor, 1968).

Important for the years after 1740 are *The Letters* of David Garrick, admirably edited by D. M. Little and G. M. Kahrl, 3 vols (London, 1963).

Valuable information on provincial conditions may be found in *A Sketch of the Life . . . of Mr Anthony Aston . . . Written by Himself*, which was prefixed to *The Fool's Opera* (1731), and has been reprinted with other Aston material by Watson Nicholson, *Anthony Aston Stroller and Adventurer* (South Haven, Mich., 1920).

Provincial conditions and many other matters are treated by Cibber's eccentric daughter in her autobiography, *A Narrative of the Life of Mrs Charlotte Charke* (1755); this was reprinted in the fourth volume (1929) of *Constable's Miscellany of Original and Selected Publications in Literature*, 6 vols (London, 1928–9).

Of the numerous theatrical memoirs published during the eighteenth century, Charles Gildon's *Life of Thomas Betterton* (1710) is still worth attention.

A good example of its sensational kind is the immensely popular *Authentick Memoirs of Mrs Ann Oldfield*, which ran to six editions in its publication year (1730).

*Memoirs of the Life of David Garrick Esq* (1780), a two-volume account by Thomas Davies, contains information about the early career of Garrick to be found in such detail in no other source.

### (iv) *Incidental references by contemporaries to players and repertory*

The shorthand diary kept between 1659 and 1699 by an indefatigable theatre-goer, Samuel Pepys, has been reprinted in several editions since its first transcription in 1825; its numerous references to plays and actors have been collected by Helen McAfee in *Pepys on the Restoration Stage* (New Haven, Conn., and London, 1916).

The controversial literature provoked by Jeremy Collier's diatribe *A Short View of the Immorality and Profaneness of the English Stage* (1698) contains much information about plays and players in its corpus of invective; it is well documented with a good bibliography by J. W. Krutch, *Comedy and Conscience after the Restoration* (New York, 1924).

The first half of the eighteenth century saw a steady increase in newspaper and periodical coverage of theatrical events. A good guide to this material is C. H. Gray's *Theatrical Criticism in London to 1795* (New York, 1931).

### (v) *Contemporary analyses of stage technique*

David Garrick's anonymously published *Essay on Acting* (1744) criticizes his own Macbeth. The egregious Samuel Foote anonymously compared Garrick, Quin and Barry in his *A Treatise on the Passions so far as they regard the Stage* (1741) and reviewed English comic acting style in *The Roman and English Comedy Considered and Compared* (1747). Aaron Hill's opinions were expressed in his periodical, *The Prompter* (1734–6); in his poem, *The Art of Acting* (1746); and in his *Essay on the Art of Acting*, published posthumously with his *Works* in their four-volume edition of 1753. John Hill published *The Actor : or, A Treatise on the Art of Playing* in 1750, and used the same title for a return to the subject in 1755. Useful extracts from such early attempts to provide a rationale for acting technique, and much background information about their authors, may be found in the compilation *Actors on Acting*, ed. Toby Cole and Helen Krich Chinoy (New York, 1949), which has been frequently reprinted.

(vi) *Prologues, epilogues and theatre satires*

Very valuable information about players and repertory may be derived from the prologues and epilogues written for particular theatrical occasions and often published with early editions of the plays they helped to frame. A most useful collection of these has been made by Autrey Nell Wiley, *Rare Prologues and Epilogues 1642–1700* (London, 1940). In particular the important work of Dryden in this field has been edited by W. B. Gardner, *The Prologues and Epilogues of John Dryden* (New York, 1951).

Also of interest, though allowance must regularly be made for sweeping statements and prejudice, are references to players and to repertory fashions in the ephemeral satires of this period, popular both in verse and in prose. Robert Gould's 'Satyr against the Play-House', written in 1685 and published with his *Poems* in 1689, is a work of this kind, reprinted by Montague Summers in an Appendix to his *Restoration Theatre* (London, 1934). *Covent Garden Drollery*, a collection of such fugitive pieces published in 1672, has also been edited by Montague Summers (London, 1927). A tendentious version of Horace's *Ars Poetica* with scathing satire on John Rich was published anonymously by James Miller in 1731 under the title *Harlequin Horace*, and ran to several editions. Several dramatic pieces in this period were devoted entirely to theatrical topicalities, and others contained a high proportion of this material: they are listed and described by Dane Farnsworth Smith in his most useful study *Plays about the Theatre in England 1671–1737* (New York, 1936).

(c) SELECTED MODERN STUDIES

(i) *General surveys*

The substantial introductory chapters to *The London Stage*, Parts 1–5, and to Allardyce Nicoll's *History of English Drama*, Vols I–II (see (a) (i) and (ii) above), deal with all aspects of the presentation of plays.

Leslie Hotson, *The Commonwealth and Restoration Stage* (Cambridge, Mass., and London, 1928), gives a closely documented account of the earlier part of the period. With his work should be read two important articles which have appeared in the Society for Theatre Research's quarterly *Theatre Notebook*: William van Lennep, 'The Death of the Red Bull', *Theatre Notebook*, XVI (Summer 1962), pp. 126–34, and John Freehafer, 'The Formation of the London Patent Companies in 1660', *Theatre Notebook*, XX (Autumn 1965), pp. 6–30.

A good general impression of theatre conditions can be gathered from two works by Montague Summers, both well documented and illustrated: *The Restoration Theatre* (London, 1934) and *The Playhouse of Pepys* (London and New York, 1935).

Alwin Thaler's *Shakspere to Sheridan* (Cambridge, Mass., and London, 1922) provides much miscellaneous information about company management, with valuable illustrations.

### (ii) *The theatres*

The physical stage conditions of the London theatres have been examined by W. J. Lawrence, *The Elizabethan Playhouse and other Studies*, 2 series (Stratford-upon-Avon, 1912–13), and *Old Theatre Days and Ways* (London, 1935). Lily B. Campbell's *Scenes and Machines on the English Stage during the Renaissance* (Cambridge, 1923) is relevant to conditions prevailing at the Restoration. Richard Southern, in *Changeable Scenery: Its Origin and Development in the English Theatre* (London, 1952), carries the history forward, as does A. S. Jackson (for the earlier part of the period) in 'Restoration Scenery, 1656–80', *Restoration and Eighteenth Century Theatre Research*, III (1964). L. J. Martin's article 'From Forestage to Proscenium: A Study of Restoration Staging Techniques', *Theatre Survey*, IV (1963), deals with a particular development. Edward A. Langhans has discussed 'Wren's Restoration Playhouse' in *Theatre Notebook*, XVIII (1964), and offers 'A Conjectural Reconstruction of the Dorset Garden Theatre' in *Theatre Survey*, XIII (1972).

### (iii) *Special studies in theatre conditions*

Though the professional theatre in London with its rival houses and managements occupies the central position in any account of English acting and playgoing during this period, much valuable work has been done on other features of the entertainment world. Eleanore Boswell's study of conditions at court performances, *The Restoration Court Stage 1660–1702* (Cambridge, Mass., 1932), discusses one production, that of Crowne's *Calisto*, in very great detail. Sybil Rosenfeld has considered *Strolling Players and Drama in the Provinces*

(Cambridge, 1939) for the period 1660–1765, and also *The Theatre of the London Fairs in the Eighteenth Century* (Cambridge, 1960). Players and repertories at the Smock Alley Theatre in Dublin are surveyed with other Irish theatre before 1720 by W. S. Clark, *The Early Irish Stage* (Oxford, 1955); useful material on Dublin theatre in the eighteenth century is presented by E. K. Sheldon in *Thomas Sheridan of Smock Alley 1719–1788* (Princeton, N.J., 1967).

(iv) *Biography of actors and managers*

Among the numerous modern biographies of individual players from this period R. W. Lowe's *Thomas Betterton* (London, 1891) still holds its place, while R. H. Barker on *Mr Cibber of Drury Lane* (New York, 1939) and W. W. Appleton on *Charles Macklin: an Actor's Life* (Cambridge, Mass., and London, 1961) are of particular value.

On David Garrick much has been written in recent years. Both Carola Oman, *David Garrick* (London, 1958), and K. Burnim, *David Garrick: Director* (Pittsburgh, Pa., 1961), are worth consulting on the first phase of his career, which falls within this period.

The lives of most Restoration actresses are fully described by J. H. Wilson, *All the King's Ladies* (Chicago, 1958).

Very valuable for the context of theatre management in the eighteenth century are both John Loftis, *Steele at Drury Lane* (Berkeley and Los Angeles, 1952), and F. Homes Dudden, *Henry Fielding: His Life, Works and Times*, 2 vols (Oxford, 1952).

(v) *Work on acting style*

On acting style in tragedy throughout the period there is a useful popular account by B. Joseph, *The Tragic Actor* (London, 1959). Special techniques are discussed by J. H. Wilson in 'Rant, Cant and Tone on the Restoration Stage', an article which it is well worth seeking out in the not always readily available learned journal, *Studies in Philology*, LII (October 1955), pp. 592–8. Another article which is of outstanding value is by A. S. Downer, 'Nature to Advantage Dress'd: Eighteenth Century Acting', in *PMLA*, LVIII (December 1943), pp. 1002–37. Acting style and stage business in performances of Shakespeare's plays are fully discussed by A. C. Sprague in *Shakespeare and the Actors* (Cambridge, Mass., 1944). On the developing traditions in playing individual roles in Shakespeare, Toby Lelyveld has considered *Shylock on the Stage* (London, 1961), while the fully annotated pictorial survey of *Hamlet through the Ages* prepared by Raymond Mander and Joe Mitchenson (London,

1952) has much of interest for this period. R. H. Ball has exhaustively studied the major role of Massinger's *A New Way to Pay Old Debts* in *The Amazing Career of Sir Giles Overreach* (Princeton, N.J., 1939).

(vi) *Work on stage costume*

James Laver's *Costume in the Theatre* (London, 1964) is a well-produced but very general survey of the whole field indicated by its title. Only part of its sixth chapter, on costume in productions of Shakespeare, deals with the period 1660–1750, and all but two of its excellent illustrations of actors in costume and stage poses date from the third quarter of the eighteenth century or later, even if reflecting traditions of the earlier period. It is important to remember that the many modern accounts of everyday and real-life costume in this period that are now available are not guides to the costumes worn on stage, though stage fashions in comedy did follow current trends. A brief but well-documented treatment of what was worn on stage from the Restoration to the early nineteenth century is Lily B. Campbell's 'A History of Costuming on the English Stage between 1660 and 1823', which is worth taking pains to seek out in *University of Wisconsin Studies*, II (Madison, Wisc., 1918), pp. 187–223. Sybil Rosenfeld has analysed surviving account books of Christopher Rich showing costume expenses in 'The Wardrobes of Lincoln's Inn Fields and Covent Garden', *Theatre Notebook*, V (Winter 1950), pp. 15–19. Pictorial material on costume in performances of Shakespeare is provided by W. Moelwyn Merchant, *Shakespeare and the Artist* (London, 1959), with the reminder that some of the illustrations may owe more to the fancy of the artist than to stage tradition. Only with this fact in mind should the very useful collection of theatrical illustrations by Raymond Mander and Joe Mitchenson, *A Pictorial History of the British Theatre* (London, 1957), be examined.

(vii) *Work on repertory patterns*

Basic material on who played what, where and when has been assembled and calendared by several modern scholars for all or part of this period. The most comprehensive calendar is that provided by *The London Stage* (see (a) (i) above), which covers the whole period and adds many quotations and references on the plays listed. J. G. McManaway lists some 'Unrecorded Performances in London about 1700' in *Theatre Notebook*, XIX (Winter 1964–5), pp. 68–70. The last few years of the period are covered by D. MacMillan's *Drury Lane Calendar 1747–1776* (Oxford, 1938), a convenient way of examining the repertory pattern at one big London house. What evidence survives of performances outside London has also been collected and examined to some extent. Irish calendars can be found in the studies by W. S. Clark and E. K. Sheldon listed in (c) (iii) above, and Sybil Rosenfeld has used records of performances in English provincial cities for her *Strolling Players and Drama in the Provinces*, also listed in (c) (iii) above.

The repertory policy of particular managements has received some attention in scattered but valuable articles relating to this period. W. van Lennep showed how the King's Men built up their repertory in 'Thomas Killigrew Prepares his Plays for Production', in J. McManaway *et al.* (eds), *J. Q. Adams Memorial Studies* (Washington, D.C., 1948), pp. 803–8. A. L. Woehl discusses 'Some Plays in the Repertories of the Patent Houses', in *Studies in Speech and Drama in Honor of A. M. Drummond* (Ithaca, N.Y., 1944), pp. 105–22. F. T. Wood deals with 'Goodman's Fields Theatres' and their repertory policy in *MLR*, XXV (October 1930), pp. 443–56. 'John Rich and the First Covent Garden Theatre' is an article by H. P. Vincent worth looking out in *ELH*, XVII (December 1950), pp. 296–306. E. L. Avery covers 'Fielding's Last Season with the Haymarket Theatre' in *MP*, XXXVI (February 1939), pp. 283–92.

(viii) *Work on repertory fashions*

The ins and outs of repertory fashions revealed by analysis of performance records have been charted in several ways by modern scholars. External pressures like censorship and political manœuvring which affected a management's choice of programme are the subjects of many studies. P. J. Crean's article, 'The Stage Licensing Act of 1737', *MP*, XXXV (February 1938), pp. 239–55, is very valuable, and John Loftis, *The Politics of Drama in Augustan England* (Oxford, 1963), is indispensable. Fluctuations of public taste which brought particular types of play or the work of this or that author into favour at various points in this period have also received attention. V. C. Clinton-Baddeley discusses *The Burlesque Tradition in the English Theatre after 1660* (London, 1952), and Leo Hughes works through the period in *A Century of English Farce* (Princeton, N.J., and London, 1956). The pantomime craze is fully documented by E. L. Avery, 'The Defense and Criticism of Pantomimic Entertainments in the Early Eighteenth Century', to be found in *ELH*, V (June 1938), pp. 127–45. *Gay's Beggar's Opera: Its Content, History and Influence* (New Haven, Conn., 1923) is an elaborate survey of the whole ballad opera fashion by W. E. Schultz.

Shakespeare has been the favourite playwright among scholars who compile popularity statistics for this period. G. C. D. Odell, *Shakespeare from*

*Betterton to Irving*, 2 vols (New York, 1920, and London, 1921), holds its place as a general guide to the fortunes of Shakespeare's plays during the period, and C. B. Hogan has calendared eighteenth-century performances in *Shakespeare in the Theatre 1701–1800*, 2 vols (Oxford, 1952–7). A. H. Scouten has contributed two important articles to publications worth hunting out in an academic library: 'Shakespeare's Plays in the Theatrical Repertory when Garrick came to London', to be found in *Studies in English* (Texas University, 1944), pp. 257–68; and 'The Increase of Popularity of Shakespeare's Plays in the Eighteenth Century', *SQ* ,VII (Spring 1956), pp. 189–202. Evidence for an early pressure group is reviewed by E. L. Avery, 'The Shakespeare Ladies' Club', *SQ*, VII (Spring 1956), pp. 153–8. Work on the versions in which Shakespeare's plays were seen during this period, and on the fortunes of individual Shakespearian plays, includes Hazelton Spencer, *Shakespeare Improved* (Cambridge, Mass., 1927); G. C. Branam, *Eighteenth Century Adaptations of Shakespearean Tragedy* (Berkeley and Los Angeles, 1956); Max Schulz, '*King Lear*: a Box-Office Maverick among Shakespearian Tragedies on the English Stage 1700–01 to 1749–50', *Tulane Studies in English*, VII (1957), pp. 83–90; and A. H. Scouten and Leo Hughes, 'A Calendar of Performances of *1 Henry IV* and *2 Henry IV* during the First Half of the Eighteenth Century', *JEGP*, XLIII (January 1944), pp. 23–41.

The fortunes of other pre-war playwrights are dealt with by A. C. Sprague, *Beaumont and Fletcher on the Restoration Stage* (Cambridge, Mass., 1926), and R. G. Noyes, *Ben Jonson on the English Stage, 1660–1776* (Cambridge, Mass., 1935). A most important article on the way Restoration managements handled pre-war manuscript plays is by Alfred Harbage, 'Elizabethan-Restoration Palimpsest', *MLR*, XXXV (July 1940), pp. 287–319.

Two of the most popular playwrights from the rising generation of Restoration writers have received special study: A. M. Taylor sees Otway as *Next to Shakespeare* (Durham, N.C., 1950), and E. L. Avery traces the fortunes of *Congreve's Plays on the Eighteenth Century Stage* (London, 1951).

## III Plays and playwrights

### (a) GENERAL

The most useful bibliographies of Restoration and early eighteenth-century drama are M. Summers, *A Bibliography of the Restoration Drama* (London, 1934); A. Nicoll, *A History of English Drama 1660–1900*, 6 vols (Cambridge,

1952–9); A. Harbage, *Annals of English Drama 975–1700*, rev. S. Schoenbaum (London, 1964); G. L. Woodward and J. G. McManaway, *A Check-List of English Plays 1641–1700* (Chicago, 1945), with a *Supplement* by F. Bowers (Charlottesville, 1949); and the first five vols of *The London Stage 1660–1800*, ed. E. L. Avery, *et al.*, 11 vols (Carbondale, Ill., 1960–8).

Books dealing with the theatre are J. Genest, *Some Account of the English Stage, from the Restoration to 1830*, 10 vols (Bath, 1832); L. Hotson, *The Commonwealth and Restoration Stage* (Cambridge, Mass., 1928); E. Boswell, *The Restoration Court Stage 1660–1702* (Cambridge, Mass., 1932); M. Summers, *The Restoration Theatre* (London, 1934); G. E. Bentley, *The Jacobean and Caroline Stage*, 7 vols (Oxford, 1941–68); R. Southern, *Changeable Scenery: Its Origin and Development in the British Theatre* (London, 1952); R. Leacroft, *The Development of the English Playhouse* (Ithaca, N.Y., 1973). For various matters pertaining to the stage, see the volumes of *Theatre Notebook* (1945–) and *Restoration and Eighteenth-Century Theatre Research* (1962–).

Useful books on the drama include: F. W. Bateson, *English Comic Drama, 1700–1750* (Oxford, 1929; repr. New York, 1963); A. Nicoll, *A History of English Drama*; B. Dobrée, *Restoration Comedy* (London, 1924) and *Restoration Tragedy* (London, 1929); M. Summers, *The Playhouse of Pepys* (London and New York, 1935); F. C. Green, *Minuet* (London, 1935); M. Prior, *The Language of Tragedy* (New York, 1947); J. H. Smith, *The Gay Couple in Restoration Comedy* (Cambridge, Mass., 1948); T. H. Fujimura, *The Restoration Comedy of Wit* (Princeton, N.J., 1952); L. Kronenberger, *The Thread of Laughter* (New York, 1952); A. Sherbo, *English Sentimental Drama* (East Lansing, Mich., 1957); N. Holland, *The First Modern Comedies* (Cambridge, Mass., 1959); J. Loftis, *Comedy and Society from Congreve to Fielding* (Stanford, Cal., 1959); G. W. Knight, *The Golden Labyrinth* (London, 1962); S. Singh, *The Theory of Drama in the Restoration Period* (Bombay, 1963); J. R. Brown and B. Harris (eds), *Restoration Theatre* (London, 1965); J. H. Wilson, *A Preface to Restoration Drama* (Boston, 1965); E. Rothstein, *Restoration Tragedy* (Madison, Wisc., 1967); K. Muir, *The Comedy of Manners* (London, 1970); V. O. Birdsall, *Wild Civility: The English Comic Spirit on the Restoration Stage* (Bloomington, Ind., 1970); H. Hawkins, *Likenesses of Truth in Elizabethan and Restoration Drama* (Oxford, 1972); see also Vol. VI of *The Oxford History of English Literature*, by J. Sutherland (Oxford, 1969), and Vol. VII by B. Dobrée (1959).

Special topics are dealt with in the following books: J. W. Krutch, *Comedy and Conscience after the Restoration* (New York, 1924; rev. 1949, repr. 1961); K. Lynch, *The Social Mode of Restoration Comedy* (London and New York,

1926); J. Wilcox, *The Relation of Molière to Restoration Comedy* (New York, 1938); G. Alleman, *Matrimonial Law and the Materials of Restoration Comedy* (Wallingford, Pa., 1942); Leo Hughes, *A Century of English Farce* (Princeton, N.J., and London, 1956); J. H. Wilson, *All the King's Ladies* (Chicago, 1958); E. Waith, *The Herculean Hero* (New York, 1962); D. R. M. Wilkinson, *The Comedy of Habit: An Essay on the Use of Courtesy Literature* (Leiden, 1964); G. Sorelius, *The Giant Race before the Flood: Pre-Restoration Drama on the Stage and in the Criticism of the Restoration* (Uppsala, 1966); J. Loftis, *The Spanish Plays of Neoclassical England* (New Haven, Conn., 1973).

Helpful articles on the drama are A. Nicoll, 'Political Plays of the Restoration', *MLR*, XVI (1921); L. C. Knights, 'Restoration Comedy: The Reality and the Myth', *Scrutiny*, VI (1937), repr. in *Explorations* (1946); A. Harbage, 'Elizabethan-Restoration Palimpsest', *MLR*, XXXV (1940); C. Leech, 'Restoration Tragedy: A Reconsideration', *Durham University Journal*, XI (1950), and 'Restoration Comedy: The Earlier Phase', *Essays in Criticism*, I (1951); D. S. Berkeley, 'The Art of "Whining" Love', *SP*, LII (1955), and 'Préciosité and the Restoration Comedy of Manners', *HLQ*, XVIII (1955); F. W. Bateson, 'L. C. Knights and Restoration Comedy', *Essays in Criticism*, VII (1957); C. O. McDonald, 'Restoration Comedy as Drama of Satire', *SP*, LXI (1964); J. Traugott, 'The Rake's Progress from Court to Comedy', *SEL*, VI (1966); A. H. Scouten, 'Notes towards a History of Restoration Comedy', *PQ*, XLV (1966); M. Mincoff, 'Shakespeare, Fletcher, and Baroque Tragedy', *Shakespeare Survey*, XX (1967); R. D. Hume, 'Diversity and Development in Restoration Comedy', *ECS*, V (1972).

Articles on special topics are A. F. White, 'The Office of Revels and Dramatic Censorship during the Restoration Period', *Western Reserve Bulletin*, XXXIV (1931), and A. H. Scouten, 'The Increase in Popularity of Shakespeare's Plays in the Eighteenth Century', *SQ*, VII (1956). Useful collections of articles are J. Loftis (ed.), *Restoration Drama: Modern Essays in Criticism* (New York, 1966), and E. Miner (ed.), *Restoration Dramatists: A Collection of Critical Essays* (Englewood Cliffs, N.J., 1966).

Books on opera and music in the theatre are E. J. Dent, *Foundations of English Opera* (Cambridge, 1928); E. Gagey, *Ballad Opera* (New York, 1937); M. Bukofzer, *Music in the Baroque Era* (New York, 1947); W. Dean, *Handel's Dramatic Oratorios and Masques* (London, 1959); R. E. Moore, *Henry Purcell and the Restoration Theatre* (Cambridge, Mass., 1961); F. E. Haun, *But Hark! More Harmony: The Libretti in English of the Restoration Opera* (Ypsilanti, Mich., 1971); R. Fiske, *English Theatre Music in the Eighteenth Century* (London, 1973).

(b) INDIVIDUAL AUTHORS

*John Banks*

*The Unhappy Favourite; or, The Earl of Essex*, ed. T. M. H. Blair (New York, 1939).

*Aphra Behn*

*The Works*, ed. M. Summers, 6 vols (London, 1915; repr. New York, 1967); *The Rover*, ed. F. M. Link (Lincoln, Neb., 1967); F. M. Link, *Aphra Behn* (New York, 1968), is a biographical and critical study.

*Roger Boyle, Earl of Orrery*

*The Dramatic Works*, ed. W. S. Clark, 2 vols (Cambridge, Mass., 1937); K. M. Lynch has a biographical study, *Roger Boyle, First Earl of Orrery* (Knoxville, Tenn., 1965).

*William Burnaby*

*The Dramatic Works of William Burnaby*, ed. F. E. Budd (London, 1931).

*William Congreve*

The most recent edition of the plays is by H. Davis (Chicago, 1967). Discussion of the plays appears in many of the general studies cited above. The critique of *The Way of the World* by C. Brooks and R. B. Heilman in *Understanding Drama* (New York, 1945) remains valuable. Among recent studies are P. and M. Mueschke, *A New View of Congreve's 'Way of the World'* (Ann Arbor, Mich., 1958); C. Leech, 'Congreve and the Century's End', *PQ*, XLI (1962); J. Gagen, 'Congreve's Mirabell and the Idea of a Gentleman', *PMLA*, LXXIX (1964); M. Novak, *William Congreve* (New York, 1971); and A. Roper, 'Language and Action in *The Way of the World*, *Love's Last Shift*, and *The Relapse*', *ELH*, XL (1973).

*John Crowne*

*Sir Courtly Nice* has been edited by M. Summers in *Restoration Comedies* (London, 1920) and by C. B. Hughes (The Hague, 1966); *City Politiques*, ed. J. H. Wilson (Lincoln, Neb., 1967); Part 2 of *The Destruction of Jerusalem*, ed. by B. Dobrée in *Five Heroic Plays* (London, 1960).

*John Dryden*

The bibliography is by Hugh MacDonald (Oxford, 1939). The plays are in *The Dramatic Works*, ed. M. Summers, 6 vols (London, 1931–2; repr. New

York, 1968); this will be superseded by the new California edition, of which four volumes of the plays have appeared. The most recent biography is by C. E. Ward (Chapel Hill, N.C., 1961); Ward also edited the *Letters* (Durham, N.C., 1942). Also biographical is J. M. Osborn's *John Dryden: Some Biographical Facts and Problems* (New York, 1940; rev. Gainesville, Fla., 1963). Some useful critical studies are L. Teeter, 'The Dramatic Use of Hobbes' Political Ideas', *ELH*, III (1936); D. W. Jefferson, 'The Significance of Dryden's Heroic Plays', *Proceedings of the Leeds Philosophical and Literary Society*, V (1940); D. Daiches, *Critical Approaches to Literature* (Englewood Cliffs, N.J., 1956); A. C. Kirsch, 'The Significance of Dryden's *Aureng-Zebe*', *ELH*, XXIX (1962), and *Dryden's Heroic Drama* (Princeton, N.J., 1965); F. H. Moore, *The Nobler Pleasure: Dryden's Comedy in Theory and Practice* (Chapel Hill, N.C., 1963); R. J. Kaufman, 'On the Poetics of Terminal Tragedy', in B. N. Schilling (ed.), *Dryden: A Collection of Critical Essays* (Englewood Cliffs, N.J., 1963); M. W. Alssid, 'The Design of Dryden's *Aureng-Zebe*', *JEGP*, LXIV (1965); B. King, *Dryden's Major Plays* (London, 1966); R. D. Hume, *Dryden's Criticism* (Ithaca, N.Y., 1970); H. Love, 'Dryden, Durfey, and the Standards of Comedy', *SEL*, XIII (1973); R. D. Hume, 'The Date of Dryden's *Marriage A-la-Mode*', *Harvard Library Bulletin*, XXI (1973).

### Thomas Duffett

His travesties are now available in *Three Burlesque Plays of Thomas Duffett*, ed. R. E. DiLorenzo (Iowa City, 1972).

### Sir George Etherege

The standard edition is by H. F. B. Brett-Smith, 2 vols (Oxford, 1927); *The Letters of Sir George Etherege* are edited by Sybil Rosenfeld (London, 1928); the most important critical study is D. Underwood's *Etherege and the Seventeenth-Century Comedy of Manners* (New Haven, Conn., 1957). Two recent articles by R. D. Hume are 'Reading and Misreading *The Man of Mode*', *Criticism*, XIV (1972), and 'Theory of Comedy in the Restoration', *MP*, LXX (1973).

### George Farquhar

The standard edition is *The Complete Works*, ed. C. Stonehill, 2 vols (London, 1930; repr. New York, 1967). Two books are E. Rothstein, *George Farquhar* (New York, 1967), and E. N. James, *The Development of George Farquhar as a Comic Dramatist* (The Hague, 1972).

*Henry Fielding*

An older edition is *The Complete Works*, ed. W. E. Henley, 16 vols (London and New York, 1902–3), Vols VIII–XII, but the Wesleyan edition is in active preparation. The standard account of the career is W. L. Cross, *The History of Henry Fielding*, 3 vols (New Haven, Conn., 1918; repr. New York, 1945, 1963). Useful articles are L. P. Goggin, 'Development of Techniques in Fielding's Comedies', *PMLA*, LXVII (1952); C. B. Woods, 'The "Miss Lucy" Plays of Fielding and Garrick', *PQ*, XLI (1962).

*John Gay*

The plays are in *The Works*, ed. G. C. Faber (London, 1926). Two biographical and critical works are W. H. Irving, *John Gay* (Durham, N.C., 1940), and P. A. Spacks, *John Gay* (New York, 1965). For criticism of *The Beggar's Opera*, see W. Empson, *Some Versions of Pastoral* (London, 1935), and B. H. Bronson, *'The Beggar's Opera'*, *Studies in the Comic* (Berkeley, Cal., 1941).

*James Howard*

On the date of *All Mistaken*, see J. Sutherland, *N & Q*, CCIX (1962), and R. D. Hume, 'Dryden, James Howard and the Date of *All Mistaken*', *PQ*, LI (1972).

*Sir Robert Howard*

No edition of Howard's plays has appeared since *Five New Plays* (1692). A modern biography is by H. J. Oliver, *Sir Robert Howard ... A Critical Biography* (Durham, N.C., 1963). *The Country Gentleman*, by Howard and the Duke of Buckingham, has been edited by A. H. Scouten and R. D. Hume (Philadelphia, Pa., 1976).

*Nathaniel Lee*

*The Works* were edited by T. B. Stroup and A. L. Cooke, 2 vols (New Brunswick, N.J., 1955). *Lucius Junius Brutus* has been edited by J. Loftis (Lincoln, Neb., 1967).

*George Lillo*

Unfortunately there is no modern edition of Lillo's plays. W. H. McBurney has edited *The London Merchant* (Lincoln, Neb., 1965) and *Fatal Curiosity* (Lincoln, Neb., 1966). See also C. F. Burgess, 'Lillo, Sans Barnwell, or the Playwright Revisited', *MP*, LXVI (1968).

*Delariviere Manley*

*Not* Mrs Mary Manley, according to P. A. Anderson, 'Mistress Delariviere Manley's Biography', *MP*, XXXIII (1936). Anderson states that her proper name appears in her letters and her will; Delariviere was the name of the wife of Mrs Manley's father's commanding officer.

*Thomas Otway*

*The Works*, ed. by M. Summers, 3 vols (London, 1926), and ed. J. C. Ghosh, 2 vols (Oxford, 1932). See also A. Taylor, *Next to Shakespeare: Otway's 'Venice Preserv'd' and 'The Orphan'* (Durham, N.C., 1950); a recent article is by D. R. Hauser, 'Otway Preserved: Theme and Form in *Venice Preserv'd*', *SP*, LV (1958).

*Sir Charles Sedley*

*The Poetical and Dramatic Works*, ed. V. de S. Pinto, 2 vols (London, 1928).

*Thomas Shadwell*

*The Complete Works*, ed. M. Summers, 5 vols (London, 1927). The biography is by A. S. Borgman (New York, 1928). Two articles are J. H. Smith, 'Shadwell, the Ladies, and the Change in Comedy', *MP*, XLVI (1948), and R. D. Hume, 'Formal Intention in *The Brothers* and *The Squire of Alsatia*', *English Language Notes*, VI (1969).

*Thomas Southerne*

The biography is by J. Dodds, *Thomas Southerne, Dramatist* (New Haven, Conn., 1933); *The Wives Excuse*, ed. R. Thornton (Philadelphia, 1973), is the only modern printing of this play.

*Sir Richard Steele*

Biographies are by G. Aitken, 2 vols (London, 1889; repr. 1903), and C. Winton, 2 vols (Baltimore, Md., 1964, 1970). In *Steele at Drury Lane* (Berkeley, Cal., 1952) John Loftis deals with the theatrical activities. See also B. A. Goldgar, *The Curse of Party* (Lincoln, Neb., 1961). The best modern edition is by S. S. Kenny (Oxford, 1971). Two articles are P. Rogers, 'A New Letter by Steele', *English Language Notes*, VII (1969), and P. E. Parnell, 'The Sentimental Mask', *PMLA*, LXXVIII (1963).

*Sir John Vanbrugh*

B. Dobrée edited the plays in *The Complete Works*, with the letters edited by G. Webb, 4 vols (London, 1927). Among several modern editions are *The*

*Provok'd Wife* and *The Relapse*, both ed. C. Zimansky (Lincoln, Neb., 1969 and 1970).

*William Wycherley*

M. Summers edited the *Complete Works*, 4 vols (London, 1924); the plays were recently edited by G. Weales (Garden City, 1966; repr. New York, 1967). A biography is C. Perromat, *William Wycherley. Sa Vie. Son Œuvre* (Paris, 1921). Some modern studies are T. W. Craik, 'Some Aspects of Satire in Wycherley's Plays', *English Studies*, XLI (1960); K. M. Rogers, 'Fatal Inconsistency: Wycherley and *The Plain Dealer*', *ELH*, XXVIII (1961); J. Auffret, 'Wycherley et ses maîtres les moralistes', *Études anglaises*, XV (1962); R. Zimbardo, *Wycherley's Drama* (New Haven, Conn., 1965); and *L'Épouse campagnarde* (*The Country Wife*), ed. A. Mavrocordato (Paris, 1968).

(c) ANTHOLOGIES OF TEXTS

In addition to modern editions of leading dramatists, there are some useful anthologies: *Plays of the Restoration and Eighteenth Century*, ed. D. MacMillan and H. M. Jones (New York, 1931); *British Dramatists from Dryden to Sheridan*, ed. G. H. Nettleton and A. E. Case (Boston, 1939), a collection in which pains have been taken over the texts; *Ten English Farces*, ed. L. Hughes and A. H. Scouten (Austin, Texas, 1948; repr. 1970); *Six Restoration Plays* (Boston, 1959) and *Six Eighteenth-Century Plays* (Boston, 1960), ed. J. H. Wilson; *Five Adaptations of Shakespeare*, ed. C. Spencer (Urbana, Ill., 1965); *Burlesque Plays of the Eighteenth Century*, ed. S. Trussler (London, 1969); and *Eighteenth-Century Afterpieces*, ed. R. W. Bevis (London, 1970).

# Index